THE HISTORY OF
THE FORMER HAN DYNASTY

BY

PAN KU

Translation, Volume One

FIRST DIVISION
The Imperial Annals

Chapters I–V

A Critical Translation with Annotations

by

HOMER H. DUBS
Acting Professor of Philosophy in Duke University

With the Collaboration of
JEN T'AI and P'AN LO-CHI

———

BALTIMORE
WAVERLY PRESS, INC.
1938

To

DR. J. J. L. DUYVENDAK

University of Leyden

INTRODUCTORY NOTE

In 1929 the American Council of Learned Societies entered upon the execution of a long-term plan for broadening the range of American humanistic scholarship through the development of certain fields of study that were little cultivated or even almost neglected. It was obvious that among such fields, that of Far Eastern studies was one the cultivation of which was not only intrinsically and relatively exceedingly worthwhile but imposed itself with peculiar urgency upon American scholars.

The first requisite of such a step as the Council proposed to take was a body of highly trained scholars, and since there was no such group in the United States in 1929, it had to be brought into being. Scholars, especially in such fields as Chinese and Japanese, cannot be produced in a single academic generation, but after nearly a decade the Council's efforts, aided by the interest and good will of the university world and by generous support from the Rockefeller Foundation and the Carnegie Corporation, have achieved a gratifying success, and at present a number of scholars who have benefited from years of study in the United States, in Europe, and in China and Japan, occupy positions in a dozen universities, where they teach various aspects of Far Eastern civilization, history, and culture, and conduct research along the lines of their varied interests. It is not too much to expect that original investigations in these fields, based upon thorough command of their difficult skills, linguistic and other, will make increasingly important contributions to the product of American scholarly research.

But only a few, relatively speaking, of the American scholars who have an interest in Chinese and Japanese history and in the social, political, and economic life of those countries, and who also have a justifiable desire to study Far Eastern problems for themselves, can hope to acquire control of the necessary tools. While the difficulties of learning the languages of China and Japan have perhaps been exaggerated, and while it may be confidently expected that those difficulties will be lessened by improvements in methods of instruction to which increasing attention is being devoted, the linguistic obstacle will doubtless always be considerable.

An immediate problem, therefore, is how to make it possible for historians, economists, political scientists, and other scholars to carry on their studies without a language equipment such as is taken for granted, and is, indeed, a *sine qua non*, in investigating the history and the social, economic, and political phenomena of Western Europe and South America. One solution of this problem, though at best a partial one, would be the translation of large bodies of essential Chinese and Japanese materials into one or another of the most widely used Western languages.

A dream of the Council, perhaps unrealizable, is a vast *Bibliotheca Sinica* not unlike, let us say, the Loeb Classical Library, in which would appear each year, through international collaboration, numerous important Chinese works, ancient as well as modern, in English, French, or German translation, and which would constitute a rapidly increasing store of authoritative sources for the use of specialists who have not the benefit of complete sinological training.

It may be over-optimistic to offer the present volume, containing a section of one of the most important of Chinese histories, as a first step in the execution of so ambitious a project, although if it could be so regarded it would be an appropriate beginning, but it is at least a demonstration, and its preparation has been a means of acquiring valuable experience.

The selection of the work to be translated, as well as of the translator, Dr. Dubs, and the general oversight of the project has been the responsibility of the Council's Committee on the Promotion of Chinese Studies, whose chairman, Dr. Arthur W. Hummel of the Library of Congress, and secretary, Mr. Mortimer Graves of the executive staff of the Council, have given constant attention to the enterprise.

The Committee early reached the decision that the experiment in translation could most usefully be conducted with a unit section of one of the so-called dynastic histories of China, which form one of the finest known bodies of historical documentation and which are, in fact, an almost contemporary record of the great sweep of Chinese history during more than twenty centuries. Early in 1932, accordingly, a sub-committee, composed of Clarence H. Hamilton of Oberlin College, Nancy Lee Swann of the Gest Chinese Research Library, then located at McGill University in Montreal but since acquired by the Institute for Advanced Study at Princeton, New Jersey, and Charles S. Gardner of Harvard University, made a study of the dynastic histories and recommended that the history of the T'ang dynasty (618–906 A.D.) or the history of one of the Han dynasties (206 B.C.–221 A.D.) should be selected for translation, leaving the final choice to be determined by the special interests of the scholar who might be invited to undertake the task. An invitation was then extended to Dr. Homer H. Dubs, professor of philosophy in Marshall College, and author of numerous works on Chinese culture, to assume direction of the work, and he fixed upon the history of the Former

Han Dynasty (206 B.C.–23 A.D.) or *Ch'ien-Han Shu* as the work to be translated.

The undertaking was made possible by a generous grant from the Carnegie Corporation, sufficient to finance it for a period of three years. The coöperation of the Library of Congress, through its Division of Orientalia, enabled Dr. Dubs and his assistants to carry on their work in an ideal environment, with all the resources in materials and personnel of one of the most important Chinese collections in the world, at their disposal. For three years, from September, 1934, to September, 1937, Dr. Dubs worked uninterruptedly in the Library of Congress with the collaboration of Mr. Jen T'ai until July, 1936, of Mr. C. H. Tsui from July to September, 1936, and of Mr. P'an Lo-ch'i from the latter date to September, 1937.

During this period Dr. Dubs devoted himself to the translation of the Imperial Annals, or *Ti-chi*, which form the chronological background of the history and comprise about a sixteenth of it, and the first five chapters of this section are presented herewith in this first volume. The remaining chapters, VI to XII, will, it is hoped, be published in due course, as volumes two and three. Two companion volumes to the Imperial Annals have been completed by Dr. Dubs and are now being prepared for the printer; these are a volume of prolegomena, which will contain a biography of the author, together with a history of the text, and other apparatus, and a volume consisting of an onomasticon. Thus Dr. Dubs's work should result in the publication of five volumes. He has, furthermore, been able to work carefully, through other parts of the history, especially its numerous biographical memoirs, but the continuation and publication of these sections must depend upon further financial and scholarly support.

Upon the conclusion of his triennium in the Library of Congress, Dr. Dubs was appointed to a position on the faculty of Duke University, where he is now able to devote a part of his time to the completion of the work and to its preparation for the press.

The American Council of Learned Societies hopes that the instalment now presented will serve to illustrate the importance of making available in translation some of the basic sources of Chinese history, and that it may, in fact, prove to be but a first step towards the undertaking of the larger task referred to above, the urgency of which becomes, in these closing days of 1937, more than ever apparent.

In conclusion, the Council desires to express its grateful appreciation of the generous assistance that it has received from the Carnegie Corporation of New York, of the indispensable collaboration of the Library of Congress, of the careful attention given to the work by its own Committee on the Promotion of Far Eastern Studies, and of the laborious devotion to this task of Dr. Dubs and his Chinese assistants.

It also desires to acknowledge its special indebtedness to Professor J. J. L. Duyvendak of the University of Leyden, who has given the translation much careful reading and who has been throughout the entire course of the work a valued critic and adviser.

WALDO G. LELAND

American Council of Learned Societies,
Washington, D. C.

FOREWORD

The *History of the Former Han Dynasty* is, as its own "Introductory Memoir" says, an "encyclopedia of scholarship" dealing with the Chinese world of the first two centuries B.C. The first volume of translation herewith presented will form the second volume of the completed series of five, one of prolegomena, three of translation, and one of glossary. This volume begins the translation of the first division in the *History*, the so-called "Imperial Annals," which deal with the emperors and the political history of the empire from 209 B.C. The two succeeding volumes of translation complete the translation of this division. The volume of prolegomena will contain a translation of the author's own important "Introductory Memoir" (the hundredth chapter of the *History* itself), lives of the author and of others who worked on the book, a discussion of the texts and their tradition, and a list of the important commentators who have concerned themselves with the *History*, and their works. The final volume will be an onomasticon or glossary of the proper names, the inclusion of which in the notes would have made them unwieldy, and an index.

I wish to record my indebtedness to those institutions and persons who have made the appearance of this work possible: to the Carnegie Corporation of New York for its generous financial support; to the American Council of Learned Societies for its administration of the enterprise and for its financial assistance in publication; to the Committee on Chinese Studies of that Council, particularly to its chairman, Dr. Arthur W. Hummel, and its secretary, Mr. Mortimer Graves, for their initial impetus, their continued enthusiasm, and their helpful criticism. Dr. Hummel, in addition, as Chief of the Division of Orientalia at the Library of Congress, has added to his helpful care in the process of translation complete access to the riches of the collection under his charge. But most of all I am grateful to Dr. J. J. L. Duyvendak of the Sinologisch Instituut, University of Leyden, who has gone patiently over my translation and made numerous and invaluable suggestions for its improvement.

I owe much, too, to my two collaborators, Messrs. T'ai Jen and L. C. P'an. They have saved me from innumerable blunders, suggested many happy renderings, and discovered much collateral material. Without their scholarship and patient industry this translation would have been much the poorer.

I have not, however, hesitated to disagree with the opinions of these friends, and I accept the ultimate responsibility for the translation as it stands.   I shall be grateful for the many suggestions towards its improvement that can doubtless be made.

HOMER H. DUBS

Library of Congress,
Washington, D. C.
June 28, 1937.

ABBREVIATIONS

HS—the *History of the Former Han Dynasty*. Arabic numerals followed by a colon refer to the chapters (卷) of that history; roman letters before the colon to part (上, 下) of the chapter; arabic numerals after the colon to the pages of Wang Hsien-ch'ien's edition, the *Ch'ien-Han-shu Pu-chu*; the letters *a* and *b* refer to the recto and verso sides of those pages respectively.

SC—The *Shih-chi*, by Szu-ma Ch'ien. The edition used is the photographic reprint of the imperial 1747 edition printed by the Han-fen-lou, Shanghai, 1916. *SCHC* denotes the edition by Kame-ta-ro Takigawa, Tokyo, 1934.

Mh—*Les Mémoires historiques de Se-ma Ts'ien*, traduits et annotés par Édouard Chavannes, 1895–1905. Capital roman numerals denote volumes; arabic numerals, pages. *Ind.* denotes his indexes, *no.* indicating the number of that listing, *sub* a listing under some word.

HHS—the *Hou-Han-shu*, the *History of the Later Han Dynasty*, by Fan Yeh (398–445). The "Treatises" are however the work of Szu-ma Piao (ca. 240–304). Quotations are by the paging in Wang Hsien-ch'ien's edition, *Hou-Han-shu Chi-chieh*. Numbers of its chapters are preceded by An., Tr., or Mem., referring to the number of the Annals, Treatise, or Memoir in that book.

Roman numerals in the margin of the translation followed by *a* or *b* indicate the paging of Wang Hsien-ch'ien's edition. Quotations and references will be made to this paging.

Numbers in parentheses following the name of a person or book are the dates of that person or book; unless specified, dates are A.D. Where the dates of birth or death cannot be found, *fl.* indicates that the person was mentioned as living (e.g., holding office, etc.) at that time. *Fl. dur.* (flourished during) precedes the dates of the dynasty or year-period in which the person was living.

Names of places have been checked with the 1933 *Postal Atlas of China* to determine their present names. Orthography (except in the case of provinces and commonly used names) is, with unimportant deviations, in accordance with that of Giles.

Other abbreviations have their common meanings.

For names of persons, places, and official titles, cf. Glossary of Names. This Glossary contains much additional information. Many of the

xi

Memoirs in the *HS* are summarized in those accounts. Without the material in the Glossary, the accounts in the Imperial Annals cannot be fully understood.

The reader's indulgence is asked for the translations of Chinese official titles. No translation into another language can be exact; our translations are merely intended to be suggestive; in each case the reader is referred to the Glossary for a more exact meaning of the title. Only because a romanized transliteration of titles so often results in meaningless words is a translation attempted, and not always then.

TABLE OF CONTENTS

THE HISTORY OF THE FORMER HAN DYNASTY

CHAPTER I

INTRODUCTION

The first chapter in the *History of the Former Han Dynasty* contains an account of the rise of Liu Chi, who became Emperor Kao-tsu and the founder of the Han dynasty, and of the important events in his reign. In accordance with the canon of Chinese historical writing that the most reliable account is to be obtained by copying sources practically verbatim, this chapter is largely a copy of the chapter devoted to Kao-tsu in Sze-ma Ch'ien's *Historical Records* or *Shih-chi*, together with additions taken from the *SC* chapter on Hsiang Yü. Those chapters were probably themselves largely copied from the *Ch'u-Han Ch'un-ch'iu* by Lu Chia, who presented his book to Kao-tsu in 197 B.C. His book is now lost, but it was preserved in T'ang times, and notations of the information it contained in addition to what is found in the *HS* are found in the notes. Very little indeed is so noted. Probably this book was allowed to disappear because practically everything in it had been incorporated into the *History*.

We have thus in the first part of this chapter an account of the conflict that arose after the death of the First Emperor of the Ch'in dynasty, taken from documents contemporary with those events. The second part of the chapter contains the chronicle of events in Kao-tsu's reign after he assumed the title of Emperor. This part of the chapter is also copied largely from the corresponding chapter in the *SC*, but there are significant additions, especially among the imperial edicts recorded for that period. Pan Ku seems to have had access to a collection of imperial edicts preserved in the archives at the capital and to a set of annals of important events kept by imperial officials. Since he admired Szu-ma Ch'ien so greatly, he made Szu-ma Ch'ien's account the basis of his own account, and added to it or corrected it at the few places where changes seemed necessary.

The Imperial Annals, the first of which constitutes this chapter, are merely the chronological summary of the *History of the Former Han Dynasty*, a typical Chinese encyclopedic history. In this *History* the twelve Annals constitute only about one twentieth of the whole work.

1

It is therefore not to be expected that the Annals should give the whole story of any reign or even any detailed account of the events in it.   Pan Ku realized that history cannot be broken off at the death of each emperor.   He conceived of history as the record of the deeds of individuals, so he put into his Memoirs and Treatises many facts that are essential to a full understanding of historical movements.   While this chapter does contain many more details than usually appear in annals, yet much additional material is to be found in the relevant Memoirs.   We have summarized in the Glossary the important Memoirs bearing on this and other reigns; it is suggested that the reader consult the Glossary *sub* the names of places and persons in each chapter.   He will find there many events not to be found in the Annals.   Pan Ku limited himself to one dynasty because the immense wealth of material at his command made a limitation of scope imperative.   He has indeed been criticized for the great length to which his history grew, yet that great length was needed for an adequate picture of this unusual period.   Because his history was planned as an encyclopedia rather than as a straightforward account, the extraordinarily complete picture given by Pan Ku will not be available until the whole of this long *History* has been translated.

*   *   *

The account of the rebellion against the Ch'in dynasty and the rise of Kao-tsu, given in the first part of this chapter, is quite logical and is told in detail.   The China of that day was still largely confined to the Yellow River valley.   In 209 B.C., at the opening of revolt, the imperial capital was at Hsien-yang, near the present city by the same name in Shensi.   Central Shensi, then called Kuan-chung, is a great natural fortress, with mountains and the Yellow River making a formidable barrier to invasion.   To the east, Kuan-chung was entered chiefly by the Han-ku Pass, which is easily defensible.   Within this fortress is the Wei River valley, then very fertile and well populated.   This region had been the seat of the Ch'in state, which had conquered China and whose king had taken the proud title of the First Emperor in 221 B.C. He had extinguished all the feudal nobility and had divided China into thirty-six commanderies, each governed by an official appointed by himself.

Southwest of Kuan-chung in the mountainous southwestern Shensi was the Han-chung Commandery, from which difficult roads led to the commanderies of Pa and Shu in the present Szechuan.   This region had not yet been fully civilized; it was still a region of exile.   Here was soon to be established the kingdom of Han$_s$, to which Liu Chi was appointed.

Travel east of Kuan-chung went chiefly down the Yellow River valley
to the place where the great coastal plain begins to broaden out.   There
was also a road across the mountains of eastern Shensi and up the Fen
River valley, which debouched through mountain passes onto the great
plain in the present central Hopei.   Because of its difficulties, traffic
usually took the other road via the Yellow River valley.   The northern
road was the one followed by Han Hsin in his conquest of Chao, Yen,
and Ch'i in 205-3 B.C.   In the narrow east and west corridor which is
the Yellow River valley east of Kuan chung, lay the city of Jung-yang,
which Kao-tsu long made his headquarters when fighting Hsiang Yü,
and where he was besieged by the latter and almost captured.   Here
too was the immense granary of Ao, on a mountain by the shore of the
Yellow River.   It contained so much grain that for three years Kao-tsu's
forces, numbering hundreds of thousands, continued to draw food from
this granary, and yet did not exhaust it.   Its location made it easily
defensible; Hsiang Yü's failure to garrison adequately this stronghold
left him without an appropriate base of supplies to fight Kao-tsu and
eventually brought about his defeat.   At the place where the plain
starts to broaden out had been the last capital of the ancient state of
Han$_h$.

The Yellow River at that time turned north from its present bed near
the place where the Peiping-Hankow railroad now crosses the River,
and flowed northeast, following approximately the present Grand Canal,
until it emptied into the sea near the present Tientsin.   Between this
channel of the Yellow River and the Gulf of Chihli (then called the
P'o Sea) had been the ancient state of Ch'i, one of the richest parts of
China.   West of the Yellow River had been the ancient state of Chao,
and north of Chao, Yen.   South of the Shantung promontory, in the
present northern Kiangsu, was P'eng-ch'eng, the last capital of the
ancient state of Ch'u.   Not far away was the birthplace of Liu Chi.
To the south in the seaboard plain, across the Yangtze River, was the
K'uai-chi Commandery, which had formerly been the state of Wu,
from which arose Hsiang Yü and his uncle.

The remainder of the present China, outside the Yellow River valley and the seaboard plain, had not yet become important.   Even
the Hsiang River valley, which later became the kingdom of Ch'ang-
sha, was still considered as "low, damp, and poverty-stricken," and
was used as a place of exile.   Present Fukien was the seat of a semi-
independent barbarian kingdom, Min-yüeh; present Kwangtung was
the seat of another barbarian kingdom, Nan-yüeh.   The First Emperor had conquered these regions and had sent convicts there as

colonists, but these regions were still sparsely settled, largely barbarous, and played only a small part in the Chinese politics of the time. The significant regions of China, in which most of the matters related in this chapter occurred, were Kuan-chung, where was the capital, the narrow valley where the Yellow River flows eastwards, and the seaboard plain, where had been located the flourishing states that had been conquered by Ch'in. Among these states there started the revolt which finally conquered Ch'in.

In the background of this revolt there lay the exactions and cruelly overwhelming force wielded by the First Emperor. After his death, his son, the Second Emperor, continued his harsh policy. The people's resentment had gradually accumulated and a spark set it aflame.

Ch'en Shê was an ambitious farm boy who became one of the chiefs in a levy of men made in the present southern Honan, which had been part of the ancient kingdom of Ch'u. In the late summer of 209 B.C., a bad rain prevented this levy from reaching its destination on time. According to the Ch'in laws, the officers and men of the levy would have been condemned to death; they accordingly conspired to rebel. As a slogan they falsely called themselves partisans of Fu-su, the displaced heir of the First Emperor, and fabricated miracles to legitimize themselves. The rebellion was not thus at first openly directed against the dynasty, but was merely the act of men driven to desperation by over-harsh laws.

Success in capturing important cities and the favorable response of the people led Ch'en Shê to call himself the King of Ch'u and appoint subordinate generals to overrun the surrounding country. These generals found themselves welcomed by the people, and set themselves up as kings of the regions which they controlled. Soon much of eastern China was aflame.

The Ch'in forces were sent to put down the rebellion, with Chang Han, a very capable general, at their head. He defeated Ch'en Shê and relieved the siege of an important city. Ch'en Shê's important generals were likewise defeated, and he fled eastwards into the present northern Kiangsu, where he was assassinated by his own charioteer.

But neither the death of Ch'en Shê nor the continued successes of Chang Han could stop the rebellion. Ambitious men all over eastern China saw their opportunity, excited their neighbors to arise and massacre the officials appointed by the Ch'in dynasty, and put themselves at the head of a rebel force. Against such a wholesale uprising even the ablest general could do little, for he could not be everywhere. Soon the less able rebel generals subordinated themselves to the more successful ones.

In the present southern Kiangsu, an uncle and nephew, Hsiang Liang and Hsiang Yü, murdered the Commandery Administrator, took his army, and marched north. They were descendants of the famous generals in Ch'u, and as they came north other generals came to them with their armies. They set up a successor to Ch'en Shê in the person of a scion from the ancient kings of Ch'u, thus legitimizing their rebellion and bringing further recruits. Their capital was put at P'eng-ch'eng, in the present northern Kiangsu.

Among the generals who had previously come to Hsiang Liang was Liu Chi, the future Kao-tsu. (There is no evidence that he used the name Liu Pang until after his coronation, when that name was tabooed.) He was a former village official who had become a bandit as the result of official oppression and bad luck, and had been summoned with his followers when the chief town of his commandery intended to rebel. He killed its vacillating magistrate when the magistrate changed his mind and refused to rebel, then he made himself master of P'ei, a city in the present northern Kiangsu, together with surrounding cities. From that time he was known as the Lord of P'ei. A subordinate who had been left in charge of Feng went over to another rebel general who had a better pedigree than Liu Chi, and Liu Chi was unable to retake Feng. He finally applied to Hsiang Liang, who gave him troops and enabled him to recapture Feng. When Chang Han defeated and killed Hsiang Liang, Liu Chi attached himself closely to Hsiang Yü and was made a marquis by the King of Ch'u.

Meanwhile rebellion had flared throughout the present Shantung and Hopei. The King of Chao was besieged by the Ch'in forces at Chü-lu in central Hopei and sent to Ch'u for rescue. At that time two projects required the urgent attention of Ch'u: the raising of the siege at Chü-lu and the carrying of the war to the capital of the dynasty at Hsien-yang, in Kuan-chung. The ablest generals, including Hsiang Yü, were sent north, and Liu Chi was sent west.

The General-in-chief in charge of the army sent to the relief of Chü-lu proved dilatory and incompetent, so Hsiang Yü boldly killed him and took charge of the army. Hsiang Yü's prestige was so high that generals from other parts of the country joined him in rescuing Chao. When he crossed the Chang River he boldly burnt his boats and destroyed all but three days' provisions, then advanced to the attack. In nine battles he defeated the besiegers, captured their general, burnt their camp, and raised the siege. The fame of this deed brought to Hsiang Yü's standard the outstanding generals of the country. Then he turned his attention to Chang Han.

Chang Han had been fighting rebels for almost two full years; they had gained in strength in spite of his victories. A defeated general could expect little but execution from the harsh authorities at the capital. Chang Han was said to have lost over a hundred thousand men in those two years. The imperial authority was then in the hands of a eunuch Chancellor of State, who had slaughtered his enemies. Chang Han was now defeated in battle by Hsiang Yü, and, when the latter promised him a kingdom, Chang Han was ready to surrender, although his army was said still to contain more than two hundred thousand soldiers. When the surrendered army showed signs of discontent at this action of its generals, Hsiang Yü had it massacred at night. Then he started for Hsien-yang with an army said to be of four hundred thousand men.

Meanwhile Liu Chi had worked his way westwards. He had been sent off with a totally inadequate force and with the promise that the person who conquered the capital would be made the king of that region. He spent a whole year going westwards, gathering recruits, preaching rebellion, making friends, and fighting with the Ch'in armies, usually, but not always, successfully. When he reached the borders of Kuan-chung, he first sent a messenger into that region to preach rebellion, then avoided the easily defensible Han-ku Pass, made a detour to the southwards, and entered the lightly defended Wu Pass. After tricking and crushing the Ch'in army sent against him, he arrived at the suburbs of the capital, which was empty of troops. There, in Nov./Dec. 207 B.C., the last ruler of the Ch'in dynasty came and surrendered to him. Kao-tsu later dated the beginning of his reign with this event.

Liu Chi showed himself generous and kindly. Instead of looting the city, he sealed up the imperial palaces and treasuries and moved his troops out of the capital, for Hsiang Yü might ask for an accounting of its treasures. Hsiao Ho, his future Chancellor, took the charts and registers out of the imperial chancellor's office. Through their possession, Liu Chi was later able to know the strategic points of the empire, the size of the population, and the people's grievances. Liu Chi gathered the leaders of the region and announced to them that he had been promised the kingship of Kuan-chung and that he was going to agree with them on a code consisting of only three articles: death for murder, proportionate punishment for robbery and assault, and the repeal of all other penal laws. While this drastic abrogation of the detailed and vexatious laws in effect in Ch'in could not be entirely carried out, yet it actually meant a great lightening of the people's burdens and secured for Liu Chi their good will. Then Liu Chi sent a guard to the Han-ku Pass.

When Hsiang Yü reached that Pass and found it barred, he forced it and marched on to the capital. Not only was he enraged that Liu Chi should have dared to try to keep him out (an act of rebellion by a subordinate against his Commander-in-chief), but he was jealous that another person should have captured the capital. With an overwhelming force, he hastened to crush Liu Chi. But the latter was forewarned and came to make apologies. With lordly generosity, Hsiang Yü accepted them, especially since the treasures of the capital had been left for him to loot. He marched into the capital, massacred its people, killed the surrendered King, and burnt the imperial palaces. That fire was the real "Burning of the Books," for in the imperial palaces there had been preserved the proscribed literature for the use of the imperial Erudits and officials. Those fires did not cease until the third month.

Hsiang Yü proceeded to divide the conquered empire. It was a military man's division. The King of Ch'u, who had done little but reign, was nominally elevated to be Emperor, but really exiled to southern Hunan, where an emissary of Hsiang Yü soon assassinated him. Hsiang Yü made himself King of Ch'u and Lord Protector of the Empire, with Kiangsu, southern Shantung, and parts of Honan and the Yangtze valley as his territory. The agreement about making the conqueror of Kuan-chung its king was disregarded; Liu Chi was made King of Han$_s$, a region located in southwestern Shensi and Szechuan. Kuan-chung was divided into three kingdoms, with the three generals of Chang Han's surrendered army as its kings. Chang Han was put in that kingdom which bordered upon Han$_s$, to serve as a buffer against Liu Chi. Those generals and nobles who had conquered parts of the country and had followed Hsiang Yü to the capital were confirmed as kings of their territory. In so doing, a few former kings had to be moved, and T'ien Jung, who had conquered Ch'i (northern Shantung), but had refused to submit to Hsiang Yü, was left out. P'eng Yüeh, a bandit chieftain in eastern Honan, was likewise neglected.

Liu Chi saw that any opposition to this unjust division was useless, so went to his capital, burning the bridges behind him; Hsiang Yü and the other generals went to their kingdoms. A month later Liu Chi returned, surprised and defeated Chang Han, and besieged him in his capital. Then Liu Chi overran Kuang-chung. In Ch'i, T'ien Jung likewise attacked the kings that Hsiang Yü had appointed to that region, and made himself king.

Hsiang Yü attacked Ch'i first, for it was nearer his own kingdom and he was told that Liu Chi had no designs on the east. He defeated T'ien Jung, who was then assassinated. But Hsiang Yü's excesses in the conquest of Ch'i so roused the people that the dead King's brother was able to raise an army to continue the struggle. Meanwhile Liu Chi had established himself firmly in Kuan-chung and invaded Honan as far as Lo-yang. When the assassination of the new Emperor by an emissary of Hsiang Yü became known, Liu Chi preached a crusade against the murderer, persuaded and compelled five kings to follow him, and marched east with a coalition army said to comprise five hundred and sixty thousand men. He captured and entered Hsiang Yü's capital, P'eng-ch'eng. Hsiang Yü was in Ch'i; with thirty thousand picked troops, he reached P'eng-ch'eng by forced marches, and surprised the coalition army at the city where it had been feasting, crushing it utterly. A hundred thousand men were forced into the rivers and drowned.

Liu Chi escaped and fortified himself in Jung-yang (near the present Cheng-hsien, Honan). There he was reinforced by new troops from Kuan-chung and elsewhere. Then he sent emissaries to stir up rebellion against Hsiang Yü in Anhui, and sent Han Hsin, who was his titular General-in-chief, to conquer Shansi and Hopei, and thence to press into Shantung.

When Hsiang Yü proceeded to besiege Liu Chi in Jung-yang, Liu Chi was now able to offer peace, dividing China in half, with only that part west of Jung-yang for his own. Hsiang Yü refused and pressed the siege. Liu Chi had to escape and permit the city to be captured; he returned to his impregnable fortress of Kuan-chung, and drew Hsiang Yü into northern Hupeh by going out of the southern part of Kuan-chung. Meanwhile P'eng Yüeh was looting near P'eng-ch'eng, so Hsiang Yü had to return to his capital. Then Liu Chi recaptured the cities he had lost in Honan. When Hsiang Yü returned to Honan, Liu Chi fled, but sent assistance to P'eng Yüeh, who burnt Hsiang Yü's stores. When Hsiang Yü pursued P'eng Yüeh, Liu Chi crushed the army Hsiang Yü had left behind and took possession of his treasures. Meanwhile Han Hsin, in a brilliant campaign, had conquered the region into which he had been sent, and had established himself in Ch'i.

Liu Chi entrenched himself in the hills northwest of Cheng-hsien, where he could draw food from the immense granary at Ao. There he was besieged by Hsiang Yü. But Anhui and Shantung revolted against Hsiang Yü; P'eng Yüeh cut off his supplies, and finally Hsiang Yü had to make peace and agree to the same division of the country as that previously proposed by Liu Chi.

When Hsiang Yü returned east, Liu Chi, disregarding the treaty, pursued him with fresh troops. By promises of territory, he induced Han Hsin, P'eng Yüeh, and others to unite with his forces. Together they besieged Hsiang Yü in his camp near his capital. By a trick they got him to flee from his camp with a body of cavalry, pursued, and killed him in Dec./Jan. 203/2 B.C.

Liu Chi now feared Han Hsin most, so he rode into Han Hsin's entrenchments, took away his army, and appointed him King of Ch'u. Ch'i was too valuable a territory to be left to anyone who might rebel. Liu Chi also sent his generals to overrun Ch'u and extinguish rebellion there.

Liu Chi's nobles and adherents now proposed to make him Emperor. He declined the requisite number of times, and was enthroned on Feb. 28, 202 B.C. He proceeded to organize his empire and appoint his followers as marquises or kings. At a great banquet, he tactfully declared that his success had been due to Chang Liang, his chief advisor, Hsiao Ho, his Chancellor, and Han Hsin, his best general. The organization of the empire was largely the work of Hsiao Ho, who had done no fighting, but whom Kao-tsu esteemed most highly among all his nobles. Because of its natural strength, Kao-tsu moved his capital from Lo-yang to Ch'ang-an in Kuan-chung (Shensi).

*   *   *

During the remainder of his reign, Kao-tsu was chiefly occupied in putting down a series of revolts, and in appointing his sons and relatives to the kingdoms thus vacated. When Kao-tsu took the throne, there were seven kings in the empire who were not members of the imperial family, and no members of the imperial family who were kings. Gradually the kings who were not members of the imperial family revolted or were disposed of. The first to revolt was Tsang Tu, who had been a follower of Hsiang Yü and had been appointed by him as King of Yen, with his capital at the present Pei-p'ing. Kao-tsu marched against him, captured and executed him, and made his own boyhood companion and best friend, Lu Wan, the King of Yen. Then Li Chi, who was a marquis and had previously been a general of Hsiang Yü, but had submitted to Kao-tsu, became afraid of treachery, and rebelled. He was routed. Han Hsin, now King of Ch'u, failed to deliver up promptly a friend who had taken refuge with him and who had been proscribed by Kao-tsu; Kao-tsu marched to Ch'u with an army, caught Han Hsin unprepared, and arrested him. He was imprisoned, then pardoned and made a marquis, but kept at court where he could be watched.

Han$_w$ Hsin had been made King of Han$_h$ in Honan. But Kao-tsu wanted that territory free from possible rebels, so in the spring of 201, he moved Han$_w$ Hsin to be King of a new Han$_h$, located in the present

Shansi. That autumn, the Huns besieged Han_w Hsin in his capital. Kao-tsu suspected his loyalty and made the mistake of sending him a letter reproving him; whereupon Han_w Hsin became suspicious of Kao-tsu's intentions and went over to the Huns. Kao-tsu himself took the field and routed Han_w Hsin, but Han_w Hsin's generals and the Huns continued to make incursions and to stir up trouble. At Lou-fan, Kao-tsu's soldiers were almost frozen to death; at P'ing-ch'eng, Kao-tsu was almost captured by the Huns. The invaders were finally driven out.

At the court of his son-in-law, Chang Ao, King of Chao, Kao-tsu did not bother to be polite; the scrupulous Chancellor of the kingdom was enraged, and ambushed Kao-tsu the next time he traveled through the kingdom. A premonition saved Kao-tsu's life. When the conspiracy was discovered, its members committed suicide and Chang Ao was degraded to be a marquis.

Then in Sept./Oct. 197, Ch'en Hsi, whom Kao-tsu sincerely trusted, and who had been made Chancellor in Tai (southwestern Chahar), was induced by Han_w Hsin to revolt. Kao-tsu was unprepared for another revolt; he rushed to Han-tan (in Hopei), but found himself without an army. Even an urgent call for troops was slow in bringing results. Kao-tsu spent the winter in Han-tan waiting. Not until spring was Ch'en Hsi's power broken and Han_w Hsin killed as he came to Ch'en Hsi's aid. Ch'en Hsi was pursued and killed the next winter.

Meanwhile, in the capital, the Empress *née* Lü had become so alarmed and suspicious that she lured Han Hsin into the palace and executed him. P'eng Yüeh had sent troops to the assistance of Kao-tsu at Han-tan, but had failed to come himself; whereupon Kao-tsu impatiently and angrily sent a rebuke to P'eng Yüeh. Then P'eng Yüeh himself wanted to go to Kao-tsu. He was however warned that the Emperor would probably execute him in anger. So he feigned illness. Then a disgruntled official went to Kao-tsu and informed him that P'eng Yüeh was planning rebellion. Kao-tsu thereupon had P'eng Yüeh arrested, dismissed him from his kingdom, and sent him into exile. On the way he met the Empress; she promised to plead for him, but instead she had Kao-tsu informed that P'eng Yüeh was again planning to revolt, whereupon he was executed. The remaining loyal kings who were not members of the imperial family were now very suspicious, wondering when their turn would come.

Ch'ing Pu had been Hsiang Yü's Commander-in-chief, and had been made King of Chiu-chiang. An emissary of Kao-tsu had induced him to rebel against Hsiang Yü; he had been compelled to flee to Kao-tsu in Jan./Feb. 204 with a very few men. Kao-tsu then used him to stir up trouble for Hsiang Yü in the lower Yangtze region, and gave him a kingdom in southern Anhui and northern Kiangsi. After the execution of Han Hsin and P'eng Yüeh, Ch'ing Pu became very nervous, and started to collect troops so as not to be caught defenseless. Word of this move was brought to Ch'ang-an, and an envoy was sent to investigate; Ch'ing Pu feared what was coming, and put his army into the field in open rebellion. He was an able general and fighter; he routed two neighboring kings belonging to the imperial house, killing one of them. But Kao-tsu had kept a large standing army ready for emergencies; he was himself ill, nevertheless he took the field against Ch'ing Pu, routed him in northern Anhui, drove him south, and finally compelled him to flee. Ch'ing Pu was killed by the people at a stopping-place.

After the death of Ch'ing Pu, no one else dared to rebel; indeed it is very doubtful that even he would have rebelled had he not felt that there was no other way to escape execution. It was discovered however that Lu Wan, the King of Yen, had had secret communication with the Huns and with Ch'en Hsi. Lu Wan had been afraid that he would be the next king to be dispossessed and killed, so had dallied with the thought of rebellion. Kao-tsu sent an emissary to investigate the matter. Some evidence was unearthed and Kao-tsu summoned Lu Wan to court. He claimed illness, so the Emperor sent two generals to attack him. Lu Wan did not think of resisting the imperial forces; he took his family and several thousand troops and moved just outside the Great Wall, hoping for a chance to come to court and beg his old friend for pardon. The Emperor's death deprived him of that chance, and he fled to the Huns, who gave him a kingdom.

There was left now only one king not of the imperial house—the King of Ch'ang-sha. His kingdom was so small and unimportant that it was not worth while to disturb him. Kao-tsu's suspicions had eliminated almost all those not of his own family and had put his clan and the men from his prefecture into practically all the important positions. At his death, nine of Kao-tsu's sons and relatives occupied kingdoms.

Kao-tsu was ill before he started out against Ch'ing Pu; a wound from a stray arrow became infected and killed him seven months later. While he was suffering from this wound, the problem of the succession to the throne became acute. As a political move in 205, ten years previously, Kao-tsu had appointed Ying, the son of the Empress *née* Lü, as his Heir-apparent. The boy was now fifteen. He had been domineered over by his mother, and had turned out to be a weakling. Kao-tsu was not pleased with him, saying openly that Ying was not like himself. Kao-tsu's favorite concubine was the Lady *née* Ch'i, whose son, Ju-yi, was only nine. Kao-tsu liked the boy greatly and said, "He is like me." The Empress hated the Lady *née* Ch'i bitterly, and Kao-tsu realized that after his death the Empress would probably try to injure the Lady *née* Ch'i and Ju-yi. For Kao-tsu it was a choice between a weak heir with a strong and capable but cruel mother, and a mere child with a beloved mother. The Lady *née* Ch'i's pleadings finally brought Kao-tsu to the point of ordering the feast at which he would announce the change. But during that feast he found that Ying had secured the following of certain learned men whom Kao-tsu had been unable to attract, and so refused to change the succession.

When Kao-tsu died, on June 1, 195 B.C., the Empress *née* Lü was at first uncertain whether her party would be able to enthrone her son. She concealed the death for four days and toyed with the notion of assassinating the prominent generals who might stand in the way of her son. But she soon saw that this policy was not really feasible, so distributed rewards to them liberally, and succeeded in enthroning her son on the day of Kao-tsu's burial, twenty-two days after his death.

Kao-tsu was probably forty when rebellion first broke out against the Second Emperor. His early life had been spent in farming, holding a village office, and finally, as a bandit chieftain. His ability to make decisions rapidly and surely and his willingness to consult with and take advice of others were powerful assets. He was ambitious, yet he recognized the abilities of others, and realized that he must depend on others for his own greatness. He had the ability to choose the right man for the place. Han Hsin was utterly undistinguished, a common soldier who had been a mere peasant and a beggar, when Hsiao Ho recommended him to Kao-tsu; he was immediately made General-in-chief. Kao-tsu's personality attracted to him able men and kept them loyal. Hsiao Ho, his Chancellor, was his former official superior. He had been Chief Official in the prefecture where Liu Chi was a village official; when the Prefect showed himself incapable, Hsiao Ho assisted in summoning Liu Chi, helped to make him Prefect, and became his loyal follower. Li Yi-chi, a garrulous Confucian, was so attracted by the sight of Liu Chi that he voluntarily came to him.

As a general, Kao-tsu showed great but not superlative capacity. He won most of his battles, but lost a respectable number of them. His tactics in the campaign against Hsiang Yü were admirable. Liu Chi refused to fight a pitched battle and kept Hsiang Yü running from one part of the country to another, then defeated Hsiang Yü's generals when Hsiang Yü had gone. Hsiang Yü never lost a battle in which he commanded, yet Liu Chi succeeded in eliminating him. It was as a politician that Kao-tsu showed himself most capable; he drew away from Hsiang Yü his capable subordinates, inducing them to revolt or stirring up Hsiang Yü to suspect and dismiss them. Kao-tsu was himself suspicious of even his greatest intimates and was quite careless about good manners. But he was just and not opinionated, so that he was quite ready to make changes. He was favored by circumstances in many ways, but he also created his circumstances. His achievements mark him as one of the world's great men.

* * *

The accession of Kao-tsu marks, in at least two important circumstances, an epoch in Chinese history. In the first place, it marks the final breakdown of the ancient aristocracy.

The Ch'in dynasty had disestablished all noble titles. But the noble families remained, and retained much of their prestige. A large number of the early leaders against the Ch'in dynasty were aristocrats. Hsiang Liang and Hsiang Yü, who became the dominant leaders, were members of the family which had given generals to the state of Ch'u, and owed much of their success to their family's prestige. When they killed the Administrator of K'uai-chi, the people came to them because of their family's reputation. That reputation likewise brought them important recruits when they started north. When Hsiang Yü killed Sung Yi, his family's prestige enabled the former to secure the following of the army. The first leaders in Ch'i, T'ien Tan, T'ien Fu, T'ien Tu, T'ien An, T'ien Jung, T'ien Kuang, and T'ien Heng were all of the princely family in Ch'i. Wei Chiu, who became King of Wei_h, was a scion of the ancient princes of Wei_h. Chao Hsieh, the first King of Chao after the rebellion began, was a descendant of the kings of Chao. Han Ch'eng, the first King of Han_h, was likewise a descendant of its kings. King Huai, the third King of Ch'u, was a grandson of the older King Huai of Ch'u. Indeed, there was a distinct tendency in all the states to make the descendant of some noble family the titular ruler of the state, although that state might have been conquered by a commoner. The commoner took a subordinate position, such as Chancellor or General-in-chief. Ch'en Ying was offered the kingship in Ch'u by the people, but he refused, for he did not come from a noble family.

On the other hand, some of the early leaders, especially the earliest ones, were commoners. Few aristocrats would risk themselves until the people had taken the lead. Ch'en Shê, who inaugurated the revolt and became the first King of Ch'u, was a commoner. So were Ching Chü, the second King of Ch'u, whose reign lasted only three months,

Wu Ch'en, the first King of Chao, Chang Erh, the Lieutenant Chancellor and finally the King of Chao, Ch'en Yu, the General-in-chief of Chao who made himself King of Tai, Han Kuang, the first King of Yen, and others, including Liu Chi.

But the aristocrats did not do so well in the test of severe competition. Indeed they did so poorly that in the apportionment of kingdoms after the downfall of the Ch'in dynasty, Hsiang Yü contemptuously disregarded birth. Thirteen kingdoms were given to commoners and only six to scions of noble families. Three of these nobles were given their kingly assignments merely because they had followed along in the train of Hsiang Yü, so that he could not very well dismiss them; they were degraded by being removed to kingdoms smaller than those they had previously occupied. Two more were appointed to Ch'i, which seems to have had stronger aristocratic prejudices than other parts of the country. The only aristocrat who really distinguished himself was Hsiang Yü. One king, Han Ch'eng, had shown himself so weak that Hsiang Yü killed him and put a commoner in his place. When King Huai dared to oppose Hsiang Yü, the latter had him exiled and assassinated. The T'ien family in Ch'i showed some vigor, but it was crushed. Thus the drastic testing of war eliminated most of the noblemen very soon after the revolt began.

The result of this debacle among the aristocracy was a turning of popular opinion away from the aristocrats and a strengthening of its attitude to those commoners who had dared to set themselves up as leaders. Liu Chi's followers were practically all commoners, and came, especially at first, mostly from his own district, P'ei. Only one aristocrat achieved any distinction in his group—Chang Liang, whose family had given the Chancellors to Han_h. He acted as Liu Chi's advisor; in physique he was sickly and weak, and as a general he was a failure, although as a strategist he was excellent. Practically all of Kao-tsu's nobles were self-made men who had achieved distinction in the hurly-burly of war. His Empress had an aristocratic surname, Lü, but her family had no aristocratic connections.

The accession of Kao-tsu thus represents a popular movement. He seems to have caught the popular imagination; he maintained personally the bearing and habits of a peasant rather than those of an aristocrat. He was continually squatting down—something that, in those days before the introduction of chairs, no cultivated person would do and all peasants did. The language he used so vituperatively was that of a peasant, so that many cultivated persons avoided him. Yet his very evident desire to help the common people attracted to him such people

as Li Yi-chi (cf. 43:1b). The common people turned to Liu Chi and
helped him. The old gentleman Tung (1A: 31a) advised Liu Chi to
use the assassination of Emperor Yi as a pretext for a league against
Hsiang Yü. Thus the accession of Kao-tsu marks the definite ending of the ancient aristocratic tradition. He showed that even the
highest position does not require aristocratic descent.

Yet the aristocratic prejudice was not thus easily exorcised. For
Kao-tsu himself there was fabricated a long pedigree, tracing his descent
to the nobility of Chin and the early emperors; this pedigree served to
convert many followers. The families he ennobled became as aristocratic as the old nobility had been. But there was a great difference,
for the Han nobility was under the thumb of the emperor. The com-
monest punishment for crime was deprivation of noble rank. One
after another family was deprived of its rank, so that very few noble
families lasted more than a century. With kingdoms and marquisates
thus enduring only for a time and revokable for cause, hereditary
nobility counted for much less than before. Under such circumstances
the aristocratic prejudice was greatly weakened, until at last it disappeared.

In the second place, the accession of Kao-tsu marks the victory of
the Confucian conception that the imperial authority is limited, should
be exercised for the benefit of the people, and should be founded upon
justice, over the legalistic conception of arbitrary and absolute sov-
ereignty. While Kao-tsu and his successors technically remained absolute sovereigns, in practise their powers were much limited by custom.

The theory and practise of government in the Ch'in state and empire
was that of centralized absolutism. The Ch'in ideal of government was
that "none will dare not to do what the ruler likes, but all will avoid
what he dislikes" (*The Book of Lord Shang*, Duyvendak, p. 292). The
primary concern of Lord Shang's theorizing, like that of Macchiavelli,
was to make the ruler all powerful. In this respect, the First Emperor
of the Ch'in dynasty was a thorough-going exemplar of the legalist theory.

While Kao-tsu adopted many of the Ch'in practises, he nevertheless
realized that what the people most condemned in the Ch'in rule was
precisely this unreasoning absolutism, and he carefully avoided any
semblance of such absolutism. He realized that he was handicapped
by his peasant birth, and knew that he must gain the good-will of the
people in order to maintain his rule. Hence he consciously adopted the
policy of always considering the interests of the people and the requirements of justice and righteousness. Before he entered Kuan-chung, he
sent an emissary to its people in order to acquaint them with his virtuous

intentions. At the surrender of the Ch'in king, he was careful to be generous and indulgent and to avoid plundering the people. One of his first official acts in Ch'in was to summon the people and inform them that he was doing away with the severe and cruel laws of Ch'in—an act which helped him greatly when he had later to reconquer the region. He refused to exact food from the people for his army, preferring to use that stored up in the government granaries. When Hsiang Yü gave him a kingdom in Han₃, he asserted that injustice had been done because a covenant had been broken. He exempted from taxes those people who had been too heavily burdened in furnishing the armies with supplies, and granted his soldiers various and increasing exemptions. He continued the practise of giving the representatives of the people the position of *San-lao*, and had them advise with the officials so that the people would have a direct voice in government. He granted general amnesties on all appropriate occasions. He had his soldiers who had died in battle enshrouded and encoffined and sent home to be buried at official expense. He appointed caretakers for the graves of the great kings, in order that their hungry manes might not disturb the country. He waited to assume the title of Emperor until it was formally offered him by his followers, and then accepted it because "the vassal kings would be favored by it and they considered it to be an advantage to all the people in the world." At his accession he freed all slaves and restored to civil rights all refugees and exiles. He granted aristocratic ranks to all his soldiers. He fixed the amount of the military tax so that the people would not be oppressed by exactions.

More important still, soon after his accession he adopted the practise of not taking the initiative in appointing any of his relatives or sons to any kingdoms or nobilities, but acting only at the suggestion of his followers. Of course it was always possible to give hints to others about what the Emperor wanted to be done. Yet this practise that the Emperor acts only at the suggestion of others became a real check upon absolutism. At first it seems to have been confined to the enfeoffment of the emperor's sons, but later it was extended to other important matters, so that the standard practise in enacting an administrative measure, even the appointment of an Empress, came to be that some official or group would memorialize the Emperor concerning what they thought should be done, and the Emperor approved the suggestion.

This custom, that the ruler acts at the suggestion of his important subordinates, was a real and often effective limitation upon the imperial power. When the Emperor Hsiao-hui died, the Empress Dowager *née* Lü was unable to obtain any effective power until one of the great officials suggested to her that she appoint her two nephews to the highest positions in the government and members of her own family as kings. Until that suggestion was made, she could only spend her time weeping helplessly. After it had been made, she rewarded very highly the person who first suggested it (cf. Glossary, *sub* Liu Tse). When this custom was disregarded by the ruler, the results were disastrous. After the Empress Dowager *née* Lü had dismissed the son of Emperor Hui from the throne, she asked the high officials to suggest his successor. The Emperor had had only this one son, although the Empress Dowager had enfeoffed six other babes on the pretense that they were his sons. The officials refused to suggest any of them for the throne, and the Empress Dowager, on her own motion, appointed one of these babes as Emperor. But the officials, by refusing to suggest him, had disclaimed responsibility for him, and, when the Empress Dowager died, they selected a son of Kao-tsu as the new emperor and killed this boy whom the Empress had put upon the throne.

This Han custom was expressed most forcibly after the death of the Empress Dowager *née* Lü. The high officials sent someone to tell her nephew, Lü Lu, who was then in control of the army, that "the establishing of the kings . . . was a matter all done after discussion with the great officials, announcement, and information to the vassal kings. The vassal kings considered it suitable." Lü Lu was warned that if he tried to do anything contrary to the will of the great officials, the greatest disaster would come upon him. So strongly did he realize the truth of the assumption behind those words, namely that the rule of the emperor is not absolute, but is vested in him in consultation with the great officials, that he finally (though too late) resigned his powers. After the extermination of the Lü family, the next emperor was chosen by the high officials and the heads of the Liu family.

The Han rulers also recognized the principle that the empire belonged, not to Kao-tsu alone, but also to his followers and associates, for they had helped him to conquer it. As long as any of Kao-tsu's companions were alive, they and no others were given the important positions in the government. Perhaps this was the reason that the high officials tolerated the Empress Dowager *née* Lü as long as she was alive. She had taken an active part in the conquest of the country. In 179, Emperor Wen gave additional rewards to those of Kao-tsu's followers who were still alive, and sought out some thirty of his followers who had not been previously rewarded. For this reason, until 176, the imperial chancellors were all military men. Not until 150 was there an imperial chancellor who had not been a follower of Kao-tsu, and then it was Chou

Ya-fu, the son of Kao-tsu's General, Chou P'o, who had also been
Chancellor under Emperor Wen. The first chancellor who was not even
a son of Kao-tsu's followers was Wei Wan, appointed in 143 B.C. Thus
Kao-tsu's followers controlled the government for sixty years after his
accession. Even after that time, the government made an effort to
continue the marquisates of Kao-tsu's outstanding followers, in spite of
the lack and derelicitions of their heirs. As Kao-tsu said in an edict of
196 B.C., "I, by the spiritual power of Heaven and by my capable
gentlemen and high officials, have subjugated and possess the empire.
. . . Capable men have already shared with me in its pacification. Should
it be that any capable persons are not to share with me in its comfort
and its profit?" The emperor was thus limited by the necessity of
giving high office to those who did outstanding services to the state.

Since the government cultivated popular support and the Emperor
recognized that he depended upon his officials, it was quite natural that
Kao-tsu should have initiated the procedure which finally brought about
the Chinese imperial civil service examination system. In an edict of 196
B.C., possibly at the instigation of Hsiao Ho, Kao-tsu ordered the officials
to send to the Chancellor of State all people of excellent reputation and
manifest virtue, so that their accomplishments and appearance could be
recorded and they could be given positions. Emperors Wen and Wu continued this practise, and the examination system gradually grew out of it.

We have said that this conception of imperial rule as limited by consultation with the high ministers and by moral considerations was specifically Confucian. This doctrine is to be found in the *Book of History*,
where the great rulers consult their ministers on all important matters.
It is the outgrowth of the attitude represented in that *Book* (II, III, iv, 7),
that Heaven sees as the people see, in Mencius (VII, II, xiv, 1), when he
says that the sovereign is inferior to the people and the spirits, and in
Hsün-tzu (IX, 4), "The prince is the boat; the common people are the
water. The water can support the boat, or the water can capsize the
boat." The Han dynasty became the first great patrons of Confucianism and under Emperor Wu that philosophy became an important
influence in the theory of government and in the training of government
servants. It has not always been realized that this Confucian influence
began with Kao-tsu.

Kao-tsu was not himself a Confucian. He seems indeed to have had,
especially in his earlier days, a deep dislike for the learned pedants of
the time. It is said, in the biography of Li Yi-chi, that before 207 B.C.,
probably when Kao-tsu had just started out as a general, some literati
came to him in full costume, with their literati's bonnets on, and that

Kao-tsu, in order to show his contempt for them, suddenly snatched off a bonnet and urinated into it. It is also told that when, in May 205, Shu-sun T'ung came to Kao-tsu and wore his literatus's robes, Kao-tsu hated it, so that Shu-sun T'ung changed and wore short clothes like those worn in Ch'u. Thus Kao-tsu had an aversion to the sight of the Confucian literatus.

That fact does not however warrant us in holding that Kao-tsu disliked Confucianism and was not influenced by it. Quite the contrary seems to have been the case. In Kao-tsu's father's home, four sons grew to maturity. The two oldest sons seem to have been farmers; Liu Chi, the third to grow up, studied military matters and became the Chief of a *T'ing*; Liu Chiao, the youngest, was sent to the state of Lu, which was not far from the homestead, and studied with three Confucian teachers. Later he studied the *Book of Odes* with Fou-ch'iu Po, a disciple of Hsün-tzu, who became the most outstanding member of the Confucian school. After Liu Chiao had been made the King of Ch'u, he summoned the three Confucian teachers with whom he had studied in his youth, and honored them as his Palace Grandees. In the time of the Empress Dowager *née* Lü, he sent his own son to study under Fou-ch'iu Po. Liu Chiao is furthermore said to have been very fond of the *Book of Odes* and to have himself written a commentary on it. Thus Liu Chiao, the younger brother of Kao-tsu, was himself a devoted and life-long Confucian, who secured an excellent Confucian classical education at the center of Confucian culture.

Liu Chiao was an intimate follower and companion of Kao-tsu from the time that Kao-tsu started out as a general. Kao-tsu left his older brother, Liu Chung (the oldest, Liu Po, had died previously), and Shen Yi-chi at the homestead to care for his father and wife, and took his other friends and followers with him to swell his army. It is said specifically that when Kao-tsu became Emperor, Liu Chiao waited upon him. He and Lu Wan, a boyhood friend, were the two persons closest to the Emperor. They had access to his private chambers, served as intermediaries, carried messages, and helped him to decide matters and make secret plans. Through his brother, much Confucian influence undoubtedly reached Kao-tsu. No one else of any education had as close relations with him; while Kao-tsu disliked the pedant and the pedant's appearance, yet he probably welcomed the Confucian teaching when it came to him divorced from the pedant.

There were several others who undoubtedly influenced Kao-tsu towards Confucianism. The earliest was Chang Liang, who came to Kao-tsu in February 208. He was not a literatus, but a politician, the descendant of the chancellors in Han_h. He was a well-educated man, and on occasion is represented as using classical allusions to back up advice on politics in a thoroughly Confucian manner. Kao-tsu respected him very highly, and publicly recognized him as his best advisor.

Li Yi-chi was a well-read Confucian who came to Kao-tsu in March/April 207. He was known to the people of his town as a Master or teacher, *sheng*, and came voluntarily to call upon and advise Kao-tsu. The latter contemptuously squatted upon the *k'ang* with two maids washing his feet, as he received him. But Li Yi-chi was more than a pedant, even though he probably wore his literatus's robes on that occasion. He was over sixty years old, six feet tall (English measure), and fearless. He reproved Kao-tsu for his discourtesy; the latter, who seems to have been trained to respect his elders, was impressed by the old man, arose, dismissed the maids, begged Li Yi-chi's pardon, and escorted him to the seat of honor. At that time Kao-tsu could not afford to lose any worthwhile advice; Li Yi-chi delighted him with stories of earlier times, then gave him direction and assistance in capturing a neighboring city. For that Kao-tsu rewarded him; the old man was quite garrulous; he had earned the nickname of "the Mad Master," and Kao-tsu liked him. At the time, Kao-tsu was giving honorary titles to those of his followers who distinguished themselves; to Li Yi-chi he gave the title of Baronet Enlarging Our Territory. Kao-tsu respected the old man, consulted with him about important matters, and sent him as a confidential envoy on important commissions.

In April 205, when Kao-tsu came to Lo-yang, the old gentleman Tung, who was a *San-lao* or leader of the people, stopped him and advised him, in thoroughly Confucian terms, to declare a crusade against Hsiang Yü because the latter had caused the assassination of his superior, the Emperor Yi. This practise, that of leading a military force to chastize a wicked ruler, is typically Confucian; in the *Book of History* Kings T'ang and Wu are both said to have led such a crusade and to have founded their dynasties in so doing. The notion was welcomed by Kao-tsu; he found it worked, for it enabled him to lead a coalition army of 560,000 men with five kings against Hsiang Yü, and to capture his capital. After this experience, Kao-tsu would not have looked with disfavor upon a teaching that so helped him against his enemy. Confucianism now became to him a most useful and helpful philosophy.

Shu-sun T'ung had been made an Erudit by the Second Emperor, and had served Hsiang Yü as an Erudit. When, in May 205, Kao-tsu captured P'eng-ch'eng, Hsiang Yü's capital, Shu-sun T'ung, who followed the policy of making himself useful to whoever was in power, surrendered to Kao-tsu. He pleased Kao-tsu with stories of fighting and war, avoiding any typically Confucian teaching. Kao-tsu made him an Erudit and gave him a title. When Kao-tsu ascended the throne, Shu-sun T'ung arranged the ceremony.

After the court had been established, Kao-tsu found himself at a loss without any court ceremonial. He himself believed in simple direct intercourse without bothering about ceremonial. Possibly what he most disliked in Confucianism was its excessive ceremonialism. Now Kao-tsu's courtiers, who were his old camp-companions, were behaving in the court just as they did in camp. Especially when under the influence of liquor, they quarrelled, shouted, acted mannerlessly, and even pulled out their swords and hacked at the columns of the palace. Kao-tsu was very much worried, for he saw that this sort of conduct must somehow be stopped. Shu-sun T'ung offered to remedy the matter by arranging a court ceremonial. Kao-tsu saw that something of that sort was necessary, so told him to go ahead, with the admonition, "Make it easy." Shu-sun T'ung called some thirty odd literati from Lu, and with them created a court ceremonial by mixing the Confucian ceremonial with that of the Ch'in court. After more than a month of preparation, the ceremonial was performed out in the country before Kao-tsu, who approved it, and had it put into practise at the court of November 201. After the ceremony Kao-tsu was so impressed that he said, "Now, I have today known what is the greatness of being an Emperor." Thus Kao-tsu even accepted a semi-Confucian ceremonial for his court.

Lu Chia came to Kao-tsu possibly at the same time as Li Yi-chi, for we find them associated together only a few months later. He was also a highly educated man and was sent as an envoy to Ch'ao T'o, King of Nan-yüeh, whose capital was at the present Canton. After his return in 196 or 195 B.C., he is said to have quoted the *Book of Odes* and the *Book of History* to Kao-tsu, whereat the latter scolded him and said, "I got the empire on horseback; why should I bother with the *Book of Odes* or the *Book of History*?" Lu Chia replied, "You got it on horseback, but can you rule it from horseback?" Then he proceeded to quote cases, from ancient history, of kings who had lost their thrones through their wickedness, concluding with the Ch'in dynasty, which Kao-tsu had himself overthrown. Kao-tsu blushed for shame and asked Lu Chia to write a book explaining why these rulers had lost their kingdoms. That book has come down to us. It is a piece of thoroughly Confucian exhortation, which argues that the rise and fall of dynasties depends on their virtue. It is said that when each chapter was completed, Lu Chia read it to Kao-tsu, who praised it and gave the book its

title, the *Hsin-yü*, "New Discourses." This event undoubtedly deep-
ened Kao-tsu's gradual conversion to Confucianism.

As his experience of statecraft increased and as he saw deeper into the
necessities of an empire, Confucianism thus looked more and more attrac-
tive. It is recorded that when in December/January 195/4 Kao-tsu
passed through Lu, he sacrificed a suovetaurilia to Confucius, but this
record is very likely unhistorical.

The climax of Kao-tsu's allegiance to Confucianism came 'when he
proposed to change the succession to the throne. Chang Liang, Shu-sun
T'ung, and others remonstrated with Kao-tsu against this change, but
without effect. Because of Kao-tsu's lack of manners, some Confucians
had refused to come to his court. Kao-tsu had by this time realized
how deep was the influence of the Confucians with the people. He
knew that just as he had won the throne, so his successors could only
keep it by securing the respect of the people. When, in the first part
of 195 B.C., Kao-tsu came actually to change the succession, and found
that his Empress had succeeded in bringing to follow her son, Ying, four
outstanding Confucians who had previously refused to come to Kao-tsu,
he refused to change the succession, for he knew how powerful was their
influence. Thus Kao-tsu finally bowed to the influence of Confucianism.

The gradual turning of Kao-tsu to Confucianism does not mean that
other philosophies had no influence. Chang Liang was much more a
Taoist than a Confucian. The imperial administration was taken over
from the Ch'in court, and brought with it much Legalist influence.
Ts'ao Ts'an was a devotee of Lao-tsu. It was only gradually that Confucianism came to have nominally exclusive sway as a philosophy in the
Han court. Under Emperor Wen, there were Erudits who specialized in
the non-Confucian philosophers; the only Confucian erudit at his court
was Chia Yi. It was not until 141 that Emperor Wu forbade the promotion of scholars who were learned in the non-Confucian teachings. Even
after that, many Legalist practises persisted. Thus the victory of Confucianism was only a gradual growth, yet it was a natural continuation
of the development in Kao-tsu's own thought.

*   *   *

The tremendous achievement of Kao-tsu in rising from the status of a
farmer boy to Emperor against the keenest competition, early attracted
the attention of thoughtful persons and led them to state reasons for
his victory. At a grand feast after Kao-tsu's accession, he is said to have
asked his courtiers to name the reasons for his victory. Kao Ch'i and

Wang Ling declared that although Kao-tsu was unmannerly and rude to people, while Hsiang Yü was kind and respectful, yet Kao-tsu rewarded his associates adequately, sharing his conquests with them, whereas Hsiang Yü was suspicious of capable people, did not give them any recognition for their victories, and kept the fruits of victory for himself and his family. Kao-tsu replied that there was an additional factor: Hsiang Yü did not trust his most capable advisor, whereas Kao-tsu succeeded because he could make use of his followers—a most tactful speech.

Kao Ch'i and Wang Ling undoubtedly hit upon a most unfortunate defect in Hsiang Yü. He seems to have been jealous of anyone else who achieved any military glory. He probably minimized other people's achievements. He had several uncles and cousins who had to be taken care of, so that he was not free to give the best territory to others. He also seems to have been suspicious of those who were not of his own clan. (Kao-tsu was also suspicious, but he trusted the men of P'ei, who were his early followers, and gave them high positions.) As a consequence, the best of Hsiang Yü's followers left him or rebelled. Han Hsin came to Kao-tsu because Hsiang Yü had rebuffed him. Ch'ing Pu, Hsiang Yü's Commander-in-chief, rebelled and came to Kao-tsu because of the treatment he had received from Hsiang Yü. At the division of the territory, the kings complained that Hsiang Yü had given himself too much of the best territory. Hsiang Yü's unfortunate temperament thus more than undid all he accomplished by his wonderful military ability.

About 22 A.D. Pan Piao, Pan Ku's father, wrote his *Discussion on the Destiny of Kings* (cf. ch. 100), in which he argues that Kao-tsu's rise was not due to chance, as many were saying, and enumerates five reasons for that victory: (1) his descent from Yao, (2) his unusual body and features, (3) his military success, (4) his liberality, perspicacity, benevolence, and consideration for others, and (5) his keenness in judging others and in selecting his subordinates. He adds that Kao-tsu was faithful and sincere; he made far-reaching plans and was willing to accept the advice of others; he did not hesitate, but acted promptly; and he was favored by the supernatural powers with marvellous events. Pan Piao concludes that Kao-tsu's success was due to supernatural influence. His list of reasons undoubtedly contains much insight. There have been very many other such lists, from early Han times down.

We mention here three further factors. First, Kao-tsu made the people feel that he was governing in their interests. This factor appeared in his conception of rule as ethical, not an arbitrary absolutism.

Secondly, there was probably a general fellow-feeling among the common people for this commoner who was aspiring to the supreme position. The oppression of the aristocrats, which culminated in the cruelties of the Ch'in dynasty, brought about a reaction in popular feeling, so that many common people came to prefer for their ruler a commoner to an aristocrat. Especially when the aristocrats showed their weakness as generals in competition with others, this feeling was bound to have been intensified. The actions of Hsiang Yü, the outstanding aristocrat, did not help matters. His carelessness for the people's lives became notorious. At the storming of Hsiang-ch'eng, in June 208, he massacred every living thing in the city. In July/August 207, when the surrendered army of Chang Han threatened trouble, he had the whole army massacred, said to be more than twenty thousand men. Such acts were sure to set the common people against the aristocrats. By contrast, Kao-tsu took care to be generous and mild. When, in October 208, the older generals of King Huai had to select someone to go west and attempt to capture the Ch'in capital, they chose Kao-tsu rather than Hsiang Yü, because of the reputation for destructiveness that Hsiang Yü had acquired at Hsiang-ch'eng, and because of Kao-tsu's reputation for generosity. They were afraid that the news of Hsiang Yü's approach would nerve the people of Kuan-chung to defend their country vigorously, in which case it would be impregnable. Kao-tsu acquainted these people with his mild purposes, and they made no move to support their rulers, so that the capital fell. After Kao-tsu had acquired their confidence and got them to mount their natural barriers, Hsiang Yü did not even attempt to invade Kuan-chung.

Kao-tsu's generous and kindly treatment of the people thus brought to him the fellow-feeling of the people. They realized that he was one of them. More than once the leaders of the people came to him with important advice. His lack of manners and use of churlish language towards even his most distinguished followers probably accentuated the kindly feeling of the people to him. He won because he manipulated public opinion in his favor; that feeling was so strong two centuries later that, at the downfall of his dynasty, only another Han dynasty with the same surname could gain the throne.

In the third place, Kao-tsu introduced not only new ideas, but also new blood into the government. His nobles were self-made men who fought their way to distinction. His government was organized by Hsiao Ho. The latter was a personal friend and fellow-villager of Kao-tsu, who had been promoted to be Chief Official in P'ei because of his skill in the law. He was a trained administrator, and was put in charge of Kuan-chung as Chancellor while Kao-tsu went out fighting. Hsiao Ho thus administered Kao-tsu's base and organized Kao-tsu's supplies. He furthermore enacted the fundamental laws of the Han empire and gave to the government its organization. He performed this task so well that for half a century afterwards, his successors merely followed in his footsteps. He built the imperial palaces in a grander style than Kao-tsu had conceived of, because he knew that this magnificence was necessary to impress the people. When the campaign against Hsiang Yü was over, Kao tsu awarded to Hsiao Ho the first place in the court and gave him the title of Chancellor of State, even though he had done no fighting, for Kao-tsu realized the importance of Hsiao Ho's work. To the frugal and simple administration of government by Hsiao Ho and his assistants must be credited much of Kao-tsu's success. After Hsiao Ho, except for his immediate successor and the Empress *née* Lü's uncle, both of whom were not important historically, the high title of Chancellor of State was not used again, so great was the respect of the dynasty for Hsiao Ho.

Whether we shall ever be able to state all of the reasons for the success of Kao-tsu is doubtful. His own personality, the mistakes of his opponents, especially of the Ch'in dynasty and Hsiang Yü, Kao-tsu's cultivation of the people's good will, the fellow-feeling of the people for this commoner, and the ability of the new blood he introduced into the government, especially Hsiao Ho, are undoubtedly important factors.

Chapter I

THE FIRST [IMPERIAL ANNALS]

THE ANNALS OF [THE EMPEROR][1] KAO [TSU]

PART I

漢　高　高　中
書　紀　祖　陽
一　第　沛　里
　　一　豐　人
　　上　邑　也

Kao-tsu was a man from the hamlet of Chung-yang [in the district] town of Feng, [prefecture[2] of] P'ei.

[1] Wang Nien-sun (1744–1832) shows that the word *ti* 帝 was not originally in the title of the first twelve chapters, and that these chapters were merely called "Annals." The Ching-yu ed. (1034–5), prepared in the Imperial Academy, has not this character in the title of the first twelve chapters. Ch. 100B, in summarizing each chapter, likewise does not use *ti*. In *HS* 31: 22a, a cross reference is made to ch. 1, and *ti* is not used. Yen Shih-ku (581–645) in a comment in ch. 2 refers to ch. 1 without using *ti*. Elsewhere references in the text and by Yen Shih-ku similarly do not use this word. Wang Hsien-ch'ien (1842–1918) adds that the Ch'ien-tao ed. (1171) likewise does not use *ti* or divide the chapters into parts, and that Yen Shih-ku divided the chapters into parts. The words that have been supplied in the heading of this chapter are in the present text or in the Chinese table of contents.

The first part of this chapter is copied, almost verbatim, from *SC* ch. 7 and 8, with very few significant variations. Not until the second part of the chapter is much new material added. This practise of copying verbatim from earlier sources is the common practise in writing Chinese history; the *SC* does it constantly. It does not constitute plagiarism in China, it was merely the commonly accepted practise and is considered the surest method of securing dependable records. In ancient times no credit needed to be given to works from which passages were copied, for no credit was expected, and educated persons (who knew the books and whose opinion was alone worth while) would know whence statements were taken. The *HS* says in its introduction (100B: 1a) "Hence I have scrutinized and have taken from the previous records, and have put together and compiled what I have heard."

[2] In the Ch'ing period a *hsien* 縣 was a sub-division of a pre-

2a His family name was Liu.   One day the old dame, 姓　嘗　陂　是　冥
his mother, was resting upon the dyke of a large pond 劉　息　夢　時　父
2b when she dreamed that she had a meeting with a 氏　大　與　雷　太
supernatural being.[1]   At the time there was thunder 母　澤　神　電　公
and lightning, and it became dark.   When [Kao-tsu's] 媼　之　遇　晦　往
father, the *T'ai-kung*,[2] came to look for her, he saw a

fecture 府; in Han times, however, as Chavannes remarks (cf. *Mh*, II, 531), there was
no administrative division between a *hsien* and a commandery, hence I have followed
him in translating *hsien* for Han times as "prefecture."   The Han dynasty's commandery
郡 corresponded roughly to the modern province in that it was the primary subdivision
of the country, although the ancient term 州, which I have translated "province," was
later also put into use.   Under the Ch'in dynasty, there were 36 commanderies; under
the Han the number kept increasing until there were 108.

A "district town" 鄉邑, was a walled city which was the administrative center
for a subdivision of a prefecture.   In ancient times the 都 was a large walled city and
the 邑, was a small walled town; under the influence of the Lord of Shang, Kung-sun
Yang, the Ch'in dynasty had organized towns into districts, which districts were
often given the name of their walled towns.   The districts were subdivided into *t'ing*
(cf. p. 29, n. 3), and the *t'ing* were further subdivided into hamlets.

It is an interesting fact that quite a few of Kao-tsu's early followers came from the
same district as he: Hsiao Ho, Ts'ao Ts'an, Wang Ling, Chou P'o, Fan K'uai, Hsia-
hou Ying, Chou Hsieh (cf. *HS* ch. 41), Chou Ho, Chou Ch'ang, and Jen Ao (cf. *HS*
ch. 42); while his general Lu Wan came from the same hamlet as Kao-tsu.

[1] A supposed ancestor of Kao-tsu, Liu Lui, is said to have tamed dragons—thus the
story about Kao-tsu's conception would appear natural.   The reliable commentators
do not even give the surname of his mother.   Huang-fu Mi (215–282), a decidedly
unreliable source, says, "The old dame was probably surnamed Wang 王."   She died
before Kao-tsu came to the throne, so that her surname was not preserved.

Shen Ch'in-han (1775–1831) notes that the *T'ai-p'ing Huan-yü Chi* (written by Yo
Shih, 930–1007) tells that 6 *li* north of the city of Feng there was a large marsh.   The
Book of Odes, I, xii, x, 1 (Legge, p. 213) has a similar passage, "By the dyke of that
marsh. . . . There is the beautiful lady."

The word *yü* 遇 is said by Yen Shih-ku to mean "a meeting; to meet without having
an appointment is called *yü*."   Wang Min-sheng (1720–1798) adds that sexual intercourse is implied.   Shen Ch'in-han (1775–1831) adds that the conception here is
similar to that in the stele of 175 A.D. to the Emperor Yao, which says, "Ch'ing-tu
had intercourse with a red dragon, and gave birth to Yi Yao," [Yi was the surname of
Yao], and the Ling-t'ai stele at Ch'eng-yang, which says, "She wandered and glanced
around on the shore of the [Yellow] River, and, affected by intercourse with a red
dragon, she then gave birth to Yao."   This account thus likens Kao-tsu to his supposed ancestor, Yao.

[2] *T'ai-kung* 太公 is a term of respectful address for an aged and respected grand-

壯試吏爲泗上亭長廷中吏無所不
也常有大度不事家人生產作業及
股有七十二黑子寬仁愛人意豁如
祖高祖爲人隆準而龍顏美須髯左
視則見交龍於上已而有娠遂產高

scaly dragon[1] above her. After that she was with child and subsequently gave birth to Kao-tsu.   248 B.C.

Kao-tsu was a man with a prominent nose and a dragon forehead. He had a beautiful beard on his 3a chin and cheeks. On his left thigh were seventy-two black moles.[2] He was kindly disposed to others, benevolent, and liked people. His mind was vast. He always had large ideas and so did not follow the same productive occupations [as those followed by] the members of his family. When he grew up, he took the tests for officials, and was made Chief of the Szu-shui T'ing.[3] There was none of the officials in the

father. It merely means, "the aged and respected head of the family." Huang-fu Mi (215–282), who is not reliable, says that his name was Chih-chia 執嘉. Wang Fu (i & ii cent.) said that his name was T'uan 煓. Chang Shou-chieh (fl. 737) quotes the Ch'un-ch'iu Wu-ch'eng (now lost, written before 386), as saying, "The old dame Liu [Kao-tsu's grandmother] dreamed [about] a red bird like a dragon playing [with her]. After that she gave birth to Chih-chia." None of these sources is reliable; perhaps Kao-tsu's father, like his sons, had no given name.

[1] The HS writes 交; the SC (8: 2a) writes chiao 蛟; so does Hsün Yüeh (148–209) in his Han-chi, and the Wen-hsüan (ca. 530). Wang Hsien-ch'ien says that HS ch. 51 reads as HS ch. 1 does, but we have not been able to find this passage. He also says that these two characters were interchanged. Hence we have followed the SC, for the HS is copying it here. The Kuang-ya (by Chang Yi, fl. 227–233) says, "When it has scales it is called a chiao dragon." The Shuo-wen (ca. 100) defines chiao as follows: "A sort of dragon. When in a pool there are 3600 fish, the chiao comes and is made their leader. He is able to lead the fish and to fly. If a basket fish trap is put in the water, he thereupon leaves." Couvreur (Dict. Classique) says that the chiao is a crocodile. Cf. 6: 29a and note 29.2.

[2] Seventy-two was a mystic number, being the number of the days of each year attributed to each of the five elements, the number of ancient sovereigns who had performed the feng and shan sacrifices, the number of the metals, etc. Cf. Mh II, 325, n. 6. It was also the number of the Ch'ih-yu brotherhood, cf. Granet, Chinese Civilization, p. 197.

[3] The t'ing 亭 was an administrative division usually composed of ten hamlets 里, each of 25 to 50 families. Stein (Serindia, II, 748) found that, at the boundary, a t'ing was expected to maintain a tui 隊 or company (whose average effective strength was 150 men), both as to personnel and supplies. Probably something of the same sort was required in China proper in times of war. Ten t'ing usually made a district 鄉. Cf. Mh II, 236, n. 1.

The chief of a t'ing had charge of both a military and civil affairs of the t'ing.

great hall[1] whom he did not dare to treat cavalierly.

He liked wine and women. He frequently went to an old dame Wang and an old lady Wu to buy wine **3b** on credit. While he was sleeping off the effects of the wine, the old lady Wu and the old woman Wang frequently saw wonderful sights above him.[2] Every time Kao-tsu came to buy wine, he would stay and drink, and they would sell several times [as much as usual],[3] and when they saw the wonderful sights, at the end of the year, these two shop-keepers often broke up his accounts[4] and forgave his debt.

Kao-tsu was frequently made to do fatigue duty in Hsien-yang, and had free access to see the Emperor of the Ch'in [dynasty]. Moved in spirit he would heave a deep sigh and say, "Ah! A real man should be like this."

A man of Shan-fu, the old gentleman Lü, was a good friend of the magistrate in [the city of] P'ei. **4a** In order to escape a feud, he came to [the magistrate] as his guest and consequently settled there. When the eminent and distinguished persons and officials of P'ei heard that the magistrate had an important

狎侮好酒及色常從王媼武負貰酒時飲醉臥武負王媼見其上常有

怪高祖每酤留飲酒讎數倍及見怪歲竟此兩家常折券棄責高祖常

繇咸陽縱觀秦皇帝喟然大息曰嗟乎大丈夫當如此矣單父人呂公

善沛令辟仇從之客因家焉沛中豪傑吏聞令有重客皆往賀蕭何為

Ying Shao (ca. 140–206) writes, "In ancient times he was called 'The Bearer of the Crossbow.'" In Han times he used all five weapons: crossbow, lance, sword, bow, and cuirass.

Instead of "the Szu-shang *T'ing*", the *SC* (*Mh* II, 336) reads "the Szu-shui *T'ing*", which reading is confirmed by *HHS*, Tr. 20: 13b. *Shang* is an error for *shui*.

The *Kua-ti-chih* 5: 5b (vii cent.) said, "The Szu-shui *T'ing* is in Hsü-chou, 100 paces east of P'ei Hsien, and has a temple to Kao-tsu."

[1] Yen Shih-ku writes, " 'In the great hall' [means] in the great hall of the commandery headquarters."

[2] The *SC* reads differently: these women "often saw a dragon above him and wondered at it." *HS* 100A: 11a reads, "He had prodigies of dragons and snakes."

[3] Chao Yi (1727–1814) suggests an interpretation for this sentence similiar to the story in *HS* 8: 3a, that when Emperor Hsüan, as a young man, bought cakes, he made them popular, so that the seller made great sales.

[4] Accounts were kept on pieces of bamboo or wood.

主吏主進令諸大夫曰進不滿千錢坐之堂下高祖爲亭長

素易諸吏乃紿爲謁曰賀錢萬實不持一錢謁入呂公大驚

起迎之門呂公者好相人見高祖狀貌因重敬之引入坐上

坐蕭何曰劉李固多大言少成事高祖因狎侮諸客遂坐上

坐無所詘酒闌呂公因目固留高祖竟酒後呂公曰臣少好

guest, they all went to congratulate him.[1] Hsiao Ho was the superintendant of officials and took charge of the offerings. He made announcement to the prominent guests, saying, "Anyone who comes presenting less than a thousand cash will be directed to sit below the [main] hall." Although Kao-tsu was [only] Chief of a *t'ing*, he used to treat his fellow-officials contemptuously, so he falsely had written on his card: "I come to congratulate [with an offering of] ten thousand cash." Really he did not bring even one cash.

When his card was sent in, the old gentleman Lü was greatly surprised, arose, and welcomed him at the door. [Now] the old gentleman Lü liked to physiognomize[2] people and it was because he noticed Kao-tsu's appearance and features that he greatly honored him. He escorted him in and seated him at the seat of honor. Hsiao Ho said, "Liu Chi **4b** certainly talks very big, but he achieves little." Because Kao-tsu was contemptuous of the guests, he thereupon seated himself on the place of honor without any signs of nervousness. When the drinking drew to an end,[3] the old gentleman Lü glanced at Kao-tsu in such a way as definitely to detain him. After the drinking was over, the old gentleman Lü said, "Your servant, from his youth,

[1] Such congratulations necessitate the bringing of gifts, in this case, of money, and a feast in return.

[2] It is still a common practice in China to tell a person's fortune by 'reading his face.' This is the practise referred to. Hsün-tzu (ca. 320-235 B.C.) attacks this practise (cf. his ch. V). Wang Ch'ung (29–97) defends it in the *Lun-heng*, ch. ii (Forke p. 305), and quotes this passage.

[3] So that some of the guests were leaving. Guests do not necessarily stay through a feast. Wen Ying (fl. ca. 196–220) says, "It says that of those who drank wine half had left and half were [still] present."

has liked to physiognomize people. I have physiognomized many people. [But] none of them had [as auspicious] a physiognomy as yours, Chi. You, Chi, should take care of yourself. There is a daughter born to your servant whom I would like to make your hand-maid."[1]

When the feast was over, the old lady Lü was angry with the old gentleman Lü, and said: "Previously you, sir, have always wanted to hold this girl precious in order to give her [in marriage] to some distinguished person. The magistrate of P'ei is your good friend. He has asked for her, but you would not give her to him. Why did you yourself thus senselessly promise to give her to this Liu Chi?" The old gentleman Lü replied, "This is not anything that children or women can understand." In the end he gave her to Kao-tsu. The daughter of the old gentleman Lü was [later] the Empress [*née*] Lü and gave birth to the Emperor Hsiao-hui and the Princess Yüan of Lu.

5a   Kao-tsu once asked for leave to go home to his fields. While the Empress [*née*] Lü and her two children were in the fields,[2] an old man went by and asked for a drink; the Empress [*née*] Lü therefore fed him. The old man physiognomized the Empress and said: "Madam will be the most honorable **5b** personage in the world." She [then] asked him to physiognomize her two children. When he saw the Emperor Hsiao-hui, he said, "The reason that

---

[1] He uses a set expression for "wife," which is literally, "the concubine of the dust-pan and broom." The word "concubine" gives it a depreciatory turn. Cf. *Mh* II, 328, n. 3.

[2] The *SC* says that they were weeding. At the time, the Empress Lü was merely a peasant woman; the historian respectfully uses the title later bestowed upon her. So with the children.

相人相人多矣無如季相願季自愛臣有息女願爲箕帚妾酒罷呂媼

怒呂公曰公始欲奇此女與貴人沛令善公求之不與何自妄許與

劉季呂公曰此非兒女子所知卒與高祖呂公女即呂后也生孝惠帝

魯元公主高祖嘗告歸之田呂后與兩子居田中有一老父過請飲呂

后因餔之老父相后曰夫人天下貴人也令相兩子見孝惠帝曰夫人

所以貴者乃此男也相魯元公主亦皆貴老父已去高祖適從旁

舍來呂后具言客有過相我子母皆大貴高祖問曰未遠乃追及

問老父老父曰鄉者夫人兒子皆以君君相貴不可言高祖乃謝

曰誠如父言不敢忘德及高祖貴遂不知老父處高祖爲亭長乃

目竹皮爲冠令求盜之薛治時時冠之及貴常冠所謂劉氏冠也

Madam will be such an honorable personage is this boy." He physiognomized the Princess Yüan of Lu [and said] also, "Both will be honorable personages."

When the old man had gone, Kao-tsu happened to come in from a neighboring dwelling. The Empress *née* Lü told him everything, "A stranger has gone by who physiognomized me and the children, [and told me that] we would all be very honorable personages." When Kao-tsu questioned her, she added, "He has not yet gone far." So he went after him and caught up with him. When he questioned the old man, the old man said, "The madam and children whom I have just looked at are all like you, sir [in princely signs].[1] Your physiognomy, sir, is honorable beyond all telling." Kao-tsu thereupon thanked him, saying, "If it should really happen as you say, I shall not dare to forget what you have done for me." When Kao-tsu became an honorable personage, no one knew where the old man was.

When Kao-tsu was the Chief of a *t'ing*, he constructed a hat of bamboo-skin and ordered his thief-catcher to go to Hsieh to have it perfected.[2] From **6a** time to time he wore it. When he became an honorable personage, he wore it constantly; it is

[1] The *SC* reads 似 for the *HS* 以. Ju Shun (fl. dur. 189–265) and Ch'ien Tao-chao (1744–1813) think that the *SC*'s reading should be adopted. The *Han-chi* 1: 3a however reads, "The [princely signs of] the madam and children are due to your power, sir," and Yen Shih-ku wishes to read this passage similarly. The *Lun-heng* (by Wang Ch'ung, 29–97) reads like the *SC*. We have adopted its reading.

[2] Ying Shao writes that anciently there were two subordinates to the Chief of a *t'ing*: one, called the *T'ing-fu* 亭 父, whose duty it was to open and shut the gates, sweep and clean [streets]; the other, called the Thief-catcher *ch'iu-tao* 求 盜, pursued and caught robbers and thieves. Chavannes (*Mh* II 330) did not understand that *ch'iu-tao* was the name of an officer, so mistranslated this sentence.

For an account of this ceremonial article, cf. Glossary *sub* Hat of the House of Liu.

called the "Hat of the House of Liu."

Kao-tsu, in his capacity as the Chief of a *t'ing*, had to escort convict laborers[1] to Mount Li for the prefecture. Many [of the convict laborers] escaped on the way. He thought to himself that before he arrived [at his destination] all of them would have escaped. When [the party] got to the Tse-chung *T'ing*, west of Feng, he stopped to drink. At night he unbound and set free all the convict laborers he was escorting, saying, "Gentlemen, all go away. From this time on I too will abscond."[2] Some ten odd of the stout fellows among the convict laborers were willing to follow him.

Kao-tsu, under the influence of liquor, was 6b traversing the marsh [one] night. He had ordered a man to go in front. The man who was in front returned and reported, "Up ahead there is a large serpent blocking the path. We had better go back." Kao-tsu was drunk and said, "When a strong man walks along, what is there to fear?" Then he went ahead, drew his sword, and cut the serpent in two.[3] The serpent was divided into two

蛇當徑願還高祖醉曰壯士行何畏乃前拔劍斬蛇

被酒夜徑澤中令一人行前行前者還報曰前有大

皆去吾亦從此逝矣徒中壯士願從者十餘人高祖

亡之到豐西澤中亭止飲夜皆解縱所送徒曰公等

高祖以亭長爲縣送徒驪山徒多道亡自度比至皆

---

[1] Enslavement or convict labor was a common punishment; a criminal could be sentenced to enslavement for a number of years. The First Emperor used these convicts on his works. As a guard, Kao-tsu was personally responsible for each prisoner, and would be punished if one was lost.

[2] Since he had lost his prisoners, Kao-tsu could not return home, and also became a fugitive.

[3] The *San-fu Huang-t'u* (quoted in iii cent.; prob. completed by 587) 6:2a, b sub *Ling-chin Nei-fu*, says, "When the Grand Emperor [Kao-tsu's father] was an humble person, he wore a sword that was three feet long. On it there were unintelligible words engraved. Tradition says it was made just at the time when 'Kao-tsung of the Yin [dynasty, i.e., the Emperor Wu-ting, reigned 1324–1266 B.C.] attacked the Demon region.' [A quotation from the *Book of Changes*, hexagram 63, Legge, p. 205. The 'Demon region' was among the Western Jung.] When the Grand Emperor was travelling around Feng and P'ei, in the middle of the mountains, at a temporary lodge in an obstructed valley there was a man casting metal. The Grand Emperor stopped beside him and asked him, 'What implement are you casting?' The workman laughingly said, 'I am casting swords for the Son of Heaven. Be careful and do not speak.' He [later] said, 'If I could secure the sword which you, sir, are wearing, mix it [with the metal], and cast it, then it would make a marvellous implement, which could conquer and subjugate the world. The essence of the Pleiades is helping, the [ele-

今者赤帝子斬之故哭人乃以嫗爲
殺嫗曰吾子白帝子也化爲蛇當道
哭嫗曰人殺吾子人曰嫗子何爲見
來至蛇所有一老嫗夜哭人問嫗何
蛇分爲兩道開行數里醉困臥後人

parts and the way cleared. After walking several *li*, he was overpowered by drink[1] and slept. When a man [who came along] afterwards reached the place where the serpent had been, an old woman was weeping there in the night. The man asked the old woman why she wept, and the old woman replied, "A man killed my son." The man said, "How did your son come to be killed?" and the old woman replied, "My son is the son of the White God. He metamorphosed himself into a serpent and blocked the way. Just now the son of the Red God has cut him in two; hence I weep [for him]."[2] Now the man thought that the old woman was not speaking the

ment] wood is decreasing and [the element] fire is increasing [water was the element by which the Ch'in dynasty is said to have ruled, and fire the element of the Han dynasty]—this is an unusual omen.' The Grand Emperor loosened his *pi-shou* [a sword with its point in the form of a spoon], and threw it into the furnace. When the sword was completed, he killed three victims in order to anoint [the sword] with the blood of the sacrifice. The workman asked him where he had gotten this [sword which had been melted], and the Grand Emperor replied, 'At the time of King Chao-hsiang of Ch'in [306–251 B.C.], I was going along a path in the fields and a rustic gave it to me, saying, "This is a supernatural thing from the time of the Yin [dynasty]." ' The workman thereupon took the sword and gave it to the Grand Emperor. The Grand Emperor therefore gave it to Kao-tsu. Kao-tsu wore it, and this it was which cut in two the white snake. When he had subjugated the world, he stored it in the treasury for valuables. The guardian of the storehouse saw a white vapor like a cloud coming out of the door, in shape like a dragon or snake. The Empress [*née*] Lü changed the treasury's [name] and called it, 'The Storehouse for Supernatural Metallic [Objects].' When the Emperor Hui came to the throne, he used this treasury to store the [imperial] reserved military equipment, and its name was called, 'The Palace Office for Supernatural Metallic [Objects, i.e., *ling-chin nei-fu*]." The *Chin Dynastic History*, in the *Treatise on Carriages and Clothes*, says, "In the time of the Emperor Hui, the military treasury was burnt by fire." The *Shih-chi Cheng-yi* (pub. 737) quotes the *Kua-ti-chih*, (vii cent.) as saying, "The Ditch [Where] the Snake Was Cut in Two 斬蛇溝 has its source in the territory of Chung-p'ing, P'ei Hsien, Hsü-chou, [in present Kiangsu]. Hence old people say, 'It is the place where Kao-tsu cut in two the snake.' [It flows] to [a place] 15 *li* west of the *hsien*, where it flows into the P'ao 泡 River."

[1] The *SC*, the Official ed. of the *HS* (1739) the Academy ed. (prob. 1124), and Lin Chih-lung's ed. (1581) read 因; Chou Shou-ch'ang (1814–1884) points out that 困 gives a much better sense. We have followed him.

[2] Ying Shao comments, "Duke Hsiang of Ch'in [777–766 BC], from the time that

truth, and wanted to trouble her.[1] Therefore the old woman suddenly disappeared. When the man [who came along] afterwards reached [the place where Kao-tsu was], Kao-tsu had awakened, [and so] he told Kao-tsu [about it]. Then Kao-tsu privately rejoiced in heart and took confidence in himself, while his followers daily feared him more and more.

The First Emperor of the Ch'in dynasty once[2] said, "In the southeast there is the emanation of a Son of Heaven."[3] Thereupon he travelled to the east in order to check and obstruct [his rival].

東南有天子氣於是東游
日益畏之秦始皇帝嘗曰
祖乃心獨喜自負諸從者
後人至高祖覺告高祖高
不誠欲苦之嫗因忽不見

he dwelt in the west [771 B.C., cf. *Mh* II, 14f], took as his lord the spirit of Shao-hao [supposed to have reigned 2598–2515 B.C.], made the Western Sacred Place [120 *li* southwest of Ch'in 秦 Hsien, Kansu] and sacrificed to the White God [the *SC* says that he sacrificed to a Lord on High 上帝, cf. *Mh* II, 59]. In the time of Duke Hsien [384–362 B.C.] at Yo-yang it rained metal, which was considered an auspicious [omen]. He also made the Ch'i Sacred Place [in Yo-yang] and sacrificed to the White God, Shao-hao, who has the virtue of metal. The Red God is a descendant of Yao, and refers to the Han [dynasty]. The killing makes plain that the Han [dynasty] must destroy the Ch'in [dynasty]."

This incident was applied by Liu Hsiang to the theory of the five elements. The relationship of the elements to each other was differently conceived by different theorists. One theory was that metal overcame wood, wood overcame earth, earth overcame water, water overcame fire, fire overcame metal, and so on. Another theory was that wood gave birth to fire, fire gave birth to earth, earth gave birth to metal, metal gave birth to water, water gave birth to wood, and so on (cf. Forke, *Lun-heng*, vol. II, App. I). Chang Ts'ang (d. 152 B.C.) held that the Han dynasty ruled by virtue of the element water; Chia Yi (200-168 B.C.), followed by Szu-ma Ch'ien, held that the Ch'in dynasty ruled by virtue of water, and was overcome by the Han dynasty because the latter ruled by virtue of earth. Liu Hsiang (76-6 B.C.) and his son, Liu Hsin, however argued from the passage in the text that the Han dynasty ruled by virtue of the element fire, whose color is red, and that the Ch'in dynasty ruled by virtue of wood, which gave birth to fire (cf. *HS* 25 B: 23b). Wang Mang adopted this latter theory and argued that since he was descended from the Yellow Emperor, whose virtue is earth, and since earth is born of fire, he must succeed the Han dynasty. Ying Shao's interpretation is still different: the Ch'in dynasty reigned by virtue of metal, which was overcome by fire, the virtue of the Han dynasty. Thus history was interpreted to yield a philosophical theory of the elements and that was used to prognosticate events and legitimize usurpation.

[1] The *SC* has 笞 "beat," instead of the *HS*'s *k'u* 苦 "trouble." Hsü Kuang (ca. 352–425) says that one text of the *SC* writes *k'u*, and Shen Ch'in-han quotes a similar passage from the *Lü-shih Ch'un-ch'iu* (possibly ii cent.) Bk. XXII, ch. iii, also using *k'u*.

[2] The *SC* has 常 "continually," instead of the *HS* 嘗 "once."

[3] Wang Ch'i-yüan (xix cent.) notes that the *Chin Dynastic History*, in the *Treatise*

以獸當之高祖隱於芒碭山澤間呂后與
人俱求常得之高祖怪問之呂后曰季所
居上常有雲氣故從往常得季高祖又喜
沛中子弟或聞之多欲附者矣
秦二世元年秋七月陳涉起蘄至陳自立

Kao-tsu was hiding among the mountains and **7b**
marshes of Mang and Tang. The Empress [*née*]
Lü sought him, together with some men, and always
found him. Kao-tsu was surprised and asked her
about it. The Empress [*née*] Lü replied, "Above the
place where you, Chi, are, there is always a misty
emanation. So we follow after it and always find
you, Chi."[1] Kao-tsu was again glad. When some
of the young men in P'ei heard of it, many wanted
to attach themselves to him.

In the first year of the Second Emperor of the Sec. Emp.
Ch'in dynasty, in the autumn, the seventh month,[2] Yr. I
Ch'en Shê arose at Chi$_1$ and came to Ch'en$_2$, setting 209 B.C.
himself up as King of Ch'u.[3] He sent Wu Ch'en, Aug./Sept.

on Astronomy, says, "The emanation of the Son of Heaven is
red within and yellow without on all sides. In the place where
it appears there must be either a king or the Son of Heaven.
If there is a place to which he is going to travel, that place also
beforehand produces this emanation. Sometimes there are the gates of a city indistinctly
in the midst of the vapor or emanation. . . . Sometimes the emanation is like a person
clothed in black clothes without hands to the west of the sun. Sometimes it is like a
dragon-horse [an auspicious kind of horse]. Sometimes there is a mixed emanation
rising towards heaven. These are all the emanations of an emperor or king."

[1] Wang Hsien-shen (1859–1922) says that the *Shih-chi Cheng-yi* (737) quotes Yen
Shih-ku as saying that Ching Fang (i cent. B.C.) in his *Yi-chao-hou* says, "How can
a sage who is hiding be known? In all directions there always is a great cloud with
all five colors, yet it does not rain. Below it there is then a sage hiding himself.
Thus the Empress [*née*] Lü looked at the cloudy emanation and found him." This
comment is lacking in the present text.

[2] P'ei Yin (fl. 465–472) quotes Hsü Kuang (ca. 352–425) as saying "Kao-tsu was at
this time in his 48th year." Dates will be given in accordance with the calendar in
"Variétés Sinologiques," vol. 29, Père P. Hoang, *Concordance des Chronologies Néoméniques*, Shanghai 1910. But its Gregorian dates will be changed to Julian dates, in accordance with the common usage of historians and astronomers.

[3] Li Chi (fl. ca 200) explains, "The [state of] Ch'in had destroyed [the state of]
Ch'u, [hence] the people of Ch'u hated Ch'in. Hence [Ch'en] Shê, because of the
people's desire, called himself the King of Ch'u, according with the people's hopes."

Chang Erh, and Ch'en Yü to overrun[1] the region of
8a Chao.   In the eighth month, Wu Ch'en set himself up
Sept. as the King of Chao, and most of the commanderies
and prefectures, in responding to [Ch'en] Shê, killed
Oct. their chief officials.   In the ninth month, the magistrate of P'ei wanted to have P'ei also respond to
[Ch'en Shê].   The Chief [Jailor] and the Superintendent of the Officials, Hsiao Ho and Ts'ao Ts'an,
said [to him], "You, sir, have been an official of the
Ch'in [dynasty] and now wish to rebel against it,
and lead the young men of P'ei [in rebellion].   We
are afraid that they will not follow you.   We wish
that you, sir, will summon back all those who have
fled outside [the city].[2]   You can get several hundred men.   Then by using them you can coerce the
people, and the people will not dare but follow you."
So he ordered Fan K'uai to summon Kao-tsu.
Kao-tsu's followers had at this time reached [the
number of] several hundred.[3]   Then Fan K'uai
came in the train of Kao-tsu [to P'ei].

The magistrate of Pei had however repented [for
what he had done], for he had feared that there would
be trouble, and so had closed the city [gates] and defended the city wall.   He wanted to execute Hsiao
[Ho] and Ts'ao [Ts'an].   Hsiao [Ho] and Ts'ao
[Ts'an] were afraid, escaped over the city wall, and
took refuge with Kao-tsu.   Kao-tsu then wrote [a
message on a piece of] silk and shot it over the city

[1] Yen Shih-ku (581–645) says, "Whenever it says 略 地, it
always means to take it as one goes along with little labor or
force."

[2] Yen Shih-ku writes, "At that time they suffered from the
oppressive government of the Ch'in [dynasty]. Taxes were
heavy and *corvée* labor much.   Hence there were those who
fled and escaped to avoid the officials."

[3] The *SC* says, "Almost a hundred."

為楚遣武臣張耳陳餘略趙地八月武臣自立為趙王郡縣多殺長吏
以應涉九月沛令欲以沛應之掾主吏蕭何曹參曰君為秦吏今欲背之
帥沛子弟恐不聽願君召諸亡在外者可得數百人因以劫衆衆不敢不
聽乃令樊噲召高祖高祖之衆已數百人矣於是樊噲從高祖來沛令後
悔恐其有變乃閉城城守欲誅蕭曹蕭曹恐踰城保高祖高祖乃書帛射

38

城上與沛父老曰天下同苦秦久矣今父老雖爲沛令守諸侯

並起今屠沛沛今共誅令擇可立立之以應諸侯即室家完不

然父子俱屠無爲也父老乃帥子弟共殺沛令開城門迎高祖

欲以爲沛令高祖曰天下方擾諸侯並起令置將不善一敗塗

地吾非敢自愛恐能薄不能完父兄子弟此大事願更擇可者

wall, saying to the elders of P'ei, "The world[1] has already been filled for a long time with bitterness against the Ch'in [dynasty]. Although you are now defending the city for the magistrate of P'ei, the nobles are all rising and they will immediately slaughter [the people of] P'ei. Now if [you, people of] P'ei, together execute your magistrate, select **8b** someone who is able to lead you, make him your leader, and make common cause with the nobles, your houses and families will thereupon be safe; otherwise old and young will all be slaughtered. Do not allow [that to happen]." So the elders led the young men and together they killed the magistrate of P'ei, opened the city gates, and welcomed Kao-tsu [in].

They wanted him to be the magistrate of P'ei, [but] Kao-tsu said, "At present the world is in disorder. The nobles have all risen [in arms]. If now[2] you should set as your commander someone who is not capable, after a single defeat, you will be trampled to the ground. It is not that I am concerned about my own safety; I fear that I am not capable enough and that I shall not be able to keep you safe, elders and brothers.[3] This is an important matter. I hope that you will select again[4] a

---

[1] Lit. "All under heaven." The ancient Chinese, like the Romans, thought of their country as being the [known] world, or all of it that counted.

[2] Reading 今 with the Southern Academy ed. (1530), the Fukien ed. (1549), the Official ed. (1739), and the *SC* instead of the present 介.

[3] Yen Shih-ku (581–645) says, "Of the people in a village or town, those who are aged and older [than the speaker] are the group of 'fathers and older brothers' [we have translated this binomial 'elders']; those who are young and younger [than the speaker] are the group of 'sons and younger brothers' [we have translated 'brothers'], hence he addressed them all."

[4] Reading 更 with the Southern Academy ed. (1530), the Fukien ed. (1549), the Official ed. (1739) and the *SC*, instead of 吏.

39

more capable person." Hsiao [Ho], Ts'ao [Ts'an], and the others were all civil officials. They were concerned about their own safety, and feared that, if things should not turn out [successfully], the Ch'in rulers would later destroy them together with their families and kindred. So they every one withdrew in favor of Kao-tsu. The elders all said, "For a long time we have heard of wonders and prodigies concerning Liu Chi, and that he was worthy to become an honorable personage, and moreover that in divination, no one's [lot was ever] nearly as auspicious as that of Kao-tsu." Kao-tsu refused several times, but no one in the crowd was willing to undertake [the office]. So Kao-tsu was set up as Lord of P'ei.[1] He worshipped[2] the Yellow Emperor, sacrificed to

9a, 9b Ch'ih-yu in the great [prefectural] hall of P'ei, and

種族其家盡讓高祖諸父老皆曰平
生所聞劉季奇怪當貴且卜筮之莫
如劉季最吉高祖數讓衆莫肯爲高
祖乃立爲沛公祠黃帝祭蚩尤於沛

蕭曹等皆文吏自愛恐事不就後秦

[1] Meng K'ang (ca. 180–260) says, "[The rulers of] Ch'u had formerly usurped the title of King, and their rulers in the prefectures were made *kung* 公. Ch'en Shê was made the King of Ch'u; P'ei *kung* [i.e., Kao-tsu] arose in response to [Ch'en] Shê, hence he conformed to the regulations of [the state of] Ch'u and called [himself] *kung*." In the time of the Chou dynasty, the *kung* were the highest of the noble ranks, and the word is accordingly to be translated 'Duke.' In Ch'u however somewhat different practices had prevailed. At this time the feudal ranks had broken up; the Han dynasty preserved only the titles, Kings, Marquises, and Baronets. In Ch'u the *kung* were members of the official hierarchy rather than nobles; hence we have translated *kung* in this and similar titles as 'Lord'. *Kung* was also commonly used to denote a father or aged person. Cf. p. 28, n. 2. From this time until he was made King of Han₃, Kao-tsu is regularly styled 'the Lord of P'ei.' Cf. *Mh* II, 335, n. 1.

[2] The distinction between the two words used for the worship of these two gods is not exact. *Chi* 祭 (here translated "sacrificed to") seems to have been the general term for sacrifices. The *Li-chi*, ch. XX, uses *chi* as the title of its chapter on the various kinds of sacrifices. The *Shuo-wen* says, "*Chi* is to worship. [It comes] from 'worship' and a hand holding meat." Of *tz'u* 祠 (here translated "worshipped"), the *Shuo-wen* says, "The spring sacrifice (*chi*) is called *tz'u*. Few objects and many words [are used. It comes] from 'to worship' and the sound *szu*. In the second month of spring, in the *tz'u*, sacrificial animals are not used. Jade tablets and circlets together with leather (furs) and silk are used." But this sacrifice of Kao-tsu was made in October. The *Chou-li* ch. XIX (Biot's trans. p. 454) says, The *Szu-szu* [an official]

廷而釁鼓旗幟皆赤由所殺蛇白帝子所殺者赤帝子故

也於是少年豪吏如蕭曹樊噲等皆爲收沛子弟得三千

人是月項梁與兄子羽起吳田儋與從弟榮橫起齊自立

爲齊王韓廣自立爲燕王魏咎自立爲魏王陳涉之將周

anointed his drums with blood.[1]　His standards and[2] pennons were all red,[3] because the snake which was killed was the son of the White god and the killer was the son of the Red god.　Because of this [fact] all the **10a** younger braves and officials, like Hsiao [Ho], Ts'ao [Ts'an], Fan K'uai, and others, gathered together the youths of P'ei [for Kao-tsu.　Thus he] secured three thousand men.[4]

In this month, Hsiang Liang and his older brother's **Oct.** son, [Hsiang] Yü, arose in Wu; T'ien Tan, together with his cousins, [T'ien] Jung and [T'ien] Heng, arose in Ch'i, setting himself up as King of Ch'i. Han Kuang set himself up as the King of Yen. Wei Chiu set himself up as King of Wei_b.　A general of Ch'en Shê, Chou Chang, [led an army]

"establishes the great sacrifices, which use jade, silk, and pure victims.　He establishes the second class sacrifices, which use victims and silk.　He establishes the inferior sacrifices, which use victims."　Then *tz'u* is a sacrifice of the first rank.

The difference between these two words then seems to have been that *chi* was a general term for sacrifice, whereas *tz'u* denoted a worship mainly verbal and of the first rank.

[1] Yen Shih-ku says, "Anciently people, when they had newly completed a bell or a three-legged cauldron, had to anoint it with blood."　This procedure was an aspersion of the blood of the sacrificed animal upon an object.　The aspersing of the newly-made war-drums made them efficacious.　Cf. *Mh* II, 336, n. 1.

[2] Wu Jen-chieh (ca. 1137–1199) and Wang Hsien-ch'ien think that "standards" should be read with the preceding sentence and "pennons" with the next.　Yang Shu-ta (1885–present) shows that these two words are generally read together and that there is no reason to separate them.　The correctness of his view is shown by the similar phrase in 1B: 26a.

[3] Chu Tzu-wen (lived before 1195) remarked that the last part of this sentence, beginning with "because," is an interpolation, since it repeats what had previously been said.　But the story referred to was one of the important justifications of Kao-tsu's claim to the throne (cf. 100A: 8a), hence it is deservedly emphasized.

[4] Some sentences in the *SC* are omitted here.

west through the Pass[1] to Hsi[4].　The Ch'in general, Chang Han, repulsed and routed him.

Yr. II　In the second year [of the Second Emperor of
10b the] Ch'in [dynasty], the tenth month,[2] the Lord
Nov. of P'ei attacked Hu-ling and Fang-yu, then he returned and guarded [the town of] Feng.　P'ing, the
Inspecting [Secretary] of the Szu-shui[3] [commandery]
led an army to besiege Feng.　On the second day, [the
Lord of P'ei] made a sortie, fought with [the Inspector's army] and routed it.　[Then] he ordered
Yung Ch'ih to guard [the town of] Feng.

Dec.　In the eleventh month, the Lord of P'ei led troops
to Hsieh.　The troops of the Administrator of the
Szu-shui[3] [commandery] for the Ch'in [dynasty],
Chuang, were defeated at Hsieh, and fled to Ch'i.[4]
The Lord of P'ei's Junior Major[5] captured and killed
11a him.　Then the Lord of P'ei returned, encamped at
K'ang-fu, and went to Fang-yü.

The King of Chao, Wu Ch'en, was killed by his
Jan. general.[6]　In the twelfth month, the King of Ch'u,

[1] When 關 is used alone, it usually refers to Han-ku Pass.
The Ch'in dynasty's capital was beyond the pass.

[2] This was the first mònth of the official year.　Cf. App. II.
The HS differs in its order of events here from the SC ch. 7
& 8, because the HS attempts to follow a strictly chronological
order of events, following SC ch. 16.

[3] We have emended the 川 of the text to 水.　HS ch. 28
and 20 speak of a Szu-shui Commandery, but there was no place
by the name of Szu-ch'uan.　These two characters are alike in
the seal script and were easily confused.　Chavannes (Mh II,
337) has failed to note this necessary emendation.

[4] The location of this place is not certain; HS 28Aiii: 10a mentions a town 70 li south of the present T'eng Hsien, Shantung
by this name, which might have been the place.　Wang
Hsien-ch'ien points out that 39:10b tells that Ts'ao Ts'an
attacked Yüan-ch'i and K'ang-fu.　Ch'i might then be Yüan-
ch'i, q. v. in Glossary.

[5] His Junior Majors at that time were K'ung Chü, Ch'en
Ho, and T'ang Li, according to Chou Shou-chang.　They are
named in ch. 16.

[6] SC 16: 4a names his murderer as Li Liang 李良.

公左司馬得殺之沛公還軍亢父至方與趙王武臣爲其將所殺十二月楚
破之令雍齒守豐十一月沛公引兵之薛秦泗川守壯兵敗於薛走至戚沛
秦二年十月沛公攻胡陵方與還守豐秦泗川監平將兵圍豐二日出與戰
章西入關至戲秦將章邯距破之

王陳涉爲其御莊賈所殺魏人周市略地豐沛使人謂雍齒曰豐故梁

徙也今魏地已定者數十城齒今下魏魏以齒爲侯守豐不下且屠豐

雍齒雅不欲屬沛公及魏招之卽反爲魏守豐沛公攻豐不能取沛公

還之沛怨雍齒與豐子弟畔之正月張耳等立趙後趙歇爲趙王東陽

甯君秦嘉立景駒爲楚王在留沛公往從之道得張良遂與俱見景駒

Ch'en Shê, was killed by his charioteer, Chuang Chia.[1]

A man of Wei[h], Chou Fu, overran the regions of Feng and P'ei. He sent men to say to Yung Ch'ih, "Feng was formerly a colony of Liang. Already several tens of cities in the region of Wei[h] have been subjugated. If now you, [Yung] Ch'ih, come under the rule of Wei[h], then the state of Wei[h] will make you, [Yung] Ch'ih, a marquis and put you in charge of Feng. If you do not submit, then I will massacre [the people of] Feng." Yung Ch'ih had not previously wanted to be subordinate to the Lord of P'ei, so when [the state of] Wei[h] summoned him, he immediately rebelled [against the Lord of P'ei] and guarded Feng for [the state of] Wei[h]. The Lord of P'ei attacked Feng, but could not take it. [Then] the Lord of P'ei returned to P'ei.[2] He held a grudge against Yung Ch'ih because he had rebelled against him together with the youths of Feng.

In the first month, Chang Erh and others set up a **11b** descendant of [the kings of] Chao, Chao Hsieh, Feb. as King of Chao. The Baronet Ning of Tung-yang and Ch'in Chia set up Ching Chü as King of Ch'u at Liu[2]. The Lord of P'ei went to attach himself [to Ching Chü]. On the way he got Chang Liang. Thereupon they together visited Ching Chü, and asked him for troops to attack Feng. At that time

[1] SC 48: 7b says that the murder was committed "in order to surrender to Ch'in." Chuang Chia was killed by Lü Ch'en. Cf. 31: 7a.

[2] The SC adds that Kao-tsu (the Lord of P'ei) was sick. In this section, the HS is not copying the SC literally; it adds and omits phrases and sentences.

Chang Han was pursuing[1] [the army of] Ch'en. A detached general,[2] Ssu-ma Yi, brought an army north to subjugate the region of Ch'u; he massacred [the people of] Hsiang, [and then] went to Tang.

12a The Baronet Ning of Tung-yang and the Lord of P'ei led their troops westwards and fought with [this general] west of Hsiao without success. So they returned, raised troops, and collected them at Liu₂.

Mar. In the second month, [the Lord of P'ei] attacked Tang; after three days he took it by storm.[3] Then he collected the soldiers [that had been in] Tang and secured six thousand men. He united them to his former [troops; thus] altogether [he had] nine thou-

Apr. sand men. In the third month he attacked the city of Hsia-yi and took it by storm. Then he turned

May back and attacked Feng, but did not take it. In the fourth month, Hsiang Liang attacked and killed Ching Chü and Ch'in Chia and stopped at Hsieh.[4] [So] the Lord of P'ei went to interview him. Hsiang Liang added to the Lord of P'ei's troops five thousand men and ten generals who were Fifth [Rank] Grandees. [Then] the Lord of P'ei returned, led his army to attack Feng, and took it by storm. Yung Ch'ih fled to Wei_h.[5]

June In the fifth month, Hsiang Yü captured Hsiang-

[1] Yen Shih-ku says that 從 means "to pursue" and quotes in substantiation the *Preface* to the *Book of History*, verse 14, (Legge, p. 5).

[2] Liu Pin (1022–1088) and Wang Hsien-ch'ien suggest reading "general" with the succeeding proper name.

[3] Yen Shih-ku writes, "拔 is to break into a walled city or town and take it. It is like pulling up a tree and getting both its trunk and roots."

[4] Hsiang Liang wanted to do some king-making on his own account. Since Ching Chü had not done much for him, Kaotsu felt quite free to go over to Ching Chü's successor.

[5] Wei_h was the state to which Yung Ch'ih had given his allegiance. Kao-tsu's steadfast purpose to recapture Feng and punish a traitor deserves attention.

請兵以攻豐時章邯從陳別將司馬尽將兵北定楚地屠相至碭東

陽甯君沛公引兵西與戰蕭西不利還收兵聚留二月攻碭三日拔

之收碭兵得六千人與故合九千人三月攻下邑拔之還擊豐不下

四月項梁擊殺景駒秦嘉止薛沛公往見之項梁益沛公卒五千人

五大夫將十人沛公還引兵攻豐拔之雍齒奔魏五月項羽拔襄城

還項梁盡召別將六月沛公如薛與項梁共立楚懷王孫心爲楚懷王

章邯破殺魏王咎齊王田儋於臨濟七月大霖雨沛公攻亢父章邯圍

田榮於東阿沛公與靳梁共救田榮大破章邯東阿田榮歸沛公項羽

追北至城陽攻屠其城軍濮陽東復與章邯戰又破之章邯復振守濮

陽環水沛公項羽去攻定陶八月田榮立田儋子市爲齊王定陶未下

ch'eng by storm, [then] returned. Hsiang Liang [next] summoned all the detached generals. In the sixth month the Lord of P'ei came to Hsieh, and, with Hsiang Liang, both together set up the grandson of King Huai of Ch'u, Hsin, as King Huai of Ch'u.[1]   July

Chang Han[2] routed and killed the King of Wei[b], [Wei] Chiu, and the King of Ch'i, T'ien Tan, at Lin-chi.

In the seventh month there was a great prolonged rain. The Lord of P'ei attacked K'ang-fu.[3] Chang Han besieged T'ien Jung at Tung-a. The Lord of P'ei and Hsiang Liang together rescued T'ien Jung and routed Chang Han's [army] completely at Tung-a. [Thereupon] T'ien Jung attached himself to the Lord of P'ei. Hsiang Yü pursued the fleeing[4] troops to Ch'eng-yang. He attacked the city and massacred its [people], then encamped his army east of P'u-yang. Again he fought a battle with Chang Han, and again routed him. Chang Han again rallied [his forces] and defended P'u-yang, encircling it with water. The Lord of P'ei and Hsiang Yü went to attack Ting-t'ao. In the eighth month, T'ien Jung set up the son of T'ien Tan, [T'ien] Fu, as King of Ch'i. Since Ting-t'ao had not yet fallen, the Lord of P'ei   Aug.

   12b

   13a

   Aug./Sept.

[1] The *SC* does not mention Kao-tsu as being prominent in setting up this king.

[2] This paragraph is taken from *SC* ch. 6 (*Mh* II, 206) or its source.

[3] At this point the *HS* resumes copying *SC* ch. 8.

[4] Wei Chao (197–273/4) says that 北 is the ancient word for *pei* 背 "turn the back upon." Wang Nien-sun shows from the *Shuo-wen* and the *Kuang-ya* (by Chang Yi, fl. 227–233) that these two words were interchanged. He quotes a passage from the *Kuan-tzu* (iii cent. B.C.) ch. 31: 3b saying that the first word above "means to turn the back upon one's lord." He says that this word takes the meaning of turn the back upon, hence to be defeated and to flee is also denoted by this word. He also quotes the *Tso-chuan*, Dk. Huan, yr. IX (Legge, p. 53) where the word has the same meaning. Anciently these two words had the same pronunciation, hence were interchanged.

together with Hsiang Yü went westward to overrun the territory as far as Yung-ch'iu. They had a battle with the Ch'in [dynasty] troops and defeated them severely. They beheaded Li Yu, the Administrator of San-ch'uan. [Then they] returned and attacked Wai-huang, [but] Wai-huang did not yet submit [to them].

Since Hsiang Liang had twice routed the Ch'in [dynasty] armies, he became arrogant. Sung Yi admonished him, but he would not listen. [The state of] Ch'in reinforced the army of Chang Han.
Sept./Oct. In the ninth month, Chang Han, after having put gags¹ into the mouths of his men, attacked Hsiang Liang by night at Ting-t'ao, and routed his [army] completely, killing Hsiang Liang. At this time there had been continuous rains from the seventh month to the ninth month. The Lord of P'ei and Hsiang Yü were just then attacking Ch'en-liu. When they heard that [Hsiang] Liang was dead, the officers and soldiers were afraid, so [the Lord of P'ei and Hsiang Yü], together with the general Lü Ch'en, led the army [away] and went to the east, moving King
13b Huai from Hsü-yi and establishing the capital at P'eng-ch'eng. Lü Ch'en encamped east of P'eng-ch'eng; Hsiang Yü encamped west of P'eng-ch'eng; and the Lord of P'ei encamped at Tang.

The younger brother of Wei Chiu, [Wei] Pao, set himself up as King of Wei_h.²
Oct./Nov. In the intercalary ninth month, King Huai united the armies of Lü Ch'en and Hsiang Yü, commanding [the united army] in person. He made the

---

¹ 銜枚. Cf. *Mh* II, 341, n. 2. Chinese generals, in a night attack, had their men hold sticks of wood, like chop-sticks, in their mouths, to prevent talking.

² In this and the next paragraph, the *HS* departs from the *SC* ch. 8. This paragraph is taken from *SC* 16: 6b (*Mh* III, 63) or its source (it is contradicted in *SC* 90:1b). The next paragraph is taken from *SC* ch. 7 (*Mh* II 260, 261).

沛公與項羽西略地至雍丘與秦軍戰大敗之斬三川守李由還攻外黃外黃

未下項梁再破秦軍有驕色宋義諫不聽秦益章邯兵九月章邯夜銜枚擊項

梁定陶大破之殺項梁時連雨自七月至九月沛公項羽方攻陳留聞梁死士

卒恐乃與將軍呂臣引兵而東徙懷王自盱台都彭城呂臣軍彭城東項羽軍

彭城西沛公軍碭魏咎弟豹自立爲魏王後九月懷王并呂臣項羽軍自將之

先入關獨羽怨秦破項梁奮勢願與沛公西入關懷王諸老將皆曰項羽為人慓悍

救趙初懷王與諸將約先入定關中者王之當是時秦兵彊常乘勝逐北諸將莫利

鹿城秦將王離圍之趙數請救懷王乃以宋義為上將項羽為次將范增為末將北

青為令尹章邯已破項梁以為楚地兵不足憂乃渡河北擊趙王歇大破之歇保鉅

以沛公為碭郡長封武安侯將碭郡兵以羽為魯公封長安侯呂臣為司徒其父呂

Lord of P'ei the chief of the Tang Commandery, and appointed him as the Marquis of Wu-an commanding the troops of the Tang Commandery. He made [Hsiang] Yü the Duke of Lu, and appointed him as the Marquis of Ch'ang-an. Lü Ch'en was made Minister over the Masses; his father, Lü Ch'ing, was made Chief Chancellor.

When Chang Han had crushed Hsiang Liang, he thought that the troops in the region of Ch'u were not worth serious attention, so he crossed the [Yellow] River, went northward, attacked the King of Chao, [Chao] Hsieh, and routed his [army] completely. [Chao] Hsieh [then] took refuge in the city of Chü-lu. A general of the Ch'in [dynasty], Wang Li, besieged him. [The state of] Chao several times requested rescue. Then King Huai made Sung Yi First [Ranking] General, Hsiang Yü the Second General, and Fan Tseng the Lowest General, to go north and rescue [the state of] Chao. **14a**

Formerly King Huai had made a covenant with the generals [to the effect that] he who would first enter and subjugate Kuan-chung would be made its king. [But] at that time the troops of the Ch'in [dynasty] were strong and very often took advantage of their victories to pursue the fleeing, [so that] none of the [Ch'u] generals [thought it of] any advantage to be first in going thru the pass. [Hsiang] Yü alone, who held a grudge against [the forces of Ch'in] for having routed Hsiang Liang, was seething with energy and wanted to go west and enter through the pass with the Lord of P'ei. [But] the older generals of King Huai all said: "Hsiang Yü in character is fiery, violent, and very destructive.[1] When he attacked Hsiang-ch'eng, he left nothing alive;[2] wherever he passes, he destroys and exterminates.   In addition, although [the state of] Ch'u has several times [attempted to] advance and conquer, both of the former [leaders], King Ch'en [Shê] and Hsiang Liang, have been defeated.   It is **14b** better to send instead a person of outstanding qualities who will abide by just conduct as he goes to the west, and have him announce and proclaim [our purposes] to the elders of [the state of] Ch'in. The elders of Ch'in have already been filled with bitterness about their rulers for a long time.   If now [our state] can indeed secure a person of outstanding qualities to go, and if he does not exploit or tyrannize [over the people], it is possible that [the state of Ch'in] could be conquered.   Hsiang Yü should not be sent.   Only the Lord of P'ei is habitually generous and an outstanding person."   In the end [the King] did not permit [Hsiang] Yü [to go], but sent the Lord of P'ei to go to the west to collect the scattered soldiers of King Ch'en [Shê] and of Hsiang Liang. Then he went by way of Tang to Ch'eng-yang.[3] [Next] he went to Chiang-li and attacked the walled camp of the Ch'in armies, routing the two [Ch'in] armies.[4]

禍賊嘗攻襄城襄城無噍類所過無不殘滅且楚數進取前陳王項梁
皆敗不如更遣長者扶義而西告諭秦父兄秦父兄苦其主久矣令誠
得長者往毋侵暴宜可下項羽不可遣獨沛公素寬大長者卒不許羽
而遣沛公西收陳王項梁散卒乃道碭至陽城與杠里攻秦軍壁破其

[1] The *SC* has 狷 "treacherous," instead of the *HS*'s 禍 "causing destruction"; these two words are however written almost alike in the seal character, so that the *HS*'s reading is probably the original one, for Hsiang Yü was not particularly treacherous.

[2] Lit. "no creature was left to chew," seemingly a vigorous local expression. For the massacre at Hsiang-ch'eng, cf. 31: 11b; *Mh* II, 255.

[3] The *HS* writes Yang-ch'eng 陽城, but the *SC* writes Ch'eng-yang 城陽, inverting the words. *HS* 39:8a reads, "He attacked the army of Wang Li south of Ch'eng-yang, and also attacked Chiang-li, routing its [troops] completely." Hence the reading of the *SC* should be followed.

[4] The *SC* has a quite different reading. A commentator

二軍

秦三年十月齊將田都畔田榮將兵助項羽救趙沛公攻破東郡尉

於成武十一月項羽殺宋義并其兵渡河自立爲上將軍諸將黥布

等皆屬十二月沛公引兵至栗遇剛武侯奪其軍四千餘人并之與

In the third year of [the Second Emperor of] Yr. III
Ch'in, the tenth month, a general of [the state of] Nov./Dec.
Ch'i, T'ien Tu, rebelled against T'ien Jung and
brought his troops to aid Hsiang Yü rescue [the
king of] Chao. The Lord of P'ei attacked and
routed [the troops of] the Military Governor of the
Tung Commandery at Ch'eng-wu.

In the eleventh month, Hsiang Yü killed Sung Dec./Jan.
Yi,[1] and united his troops [with his own, then] 207 B.C.
crossed the [Chang[2]] River. He set himself up as
the First [Ranking] General; all the generals, Ch'ing
Pu and the others, became his subordinates.

In the twelfth month, the Lord of P'ei led his Jan./Feb.
troops to Li,[3] met the Marquis of Kang-wu,[4] and **15a**
took away by force his army of over four thousand
men, uniting them [with his own]. He joined armies

on the *SC* says that this passage refers to the battle at Wu-
ch'eng, with which Chavannes agrees. Cf. *Mh* II, 344, n. 2.
The *HS* dates this battle before the tenth month, in which
the *SC* says that the battle at Wu-ch'eng occurred. The
HS also mentions this battle before it mentions the rebellion
of T'ien Tu (which happened, according to the *SC*, on the
fourth day of the month, whereas the battle at Wu-ch'eng
happened on the fifteenth day). Cf. *Mh* III, 64. Hence the
battle at Chiang-li and the one at Wu-ch'eng must have been
two different events.

[1] Sung Yi was cautious and would not advance to raise the
siege of Chü-lu even though his soldiers were cold and hungry;
hence Hsiang Yü killed him. Cf. 31: 14a.

[2] Wang Hsien-ch'ien, in a note to 31: 14b, says that this was
the Chang 漳 River.

[3] The *HS* omits a sentence in the *SC* which tells that Kao-
tsu fought an unsuccessful battle with the Ch'in armies and was
forced back to Li.

[4] Ying Shao says, "He was a general of King Huai of Ch'u.
HS 16: [19b] has a Marquis Kang of Chih-p'u, Ch'en Wu
棘蒲, 剛侯, 陳武 [cf. p. 227, n. 3.]. Wu was also surnamed
Ch'ai 柴. 剛武侯 [as the present text reads] should properly
be 剛侯武. He was a general of Wei_h." Meng K'ang
(iii cent.) objects, "According to *HS* chap. 16, Ch'ai Wu arose

with those of the Wei[h] generals, Huang Hsin and Wu Man[1], [then] attacked the Ch'in army and routed it.[2]

T'ien An, the grandson of the former King of Ch'i, [T'ien] Chien, subjugated Chi-pei and followed Hsiang Yü to rescue [the state of] Chao. [Hsiang] Yü completely routed the Ch'in army below [the city of] Chü-lu. He captured Wang Li and put Chang Han to flight.

Mar./Apr.   In the second month, the Lord of P'ei, coming from Tang, went north and attacked Ch'ang-yi. He met P'eng Yüeh, and [P'eng] Yüeh assisted him in attacking Ch'ang-yi, but it did not fall. The Lord

15b of P'ei [then] went west past Kao-yang. Li Yi-chi, who was superintendent of the gate to a hamlet,[3] said: "Many generals have passed through this place; as I see it, the Lord of P'ei has the greatest plans [of them all]." So he asked to see the Lord of P'ei.

as a general at Hsieh, went to Pa-shang, and entered Han [-chung]. He was not a general of King Huai, and also not a general of Wei[h]. According to custom, he should not be called by his posthumous name." Yen Shih-ku also objects to Ying Shao's statement and declares that he has no evidence for it. Wu Jen-chieh (ca. 1137–1199) says, "This man is *Kang-wu Hou* and [the text] certainly cannot be changed to make him Ch'en Wu." He however proceeds to attempt to identify Ch'en Wu with the General of P'u or General P'u 蒲 將 軍, who is said in 31: 11a to have been a subordinate of Hsiang Liang and who consequently became a general of King Huai after the death of Hsiang Liang. But there seems to be no evidence for this identification and Wei Chao says that P'u was a surname. Ying Shao seems to have identified the Marquis of Kang-wu with General P'u and with Ch'en Wu. In all probability the surname and given name of the Marquis of Kang-wu have merely been lost.

[1] The *SC*, the Fukien ed. (1549) and the Wang Wen-shen ed. (1546) of the *HS* write Wu Man's given name as 蒲. The *SC* adds the title 申 徒 of Wei[h]. The Ch'ien-tao ed. (1167) writes as in the text.

[2] This event and the next few events, down to the attack upon Ch'ang-yi, are taken from *SC* 16: 7a, b (*Mh* III, 65; which is not a complete translation).

[3] The commentary of Ho Hsiu on Kung-yang's Commentary, written by the end of the later Han dynasty, *sub* Duke Hsüan,

魏將皇欣武滿軍合攻秦軍破之故齊王建孫田安下濟北從

項羽救趙羽大破秦軍鉅鹿下虜王離走章邯二月沛公從碭

北攻昌邑遇彭越越助攻昌邑未下沛公西過高陽酈食其爲

里監門曰諸將過此者多吾視沛公大度乃求見沛公沛公方

踞床使兩女子洗酈生不拜長揖曰足下必欲誅無道秦不宜踞見長者於是沛公起攝衣謝之延上坐食其說沛公襲陳留沛公以爲廣野君以其弟商爲將將陳留兵三月攻開封未拔西與秦將楊熊會戰白馬又戰曲遇東大破之楊熊走之滎陽

The Lord of P'ei was just then squatting on a bed, with two maids washing [his feet]. Master Li did not prostrate himself, [but] made a deep bow and said, "If your honor firmly wishes to destroy the utterly inhuman [dynasty of] Ch'in, it is not fitting that you should interview your senior squatting down." Thereupon the Lord of P'ei arose, holding up [the skirts of] his garments, begged his pardon, and conducted him to the seat of honor.[1] [Li] Yi-chi advised the Lord of P'ei to make a surprise attack upon [the city of] Ch'en-liu.[2] For that the Lord of P'ei made him the Baronet Enlarging Our Territory, and made his younger brother, [Li] Shang, the general in charge of the troops at Ch'en-liu. In the third month, [the Lord of P'ei] attacked K'ai-feng, but did not take it by storm. [Then] he went westwards, met with the Ch'in general, Yang Hsiung, fought with him at Pai-ma, also fought east of Ch'ü-yung, and routed his [army] completely. Yang Hsiung fled and went to Jung-yang, [so] the Second Emperor

(margin: Apr./May)   *(margin: 16a)*

15th year, says: "In a district there are [subdivisions] called li 里 [the word we have here translated "hamlet"]. A li [consists of] eighty houses. Eight families together [compose] a lane 巷. In a li there is an assembly house. [The li] selects some members from those who are over sixty years of age and have very good character, and calls them the Elders. One person, who is eloquent, can protect the people, and is robust, is made the Head of the li. . . . In the spring, when [the people] go to work in the fields, at dawn the Elders and Head of the li open the gate, sitting in the rooms beside the gate [to keep watch]. Those who are late in going out, coming after the [appointed] time, are not allowed to go out. In the evening those who do not return bearing firewood are not allowed to come in." The superintendent of the gate to a li was thus not an underling, but the most respected member of the hamlet (he had the privilege of riding a horse), and had underlings subordinate to him to sprinkle and sweep the streets and watch the gates.

[1] This incident has become famous.

[2] The SC adds, "So he took possession of the grain which the Ch'in [emperor] had accumulated there." Cf. Mh II, 346. Kao-tsu followed Li Yi-chi's advice.

sent a messenger to behead him as an example.
May/June In the fourth month [the Lord of P'ei] went southwards, attacked Ying-yang,[1] and massacred its
[inhabitants]. Because of Chang Liang, he thereupon overran the region of Han_h.[2]

At that time a detached general of Chao, Szu-ma
Ang, was just then wanting to cross the [Yellow]
River and enter the [Han-ku] Pass, so the Lord of
P'ei went north, attacked P'ing-yin, and closed the
ford of the [Yellow] River [to him].[3] Then] he
went southwards and fought a battle east of Lo-yang,
but his army was not victorious. So he went by way
of the Huan-yüan [Pass] to Yang-ch'eng, and
collected horses and cavalrymen for his army. In
July/Aug. the sixth month, he fought a battle with the
Administrator of the Nan-yang [Commandery],
16b [Lü] Yi, [at a place] east of Ch'ou, routed him,[4]
and overran the Nan-yang Commandery. The
Administrator of Nan-yang fled to take refuge in
his capital city, and defended [the city of] Yüan.
When the Lord of P'ei led his troops past Yüan
westwards, Chang Liang admonished him as follows:
"Although you, Lord of P'ei, want to hurry into the
Pass, the Ch'in troops are still numerous and are
holding the strategic positions. If now you do not

引兵過宛西張良諫曰沛公雖欲急入關秦兵尚衆距險今
陽守齮戰犨東大破之略南陽郡南陽守走保城守宛沛公
南戰雒陽東軍不利從轘轅至陽城收軍中馬騎六月與南
時趙別將司馬卬方欲渡河入關沛公乃北攻平陰絕河津
二世使使斬之以徇四月南攻潁川屠之因張良遂略韓地

---

[1] The *HS* has 潁川, but the second word of this name is
written 陽 in the *SC*, which is correct. Ying-ch'uan was the
name of a commandery in Ch'in and Han times (cf. glossary),
in which the city of Ying-yang was located.

[2] Chang Liang's ancestors had been for five generations the
Chancellors of Han_h, hence Kao-tsu seized that region for him.

[3] 絕河津, which Yen Shih-ku wishes to interpret, "trav-
ersed the ford." Liu T'ai-kung (1751–1805) justifies our translation, saying it implies that Kao-tsu closed the ford in order
to prevent Szu-ma Ang from getting ahead of him into the pass.

[4] The present text adds the word 大, meaning that Lü Yi
suffered a severe defeat; the Ching yu edition (1034/5) and the
SC are without this word—it is probably an interpolation.

subjugate Yüan, [the forces of] Yüan will follow you and attack you from behind, while ahead of you will be the strong [forces of] Ch'in. This is a dangerous policy." Therefore the Lord of P'ei by night led his troops to return by another route with his flags and pennons rolled up, and, when it became first light, he had already surrounded the city of Yüan with three lines. The Administrator of Nan-yang **17a** wanted to cut his own throat, [but] a man of his suite, Ch'en K'uei, said [to him]: "There is still ample time to die." Then he climbed over the city wall and interviewed the Lord of P'ei, saying [to him], "Your servant has heard that your honor has entered into a covenant that he who will first enter Hsien-yang shall be king over it. [But] at present your honor is held [here] by the defenders of Yüan. The prefectures of the commandery [in which] Yüan [is located form] several tens of adjoining walled cities; its officials and people think that they will certainly die if they surrender; hence they all defend [their cities] firmly, mounting the city walls [to guard them]. If now your honor stops to attack [Yüan] for all the days [required to capture it], many of your soldiers will inevitably be killed and wounded; [on the other hand], if you lead your troops away from Yüan, [the troops of] Yüan will certainly pursue after your honor. If your honor does the former, then you will lose [the benefit] of the covenant concerning Hsien-yang; if you do the latter, you may suffer misfortune because of this strong place, Yüan. For your honor there is no plan as good as that of making a covenant regarding its surrender, enfeoffing its Administrator, thus caus- **17b** ing him to stop here and defend it, and leading away its militia and soldiers, taking them westwards. [Then] all the cities which have not yet fallen, when they hear the news [of what has happened], will rival each other

53

in opening their gates and awaiting your honor.
[Thus] your honor will have nothing to worry about
in marching straight ahead." The Lord of P'ei

Aug./Sept. replied, "Good." In the seventh month the Administrator of Nan-yang, [Lü] Yi, surrendered, and
[the Lord of P'ei] appointed him as Marquis of Yin;
he [also] appointed Ch'en K'uei [to the income of] a
thousand families. He led the troops westward and
all [places] yielded [to him]. When he came to
Tan-shui,[1] the Marquis of Kao-wu, Sai, and the
Marquis of Jang,[2] Wang Ling, surrendered. He

18a turned back and attacked Hu-yang. He met Mei
Hsüan, a detached general of the Baronet of P o,
[Wu Jui]; with him they both attacked Hsi₅ and
Chih₅, and both [places] surrendered. [The soldiers
were ordered], wherever they went, not to be rude
nor to pillage, [so that] the people of Ch'in were
delighted. [The Lord of P'ei] sent Ning Ch'ang, a
man [originally] of Wei_h, as a messenger to [the state
of] Ch'in.

In this month Chang Han and his whole army
surrendered to Hsiang Yü, and [Hsiang] Yü made
him the King of Yung.[3] Shen Yang of Hsia-ch'iu
subjugated [the region] south of the [Yellow] River.

Sept./Oct. In the eighth month, the Lord of P'ei attacked the
Wu Pass, and entered [the state of] Ch'in. The
Chancellor of Ch'in, Chao Kao, was afraid, so he
killed the Second Emperor and sent men [to the
Lord of P'ei], desiring to make an agreement to divide
[with him] the kingship of Kuan-chung; [but] the

Oct./Nov. Lord of P'ei would not consent to it. In the ninth

---

[1] Kao-tsu was marching southwestward to avoid the Han-ku
Pass.

[2] The present text has Hsiang 襄; Wei Chao (197–273/4)
says that in Nan-yang there was a *hsien* by the name of Jang 穰,
whereas Hsiang Hsien is far from Nan-yang, where Kao-tsu
met the Marquis of this place; hence the name should be written Jang.

[3] For this incident cf. 31: 16; *Mh* II, 271–2.

攻武關入秦秦相趙高恐乃殺二世使人來欲約分王關中沛公不許
使秦是月章邯舉軍降項羽羽以爲雍王瑕丘申陽下河南八月沛公
番君別將梅鋗與偕攻析酈皆降所過毋得鹵掠秦民喜遣魏人甯昌
恢千戶引兵西無不下者至丹水高武侯鰓襄侯王陵降還攻胡陽遇
待足下足下通行無所累沛公曰善七月南陽守齮降封爲殷侯封陳

九月趙高立二世兄子子嬰爲秦王子嬰誅滅趙高遣將將兵距嶢關

沛公欲擊之張良曰秦兵尚彊未可輕願先遣人益張旗幟於山上爲

疑兵使酈食其陸賈往說秦將啗以利秦將果欲連利沛公欲許之張

良曰此獨其將欲叛恐其士卒不從不如因其怠懈擊之沛公引兵繞

嶢關踰蕢山擊秦軍大破之藍田南遂至藍田又戰其北秦兵大敗

month, Chao Kao set up Tzu-ying, the son of the
Second Emperor's older brother, as King of Ch'in. **18b**
Tzu-ying executed Chao Kao and exterminated [his
family].[1] He sent a general leading troops to resist
[the Lord of P'ei] at the Yao Pass. The Lord of P'ei
wanted to attack them, but Chang Liang said [to him],
"The troops of Ch'in are still strong. They cannot
yet be lightly esteemed. I would prefer that you
would first send men to display flags and pennons on
the mountain top in greater [number than before], in
order to make [the enemy] suspect there are troops
[with each flag], and send Li Yi-chi and Lu Chia to go
and [attempt to] persuade the Ch'in generals [to
surrender], luring them with [promises of] gain."[2]
The Ch'in generals really wished to be in peaceable
relations [with the Lord of P'ei] and the Lord of
P'ei wanted to agree. [But] Chang Liang said, "This
[reply means that] only the generals wish to rebel.
I fear that their officers and soldiers will not follow them. It is best to take advantage of [the
fact that they are] half-hearted and attack them."
[So] the Lord of P'ei sent troops around the Yao
Pass, crossing over Mt. K'uai, and attacked the Ch'in
troops, routing them completely south of Lan-t'ien.
Thereupon he reached Lan-t'ien, and again fought
[at a place] north of it, [where] the Ch'in troops
were severely defeated.　　　　　　　　　　　　Kao-tsu

In the first year [of the Emperor Kao-tsu of the Yr. I
Han dynasty[3]], in the winter, the tenth month, Nov./Dec.

[1] For this event, cf. *Mh* II, 216 f.

[2] In the *SC*, Chang Liang is made to give this advice before
Kao-tsu captures the Wu Pass, not the Yao Pass, cf. *Mh* II,
351.

[3] Kao-tsu later claimed to have begun his reign when he
entered Kuan-chung and overthrew the Ch'in dynasty, although
at that time he was merely the Lord of P'ei and was not actually
enthroned as Emperor until the fifth year afterwards. The
HS is following this later numbering of the years.

19a there was a conjunction of the five planets[1] in [the
19b constellation] Tung-ching and the Lord of P'ei
reached Pa-shang. The King of Ch'in, Tzu-ying,
in a plain chariot with white horses, with his seal-
cord tied about his neck,[2] having sealed up [for
presentation to the Lord of P'ei] the imperial seals,
the insignia and the credentials,[3] surrendered beside
Chih-tao.

元年冬十月沛公至
霸上秦王子嬰素
車白馬繫頸以組
封皇帝璽符節降
聚于東井五星

[1] For the real date of this conjunction, cf. Appendix I.

[2] The *Chan-kuo-ts'e* (iii cent. B.C.) ch. V, *sub* Ch'u, King Ching-hsiang, says,
"Marquis Ling of Ts'ai [542–529 B.C.] ... did not pay attention to his state, not
knowing that his son, Fa, was just then receiving orders from the spiritual kings [i.e.,
the ancestors] that he [the Marquis] must tie himself up with vermillion silk and
present himself [to the ancestors]."   Shen Ch'in-han remarks, "After this event, a
captive was always presented in this manner."   The biography of Liu Shou-kuang in
the *History of the Five Dynasties* says, "The King of Chin came to T'ai-yuan dragging
Liu Jen-kung by his seal-cord, and offered him in the ancestral temple."   The cord
around King Tzu-ying's neck was thus a sign of surrender.   Today on the Chinese stage
a prisoner is indicated by a cord around his neck.

[3] Wei Chao (197–273/4) writes, "The 'insignia' 符 are for generals to lead out troops.
The 'credentials' 節 are for internuncios to hold."   The *Shuo-wen* (100) says that the
former character means "a witness 信".   Szu-ma Cheng (fl. 713–742) says, "According
to the Han [dynastic] regulations, [the insignia] were made of bamboo, six inches long.
They were divided and matched together."

The *Han-Chiu Yi*, ch. I, p. 1b (written by Wei Hung, fl. 25–57; the same passage is found in the *Han-kuan Yi*, II, 13a, b), says: "The Emperor's six seals are all
of white jade with a knob [made in the shape of] a hornless dragon or tiger.   Their inscriptions read: 'The Seal of the Emperor's Command,' The Emperor's [Own] Seal,'
'The Emperor's Witnessing Seal,' 'The Seal of the Son of Heaven's Command,' 'The
Son of Heaven's [Own] Seal,' 'The Son of Heaven's Witnessing Seal,' six seals in all
皇帝行璽皇帝之璽皇帝信璽天子行璽天子之璽天子信璽凡六璽.   The 'Seal of
the Emperor's Command was used for all miscellaneous matters.   'The Emperor's [Own]
Seal' was used for correspondence with the vassal kings.   The 'Emperor's Witnessing
Seal' was used in mobilizing troops.   In summoning the great officials, there was used
the 'Seal of the Emperor's Command.'   In tablets for installing [officials or kings]
and for matters [concerning] foreign states, the 'Son of Heaven's [Own] Seal' was
used.   In serving Heaven, Earth, and the spirits, the 'Son of Heaven's Witnessing
Seal' was used.   All [documents] are sealed with Wu-tu brown mortar and a blue
cloth bag with plain white lining [covers them].   The two ends are without a crack
[and are] a tablet one foot [long, (a phrase denoting an imperial edict, according to
Li Hsien, 651–684, in *HHS*, Mem. 47: 10b)].   In the middle it was tied and inscribed.
The Emperor's girdle and seal cord have a yellow ground [and are adorned in]
six colors."   This passage seems to refer to the same sort of ancient stationery as
that described by Stein in *Serindia*, vol. IV, pl. XXI.

枳道旁諸將或言誅秦王沛公
曰始懷王遣我固以能寬容且
人已服降殺之不祥乃以屬吏
遂西入咸陽欲止宮休舍樊噲
張良諫乃封秦重寶財物府庫

Some of the generals[1] said that the King of Ch'in should be executed, [but] the Lord of P'ei replied, "When at first King Huai sent me [on this expedition], it was certainly because I am able to be generous and indulgent. Moreover, when a man has already surrendered, it would be inauspicious to **20a** kill him." So he gave him into the charge of his officials. Thereupon [the Lord of P'ei] went west and entered Hsien-yang. He wanted to stop in the palace and rest [his soldiers] in the [palace] hostels, [but] Fan K'uai and Chang Liang[2] admonished him [not to do so], so he sealed up the depositories and treasuries for the Ch'in [dynasty's] important treasures and valuable objects,[3] returned, and encamped

[1] The *SC So-yin* (by Szu-ma Cheng, fl. 713–742) quotes the *Ch'u-Han Ch'un-ch'iu* (197 B.C.) as saying, "Fan K'uai begged for permission to kill him."

[2] *HS* 40: 4a says that Fan K'uai admonished him but he would not listen; then Chang Liang added his arguments and he acceded.

[3] The *Hsi-ching Tsa-chi* (vi cent.) ch. 3, says, "When Kao-tsu first entered the palace at Hsien-yang, he went all around the storehouses and treasuries, and the gold, jade, rarities, and treasures could not be enumerated. It is said that [among] its extraordinary and strange rarities there was a blue jade five-branched lamp, seven feet and five inches [ca. 6 ft. Eng. measure] high, made [in the shape of] coiled hornless dragons holding lamps in their mouths. When the lamps are lighted, the scales all move [(turned by the heat?). Its light] is bright and luminous like the assembled stars and fills the room.

"Also there were twelve seated men cast in bronze, all of them three feet [27 in. Eng. meas.] high, arranged on a mat. Each one held a lute or a reed organ. All had sewed on them variegated colored silk [clothes] exactly like live men. Below the mat there were two bronze tubes. The upper end was several feet high and protruded behind the mat. One of these pipes was empty; in one of the pipes there was a rope as large as a finger. One man was made to blow the empty pipe and one man to make a knot with the rope. Then the group all made music just like real musicians.

"There was a lute six feet [54 in. Eng. meas.] long with 13 strings and 26 marks for the cords, each adorned with seven jewels. It was engraved with the words, 'The music of [the precious stone] Fan and Yü.' [Cf. *Tso-chuan*, Dk. Ting, yr. V, Legge, p. 760.]

"[There was] a jade flute with two tubes two feet and three inches long, with six holes. When it is blown, one sees numerous carriages, with horses, mountains, and forests in succession. It was engraved with the words, 'The flute of bright flowers.' . . .

還軍霸上蕭何盡收秦丞相府圖籍文書　十一月召諸縣豪桀曰父老苦秦苛法久　矢誹謗者族耦語者棄市吾與諸侯約先入　關者王之吾當王關中與父老約法三章耳　殺人者死傷人及盜抵罪餘悉除去秦法吏

at Pa-shang. Hsiao Ho gathered up completely from the courts of the Lieutenant Chancellor of Ch'in the charts, the registers, the documents, and the writings.[1]

Dec./Jan. 206 B.C.   In the eleventh month [the Lord of P'ei] summoned the eminent and distinguished people from the prefectures and said [to them], "Fathers and Elders, you have suffered long enough from the cruel laws of the Ch'in [dynasty]: those who spoke ill or criticized [the government] have been cruelly executed with their relatives, those who talked in private[2] have been publicly executed[3] in the market-place. I and the nobles have made a covenant that he who first enters through the passes will be king in [the region inside the passes], [therefore] I ought to be king in Kuan-chung. I am merely going to agree with you, Fathers and Elders, upon [a code of] laws

20b in three articles: he who kills anyone will be put to death; he who wounds anyone or robs [will be punished] according to his offence; as to the remainder, I am repealing and doing away with all the laws of the Ch'in [dynasty]. You, the officials

---

"There was a square mirror four feet [3 ft. Eng. meas.] wide and five feet nine inches tall, with the recto and verso sides both shining. When a man [standing] upright comes and reflects himself in it, then his image appears upside down. When he comes with his hand covering his heart, then he sees his bowels, his stomach, and his five viscera one by one without hindrance. If a person has a sickness within himself, and he covers his heart and reflects himself in it, then he can tell where his sickness is. Moreover, if a woman has evil intentions, then her gall is enlarged and her heart moves. The First Emperor of Ch'in used to use it to reflect the women of his harem. If [anyone's] gall was enlarged or her heart moved, he killed her. Kao-tsu sealed and closed them all up in order to await Hsiang Yü. [Hsiang] Yü took them all [away] to the east; it is unknown where they were after that."

[1] This very important sentence is not in the *SC* ch. 8, but is in *SC* 53: 2a. These maps seem to have been preserved in Later Han times; they are mentioned in 28Aiii: 7a, *sub* Ch'ang-kuang.

[2] Lit. "talk in pairs," i.e., plot against the government. Ying Shao says, "The laws of Ch'in forbade any gatherings of the people."

[3] 棄 市 was a regular punishment—it was "public execution"; quartering of the body after execution was called 磔, and was considered a still more severe punishment. Cf., ch. 5, n. 6.4 and *Han-lü K'ao*, ch. II, 17b.

民皆按堵如故凡吾所以來爲父兄除害非有所侵暴毋恐且吾所以軍霸上待諸侯

至而定要束耳乃使人與秦吏行至縣鄉邑告諭之秦民大喜爭持牛羊酒食獻享軍

士沛公讓不受曰倉粟多不欲費民民又益喜唯恐沛公不爲秦王或說沛公曰秦富

十倍天下地形彊今聞章邯降項羽羽號曰雍王王關中卽來沛公恐不得有此可急

使守函谷關毋內諸侯軍稍徵關中兵以自益距之沛公然其計從之十一月項羽果

and people, should all be quiet and undisturbed as previously. All that I have come for is to deliver you, Elders, from harm. I do not have [any intention of] exploiting or tyrannizing [over you]. Do not be afraid. Moreover, the reason that I have encamped at Pa-shang is merely that I am awaiting the arrival of the nobles in order to make an agreement [with them]." Then he sent people to go with the Ch'in officials to the prefectures and district cities to make known and proclaim this [matter]. The people of Ch'in were greatly rejoiced and vied [with each other] in bringing cattle, sheep, wine, and food, offering them for the enjoyment of the soldiers of the army. [But] the Lord of P'ei refused to accept them, saying, "In the granaries there is much grain; I do not wish to be a burden upon the people." [Then] the people were even more glad, and only feared lest the Lord of P'ei should not become king of Ch'in.

Someone advised the Lord of P'ei, saying, "[The region of] Ch'in is ten times as rich as [the rest of] the world; by its geographical configuration it is strong. Now I have heard that Chang Han has surrendered to Hsiang Yü and that [Hsiang] Yü has entitled him King of Yung, to be king over Kuan-chung. He will forthwith come [here], and I am afraid that you, O Lord of P'ei, will not succeed in keeping this [territory]. You might hasten to send [troops[1]] to guard the Han-ku Pass. Do not admit the army **21a** of the nobles, and levy some soldiers from Kuanchung in order to add to your [own army] and resist them." The Lord of P'ei assented to his plan and followed it.

Consequently, [when] in the twelfth month Hsiang **Jan./Feb.** Yü, leading the troops of the nobles, really wished to

---

[1] The Southern ed. (possibly x–xii cent.) and the *SC* add 兵 at this point.

go westward through the Pass, the gates of the Barrier were closed, and he heard that the Lord of P'ei had already subjugated Kuan-chung. [Thereupon Hsiang] Yü was greatly enraged and sent Ch'ing Pu and others to attack and break through the Han-ku Pass.[1] Thereupon he reached Hsi₄.[2]

A Junior Major of the Lord of P'ei, Ts'ao Wu-shang, upon hearing that [Hsiang] Yü was angry and wanted to attack the Lord of P'ei, sent men to speak to [Hsiang] Yü as follows: "The Lord of P'ei wants to be king of Kuan-chung. He has ordered Tzu-ying to be his chancellor. All the jewels and valuables [of Ch'in] have been taken [by him]." [Ts'ao Wu-shang, by this message,] was seeking [for a means] by which he could ask for a fief [from Hsiang Yü]. His Second Father, Fan Tseng, advised [Hsiang] Yü, saying, "When the Lord of P'ei was east of the mountains,[3] he was greedy for money and loved women. Now I have heard that since he entered the passes, he has not taken any precious things nor granted favors to any women. These [facts] show that his designs are

21b great. I [formerly] sent men to look at his emanation,[4] and it was all that of a dragon; it is of all colors. This is the emanation of a Son of Heaven.

帥諸侯兵欲西入關關門閉聞沛公已定關中羽大怒使黥布等
攻破函谷關遂至戲下沛公左司馬曹毋傷聞羽怒欲攻沛公使
人言羽曰沛公欲王關中令子嬰相珍寶盡有之欲以求封亞父
范增說羽曰沛公居山東時貪財好色今聞其入關珍物無所取
婦女無所幸此其志不小吾使人望其氣皆爲龍成五色此天子

[1] The *Yi-wen Lei-chi* (by Ou-yang Hsün, 557–641) quotes the *Ch'u-Han Ch'un-ch'iu* (197 B.C.) as follows: "The Lord of P'ei went west thru the Wu Pass and stopped at Pa. Master Chieh 解 advised him to send a general to defend the Han-ku Pass and not admit King Hsiang. His General-in-chief, the Second Father [Fan Tseng], came to the Barrier, [but] was not permitted to enter. He was enraged, and said, 'Does the Lord of P'ei intend to rebel?' Then he ordered [each] person to bring a bundle of firewood, wishing to burn the gates of the Barrier. Then the gates of the Barrier were opened."

[2] The Sung Ch'i ed. (xi or xii cent.) reports that the Southern ed. omits the 下.

[3] 山東. There was no commandery by this name; here and later (1A: 29a) it is used as a common noun, not a proper name.

[4] This word 氣 refers to the emanation supposed to rise from a person who will

氣急擊之勿失於是饗士旦日合戰是時羽兵四十萬號百萬沛公兵

十萬號二十萬力不敵會羽季父左尹項伯素善張良夜馳見張良具

告其實欲與俱去毋特俱死良曰臣爲韓王送沛公不可不告亡去不

義乃與項伯俱見沛公沛公與伯約爲婚姻曰吾入關秋豪無所敢取

籍吏民封府庫待將軍所以守關者備他盜也日夜望將軍到豈敢反

You should hasten to attack him and not lose [this opportunity]." Thereupon [Hsiang Yü] feasted his soldiers [in preparation for] joining battle on the morrow.

At this time [Hsiang] Yü's troops [numbered] four hundred thousand and were asserted to be a million, [while] the Lord of P'ei's troops [numbered] a hundred thousand and were asserted to be two hundred thousand—his strength was not equal [to that of Hsiang Yü]. It happened that the Junior Administrator, Hsiang Po, who was the youngest brother of [Hsiang] Yü's father, had been a constant friend of Chang Liang. In the night he galloped fast [to the Lord of P'ei's camp] to see Chang Liang and told him all the facts [about the situation]. He wanted [Chang Liang] to go away with him and not merely to die with [the Lord of P'ei. But Chang] Liang replied, "I am accompanying the Lord of P'ei in the service of the King of Han_h; I must inform him [of this danger]. To abandon him and go away would be disloyal." So he, together with Hsiang Po, interviewed the Lord of P'ei. The Lord of P'ei agreed to contract a marriage [in the family of Hsiang] Po, and said [to him], "[Since] I have entered the passes, I have not dared to take the slightest hair.[1] I have made a register of the officials and people and have sealed the courts and treasuries, awaiting [the arrival] of the General. The reason I guarded the Pass was to prevent [the entrance of] bandits. Day and night I have been hoping that the General would come;

become distinguished, presaging his future. The "dragon" is the emblem of the emperor; "five colors," instead of only one, presages an especially brilliant future, because they are identified with the five points of the compass.

[1] Referring to his action regarding the palace. Cf. 1A: 20a.

how could I have dared to rebel [against him]? I wish that you, [Hsiang] Po, would make clear [to Hsiang Yü] that I would not dare to revolt against his beneficence." Hsiang Po promised to do so. The same night, as he left to return [to his camp], he warned the Lord of P'ei, saying, "Tomorrow you yourself absolutely must come early to make an apology." Hsiang Po returned [to his camp] and told [Hsiang] Yü all that the Lord of P'ei had said, taking the opportunity [to add], "If the Lord of P'ei had not first crushed the troops of Kuan-chung,

22a how could you, sir, have been able to enter? Moreover, when a man has done you great service, it would not be auspicious to attack him. It is better to take this opportunity and make friends with him." [Hsiang] Yü promised to do so.

The next day the Lord of P'ei, followed by a hundred-odd cavalrymen, went to see [Hsiang] Yü at Hung-men, and made his apologies, saying, "Your servant has joined his efforts with yours, General, in attacking [the state of] Ch'in. You, General, have fought north of the [Yellow] River; your servant has fought south of the [Yellow] River. [Your servant] did not himself think that he could first go through the passes and be able to break [the power of] Ch'in, and meet you, General, again [at this place]. Now some evil-[minded] person has been talking [about me] and has brought about a disagreement between you, General, and your servant." [Hsiang] Yü replied, "This is what your, the Lord of P'ei's, Junior Major, Ts'ao Wu-shang, has said. Otherwise how could [I], Chi, have fallen into[1] this situation?" Thereupon [Hsiang] Yü retained the Lord of P'ei to banquet him.

[1] The Ching-yu ed. (1034), the Ch'ien-tao ed. (1171), the Wang ed. (1546) all read 生; we have emended it to 至 with the Southern Academy ed. (1530), the Fukien ed. (1549), the SC ch. 7 & 8, the Tzu-chih T'ung-chien (1084), and the Ch'ien-Han-chi (ii cent.)

令將軍與臣有隙羽曰此沛公左司馬曹毋傷言之不然籍何以生此羽因留沛

秦將軍戰河北臣戰河南不自意先入關能破秦與將軍復相見今者有小人言

不祥不如因善之羽許諾沛公旦日從百餘騎見羽鴻門謝曰臣與將軍戮力攻

伯還其以沛公言告羽因曰沛公不先破關中兵公豈能入乎且人有大功擊之

邪願伯明言不敢背德項伯許諾卽夜復去戒沛公曰旦日不可不早自來謝項

公飲范增數目羽擊沛公羽不應范增起出謂項莊曰君王爲人不忍

汝入以劍舞因擊沛公殺之不者汝屬且爲所虜莊入爲壽壽畢曰軍

中無以爲樂請以劍舞因拔劍舞項伯亦起舞常以身翼蔽沛公樊噲

聞事急直入怒甚羽壯之賜以酒噲因譙讓羽有頃沛公起如廁招樊

噲出置車官屬獨騎與樊噲靳彊滕公紀成步從間道走軍使張良留

Fan Tseng several times threw glances at [Hsiang] Yü [urging him] to attack the Lord of P'ei, [but Hsiang] Yü did not respond. [So] Fan Tseng arose **22b** and went out. He spoke to Hsiang Chuang, saying, "Our lord is not hard-hearted [enough] in character. Do you enter in order to dance a sword-dance, and take the opportunity to attack the Lord of P'ei and kill him. Otherwise you and yours will presently become his captives." [Hsiang] Chuang entered and drank a health [to the guest]. When the toast had been drunk, he said, "In our camp there is nothing to use [as entertainment]; I crave permission to dance a sword-dance." Thereupon he drew his sword and danced. [But] Hsiang Po also arose and danced, always protecting and covering the Lord of P'ei with his own body. When Fan K'uai heard that the situation was critical, he came right in, very angry.[1] [Hsiang] Yü admired his [strength and courage] and therefore granted him [a cup of] wine. Thereupon [Fan] K'uai reproached and reprimanded [Hsiang] Yü. After some moments, the Lord of P'ei arose and went to the toilet. He beckoned to Fan K'uai and went out. Leaving his chariot and his official retinue, he mounted alone, with Fan K'uai, Chin Ch'iang, the Lord of T'eng, [Hsia-hou Ying],[2] and Chi Ch'eng[3] following on foot, and fled to his army by unfrequented paths, ordering Chang Liang to stay and make apologies to [Hsiang]

[1] The SC (Mh, II, 279) states that he resolved to share the fate of Kao-tsu and forced his way in, striking down the guards in doing so.

[2] The Lord of T'eng was with Kao-tsu in two other narrow escapes: after the battle of P'eng-ch'eng and in his escape from Ch'eng-kao.

[3] The SC names Chi Hsin 紀信 instead. The SC So-yin (by Szu-ma Cheng) says that the HS reads Chi T'ung (the son of the Chi Ch'eng).

Yü. [Hsiang] Yü asked where the Lord of P'ei was, and [Chang Liang] replied, "He learned that you, General, had the intention of reprimanding him 23a so he has left and gone by a short-cut to his army. Hence he has had your servant present you with [these] jade circlets."[1] [Hsiang] Yü received them. [Then Chang Liang] also offered to Fan Tseng a large jade wine ladle, [but Fan] Tseng got angry; he struck at the wine-ladle [presented to] him, arose, and said, "We and ours are now already captives of the Lord of P'ei."

Several days after the Lord of P'ei had returned [to his camp, Hsiang] Yü led his troops west, massacred [the people of] Hsien-yang, killed Tzu-ying, the king of Ch'in who had surrendered, and burnt the palaces and courts of the Ch'in [emperor]. Nothing of what he passed by was left without injury or destruction, [so that] the people of Ch'in were gravely disappointed in their hopes.

[Hsiang] Yü sent men to return and report to King Huai [that he had conquered Kuan-chung and should be allowed to do as he liked about its rule, but] King Huai replied, "[Let it be done] according to the covenant." [So Hsiang] Yü held a grudge against King Huai because he had not been willing to order [Hsiang Yü] to go west through the passes together with the Lord of P'ei, but [had sent him] north to rescue [the state of] Chao, [thus coming too] late [to reap the benefit of] the covenant [made with the generals of] the empire [concerning the

謝羽羽問沛公安在曰聞將軍有意督過之脫身去閒至軍故
使臣獻璧羽受之又獻玉斗范增增怒撞其斗起曰吾屬今為
沛公虜矣沛公歸數日羽引兵西屠咸陽殺秦降王子嬰燒秦
宮室所過無不殘滅秦民大失望羽使人還報懷王懷王曰如
約羽怨懷王不肯令與沛公俱西入關而北救趙後天下約乃

---

[1] A pi 璧 was a circular piece of flat jade with a hole in the center, considered at the time as a very precious gift. They were made in pairs. Cf. B. Laufer, *Jade*, pp. 86f, 157f. The *K'ang-hsi Dictionary* says that the pi was circular outside (to represent heaven) and square inside (to represent earth), but Laufer mentions only those with circular holes.

日懷王者吾家所立耳非有功

伐何以得專主約本定天下諸

將與籍也春正月陽尊懷王爲

義帝實不用其命二月羽自立

爲西楚霸王王梁楚地九郡都

kingship of Kuan-chung]. So he said, "King Huai is merely one whom my family has set up. He has not [achieved] any merit or glory.[1] How did he get sole authority over the covenant? Those who really subjugated the world were the generals and myself, Chi."

In the spring, in the first month,[2] in feigned **26b** respect, he gave King Huai [the title], the Emperor Feb./Mar. Yi, [but] in reality he did not avail himself of [the Emperor's] orders.[3] In the second month[4] [Hsiang] Mar./Apr. Yü set himself up as the King Lord Protector[5] of Western Ch'u, ruling over nine commanderies in the region of [the former feudal states,] Liang and Ch'u,[6] with his capital at P'eng-ch'eng. He **27a**

●

[1] Cf. *Mh* 356, n. 1.

[2] Cf. Appendix II to this chapter.

[3] In issuing orders he did not even pretend to legitimize them by using the Emperor's name; he issued orders in his own name.

[4] The *SC* reads "in the first month"; the *Tzu-chih T'ung-chien* adopts the reading of the *HS*. The Official ed. (1739) omits this date and notes that in the Academy ed. (1124) the words "second month" are interpolated; following the Sung Ch'i edition (ca. xii cent.) they are excised.

[5] *Pa* 霸 was the title taken by or given to the outstanding feudal chiefs in the time of the later Chou dynasty. The *Pa* or Lord Protector was the dictator over or the leader of the nobles, often really taking the authority of the Chou dynasty's kings. Hsiang Yü thus chose for himself a title signifying that he was the leader or dictator of the kings.

[6] The ancient feudal state of Ch'u was, in the latter part of the Chou dynasty, roughly the region of the Yangtze valley below the gorges and the eastern seaboard as far north as Shantung. In the *SC*, chap. 129, we find a description of the various regions of China in terms of the popular divisions of the feudal states. "North of the Huai [river], the P'ei, the Ch'en, the Ju-nan, and the Nan Commanderies—these are Western Ch'u ... East of P'eng-ch'eng, the Tung-hai, Wu, and Kuang-ling—these are Eastern Ch'u ... Heng-shan, Chiu-chiang, Chiang-nan, Yü-chang, and Ch'ang-sha— these are Southern Ch'u." (*SC* 129: 10a, b.) Meng K'ang (pro. ca. 180–260) says that Southern Ch'u centered around Chiang-ling 江陵 (where was the capital of ancient Ch'u); Eastern Ch'u centered around Wu 吳 (a former feudal state with its capital at the modern Soochow, Kiangsu); and Western Ch'u centered around P'eng-ch'eng in northern Kiangsu. Hsiang Yü wanted to make P'eng-ch'eng his capital, hence he called himself the King of Western Ch'u.

The nine commanderies taken by Hsiang Yü have been identified by Wang Hsien-ch'ien as being nine of the thirty-six commanderies into which the Ch'in dynasty had divided the country. Ch'üan Tsu-wang (1705–1755) previously reached the same conclusions. They are as follows: (1) the Ch'u Commandery (the Ch'in dynasty, after

went contrary to the covenant [about making the
conqueror of Kuan-chung its king] and changed
[the Lord of P'ei's kingdom], setting up the Lord of
P'ei as the King of Han₃, to rule over forty-one
prefectures of Pa, Shu, and Han-chung, with his
capital at Nan-cheng.[1] Kuan-chung was divided
into three parts, and [over it] were set the three
generals of [the former dynasty of] Ch'in: Chang Han
became King of Yung with his capital at Fei-ch'iu;

秦三將章邯爲雍
南鄭三分關中立
漢中四十一縣都
公爲漢王王巴蜀
彭城背約更立沛

its conquest of Ch'u, separated off from this very large state five commanderies, viz.,
Chiu-chiang, Ch'ang-sha, Tung-hai, the Szu River Commandery, and Hsieh, retaining
the rest as the commandery of Ch'u. Cf. *Mh* IV, 416). Hsiang Yü's capital, P'eng-
ch'eng, was in this commandery, according to *HS* ch. 28; it also included the Han
kingdom of Huai-yang. (2) The Szu-shui 泗水 Commandery (it was later called
the P'ei Commandery), (3) the Hsieh 薛 Commandery, in Shantung; in 187 B.C. it was
called the kingdom of Lu 魯, (4) the Tung-hai 東海 Commandery, which was also
called the T'an 郯 Commandery; the Lin-huai 臨淮 Commandery of Han times, was
included in this and the Szu-shui Commanderies; the kingdom of Kuang-ling 廣陵
was also included in this commandery, (5) the Ch'ien-chung 黔中 Commandery;
this region was organized by Ch'in out of the Wu 巫, and the Chiang-nan 江南
Commanderies of Ch'u; cf. *Mh* II, 87 for this event, also *Mh*, 133, n. 1, 34°; but
Ch'ang-sha was evidently not included in it at the time, since Hsiang Yü had made
the Emperor Yi its suzerain with his capital at Ch'en₁ (cf. 1A: 30a). After his assassination, Ch'ang-sha probably reverted to Hsiang Yü, altho nothing is said about it
in the histories; perhaps that was the motive for the assassination, (6) the K'uai-chi
會稽 Commandery; the Tan-yang 丹陽 Commandery belonged to it; the commanderies of Chang 鄣 and Wu 吳 were divided from it in Ch'u and Han times; (7) the
Nan-yang 南陽 Commandery; this was the region where the ancient states of Hanₕ,
Liang, and Ch'u met; it included the cities, Yuan, Shê, Sui and Teng 鄧, (8) the
Tang 碭 Commandery, which later became the kingdom of Liang 梁 in modern
Honan; it included also the later Chi-yin 濟陰, Ch'eng-liu and Shan-yang 山陽
commanderies, and (9) the Tung 東 Commandery; this commandery had been organized
by Ch'in out of twenty cities of the state of Weiₕ in modern Kiangsu, cf. *Mh* IV, 212.

[1] Kao-tsu was thus practically banished to southwestern Shensi and Szechuan, outside of central China.

臨菑徙趙王歇爲代

土趙相張耳爲常山王漢王怨羽之背約欲攻之丞相蕭何諫乃止

燕王韓廣爲遼東王燕將臧荼爲燕王都薊徙齊王田市爲膠東王齊將田都爲齊王都

陵番君吳芮爲衡山王都邾故齊王建孫田安爲濟北王徙魏王豹爲西魏王都平陽徙

趙將司馬卬爲殷王都朝歌當陽君英布爲九江王都六懷王柱國共敖爲臨江王都江

王都廢丘司馬欣爲塞王都櫟陽董翳爲翟王都高奴楚將瑕丘申陽爲河南王都洛陽

Szu-ma Hsin became King of Sai with his capital at Yüeh-yang; Tung Yi became King of Ti with his capital at Kao-nu. The Ch'u general, Shen Yang, [who was formerly of] Hsia-ch'iu, became the King of Honan with his capital at Lo-yang. The general of [the state of] Chao, Szu-ma Ang, became King of Yin with his capital at Chao-ko. The Baronet of Tang-yang, Ying Pu, became King of Chiu-chiang with his capital at Liu₅. King Huai's Pillar of State, **27b** Kung Ao, became the King of Lin-chiang with his capital at Chiang-ling. The Baronet of P'o, Wu Jui, became King of Heng-shan with his capital at Chu. T'ien An, the grandson of the former King of [the feudal state of] Ch'i, [T'ien] Chien, became King of Chi-pei. The King of Weiₕ, [Wei] Pao, was shifted and made the King of Western Weiₕ with his capital at P'ing-yang. The King of Yen, Han Kuang, was [also] shifted and made the King of Liao-tung. The general of [the state of] Yen, Tsang Tu, became King of Yen, with his capital at Chi₄. The King of Ch'i, T'ien Fu, was [likewise] shifted and made the King of Chiao-tung. The general of Ch'i, T'ien Tu, became King of Ch'i with his capital at Lin-tzu. The King of Chao, [Chao] Hsieh, was shifted and made the King of Tai. The Chancellor of Chao, Chang Erh, was made King of Ch'ang-shan.

The King of Han₈ held a grudge against [Hsiang] Yü because he had gone contrary to the covenant, and [so] wanted to attack him, [but] his Lieutenant **28a** Chancellor, Hsiao Ho, admonished him, so he desisted. In the summer, the fourth month, the **May/June** nobles were discharged at Hsi₄,[1] and each went

[1] Chavannes, following Yen Shih-ku, translates this sentence as "they left the colors." Cf. *Mh* II, 358, and n. 1. Here he is very probably wrong. Ku Yen-wu (1613–1682) the founder of modern Chinese philology, says that this interpretation "does not make sense" of the phrase. It is true that *Hsi* is sometimes

to his own state. [Hsiang] Yü sent thirty thousand soldiers to follow the King of Han₅.¹ Many tens of thousands of the people of Ch'u and of the followers of the nobles admired and followed him. From Tu he went south and entered [the gorge of] Li. Chang Liang [then] asked for permission 28b to leave and return to [the state of] Hanₕ; the King of Han₅ accompanied him [back] to Pao-chung. Thereupon he advised the King of Han₅ to burn utterly the suspended roads² in order to guard against stealthy [attacks by the] troops of the nobles and also in order to show Hsiang Yü that he had no intentions of [returning] eastwards [to compete with him].

When the King of Han had arrived at Nancheng, his generals, together with the officers and soldiers, all sang Ch'i songs, [which showed that they were] thinking of returning to the east,³ and many escaped on the way and returned [home]. Han Hsin, who was Commissary Chief Commandant, also escaped and went off. [But] Hsiao Ho went after

夏四月諸侯罷戲下各就國羽使卒三萬人從漢

王楚子諸侯人之慕從者數萬人從杜南入蝕中

張良辭歸韓漢王送至襃中因說漢王燒絕棧道

以備諸侯盜兵亦視項羽無東意漢王既至南鄭

諸將及士卒皆歌謳思東歸多道亡還者韓信爲

used with the meaning, "flag," but Szu-ma Cheng in a note to *SC* 7: 19b says that it was the name of a river, and that Hsi-hsia 戲下 was quite the same sort of expression as Hsü-hsia 許下 and Lo-hsia 洛下. Cf. p. 310, n. 3.3. As to Yen Shih-ku's remark (which Chavannes quotes) that Hsiang Yü had already left Hsi₄, it is true that Hsiang Yü had come west of the Hsi River to Hung-men, where he met Kao-tsu, and then to Hsien-yang, where he burnt the palaces, but the nobles probably returned to the place where they had first encamped in order to take formal leave of each other. Formal announcement was made that their warfare was completed and each went to his kingdom. Our translation of this phrase is not however certain; Takigawa Kame-ta-ro, in his recent edition of the *SC*, agrees with Yen Shih-ku. Chang Mou-ch'ung (prob. xx cent.) quotes the *Shuo-wen*, "A *hsi* is a section of the army."

¹ Contrast Kao-tsu's former army of a hundred thousand. He evidently had to swallow much.

² They were called "Cloud-bridges 連雲棧." Cf. *Mh* II, 358, n. 3.

³ The *Shuo-wen* 3A: 8a says an *Ou* 謳 is a song of Ch'i, and Yen Shih-ku explains, "It means that they sing together (*ch'i*). Or it is said that it is a song of the region of Ch'i." The *SC* does not have the word *ou*. In the Sung dynastic history (section on music) there is a famous Han song (with the direction: to be sung with cymbals), which interestingly illustrates this passage:

治粟都尉亦亡去蕭何追還之因薦於漢王曰必
欲爭天下非信無可與計事者於是漢王齊戒設
壇場拜信爲大將軍問以計策信對曰項羽背約
而王君王於南鄭是遷也吏卒皆山東之人日夜
企而望歸及其鋒而用之可以有大功天下已定

him and brought him back. Thereupon he recommended him to the King of Han, saying, "If you really wish to contest [for the control of] the world [the emperorship], except for [Han] Hsin, there is no one else who can plan for you." Thereupon the King of Han fasted and purified himself, erected an altar on a level place, and installed[1] [Han] Hsin as General-in-chief. [Then] he asked him about what plans and stratagems [he would suggest]. [Han] Hsin replied, "Hsiang Yü acted contrary to the covenant and made you, sir King, king at Nancheng. This is a banishment.[2] Your officials and soldiers **29a** are all people from east of the mountains; day and night they are longing and hoping to return [home]. If you use this [weapon] when it is sharp, you can thereby achieve great results; [but] when

> "The Wu mountain [Szechuan] is high,
>> High and great.
> The Huai River [Kiangsu] is deep,
>> And difficult to reach.
>
> "I want to return to the east.
>> The broken bridges have not been rebuilt—
>> What I could collect would not rise high.
> To cross the waters—how can they be bridged,
>> Swelling and whirling?
> On the brink of the river I look afar,
>> And my tears fall, dampening my garments.
> A man of distant lands,
>
>> "My thoughts are of returning,
>>> But what can I do?"

Wang Hsien-ch'ien (1842–1918) thinks that the above song was probably written by one of Kao-tsu's generals or officers whose home was on the Huai River.

[1] Cf. *HS* 100A: 2b and n. 2.9, which fixes the meaning of this word.

[2] Ju Shun says that the Ch'in rulers had banished criminals to Szechuan and Han$_s$. *SC* 93: 1b and *HS* 33: 6b puts this speech into the mouth of Han$_w$ Hsin, an entirely different person.

the country has already [become] stable and the people are all themselves seeking quietude, you cannot employ it again. It is better to decide upon a plan to [press] eastwards." Thereupon he presented a plan by which [Hsiang] Yü could be outwitted and the three [states into which] Ch'in [had been divided] could easily be reunited [and taken possession of]. The King of Han was greatly delighted. Thereupon he followed [Han] Hsin's plan. He arranged and disposed his generals, leaving Hsiao Ho to collect the revenue from Pa and Shu and provision the army.[1]

June/July   In the fifth month,[2] the King of Han, leading his troops by way of Ku-tao, came out [of Han₈] and made a surprise attack on [the state of] Yung. The King of Yung, [Chang] Han, came to meet [him] and attacked [the troops of] Han₈ at Ch'en-ts'ang. The troops of Yung were defeated and fled back [to their base]. They fought [again] at Hao-chih, [where they were] again severely defeated and fled to Fei-ch'iu. Thereupon the King of Han subjugated the region of Yung; he went east to Hsien-yang; he led troops to besiege the King of Yung at Fei-ch'iu and sent his generals to seize the [neighboring] regions.[3]

When T'ien Jung heard that [Hsiang] Yü had removed the King of Ch'i, [T'ien] Fu, to Chiao-tung **29b** and set up T'ien Tu as King of Ch'i, he was very

---

[1] After 軍 the Southern Academy ed. (1528), the Fukien ed. (1549), and the Official ed. (1739) have 糧.

[2] The *SC* (*Mh* II, 360) says the "eighth" month, but that date does not correspond with Han Hsin's advice to Kao-tsu to take advantage of his soldiers' homesickness.

[3] The *SC* mentions definitely the two commanderies of Lung-hsi and Pei-ti as being overrun (cf. *Mh* II, 361; in the *SC* text, instead of the "Shang" 上 commandery we should probably read "two" 二, a common copyist's error).

民皆自寧不可復用不如決策東向因陳羽可圖三秦易幷之

計漢王大說遂聽信策部署諸將留蕭何收巴蜀租給軍食五

月漢王引兵從故道出襲雍雍王邯迎擊漢陳倉雍兵敗還走

戰好畤又大敗走廢丘漢王遂定雍地東如咸陽引兵圍雍王

廢丘而遣諸將略地田榮聞羽徙齊王市於膠東而立田都爲

齊王大怒以齊兵迎擊田都都走降楚六月田榮殺田市自立爲齊王

時彭越在鉅野衆萬餘人無所屬榮與越將軍印因令反梁地越擊殺

濟北王安榮遂幷二齊之地燕王韓廣亦不肯徙遼東秋八月臧荼殺

韓廣幷其地塞王欣翟王翳皆降漢初項梁立韓後公子成爲韓王張

良爲韓司徒羽以良從漢王韓王成又無功故不遣就國與俱至彭城

angry, and, with the troops of Ch'i, he met and attacked T'ien Tu. [T'ien] Tu fled and submitted[1] himself to [the state of Western] Ch'u. In the sixth July/Aug. month, T'ien Jung killed T'ien Fu and set himself up as King of Ch'i. At that time, P'eng Yüeh was at Chü-yeh with a band of over ten thousand men. He had no overlord, [so T'ien] Jung gave to [P'eng] Yüeh the seal of a general, and ordered him therefore to raise a revolt in the region of Liang. [P'eng] Yüeh attacked and killed the King of Chi-pei, [T'ien] An. [T'ien] Jung then united [and took possession of] the territory comprising the three [states made out of the former state of] Ch'i.[2] The King of Yen, Han Kuang, also was unwilling to be removed to Liao-tung; in the autumn, the Sept. eighth month, Tsang Tu killed Han Kuang and took possession of his territory. The King of Sai, [Szu-ma] Hsin, and the King of Ti, [Tung] Yi, both submitted to [the King of] Han_s.[3]

Hsiang Liang had previously set up a Prince [who was] a descendant of [the former kings of] Han_h, [Han] Ch'eng, as King of Han_h and Chang Liang as the Minister of the Masses in Han_h. [Hsiang] Yü, considering that [Chang] Liang had followed the King of Han_s, and that the King of Han_h, [Han] Ch'eng, had moreover not achieved anything, therefore did not send him, [Han Ch'eng], back to his state, [but took him] with himself to P'eng-ch'eng and killed

[1] At this point SC ch. 8 says that T'ien Tu was killed (cf. Mh II, 360); but the HS 31: 3b and 31: 18b both say that he submitted to Ch'u; in chap. 16 his submission is likewise implied—here the HS has corrected the SC.

[2] I.e., Ch'i, Chi-pei, and Chiao-tung.

[3] In the SC 16: 16b and in the HS 13: 5a this event is said to have happened in the eighth month (cf. Mh III, 75, n. b & c), and in the next month commanderies were made out of these kingdoms; but in SC chap. 8 the event is dated in the next year (Mh II, 362).

him. When he heard that the King of Han₅ had reunited [and taken possession of] Kuan-chung and that [the states of] Ch'i and Liang had rebelled against him, [Hsiang] Yü was very angry. He thereupon made the former prefect in Wu, Cheng Ch'ang, the King of Han_h, [with orders] to oppose [the state of] Han₅. He ordered the Lord of Hsiao, Chio, to attack P'eng Yüeh, [but P'eng] Yüeh defeated Chio's troops. At that time, Chang Liang

30a was traveling about[1] the regions of Han_h; he sent [Hsiang] Yü a letter, saying, "[The state of] Han₅ wants to secure Kuan-chung; it will act according to the covenant, and then will stop [its conquests] and not presume to go farther eastwards." For that reason [Hsiang] Yü had no thoughts of going westwards, but went northwards to attack [the state of] Ch'i.

Oct.   In the ninth month, the King of Han₅ sent his generals Hsieh Ou and Wang Hsi out [by way of] the Wu pass, using the troops of Wang Ling, and [ordering them] to go by way of Nan-yang to get the *T'ai-kung* and the Empress [*née*] Lü, [who were] at P'ei.[2] [But Hsiang] Yü heard of it and dispatched troops to oppose them at Yang-chia, [so that] they could not [go] forward.

Yr. II   In the second year, in the winter, the tenth month, Nov. Hsiang Yü sent the King of Chiu-chiang, [Ch'ing] Pu, to kill the Emperor Yi at Ch'en₁.

Ch'en Yü also held a grudge against [Hsiang] Yü, [because] he alone was not made a king; [so] he borrowed from T'ien Jung auxiliary troops to attack Chang Erh, the King of Ch'ang-shan. [Chang] Erh

[1] Su Lin (fl. 196–227) says that he was travelling about to pacify his people. Meng K'ang (ca. 180–260) says he was "overrunning" the territory and Yen Shih-ku approves this explanation.

[2] At that time, Wang Ling had several thousand men at Nan-yang and surrendered to Kao-tsu. Cf. 40:17b.

二年冬十月項羽使九江王布殺義帝於郴陳餘亦怨羽獨不王己從田榮藉助兵以

於沛羽聞之發兵距之陽夏不得前

無西意而北擊齊九月漢王遣將軍薛歐王吸出武關因王陵兵從南陽迎太公呂后

擊彭越越敗角兵時張良徇韓地遺羽書曰漢欲得關中如約卽止不敢復東羽以故

殺之及聞漢王幷關中而齊梁畔之羽大怒乃以故吳令鄭昌爲韓王距漢令蕭公角

擊常山王張耳耳敗走降漢漢王厚遇之陳餘迎代王歇還趙

歇立餘爲代王張良自韓間行歸漢漢王以爲成信侯漢王如

陝鎭撫關外父老河南王申陽降置河南郡使韓太尉韓信擊

韓韓王鄭昌降十一月立韓太尉信爲韓王漢王還歸都櫟陽

使諸將略地拔隴西以萬人若一郡降者封萬戶繕治河上塞

was defeated; he fled and submitted himself to [the King of] Han_s, [and] the King of Han_s treated him well. Ch'en Yü welcomed the King of Tai, [Chao] Hsieh, back to Chao, [and Chao] Hsieh set up [Ch'en] Yü as King of Tai.

Chang Liang returned by unfrequented paths from Han_h to Han_s, and the King of Han_s made him Ch'eng-hsin Marquis. The King of Han went to Shan, pacifying and comforting the elders of the region outside the pass.[1] The King of Ho-nan, **30b** Shen Yang, submitted [to him, so] he established the commandery of Ho-nan.[2] He [then] had the Grand Commandant in Han_h, Han_w Hsin, attack [the state of] Han_h, and the King of Han_h, Cheng Ch'ang, submitted. In the eleventh month he set up the Dec. [former] Grand Commandant in Han_h, Han_w Hsin, as King of Han_h. [Then] the King of Han_s turned round, returned [to Kuan-chung, and established] his capital at Yüeh-yang. He sent his generals to overrun territory and they captured the Lung-hsi [Commandery] by assault. Upon those who submitted with ten thousand persons or with one commandery, he conferred [the income of] ten thousand families. He repaired the Barrier[3] of the Ho-shang

[1] Kuan-wai 關 外, the region east and outside of the Han-ku Pass, i.e., in the present Honan.

[2] Cf. *Mh* II, 535, no. 10. *SC* 16: 17b says that this event happened in the eleventh (the next) month.

[3] Ch'i Shao-nan (1703–1768) says that this was the portion of the former barrier at the northern border of the Ho-shang 河 上 Commandery (the same as the later Tso-p'ing-yi 左 馮 翊 cf. Glossary), between the territory of the Huns and that of the Chinese. Previously this region had belonged to the King of Sai; when his territory was taken, the barrier was repaired. Cf. 94A: 5b. Upon the appearance of disorder in China, the Huns had probably invaded, hence this barrier was needed.

民給軍事勞苦復勿租稅二歲關中卒從軍者復家

癸未令民除秦社稷立漢社稷施恩德賜民爵蜀漢

人復畦之諸將拔北地虜雍王弟章平赦罪人二月

滎敗走平原民殺之齊皆降楚楚焚其城郭齊

故秦苑囿園池令民得田之春正月羽擊田滎城陽

[Commandery]. Regarding the pastures,[1] enclosures, gardens, and ponds of the former Ch'in [dynasty], he ordered that the common people were permitted to [make] cultivated fields of them.

205 B.C. Feb.   In the spring, the first month, [Hsiang] Yü attacked T'ien Jung at Ch'eng-yang. [T'ien] Jung was defeated and fled to P'ing-yüan and the people of P'ing-yüan killed him. All of [the state of] Ch'i [then] submitted to Ch'u, [whereupon the forces of] Ch'u burnt their outer and inner walls. [Thereupon] the people of Ch'i again rebelled against [Ch'u].

[The King of Han's] generals took the Pei-ti [Commandery] by assault, and captured Chang P'ing, the younger brother of [Chang Han], the King of Yung.

Mar. Mar. 5   [The King of Han proclaimed] an amnesty for criminals.[2] In the second month, on [the day] *kuei-wei*, [the King of Han] ordered the people to do away with the Ch'in [dynasty's] gods of the soils and grains and establish the Han [dynasty's] gods of the soils and grains. He showed his virtue and bounty and granted aristocratic ranks to the people. Because the people of Shu and Han₃ had been heavily burdened in furnishing the armies with supplies, he exempted them from the land tax and from contributions in kind for [a period of] two years. For the soldiers of Kuan-chung who were

31a

---

[1] Yen Shih-ku says, "[A place where] fowl or animals are reared is called a pasture 苑. When a pasture has a wall it is called an enclosure 囿. [Places] where [things] are planted are called gardens 園. 田 means to cultivate."

[2] A general amnesty, together with temporary exemptions from taxes, was usually ordered at the accession of a new emperor—it is now done with that connotation. The change in the gods of the land and grains was only made at the beginning of a new dynasty (not always then). Cf. *Mh* II, 363 for this custom.

一歲舉民年五十以上有脩行能帥衆爲善置以爲三老鄉一人擇鄉

三老一人爲縣三老與縣令丞尉以事相教復勿繇戍以十月賜酒肉

三月漢王自臨晉渡河魏王豹降將兵從下河內虜殷王卬置河內郡

至脩武陳平亡楚來降漢王與語說之使參乘監諸將南渡平陰津至

洛陽新城三老董公遮說漢王曰臣聞順德者昌逆德者亡兵出無名

with the armies he exempted their families [from taxes] for one year. Those among the people who were fifty years old and over, who had cultivated personalities,[1] and who were able to lead the multitude and do good, he elevated to the position of *San-lao*— one in each district. One of the district *San-lao* was selected to be the prefectural *San-lao*, who was to serve as a consultant with the Prefect, the Assistant [Prefect], and the Chief of Police. [The *San-lao*] were exempted from forced labor and garrison service, and in the tenth month were to be granted wine and meat.

In the third month, the King of Han, crossed the [Yellow] River from Lin-chin. The King of Wei, [Wei] Pao, submitted, and, leading his troops, followed [the King of Han. The King of Han] subdued Ho-nei, captured the King of Yin, [Szu-ma] Ang, and established the Ho-nei Commandery. When he came to Hsiu-wu, Ch'en P'ing escaped from Ch'u and came to submit himself. The King of Han talked with him, liked him, and so made him his Chariot-companion [with the duty of] supervising the generals.

[Going] southwards, [the King of Han] crossed [the Yellow River] at the ford of P'ing-yin, and came to Lo-yang. [There] the *San-lao* of Hsin-ch'eng, the Great Excellency Tung, stopped the King of Han and advised him, saying, "Your servant has heard that

"He who accords with virtue will shine,
    [But] he who goes contrary to virtue will be
        destroyed.
When troops are ordered out without a just cause,
The affair will therefore fail.   31b

[1] Shen Ch'in-han remarks that "[people of] cultivated personalities" later became a technical term denoting certain persons who had been recommended to the central government (as possessing this quality), just as did the terms, "filially pious and incorrupt" and "accomplished talent."

Hence it is said:

> "Make clear that he is a wrong-doer—
> Your enemy can thereupon be subdued.[1]

Hsiang Yü has acted in an inhuman [fashion]; he has banished and murdered his lord—he is the [greatest] wrong-doer in the world.   Moreover

> "He who is benevolent needs use no braves,
> He who is righteous needs use no force.

All those in your armies should wear plain garments[2] [in mourning] for [Emperor Yi] in order to announce [your purpose],[3] and the nobles will for this reason march eastwards to chastize [Hsiang Yü. Then] no one within the four seas[4] will fail to admire your virtue.   The foregoing is the procedure [used by] the three kings."[5]   The King of Han replied, "Good.   Except for you, O master, I should have heard nothing [of the kind]."   Thereupon the King of Han proclaimed a mourning for the Emperor Yi; he uncovered his arm and wailed loudly; [the whole army] mourned and lamented for three days.   He sent messengers to inform the nobles, saying, "All the world together set up the Emperor Yi, and, facing north,[6] it served him.   Now Hsiang Yü has

---

[1] The six lines above are each of four characters and rime in couplets.

[2] Mourning clothes.

[3] Liu Pin (1022-1088) says that the 之 is a gloss.

[4] I. e., no one in the world.

[5] The "three kings" have been variously identified: Yen Shih-ku says they are the great rulers of the three dynasties, Hsia, Yin, and Chou; the phrase plainly means that this practise was followed by the model rulers of ancient times.   This speech and Kao-tsu's action indicates that Kao-tsu was reversing the First Emperor's anti-Confucian policy; hence it is very significant.

[6] The emperor, on his throne, faces south; hence his subjects face north.

聞漢東既擊齊欲遂破之而後擊漢漢王以故得劫五諸侯兵

義帝者夏四月田榮弟橫收得數萬人立榮子廣為齊王羽雖

悉發關中兵收三河士南浮江漢以下願從諸侯王擊楚之殺

之今項羽放殺義帝江南大逆無道寡人親為發喪兵皆縞素

banished and murdered the Emperor Yi in Chiang-nan. It was a treasonable and inhuman [action]. We Ourselves have proclaimed a mourning for him; [Our] troops are all wearing plain garments.[1] We have sent forth the troops of Kuan-chung, and collected warriors from the three Ho [Commanderies] to sail southwards down the Yangtze and Han [Rivers].[2] We are willing to follow you, nobles and **32a** kings, to attack the one in Ch'u who has murdered the Emperor Yi."

In the summer, the fourth month, T'ien Jung's May younger brother, [T'ien] Heng, succeeded in collecting several tens of thousands of men and set up [T'ien] Jung's son, [T'ien] Kuang, as King of Ch'i. Altho [Hsiang] Yü heard that [the army of] Han₅ was coming eastwards, since he had [already] attacked [the state of] Ch'i, he wished to complete crushing it and afterwards to attack Hanₕ. For this reason the King of Han₅ succeeded in compelling the troops of five nobles[3] [to follow him] and went east- **33a**

[1] The *SC* says instead, "The nobles all wore plain garments," which makes Chavannes end the proclamation here.

[2] No campaign along these rivers is recorded in the *SC* or *HS*. Probably this phrase merely records his hopes—these rivers led into the state of Ch'u. The *Comment to the Shui-ching* (by Li Tao-yüan, d. 527) 17:22a however tells of the establishment of the Ch'ang-sha and Ch'ien-chung Commanderies in this year, implying a campaign along these rivers.

[3] The commentators have discussed variously who these five were. Chavannes's list, which is that of Yen Shih-ku (*Mh* II, 297, n. 3) is probably wrong. Chang Erh had fled from his kingdom; nowhere is he said to have had troops. Shen Yang had surrendered and his domain had been made into a commandery; hence he could not have been considered a noble. Cheng Ch'ang had also surrendered, and his kingdom had been given to Han Hsin, hence he was not among these nobles. Thus there are left only two of Chavannes's list.

The best discussion is probably that of Ch'üan Tsu-wang (1705–1755). He writes that Han₅ had by this time already completely subjugated the three states of Kuan-chung, viz., Yung, Ti, and Sai, and had made commanderies out of them, so that none of their former kings could be counted among the nobles, even tho in the succeeding passage these kings are still given their former titles. Cf. p. 81, n. 5. *HS* 13:5a also states that these commanderies were established in the eighth month of Kao-tsu's first year. *HS* 16:26a implies the same. The biography of King Pao of

wards to chastize [the state of] Ch'u. When he
came to Wai-huang, P'eng Yüeh came with thirty
thousand men to follow Han₈. The King of Han₈
installed him as the Chancellor of State in Wei_b, and
ordered him to subjugate the region of Liang.
Thereupon the King of Han entered P'eng-ch'eng,
took [Hsiang] Yü's Beauties and his valuables,
and held a great banquet. When [Hsiang] Yü
heard of it, he ordered his general to attack [the state
of] Ch'i, and himself, with thirty thousand picked
soldiers, [went] by way of Lu out of Hu-ling to Hsiao.
At dawn he attacked the army of Han₈ and fought a
great battle[1] at P'eng-ch'eng and east of Ling-pi.[2]

Wei_b (SC 90: 2a, HS 33: 1b) testifies that he was one of these
five. HS 13: 7b testifies that another was Han_w Hsin, the
King of Han_b. HS 32: 7a and SC 92: 10b inform us that
Ch'en Yü, the minister of the state of Chao, was a third (he
had sent troops). The two others were the state of Ch'i (whose
troops are said in SC 92: 4b to have joined in the attack) and
Yin. On 1A: 31a it is said that Yin had also been made into a
commandery, but that is an anticipation of what happened a
month later. HS 16: 23b says, "Yen Tse-ch'ih ... was sent
as the chancellor of Yin to attack Hsiang Chi," hence the state
of Yin, with Szu-ma Ang as King, was not ended until his
death in battle this month (cf. 1A: 33b). Or, instead of Ch'i,
it might less probably have been the state of Heng-shan. Wu
Jui, the King of Heng-shan, had been demoted from Po to
Heng-shan, which was a worse position, hence he bore a grudge
against Hsiang Yü.

Tung Chiao-tseng (1750–1822) however suggests that "five
nobles" is here merely a way of referring to "all China," just
as the similar phrase in HS 31: 29a.

[1] The Academy ed. (1124) reads "was severely defeated"
大 敗 instead of "fought a great battle" 大 戰. The Official
ed. follows the Sung Ch'i ed. (ca. xii cent.) in correcting to
read the latter.

[2] HS 31: 11a–12a makes plain what happened: "[Hsiang]
Yü came by way of Hsiao and at dawn attacked the army of
Han₈ and drove it eastwards to P'eng-ch'eng. By noon he had
severely crushed the army of Han₈. The army of Han₈ all fled
and were forced to the Ku and Szu Rivers; [then] the army of
Han₈ all fled south to the mountains. [The army of] Ch'u still
pursued and attacked it to the east of Ling-pi on the bank of the
Sui River."

人從魯出胡陵至蕭晨擊漢軍大戰彭城靈壁東

置酒高會羽聞之令其將擊齊而自以精兵三萬

魏相國令定梁地漢王遂入彭城收羽美人貨賂

東伐楚到外黃彭越將三萬人歸漢漢王拜越為

睢水上大破漢軍多殺士卒睢水爲之不流圍漢王三帀大風從

西北起折木發屋揚砂石晝晦楚軍大亂而漢王得與數十騎遁

去過沛使人求室家室家亦已亡不相得漢王道逢孝惠魯元載

行楚騎追漢王漢王急推墮二子滕公下收載遂得脫審食其從

太公呂后間行反遇楚軍羽常置軍中以爲質諸侯見漢敗皆亡

On the Sui River he completely routed the army of Han, and killed so many officers and soldiers that because of it the Sui River did not flow.[1] He surrounded the King of Han with three lines [of soldiers. But] a great wind arose from the north-west, breaking trees and blowing away houses, blowing up sand and gravel, so that the day was dark. The army of Ch'u [fell into] great disorder and the King of Han succeeded in escaping with several tens **33b** of cavalrymen. He went by P'ei and sent people to seek his family, but his family[2] had also already fled and he did not meet them. On the road, the King of Han happened upon Hsiao-hui and the [Princess] Yüan of Lu,[3] and carried them along in his chariot. [But] the cavalrymen of Ch'u pursued the King of Han. The King of Han got excited and pushed the two children so that they fell out, [whereupon] the Lord of T'eng, [Hsia-hou Ying], got down and gathered them into the chariot. Thus they succeeded in escaping.[4] Shen Yi-chi was ac-companying T'ai-kung and the Empress [née] Lü, [who were fleeing] by unfrequented paths; instead [of escaping] they met the army of Ch'u. [Hsiang] Yü constantly placed them in the midst of his army, and held them as hostages.

When the nobles saw that Han, had been de-feated, they all fled. The [former] King of Sai,

[1] Because it was blocked with corpses as the troops tried to cross it. They were fleeing northwestward.

[2] Chu Tzu-wen (before 1198) suggested that the repetition of "his family" 室 家 and of "the King of Han," 漢 王 is due to dittography.

[3] His two children by the Empress née Lü, here called by their later titles. He had also had other children by concubines.

[4] The SC says that the children fell out three times and the Lord of T'eng, Hsia-hou Ying, picked them up, until at last he remonstrated with Kao-tsu. Cf. Mh II, 300. The HS version, that they fell out only once, seems far more probable, for they were being pursued. For a further detail of that escape, cf. Glossary, sub Ting Ku.

[Szu-ma] Hsin, and the [former] King of Ti, [Tung] Yi, surrendered to Ch'u. The King of Yin, [Szu-ma] Ang, died. The older brother of the Empress [*née*] Lü, the Marquis of Chou-lü, [Lü Tse], was in charge of troops encamped at Hsia-yi. The King of Han went to him,[1] collected a few officers and soldiers, and encamped them at Tang. The King of Han went westward, passing across the region of Liang to Yü. He said to the internuncio, Sui Ho, "If you, sir, would be able to persuade the King of Chiu-chiang, [Ch'ing] Pu, and lead him to mobilize his troops in rebellion against [the state of] Ch'u, King Hsiang [Yü] would have to be detained in attacking him; if you could succeed in detaining him for several months, I would be quite certain of obtaining the empire." [So] Sui Ho went to persuade [Ch'ing] Pu and really made him rebel against [the state of] Ch'u.

34a

June In the fifth month, the King of Han encamped at Jung-yang. Hsiao Ho sent forth from Kuan-chung to go to the army all the old and weak and those not yet enregistered.[2] Han Hsin also collected troops and joined with the King of Han. Thus [the King of Han's] troops were renewed and greatly restored. They fought with [the troops of] Ch'u south of Jung-yang, between Ching and So, and routed

關中老弱未傅者悉詣軍韓信亦收兵與漢王會兵復大振與
取天下必矣隨何往說布果使畀楚五月漢王屯榮陽蕭何發
曰公能說九江王布使舉兵畀楚項王必留擊之得留數月吾
漢王往從之稍收士卒軍碭漢王西過梁地至虞謂謁者隨何
去塞王欣翟王翳降楚殷王印死呂后兄周呂侯將兵居下邑

---

[1] Wang Nien-sun says that the word 往, which is in the present text, is an interpolation; the Ching-yu ed. (1035) and the *SC* ch. 8 are without it. It has been omitted in the translation.

[2] Meng K'ang (ca. 180–260) tells that in ancient times (before the Han period) a youth was enrolled in his 20th year and tilled for three years, when he would have stores for one year and was hence conscripted into the army in his 23rd year. Ju Shu says that by law a youth was enrolled in his 23rd year as a person following his hereditary occupation 疇官 and each one followed his father in learning his hereditary occupation. If he was less than six feet two inches tall, [4 ft. 8 in. Eng. meas.], he was excused on account of his defect. The *Han-chiu-yi* (written by Wei Hung, fl. 25–57), pt. II, 5b, says that people in their 23rd year serve first as regular soldiers 正卒, after a year they serve as guards 衛士, and after another year as skilled soldiers 材官 or cavalrymen. They were trained in archery, driving, riding, galloping, fighting, and tactics. In his 56th year a soldier was superannuated on account of age, excused from

楚戰滎陽南京索間破之築甬道屬河以取敖倉粟魏
王豹謁歸視親疾至則絕河津反爲楚六月漢王還櫟
陽壬午立太子赦罪人令諸侯子在關中者皆集櫟陽
爲衛引水灌廢丘廢丘降章邯自殺雍州定八十餘縣
置河上渭南中地隴西上郡令祠官祀天地四方上帝

them.[1] They built a walled road[2] connecting with the [Yellow] River in order to get grain from the Ao Granary.

The King of Wei[h], [Wei] Pao, asked permission to return home in order to see his sick parent;[3] when he had arrived, he closed the ford at the [Yellow] River and rebelled in favor of Ch'u.

In the sixth month, the King of Han returned to Yüeh-yang. On [the day] *jen-wu*, he named the Heir-apparent and proclaimed an amnesty to criminals; he ordered the members of the noble houses who were in attendance at Kuan-chung all to gather at Yüeh-yang as a guard. *(June/July ... July 1)*

He led water to flood Fei-ch'iu;[4] Fei-ch'iu sur-rendered, Chang Han committed suicide, and the province of Yung was subjugated, some eighty odd prefectures. He [thereupon] established the commanderies of Ho-shang, Wei-nan, Chung-ti, Lung-hsi, and Shang.[5] He ordered the officials in charge of the sacrifices to make offerings to Heaven, to Earth, to the Four Directions, to the Lords on High, to the Hills, and to the Streams—at the [proper] time *(34b)*

service, relegated to the ranks of the ordinary people, and went back to his farm and village. Hsiao Ho, in sending the "old" and "unregistered," was sending those over 56 and under 23 to Kao-tsu. Cf. also 5: 3b.

[1] The *SC* ch. 8 (*Mh* II, 367) puts this battle in the sixth month, after the naming of the heir apparent; the *HS* however is in this section following *SC* ch. 7 (*Mh* II, 301f), in which no monthly datings are given; this order is preferable.

[2] *SC* 6: 14a (*Mh* II, 139 & n. 4) tells that the First Emperor built a similar walled road 甬道 from Hsien-yang (his capital) to the Kan-ch'üan Palace, and Ying Shao comments, "It says that on the outside of a road for galloping he built walls [so that when] the Son of Heaven rode in between them, people outside would not see him." Kao-tsu thus guarded the road to the granary by building walls on each side of it. Ying Shao comments on the present passage, "He feared that the enemy would seize his baggage-train, so he built walls like a street or narrow lane."

[3] His mother, according to Yen Shih-ku. Cf. 33: 1b.

[4] Where Chang Han, the King of Yung, was being besieged. Cf. 1A: 29a.

[5] The *SC* records the establishment of these commanderies at the beginning of Kao-

to sacrifice [regularly] to them.   He caused the troops in Kuan-chung to take arms and mount the Barrier at the boundary [for its defence].

In Kuan-chung there was a great famine; a *hu* of rice [or hulled millet cost] ten thousand cash [and] people ate each other.   [The King of Han] ordered the people to go to Shu and Han₈ to eat.

Aug./Sept.   In the autumn, the eighth month, the King of Han went to Jung-yang and said to Li Yi-chi, "With a kindly tongue go and persuade the King of Weiₕ, [Wei] Pao; if you are able to make him submit, I will appoint you, Master [Li, with the income of] ten thousand families in Weiₕ."   [Li] Yi-chi went, [but Wei] Pao did not listen to him.   [So] the King of Han made Han Hsin Junior Lieutenant Chancellor [and ordered him], together with Ts'ao Ts'an and Kuan Ying, all to attack [the state of] Weiₕ.   When [Li] Yi-chi returned, the King of Han asked him who was the General-in-chief of Weiₕ.   He replied, "Po Chih."   The King answered, "This [man's] mouth still smells of [mother's] milk!   He cannot resist Han Hsin.   Who is his general of cavalry?"   He replied, "Feng Ching."   [The King] answered, "This man is

35a   the son of the Ch'in general, Feng Wu-ts'ê.   Although he is capable, he is not able to resist Kuan Ying. Who is his general of foot-soldiers?"   He replied, "Hsiang T'o."   [The King] answered, "He is not able to resist Ts'ao Ts'an.   I have nothing at all to

Sept./Oct.   worry about."   In the ninth month [Han] Hsin and the others captured [Wei] Pao; he was ordered to be sent to Jung-yang.   The region of Weiₕ was subjugated and the commanderies of Ho-tung, T'ai-yüan, and Shang-tang were established.

[Han] Hsin sent men [to the King of Han] asking

tsu's second year; he had captured the territory before the end of the siege of Fei-ch'iu.   The *HS* mentions them all together at this place for convenience's sake.

誰也曰項它曰是不能當曹參吾無患矣九月信等虜豹傳詣滎陽定魏地置河東太原
尚乳臭不能當韓信騎將誰也曰馮敬曰是秦將馮無擇子也雖賢不能當灌嬰步卒將
以韓信爲左丞相與曹參灌嬰俱擊魏食其還漢王問魏大將誰也對曰柏直王曰是口
王如滎陽謂酈食其曰緩頰往說魏王豹能下之以魏地萬戶封生食其往豹不聽漢王
山川以時祠之與關中卒乘邊塞關中大饑米斛萬錢人相食令民就食蜀漢秋八月漢

上黨郡信使人請兵三萬人願以北舉燕趙東擊齊南絕楚糧道漢王與之

三年冬十月韓信張耳東下井陘擊趙斬陳餘獲趙王歇置常山代郡甲戌晦日有食

之十一月癸卯晦日有食之隨何既說黥布布起兵攻楚楚使項聲龍且攻布布戰不

勝十二月布與隨何間行歸漢漢王分之兵與俱收兵至成皋項羽數侵奪漢甬道漢

軍乏食與酈食其謀橈楚權食其欲立六國後以樹黨漢王刻印將遣食其立之以問

for thirty thousand soldiers, wishing with them [to go] northwards to take [the states of] Yen and Chao, eastwards to attack [the state of] Ch'i, and southwards to cut the roads by which provisions were brought to the Ch'u [army]. The King of Han gave them [to him].

In the third year, in the winter, the tenth month, III Han Hsin and Chang Erh went eastwards, subjugated Ching-hsing, and attacked [the state of] Chao. They beheaded Ch'en Yü and captured the King of Chao, [Chao] Hsieh. [Then] the commanderies of Ch'angshan and Tai were established.   Nov./Dec.

On [the day] *chia-hsü*, the last day of the month, Dec. 20 there was an eclipse of the sun.[1] In the eleventh Dec./Jan. month, on [the day] *kuei-mao*, the last day of the 204 B.C. month, there was an eclipse of the sun.

Since Sui Ho had persuaded Ch'ing Pu [to rebel], [Ch'ing] Pu set his troops in motion and attacked [the state of] Ch'u. Ch'u sent Hsiang Sheng and Lung Chü to attack [Ch'ing] Pu. [Ch'ing] Pu fought [with them, but] did not defeat them. In the twelfth month, [Ch'ing] Pu, with Sui Ho, by unfrequented paths, returned to Han. The King of **35b** Jan./Feb. Han gave him a part of his own troops and, together with him, he collected troops and reached Ch'eng-kao.

Hsiang Yü several times invaded and captured the walled road of Han [with the result that] the army of Han lacked food. [The King of Han] schemed with Li Yi-chi to enfeeble the power of Ch'u. [Li] Yi-chi wanted to set up the descendants of the six [ancient feudal] states in order to establish factions; the King of Han had seals engraved and was going to send [Li] Yi-chi to set them up, when he asked Chang Liang about it. Chang Liang brought for-

[1] For eclipses, cf. App. IV.

ward eight objections.[1]   The King of Han stopped eating and spit out what he had in his mouth, saying [to Li Yi-chi], "Stupid bookworm!   You've almost spoiled your daddy's business."   [Then] he ordered the seals to be quickly melted down.   He also asked Ch'en P'ing [what to do], and followed his plan.   He gave [Ch'en] P'ing forty thousand catties of [real] gold in order in Ch'u to separate the lord from his followers.

May/June   In the summer, the fourth month, Hsiang Yü besieged the [King of[2]] Han, at Jung-yang, and the King of Han, begged for peace, [offering] to cut off [the region] west of Jung-yang as [the country of] Han, [leaving the rest to Hsiang Yü.   But] his Second Father, [Fan Tseng], urged Hsiang Yü to hasten and attack Jung-yang.   The King of Han was worried over [that possibility, but] since Ch'en P'ing's [plan to bring about] a change and a separation [between the lord and his followers in Ch'u] had already succeeded, [Hsiang] Yü was, as a result, suspicious of his Second Father, [Fan Tseng].   His Second Father was [therefore] very angry, so went away,

June/July   became ill, and died.   In the fifth month, General Chi Hsin said, "The situation has become urgent. Your servant begs [for permission] to deceive [the army of] Ch'u [so that] you can thereby escape in the

36a   interval."   Therefore Ch'en P'ing at night sent out more than two thousand women by the east gate.[3] [The troops of] Ch'u thereupon attacked them from all sides.   Now Chi Hsin had mounted the King's chariot, with its yellow canopy and plumes on the

張良良發八難漢王輟飯吐哺曰豎儒幾敗乃公事令趣銷印又問陳平乃

從其計與平黃金四萬斤以間疏楚君臣夏四月項羽圍漢滎陽漢王請和

割滎陽以西者爲漢亞父勸項羽急攻滎陽漢王患之陳平反間既行羽果

疑亞父亞父大怒而去發病死五月將軍紀信曰事急矣臣請誑楚可以間

出於是陳平夜出女子東門二千餘人楚因四面擊之紀信乃乘王車黃屋

---

[1] They are enumerated in ch. 40: 6a–7a.

[2] Wang Nien-sun says that the word 王 has dropped out of this sentence; without it, the meaning is not clear. Li Shan (649–689), in the *Wen-hsüan* 14: 18b, quotes this sentence without this word. But in the *Wen-hsüan* 47: 11b, he quotes it with this word, so that in the other quotation this word must have later been deleted.   Where this passage is quoted in the *Han-chi* 3: 14a and in the *Tzu-chih T'ung-chien* 10: 7b, the word is used.

[3] In the *SC* it is said that they were armed.

左纛曰食盡漢王降楚楚皆呼萬歲之城東觀以故漢王得與數十

騎出西門遁令御史大夫周苛魏豹樅公守滎陽羽見紀信問漢王

安在曰已出去矣羽燒殺信而周苛樅公相謂曰反國之王難與守

城因殺魏豹漢王出滎陽至成皋自成皋入關收兵欲復東轅生說

漢王曰漢與楚相距滎陽數歲漢常困願君王出武關項王必引兵

left,[1] and said: "Our food is gone. The King of Han submits to Ch'u." [The soldiers of] Ch'u all called out, "Long live the King," and went to the east of the city to look at [the pretended King of Han]. Because of that, the King of Han succeeded in going out of the western gate with several tens of cavalrymen and fled. He had ordered the Grandee Secretary Chou Ho, Wei Pao, and his excellency Ts'ung to defend Jung-yang.

When [Hsiang] Yü saw Chi Hsin, he asked where the King of Han was. [Chi Hsin] replied, "He has already gone away." [Hsiang] Yü [thereupon] burnt [Chi] Hsin to death.

Meanwhile Chou Ho and his excellency Ts'ung said to each other, "It is difficult to defend a city together with a king who has made his state rebel." Hence they killed Wei Pao.

When the King of Han went out of Jung-yang, he went to Ch'eng-kao, [and] from Ch'eng-kao he entered the [Han-ku] pass. He collected troops, wanting to return eastwards, but Master Yüan advised the King of Han, saying, "Han₈ and Ch'u **36b** have opposed each other at Jung-yang for several years, and Han₈ has continually been exhausted. I wish that your Majesty would go out by the Wu pass.[2] [Then] King Hsiang [Yü] would have to lead [away] his troops and hasten southwards. Your

---

[1] According to Li Fei (prob. iii cent.) and Ts'ai Yung (133–192), the emperor's chariot had a yellow silk lining to its roof, and the "plumes" 纛 were a bunch of feathers or of yak tail hair attached to the left end of the yoke at the end of the chariot tongue or attached to the left outer horse of the quadriga. Ying Shao says that the "plumes" were made of pheasant feathers and put onto the bit of the left outside horse, but Yen Shih-ku says he is wrong. This passage, together with the foregoing comments, is the *locus classicus* for the description of the ancient imperial chariot.

[2] This route would carry him to the south of Kuan-chung; he had been east of it.

Majesty would be deeply entrenched and [remain on the defensive], so you would permit [the region] between Jung-yang and Ch'eng-kao temporarily to secure a rest. You would send Han Hsin and others to take, piece by piece, [the state of] Chao in the region north of the [Yellow] River, and make an alliance with [the states of] Yen and Ch'i. Your Majesty will thereupon [be able to] return to Jung-yang. If you do this, then [the state of] Ch'u must be prepared at many places, and its strength will be divided. When Han, has secured a rest, and fights with [Ch'u] again, the rout [of Ch'u] will be certain." The King of Han followed his plan and led out his army between Yüan and Shê; he marched and collected soldiers with Ch'ing Pu. When [Hsiang] Yü heard that the King of Han was at Yüan, he really led his troops southwards. [But] the King of Han was firmly entrenched, and did not fight with him.

In that month, P'eng Yüeh crossed the Sui [River], fought with Hsiang Sheng and the Lord of Hsieh at Hsia-p'ei, routed [their armies], and killed the Lord of Hsieh. [Hsiang] Yü had the old gentleman Chung defend Ch'eng-kao and himself went east to attack P'eng Yüeh. The King of Han led his troops north, attacked and routed the old gentleman Chung, and again encamped at Ch'eng-kao.

July/Aug.   By the sixth month, [Hsiang] Yü had already routed P'eng Yüeh and made him flee.

When he heard that [the King of] Han had again encamped at Ch'eng-kao, he thereupon led his troops west, took the city of Jung-yang by storm, and captured Chou Ho alive. [Hsiang] Yü said to [Chou] Ho: "Be my general and I will make your honor First [Ranking] General and will appoint you [with the income of] thirty thousand families." [But] Chou Ho reviled him and said: "If you do not forthwith

南走王深壁令滎陽成皋間且得休息使韓信等得輯河北趙地連燕齊君王乃復走滎陽

如此則楚所備者多力分漢得休息復與之戰破之必矣漢王從其計出軍宛葉間與黥布

行收兵羽聞漢王在宛果引兵南漢王堅壁不與戰是月彭越渡睢與項聲薛公戰下邳破

殺薛公羽使終公守成皋而自東擊彭越漢王引兵北擊破終公復軍成皋六月羽已破走

彭越聞漢復軍成皋乃引兵西拔滎陽城生得周苛羽謂苛爲我將以公爲上將軍封三萬

戶周苛罵曰若不趨降漢今為虜矣若非漢王敵也羽亨周苛并殺樅公而虜韓王信遂圍

成皋漢王跳獨與滕公共車出成皋玉門北渡河宿小脩武自稱使者晨馳入張耳韓信壁

而奪之軍乃使張耳北收兵趙地秋七月有星孛于大角漢王得韓信軍復大振八月臨河

南鄉軍小脩武欲復戰郎中鄭忠說止漢王高壘深塹勿戰漢王聽其計使盧綰劉賈將卒

二萬人騎數百渡白馬津入楚地佐彭越燒楚積聚復擊破楚軍燕郭西攻下睢陽外黃十

submit to Han₈, you may now [consider yourself] its captive. You are not a match for the King of Han." **37a**
[Hsiang] Yü boiled Chou Ho [alive] and also killed his excellency Ts'ung. Moreover he captured the King of Han_h, [Han_w] Hsin. Thereupon he besieged Ch'eng-kao. The King of Han₈ fled; alone, with the Lord of T'eng, [Hsia-hou Ying], sharing his chariot, he came out of Ch'eng-kao by the Jade Gate, went northwards, crossed the [Yellow] River, and spent the night at Hsiao-hsiu-wu. By calling himself a messenger, at dawn he [managed to] gallop into the entrenchments of Chang Erh and Han Hsin and took from them [the command of] their army. Then he sent Chang Erh northwards to collect troops in the region of Chao.

In the seventh month, there was a bushy comet in Aug/Sept. the [constellation] *Ta-chio*.[1]

When the King of Han₈ got the army of Han Hsin, he became powerful again. In the eighth Sept./Oct. month he approached the [Yellow] River, and, going southwards, he encamped at Hsiao-hsiu-wu, intending to engage in battle again. [But] the Gentleman-of-the-Palace Cheng Chung advised him to stop, that he, the King of Han, should build high his ramparts, deepen his moats, and not fight [any battles]. The King of Han followed this strategy.

He sent [out] Lu Wan and Liu Chia, leading twenty thousand soldiers and several hundred **37b** cavalry. They crossed [the Yellow River] at the Pai-ma ford, entered the territory of Ch'u, assisted P'eng Yüeh to burn the accumulated stores of Ch'u, again attacked and routed the army of Ch'u west of the suburb of Yen, and attacked and captured Sui-yang and Wai-huang, seventeen cities [in all].

In the ninth month, [Hsiang] Yü said to his Com- Oct./Nov.

[1] This comet was supposed to be an inauspicious sign. It is listed as no. 15 in John Williams, *Observations of Comets*, London, 1871.

mander-in-chief, Ts'ao Chiu, the Marquis of Hai-ch'un, "Cautiously defend Ch'eng-kao. If the King of Han wishes to provoke a battle, be careful not to engage in a battle with him. Only do not allow him to go eastwards. In fifteen days I shall certainly have subjugated the region of Liang and will again come to you, general." [Hsiang] Yü led his troops eastwards and attacked P'eng Yüeh. The King of Han sent Li Yi-chi to advise the King of Ch'i, T'ien Kuang, to cease defending himself with his troops and make peace with Han₈.

IV
Nov./Dec.

In the fourth year, in the winter, the tenth month, Han Hsin, following the plan of K'uai T'ung, made a surprise attack upon and routed [the army of] Ch'i. The King of Ch'i [thereupon] boiled Master Li [Yi-chi alive] and fled east to Kao-mi. When Hsiang Yü heard that Han Hsin had routed [the army of] Ch'i and moreover wanted to attack Ch'u, he sent Lung Chü to save Ch'i.

[As Hsiang Yü had] predicted, [the army of] Han₈ [tried] several times to provoke a battle at Ch'eng-kao, but the army of Ch'u would not come out. [Then the King of Han₈] sent people to insult [the army and its generals. After] several days, the Commander-in-chief, [Ts'ao] Chiu, was angry and

38a

crossed the Szu River with his troops. When the officers and soldiers were half-way across, [the army of] Han₈ attacked them and severely routed the army of Ch'u. [The King of Han then] took all that the state of Ch'u had of gold, jewels, goods, and riches. The Commander-in-chief, [Ts'ao] Chiu and his Chief Official,[1] [Szu-ma] Hsin, both cut their own throats on the Szu River. The King of Han₈ led his troops across the [Yellow] River and again took Ch'eng-kao, encamping at Kuang-wu

---

[1] The text here is 長 史; the second word should probably be 吏 to conform to usage elsewhere in the *HS*.

和
我十五日必定梁地復從將軍羽引兵東擊彭越漢王使酈食其說齊王田廣罷守兵與漢
七城九月羽謂海春侯大司馬曹咎曰謹守成皐卽漢王欲挑戰愼勿與戰勿令得東而已

龍且救齊漢果數挑成皐戰楚軍不出使人辱之數日大司馬咎怒渡兵汜水士卒半渡漢
四年冬十月韓信用蒯通計襲破齊齊王亨酈生東走高密項羽聞韓信破齊且欲擊楚使

擊之大破楚軍盡得楚國金玉貨賂大司馬咎長史欣皆自剄汜水上漢王引兵渡河

復取成皋軍廣武就敖倉食羽下梁地十餘城聞海春侯破乃引兵還漢軍方圍鍾離

昧於滎陽東聞羽至盡走險阻羽亦軍廣武與漢相守丁壯苦軍旅老弱罷轉餉漢王

羽相與臨廣武之間而語羽欲與漢王獨身挑戰漢王數羽曰吾始與羽俱受命懷王

曰先定關中者王之羽負約王我於蜀漢罪一也羽矯殺卿子冠軍自尊罪二也羽當

and going to the Ao Granary for food.

[Hsiang] Yü had subjugated some ten odd cities of the region of Liang when he heard that the Marquis of Hai-ch'un, [Ts'ao Chiu's, army] had been routed. Thereupon he led his troops back. The army of Han, was just then besieging Chung-li Mo [at a place] east of Jung-yang; when it heard that [Hsiang] Yü had arrived, it all fled to the precipitous and difficult [terrain at Kuang-wu.]

[Hsiang] Yü also encamped at Kuang-wu; [his army] and [that of] Han, watched each other; the strong men were suffering from [constant] military service, the old and weak were exhausted in transporting food. The King of Han and [Hsiang] Yü had an interview on the border of the stream in the gully[1] [between the two cities of] Kuang-wu, and talked [together. Hsiang] Yü wanted to fight a duel single-handed with the King of Han. [But] the King of Han rebuked [Hsiang] Yü by enumerating his faults, saying, "When at first I received orders **38b** together with you, Yü, King Huai said, 'Whoever first subjugates Kuan-chung will be made its king.' You, Yü, outraged this covenant and made me king of Shu and Han,—this was your first crime. You, Yü, murdered by a false authorization the high minister[2] who had command of the army, and exalted yourself—this was your second crime. After you, Yü, had rescued [the state of] Chao, you ought to have returned to report [to King Huai];

---

[1] Reading 澗 for 間 at the suggestion of Ho Ch'uo (1661–1722) and Chou Shou-ch'ang. The T'ai-p'ing Yü-lan, ch. 69, quoting this line from HS ch. 31, writes the former character. Cf. Glossary sub "Kuang-wu".

[2] Wen Ying (fl. ca. 196–220) says that 卿子 was at that time an honorable appellation, analogous to 公-tzu. Yen Shih-ku (581–645) approves. Kao-tsu is here referring to the murder of Sung Yi, who was the first ranking general in King Hsiang's army. Cf. 13a, 14b.

on the contrary, without authorization, you seized the troops of the nobles and went through the [Han-ku] Pass—this was your third crime.　King Huai had engaged his word that when [the troops] entered [the region of] Ch'in there would be no violence or plundering; [but] you, Yü, burnt the palaces and courts of Ch'in, dug up the tomb of the First Emperor,[1] and took for your own his riches[2]—this was your fourth crime.　In violence you also murdered the King of Ch'in, Tzu-ying, who had surrendered—this was your fifth crime.　By treachery you buried in a trench at Hsin-an two hundred thousand young men of Ch'in and gave kingdoms to their generals[3]—this was your sixth crime.　You have everywhere made the generals kings of good regions and removed and expelled their former lords,[4] making ministers and subjects to strive, rebel, and commit treason—this was your seventh crime.　You drove out and expelled the Emperor Yi from P'eng-ch'eng, making it your own capital.　You took by force the territory of the King of Han$_h$,[5] and reigned over Liang and Ch'u at the same time, giving too much [of the conquered territory] to yourself—this was your

以救趙還報而擅劫諸侯兵入關罪三也懷王約入秦無暴

掠羽燒秦宮室掘始皇帝冢收私其財罪四也又彊殺秦降

王子嬰罪五也詐阬秦子弟新安二十萬王其將罪六也皆

王諸將善地而徙逐故主令臣下爭畔逆罪七也出逐義帝

彭城自都之奪韓王地幷王梁楚多自與罪八也使人陰殺

---

[1] As a severe punishment to the First Emperor.

[2] Those sealed up by Kao-tsu in the palaces and courts as well as those in the tomb. Cf. 1A: 20b.

[3] For this incident cf. *Mh* II, 272–3.　Hsiang Yü had treacherously murdered a Ch'in army which had surrendered, numbering more than 200,000 men, saving only its three generals, Chang Han, Szu-ma Hsin, and Tung Yi, alive, who were made Kings of Yung, Sai, and Ti, respectively.

[4] Such as Tsang Tu, the general of Yen, T'ien Tu, the general of Ch'i, Chang Erh, the minister of Chao, and others who were made kings of their states, displacing the former kings. Cf. 1A: 27a & b.

[5] Cf. *HS* 1A: 29b.　Chavannes forgot the incident noted in that passage (which is in the *SC*, cf. *Mh* II, 293), so wrongly suggests emending Han$_h$ to Wei$_w$. Cf. *Mh* II, 376, n. 1.　Chang Liang, Kao-tsu's follower, had been a minister of King Ch'eng of Han$_h$, hence Hsiang Yü's mistreatment and murder of King Ch'eng would touch Kao-tsu closely.

義帝江南罪九也夫爲人臣而殺其主殺其已降爲政不平主約不信天下

所不容大逆無道罪十也吾以義兵從諸侯誅殘賊使刑餘罪人擊公何苦

乃與公挑戰羽大怒伏弩射中漢王漢王傷胸乃捫足曰虜中吾指漢王病

創臥張良彊請漢王起行勞軍以安士卒毋令楚乘勝漢王出行軍疾甚因

馳入成皋十一月韓信與灌嬰擊破楚軍殺楚將龍且追至城陽虜齊王廣

eighth crime. You sent men to assassinate the Emperor Yi secretly in Chiang-nan—this was your ninth crime. Verily, in your own character as a subject, you have murdered your lord, murdered those who had[1] already surrendered, in your government you **39a** have been unjust, and as administrator of the covenant you have been faithless. [Such deeds are what] the world cannot endure; [they constitute] treason and inhuman conduct[2]—this is your tenth crime. I, with my righteous soldiers,[3] am an associate of the nobles in punishing a merciless brigand. I should send an ex-convict to fight with you, sir—why should I then suffer the trouble of [fighting] a duel with you, sir?" [Hsiang] Yü was very angry, shot a hidden crossbow, and hit the King of Han. The King of Han was wounded in the breast, but he grasped his foot and said, "This caitiff has hit me in the toe."[4]

The King of Han suffered from his wound and lay on his bed, [but] Chang Liang strongly begged the King of Han to arise, go about among the army and allay [their disquietude] in order to quiet the officers and soldiers and not permit [the army of] Ch'u to take advantage of it to gain a victory. The King of Han went out and visited the army, [but] he suffered greatly, and consequently rode into Ch'eng-kao.

In the eleventh month, Han Hsin and Kuan Ying **Dec./Jan.** attacked and routed the army of Ch'u and killed the **203 B.C.** Ch'u general, Lung Chü. They pursued it to Ch'eng-yang and captured the King of Ch'i, [T'ien] Kuang. The minister of Ch'i, T'ien Heng, set him-

[1] Wang Hsien-ch'ien notes that 其 is here a superfluous interpolation and dittography; SC 8: 25a has this sentence without this character.

[2] The name of the most serious crime in the Chinese code.

[3] Cf. Mh II, 376, n. 2.

[4] He had the presence of mind to dissimulate the seriousness of his wound in order to avoid frightening his troops.

self up as King of Ch'i and fled to P'eng Yüeh. Han₈ set up Chang Erh as King of Chao.

When the King of Han's illness was abated, he went west through the [Han-ku] Pass [and came] to Yüeh-yang, [where he] visited and conversed with the elders, and gave them a feast. He exposed on a post in the market-place of Yüeh-yang the head of the former King of Sai, [Szu-ma] Hsin.[1] He stayed [there] four days [and then] went back to his army. It remained encamped at Kuang-wu, [so that] soldiers more and more came out from Kuan-chung, while, [on the other hand] P'eng Yüeh and T'ien Heng[2] were in the region of Liang, going back and forth and harassing the troops of Ch'u, cutting off their food supplies.

39b　When Han Hsin had routed [the forces of] Ch'i, he sent men to say [to the King of Han], "[The state of] Ch'i is a neighbor of [the state of] Ch'u. My authority is slight; if you do not make me king temporarily, I fear that I may not be able to tranquillize Ch'i." The King of Han was angry and wished to attack him, [but] Chang Liang said, "It is better to accede to [his request] and to set him up [as king,] thus causing him to defend [Ch'i] for his own sake." In the spring, the second month, [the King of Han] sent Chang Liang with a seal to establish Han Hsin as King of Ch'i.

Mar./Apr.

Aug./Sept.　In the autumn, the seventh month, he set up
Sept./Oct.　Ch'ing Pu as King of Huai-nan. In the eighth

---

[1] He had committed suicide at the Szu River; his head was exposed at Yüeh-yang because it was his former capital and he had traitorously gone over to Hsiang Yü after surrendering to Kao-tsu.

[2] The name of T'ien Heng is also in the *SC*; after being driven out by Han₈ he would hardly be helping Han₈ by harassing Ch'u, yet on the page before he is said to have fled to P'eng Yüeh, who was only an ally, not a subject of Han₈. Ch'üan Tsu-wang (1705–1755) and Wang Hsien-ch'ien hence

齊相田橫自立爲齊王奔彭越漢立張耳爲趙王漢王疾瘉西入關至櫟

陽存問父老置酒梟故塞王欣頭櫟陽市留四日復如軍軍廣武關中兵

益出而彭越田橫居梁地往來苦楚兵絕其糧食韓信已破齊使人言曰

齊邊楚權輕不爲假王恐不能安齊漢王怒欲攻之張良曰不如因而立

之使自爲守春二月遣張良操印立韓信爲齊王秋七月立黥布爲淮南

王八月初爲算賦北貉燕人來致梟騎助漢漢王下令軍士不幸死
者更爲衣衾棺斂轉送其家四方歸心焉項羽自知少助食盡韓信
又進兵擊楚羽患之漢遣陸賈說羽請太公羽弗聽漢復使侯公說
羽乃與漢約中分天下割洪溝以西爲漢以東爲楚九月歸太公
羽

month the poll-tax (*suan*) was levied for the first time.[1]

People of the northern Mo and of Yen come, bringing intrepid cavalry[2] to assist Han[s].

The King of Han issued an order that the officials should provide shrouds, coverlets, coffins, and encoffining for all the soldiers in the army who were so unfortunate as to die, and send them back to their homes. In all directions, [people's] hearts turned to him.

Hsiang Yü himself knew that he had little support and that his food supply was at an end. Han Hsin was again advancing his troops to attack Ch'u,[3] and **40a** [Hsiang] Yü was worried about him. Han[s] sent Lu Chia to talk to [Hsiang] Yü and beg for the *T'ai-kung*,[4] but [Hsiang] Yü did not listen [to him]. Han[s] again sent his excellency Hou to talk to [Hsiang] Yü. [Hsiang] Yü then made a treaty [with Han[s]] to divide the world[5] in half, making the boundary at the Hung-kou,—[the territory] west of it to be Han[s]'s and that east of it to be Ch'u's. In the ninth **Oct./Nov.** month [Hsiang Yü] sent back the *T'ai-kung* and the

think that "T'ien Heng" is an interpolation. It may however be genuine.

[1] Ju Shun writes that the comment in the *Han-Chiu-yi* (written supposedly by Wei Hung, fl. 25–57) says, "People from their fifteenth to their fifty-sixth year were required to pay the capitation tax. Each person [paid] 120 cash as one poll-tax, for the care of the arsenal, the soldiers, the chariots, and the horses." Cf. *Mh* III, 541 n. 6. But cf. Glossary, *sub* Poll-tax.

[2] Lit. "owl cavalry."

[3] For details of the situation, cf. *SC* chap. 95 or *HS* chap. 41; the Glossary, *sub* Han Hsin.

[4] Kao-tsu's father, whom Hsiang Yü was holding as a hostage, together with his wife. The *HS* says nothing about his mother, although the *SC* mentions her (but this mention is probably a mistake. Cf. p. 124 n. 1; *Mh* II, 313).

[5] The Chinese thought of their country as comprising the (known) world and the Emperor regularly spoke of his territory as "the world" 天下.

Empress [*née*] Lü. The army all shouted, "Long life." Thereupon [the King of Han] appointed his excellency Hou as the P'ing-kuo General.[1]

[Hsiang] Yü withdrew [his army] and returned to the east. The King of Han wanted to return to the west, [but] Chang Liang and Ch'en P'ing admonished him, saying, "Now Han₈ has the larger half of the world and the nobles are all its adherents, [whereas] the troops of Ch'u are. exhausted and their food is

40b gone. This is the time when Heaven will destroy it. If you do not profit by this opportunity and take [the kingdom of Ch'u], [you will be in the situation when] it is said: 'By rearing a tiger one brings misfortune upon himself.'" The King of Han followed [their counsel].[2]

---

[1] Lit. "The general who brings peace to the country." The Official ed. (1739), the *SC* 7: 28b and the *Han-chi* (ii cent.) write "baronet" 君; Wang Hsien-ch'ien and the old texts write instead "general" 將. For Kao-tsu's tribute to his excellency Hou, which is taken from the *Chu-Han Ch'un-ch'iu* (197 B.C.), cf. *Mh* II, 313.

[2] Kao-tsu's action in attacking Hsiang Yü just after he had made a treaty of peace with him does, of course, involve a breach of that treaty. But in ancient China, as in modern Europe, treaties were little respected unless keeping them was plainly to the advantage of both parties. Hsiang Yü had showed himself as little scrupulous in keeping his word as any of the leaders in his time. Cf. p. 64. In his refusal to abide by the covenant requiring him to award Kuan-chung to Kao-tsu (cf. p. 66), and in his slaughter of a surrendered army (cf. p. 90, n. 3), he had shown himself quite unscrupulous, so that he had no real claim upon Kao-tsu that might require him to keep his agreement. Kao-tsu was merely requiting Hsiang Yü with the sort of treatment he had received from him.

漢書一上

亡之時不因其幾而遂取之所謂養虎自遺患也漢王從之

張良陳平諫曰今漢有天下太半而諸侯皆附楚兵罷食盡此天

呂后軍皆稱萬歲乃封侯公爲平國將羽解而東歸漢王欲西歸

Chapter I

THE ANNALS OF [EMPEROR] KAO-[TSU]

PART II[1]

In the fifth year, in the winter, the tenth month, V
the King of Han pursued Hsiang Yü to [a place] Nov.
south of Yang-chia. [There] he stopped and encamped. He had arranged for a meeting with the
King of Ch'i, [Han] Hsin, and with the Chancellor
of State in Wei[h], [P'eng] Yüeh, to attack Ch'u;
[but even] when he reached Ku-ling, they did not
meet him. [The army of] Ch'u attacked the army
of Han[s] and severely routed it. [So] the King of
Han again went into entrenchments, digging deep
his moat, and held himself on the defensive.

He said to Chang Liang, "The nobles do not
follow [me], what can I do?" [Chang] Liang replied,
"Altho the troops of Ch'u are almost routed, you
have not yet distributed to [your followers] any
territory; it is really quite natural that they did not
come. If your Majesty is able to share the world **1b**
with them, you can get them to come immediately.
The establishment of [Han] Hsin as King of Ch'i
was not your Majesty's design; [Han] Hsin is moreover not yet sure of his position. P'eng Yüeh
originally subjugated the region of Liang; at first your

[1] In the second part of this chapter more than half of the
material in the *HS* is not to be found in the *SC* ch. 7 & 8.
It looks as if Pan Ku, when he used the *SC* for his source,
made a practise of condensing that material while preserving its
essential features, and then added what important new material
he had gathered, especially from the imperial edicts and from
memorials to the throne. In the first few pages, the *HS* is
here excerpting its material from *SC* chap. 7, which gives a
fuller account than *SC* chap. 8; a little later it turns to *SC*
chap. 8. Cf. *Mh* II, 313ff.

漢書一　高紀第一下

五年冬十月漢王追項羽至陽夏南止軍與齊王信魏相國越期會擊

楚至固陵不會楚擊漢軍大破之漢王復入壁深塹而守謂張良曰諸

侯不從奈何良對曰楚兵且破未有分地其不至固宜君王能與共天

卜可立致也齊王信之立非君王意信亦不自堅彭越本定梁地始君

Majesty installed [P'eng] Yüeh as Chancellor of State on account of Wei Pao; now [Wei] Pao is dead and [P'eng] Yüeh hopes to be king, but your Majesty did not decide [to appoint him] in good time. If now you will take [the region] north of Sui-yang to Ku-ch'eng and make P'eng Yüeh king of it all, and give the King of Ch'i, [Han] Hsin, [the region] from the east of Ch'en₂ to the ocean—[Han] Hsin's home is in Ch'u; he wants to obtain again his home town— if you can give up these territories and promise them to these two men, making each one fight for his own [interests], then Ch'u will easily be defeated." Thereupon the King of Han dispatched a messenger to cause Han Hsin and P'eng Yüeh to come. Both came, leading their troops.

Dec.   In the eleventh month, Liu Chia entered the region of Ch'u and besieged Shou-ch'un. Han₃ also sent someone to tempt the Commander-in-chief of Ch'u, Chou Yin. [Chou] Yin rebelled against Ch'u; with [forces from] Shu, he [captured and] massacred [the inhabitants of] Liu₅, raised the troops of [the kingdom of] Chiu-chiang, and welcomed [back] Ch'ing Pu; they marched together and massacred [the inhabitants of] Ch'eng-fu. In the train of[1] Liu Chia they all joined forces.

2a   In the twelfth month they surrounded [Hsiang]
Dec./Jan.   Yü's [camp] at Kai-hsia. In the night [Hsiang] Yü
202 B.C.   heard the army of Han₃ on all sides singing the songs of Ch'u,[2] and thought that [the King of Han] had

---

[1] The Fukien ed. (1549) follows the SC chap. 8 (Mh II, 378) in reading "Sui Ho" 隨何 instead of "in the train of" 隨. But chap. 7 of the SC, in telling of this event (cf. Mh II, 315) reads "in the train of." Sui Ho was Kao-tsu's Internuncio, not at all a military man; nowhere else is he said to have taken part in any fighting. HS 31: 22b likewise reads "in the train of"; 35: 1b, in recounting this incident has the same meaning. The word Ho in the SC ch. 8 must therefore be an interpolation.

[2] These songs were a stratagem on Kao-tsu's part, to induce

舒屠六舉九江兵迎黥布並行屠城父隨劉賈皆會十二月圍羽垓下羽夜聞
皆引兵來十一月劉賈入楚地圍壽春漢亦遣人誘楚大司馬周殷殷畔楚以
出捐此地以許兩人使各自爲戰則楚易敗也於是漢王發使使韓信彭越至
至穀城皆以王彭越從陳以東傅海與齊王信信家在楚其意欲復得故邑能
王以魏豹故拜越爲相國令豹死越亦望王而君王不早定令能取睢陽以北

漢軍四面皆楚歌知盡得楚地羽與數百騎走

是以兵大敗灌嬰追斬羽東城楚地悉定獨魯

不下漢王引天下兵欲屠之爲其守節禮義之

國乃持羽頭示其父兄魯乃降初懷王封羽爲

魯公及死魯父爲之堅守故以魯公葬羽於穀

gained all the territory of Ch'u, [so Hsiang] Yü fled with several hundred horsemen. Because of this fact, his army was severely defeated. Kuan Ying pursued and beheaded [Hsiang] Yü at Tung-ch'eng.[1]

[Thereafter] the territory of Ch'u was all subjugated, only [the state of] Lu[2] would not submit. The King of Han led the troops of the empire[3] [against it], intending to massacre its [inhabitants]. Because it was a state which had guarded itself faithfully and was [known for its] proper conduct and sense of human relationships,[4] [the King of Han had] the head of [Hsiang] Yü held up and shown to the elders [of Lu]; then Lu surrendered. Because King Huai had originally appointed [Hsiang] Yü as the Duke of Lu, and because when he died Lu was still firmly defended for him, [the King of Han had Hsiang] Yü therefore buried at Ku-ch'eng [with the title of][5]

homesickness in Hsiang Yü's soldiers as well as to deceive him about the extent of the rebellion against him.

[1] The *HS* is following the account in the *SC* chap. 8; but the *SC* says "killed" instead of "beheaded" (cf. *Mh* II, 379). Hsiang Yü committed suicide after being wounded more than ten times and being cornered; then Wang Yi, a cavalryman, cut off his head, and there was a fight among some of Kao-tsu's generals and soldiers over his body and the reward for it. Cf. *Mh* II, 320. For the splendid account of his final stand, parting speeches, and death, cf. *Mh* II, 316–320, also *HS* ch. 31; Glossary, *sub* Hsiang Chi.

[2] Hsiang Yü had been made a Duke of Lu (cf. 1A: 13b) and had spent some time there (cf. 1A: 33a).

[3] Lit. "of the world" 天下, indicating that he was now master of the then known world, China.

[4] This curious statement, worthy of a Confucian historian, is taken from *SC* 7: 33a. Cf. *Mh* II, 321; *HS* 88: 3a.

[5] Wang Hsien-ch'ien (1842–1918) says that, since the *SC* and chap. 31 of the *HS* add 號 "with the title of" at this point, the word should be in the text here too.

a Duke of Lu. The King of Han proclaimed a
2b mourning ceremony[1] for him. He wept and lamented, then left.

He appointed Hsiang Po and others, [altogether]
four [of Hsiang Yü's kindred], as marquises, granting
them the [imperial] surname, Liu.[2] All the people
who had been captured [and kept] in Ch'u were
[allowed] to return [home].

The King of Han returned to Ting-t'ao, rode into
the entrenchments of the King of Ch'i, [Han] Hsin,
and took away his army.[3]

The King of Lin-chiang, Kung Ao, whom Hsiang
Yü had originally set up, had previously died; his son
[Kung] Wei had been set up [by Hsiang Yü] in suc-
cession as king, [so] he did not surrender. [The King
of Han] sent Lu Wan and Liu Chia to attack him;
Jan./Feb. they captured [Kung] Wei.

In the spring, the first month, [the King of Han]
posthumously honored his older brother [Liu] Po,
entitling him Marquis Wu-ai.

[1] Reading 喪 with the official ed. (1739) instead of the present 葬. The two words here seem practically interchangeable.

[2] Hsiang Po was the person who defended Kao-tsu when he
was in danger of assassination at Hung-men. Cf. 1A: 22.
These four marquises were: Liu Chan (Hsiang Po), Marquis
of She-yang; Liu T'o, Marquis of P'ing-kao; Liu Hsiang, Marquis
of T'ao-an; the fourth is not listed in HS chap. 18, (p. 10b,
33a, and 58a, which furnish the preceding three names) nor
elsewhere; the SC merely gives his name as the Marquis of
Hsüan-wu 玄武; cf. Mh II, 322. The granting of the imperial
surname, Liu, was an especial honor.

[3] Kao-tsu was uncertain of the loyalty of Han Hsin.

城漢王為發喪哭臨而去封項伯等四人為列侯賜姓劉

氏諸民略在楚者皆歸之漢王還至定陶馳入齊王信壁

奪其軍初項羽所立臨江王共敖前死子尉嗣立為王不

降遣盧綰劉賈擊虜尉春正月追尊兄伯號曰武哀侯下

令曰楚地已定義帝亡後欲存恤楚眾以定其主齊王信習楚風俗更立為

楚王王淮北都下邳魏相國建城侯彭越勤勞魏民卑下士卒常以少擊眾

數破楚軍其以魏故地王之號曰梁王都定陶又曰兵不得休八年萬民與

苦甚今天下事畢其以赦天下殊死以下於是諸侯上疏曰楚王韓信韓王信

淮南王英布梁王彭越故衡山王吳芮趙王張敖燕王臧荼昧死再拜言大

An order was given, saying, "The region of Ch'u has already been subjugated, [but] the Emperor Yi had no heirs; We wish to be solicitous for the people of Ch'u and fix upon a king for them. The King of Ch'i, [Han] Hsin, is well versed in the customs of Ch'u— let [his kingdom] be changed and [let] him be established as the King of Ch'u, ruling over [the region] north of the Huai [River], with his capital at Hsia-p'ei. The Chancellor of State at Wei_h, the Chien-ch'eng Marquis, P'eng Yüeh, has toiled diligently for the people of Wei_h; he has humbled and abased himself to his soldiers and officers. Often with a few [followers] he has attacked a more numerous [force]; several times he has routed the army of Ch'u. Let him be made king over the former territory of Wei_h, with the title, 'The King of Liang.' His capital shall be at Ting-t'ao." [The order] also said, "The troops have not had rest for eight years. All the people have suffered severely.[1] Now [my efforts in settling the control] of the world have been brought to completion. Let an amnesty [be proclaimed] throughout the world [for all crimes] below [those deserving] capital punishment."

Thereupon the nobles sent up a petition to [the King of Han], saying: "The King of Ch'u, Han Hsin, **3a** the King of Han_h, [Han_w] Hsin, the King of Huai-nan, Ying Pu, the King of Liang, P'eng Yüeh, the former King of Heng-shan, Wu Jui, the King of Chao, Chang Ao, and the King of Yen, Tsang Tu, risking death and making repeated obeisances,[2] say

---

[1] Wang Nien-sun explains that 與 is here a meaningless auxiliary word. Cf. 4: 19b.

[2] 昧死再拜. In the time of the Ch'in dynasty the phrase 昧犯死罪 "blindly risking the commission of a crime worthy of capital punishment" (cf. *Mh* II, 126) was used in a memorial to the emperor. Chou Shou-ch'ang tells that the

to your Majesty the great King:[1] In times past the Ch'in [dynasty] acted contrary to principle and the world punished it. You, great King, were the first to capture the King of Ch'in and subjugate Kuan-chung—your achievements have been the greatest in the world. You have preserved the perishing and given repose to those in danger; you have rescued those who were ruined and have continued broken [lines of descent] in order to tranquillize all the people. Your achievements are abundant and your virtue is great. You have moreover granted favors to the vassal kings who have merit, enabling them to succeed in setting up their gods of the soil and grains.[2] The division of the land has already been settled, but positions and titles are

王陛下先時秦爲亡道天下誅之大王先

得秦王定關中於天下功最多存亡定危

救敗繼絕以安萬民功盛德厚又加惠於

諸侯王有功者使得立社稷地分已定而

former Han dynasty followed the Ch'in customs, so continued the use of this phrase, merely altering its words slightly, as in the text. When Wang Mang came to the throne, he loved to follow ancient practises, so he had officials use the phrase 稽首, "I bow my head to the earth," which is found in the Book of History. His courtiers however thought this phrase was not sufficiently humble, so wrote 稽首再拜, "I bow my head to the earth, making repeated obeisances," (found in *Mencius* V, ii, vii, 4; Legge, p. 386.) Liu Chao (fl. first half of the vi. cent A.D.) in his comment on chap. 11 of the *HHS*, quotes a memorial of Ts'ai Yung (133–192), written when he was on frontier duty, which begins, "Your servant Yung, bowing his head to the earth and making repeated obeisances, memorializes Your Majesty the Emperor 臣邕稽首再拜上書皇帝陛下" and ends, "Your servant, knocking his head on the earth as one who is worthy of capital punishment, bowing his head to the earth and making repeated obeisances, brings [this matter] to your hearing 臣頓首死罪稽首再拜以聞." Thus the Later Han dynasty combined the phraseology introduced by Wang Mang with that used earlier.

The memorial in the text uses all the stock phraseology of address to an emperor except the word, "Emperor." This memorial is not in the *SC*, altho Kao-tsu's reply is quoted there; the mention of the names of the kings presenting it leads us to think that it is genuine.

[1] Lit. "the steps below [the throne of] the great king." The Emperor is often addressed as 陛下, which phrase is equivalent to the European "Your Majesty," but is much more humble.

[2] I.e., to establish their own state and dynasty. Cf. H. Maspero, *La Chine antique*, pp. 167–171.

位號比儗亡上下之分大王功德之著於後世不宣昧死再拜上皇帝尊號漢王曰

寡人聞帝者賢者有也虛言亡實之名非所取也今諸侯王皆推高寡人將何以處

之哉諸侯王皆曰大王起於細微滅亂秦威動海內又以辟陋之地自漢中行威德

誅不義立有功平定海內功臣皆受地食邑非私之也大王德施四海諸侯王不足

以道之居帝位甚實宜願大王以幸天下漢王曰諸侯王幸以爲便於天下之民則

[still] confounded with one another, without the [proper] division of the superior [from] the inferior, so that the manifestation of your, the great King's, merits and virtue is not proclaimed to later genera- **3b** tions. Risking death and making repeated obeisances, we offer to our superior the honorable title of Emperor."

The King of Han, replied, "I, a person of little virtue,[1] have heard that [the title of] emperor should be possessed by a man eminent in talent and virtue. An empty name without [possessing] its reality should not be adopted. Now you, vassal kings, have all highly exalted me, a person of little virtue. How could I therefore occupy [such a position]?"

The vassal kings all said, "You, great King, arose from small [beginnings]; you destroyed the seditious [dynasty of] Ch'in; your majesty stirs everything within the seas;[2] moreover, starting from a secluded and mean region, from Han-chung, you acted out your majesty and virtue, executing the unrighteous, setting up the meritorious, tranquillizing and establishing the empire. Meritorious officials all received territory and the income of towns; you did not appropriate them for yourself. Your virtue, great King, has been bestowed [even to the borders of] the four seas. We, vassal kings, [find our speech] inadequate to express it. For you to take the position of Emperor would be most appropriate. We hope that you, great King, will favor the world [by doing so]."

The King of Han replied, "Since the vassal kings would be favored [by it] and since they consider it to be an advantage to [all] the people in the world, it

[1] The term regularily used for himself by the Emperor or by a king, when speaking to his subjects. It may usually be translated merely "I." Here it seems to have a special significance.

[2] I.e., everyone in the (Chinese) world.

may be done."[1]

Thereupon the vassal kings and "your servant, the Grand Commandant and Marquis of Ch'ang-an, [Lu] Wan, and others, [altogether] three hundred persons, together with the Erudit and the Chi-szu Baronet, Shu-sun T'ung, carefully selected a favorable day." In the second month, on [the day] chia-wu,[2] they presented to their superior the honorable title [of Emperor] and the King of Han ascended the imperial throne upon the northern bank of the river Szu.[3] The Queen was honored and called, "The Empress"; the Heir-apparent was called "The Imperial Heir-apparent"; the deceased old dame, [the Emperor's mother], was posthumously honored and called "The Chao-ling Lady."

An imperial edict[4] read: "The former King of Heng-shan, Wu Jui, together with his two sons and his older brother's son, followed by the troops of the many Yüeh,[5] rendered very signal service in assisting the nobles in punishing the tyrannous Ch'in [dynasty]; the nobles set him up as King, [but] Hsiang Yü took away his territory by force,

Feb./Mar.

Feb. 28

4a

---

[1] The SC tells that Kao-tsu declined the title for the customary three times before accepting. Cf. Mh, II, 380.

[2] The HS has corrected the SC here. Cf. Mh, II, 381, n. 1.

[3] This is not the River Szu 汜 in Honan, but the one in Shantung. Cf. Mh II, 381, n. 2. SC ch. 99, HS 43:14b tell that Kao-tsu ascended the throne at Ting-t'ao, which is on this river Szu. Lü Shen (prob. fl. dur. 265–330) says, "Formerly after [the Emperor Kao-]tsu of the Han [dynasty] had subjugated the world, he ascended the imperial throne at Ting-t'ao on the northern bank of the Szu River."

[4] Ju Shun says, "From the time of the Ch'in and Han [dynasties] on, only the Son of Heaven alone employed [the word 詔]." It was also used by an Empress Dowager, cf. 11: 1b, 98: 10b.

[5] The SC writes 越 where the HS writes 粵. These words were interchangeable.

可矣於是諸侯王及太尉長安侯臣綰等三百人與博士稷

嗣君叔孫通謹擇良日二月甲午上尊號漢王即皇帝位于

汜水之陽尊王后曰皇后太子曰皇太子追尊先媼曰昭靈

夫人詔曰故衡山王吳芮與子二人兄子一人從百粵之兵

以佐諸侯誅暴秦有大功諸侯立以爲王項羽侵奪之地謂

calling him [merely] the Baronet of P'o. Let the Baronet of P'o, [Wu] Jui, be established as King of Ch'ang-sha, [ruling over] Ch'ang-sha, Yü-chang,[1] the Hsiang Commandery, Kuei-lin, and Nan-hai."[2] It also said, "The ex-king of [Min-] Yüeh, [Tsou] Wu-chu, for a generation has been perpetuating the ancestral sacrifices of Yüeh; the Ch'in [dynasty] took away his territory by force, [so that] his gods of the soils and grains did not get any blood or food.[3] When the nobles were chastizing the Ch'in [dynasty, Tsou] Wu-chu himself led the troops of Min-chung to assist in destroying the Ch'in [dynasty]; [but] **4b** Hsiang Yü set him aside and did not set him up [as king]. Now we make him King of Min-yüeh, ruling over the territory of Min-chung. Let them not neglect their charges."

The Emperor thereupon went west[4] and established his capital at Lo-yang. In the summer, the fifth month, the troops were all disbanded and **May/June** returned to their homes. An imperial edict said, "The members of the noble families[5] in Kuan-

---

[1] Yü-chang is later said to belong to the kingdom of Huai-nan; *HS* chap. 34 says it belonged to Ying Pu—the inclusion of this name here may be a copyist's addition.

[2] Hsiang, Kuei-lin, and Nan-hai belonged at that time to Chao T'o, who, four years after this edict (196 B.C.) was confirmed by Kao-tsu as King Wu of Nan-yüeh (cf. 1B: 19a and *SC* chap. 113); hence the appointment of Wu Jui as king of these three regions was largely an empty gesture. The troops of Min-yüeh had come in the train of Wu Jui, hence he is made overlord of Nan-yüeh! His kingdom was really confined to Ch'ang-sha.

[3] Yen Shih-ku says, "In sacrifice blood and raw food 血 腥 are preferred."

[4] He had taken the throne at Ting-t'ao, which is in the present Shantung.

[5] Chou Shou-ch'ang (1814–1884) shows that the 諸 侯 子 were the 支 屬 of the nobles, the offshoots of the noble families. This phrase is also used in 1A: 34a, which fixes its meaning.

上賜爵各一級其七大夫以上皆令食邑非七大夫以下皆復
會赦其亡罪而亡爵及不滿大夫者皆賜爵爲大夫故大夫以
辨告勿笞辱民以饑餓自賣爲人奴婢者皆免爲庶人軍吏卒
書名數今天下已定令各歸其縣復故爵田宅吏以文法教訓
子在關中者復之十二歲其歸者半之民前或相聚保山澤不

chung are exempted [from service and taxes] for twelve years; those who have already returned [home are exempted for] half [that period].[1] As to the people who formerly had collected to take refuge in the mountains and marshes,[2] whose names and numbers have not been enregistered—the world has now been pacified, [hence] We order that each return to his prefecture and resume his former noble rank, his fields, and his habitation. The officials, using civil laws, should teach and instruct [these people]; let it be published abroad[3] that there is to be no beating nor shaming [of them]. As to those people who because of famine or hunger have themselves sold their persons to be slaves or slave-girls,[4] let them all be freed and become common people. As to the officers and soldiers in the army who have been pardoned, those who have been without crime, but are without any noble rank, and those who have not

5a attained [the rank of] Grandee, We grant them all the noble rank of Grandee. To all those who formerly [had the rank] of Grandee and upward, We grant a noble rank one step [higher]. Let it be ordered that all those who have [the noble rank of] Seventh [Rank] Grandee and upward are to be given the revenue of estates;[5] all those below [the noble rank of] Seventh [Rank] Grandee will themselves be personally

[1] The *SC* adds that they were also to receive a year's supplies 食之一歲.

[2] Brigands and outlaws.

[3] Wang Nien-sun (1744–1832) says that 辨 was anciently written for 班.

[4] This passage shows that there were private slaves in addition to those enslaved to the government as a punishment.

[5] Fu Tsan (fl. ca. 285) says that according to the regulations of the Ch'in dynasty, marquises (the highest rank in the aristocratic hierarchy) had been given the revenue of estates. Now the seventh rank and upward are so honored. Cf. Glossary, *sub* Marquis.

其身及戶勿事又曰七大夫公乘以上皆高爵也諸侯子及從

軍歸者甚多高爵吾數詔吏先與田宅及所當求於吏者亟與

爵或人君上所尊禮久立吏前曾不為決甚亡謂也異日秦民

爵公大夫以上令丞與亢禮今吾於爵非輕也吏獨安取此且

法以有功勞行田宅令小吏未嘗從軍者多滿而有功者顧不

exempted [from public service] and their households
will not be required to do public service." It also
said, "[The noble ranks] of Seventh [Rank] Grandee
and Public Chariot and above are all high ranks.
Among the members of the noble houses[1] and those
who have returned from the army are very many
with high noble ranks; I have several times ordered
the officials to give fields and habitations to them
first, and that whatever they rightfully ask of the 5b
officials should be promptly given them. There are
some people with [high] noble titles as lords of men[2]
whom the Emperor has honored, performed the
ceremonies, and set up a long time ago, [but] about
whom the officials have unexpectedly not yet
reached a decision—this is utterly unspeakable. As
to those among the people of Ch'in who in former
days were ennobled [with the ranks] of Universal
Grandee and upwards, a Chief and an Assistant[3]
should respect them as their equals. Now I do not
think lightly of [these] noble ranks, why should the
officials alone take them thus? Moreover, according to the law, those who have some achievement
and have rendered meritorious service should be
given fields and habitations; [yet] at present many of
the small officials who have never been with the
army have been satisfied, but those who have [mili-
tary] merit have nevertheless received nothing. For
a [Commandery] Administrator, a [Commandery]

---

[1] Cf. p. 103, n. 5. This passage especially indicates the correct meaning of this phrase, showing that they were distinct
from the other soldiers.

[2] Yen Shih-ku explains, "If their noble ranks were high and
they had kingdoms or estates, they themselves acted as lords
to their people, hence it says, 'Some who were lords of men.'"

[3] The heads of government bureaux were entitled Chiefs 令,
their assistants were called Assistants 丞. Prefects and their
assistants were also called chiefs and assistants, respectively.
Cf. *Mh* II, Appendix I. Two personages with the same rank
greet each other with a long bow without any prostration,
according to Ying Shao.

Commandant, or a Chief Official to act contrary to public interest and for the interests of private persons is a kind of teaching and instruction that is extremely bad. Let it be ordered that the officials should treat the holders of high noble ranks properly [in order to] conform to my wishes. Moreover there will be an inspection and examination; if there are [found] any who have not acted in accordance with my edict, they will be heavily sentenced."

6a　The Emperor held a feast in the Southern Palace at Lo-yang. The Emperor said, "Marquises and generals, do not dare to hide anything from Us. Express all your feelings. What was the reason that I have obtained the empire? What was the reason that the house of Hsiang [Yü] lost the empire?"

Kao Ch'i[1] and Wang Ling replied, "Your Majesty treats people cavalierly and is rude to them, [whereas] Hsiang Yü was kind and respected people; yet when your Majesty sent people to attack a city or overrun a region, you thereupon gave them whatever 6b they submitted, sharing your advantages with the world. Hsiang Yü was jealous of the capable and envious of the able; he [sought to] injure whoever had accomplished anything worth while and was suspicious of those who were capable. When people were victorious in battle he did not give them any glory; when they obtained some territory, he did not give others any advantage [of it]. The foregoing is the reason that he lost the empire."

The Emperor said, "You sirs, know a part, but you do not know the whole. Now, in revolving plans in the tent and in making a victory certain at a distance of a thousand *li*, I am not as good as [Chang] Tzu-fang.[2] In pacifying a state, in soothing the people, in supplying pay and provisions

---

[1] The words "Kao Ch'i" may be an interpolation. Cf. Glossary, *sub voce.*

[2] The use of Chang Liang's style by the emperor (who usually uses a person's given name) was an extremely courteous form of address.

得背公立私守尉長吏教訓甚不善其令諸吏善遇高爵稱吾意且廉問有不如詔者以

重論之帝置酒雒陽南宮上曰通侯諸將毋敢隱朕皆言其情吾所以有天下者何項氏之

所以失天下者何高起王陵對曰陛下嫚而侮人項羽仁而敬人然陛下使人攻城略地所

降下者因以與之與天下同利也項羽妬賢嫉能有功者害之賢者疑之戰勝而不與人功

得地而不與人利此其所以失天下也上曰公知其一未知其二夫運籌帷幄之中決勝千

里之外吾不如子房塡國家撫百姓給餉餽不絕糧道吾不如蕭何連百

萬之衆戰必勝攻必取吾不如韓信三者皆人傑吾能用之此吾所以取

天下者也項羽有一范增而不能用此所以爲我禽也羣臣說服初田橫

歸彭越項羽已滅橫懼誅與賓客亡入海上恐其久爲亂遣使者赦橫曰

橫來大者王小者侯不來且發兵加誅橫懼乘傳詣雒陽未至三十里自

and never permitting the communications for food to be cut, I am not as good as Hsiao Ho. In uniting a crowd of a million [men], in being sure of victory in battle, and in taking whatever [place] one attacks,[1] I am not as good as Han Hsin. [These] three are all outstanding men. I was able to make use of them— that is the reason I took the world. Hsiang Yü had one Fan Tseng, but he could not make use of him[2]—that was the reason he became my captive." The crowd of officials were glad to acquiesce.

Originally T'ien Heng had gone over to P'eng Yüeh. When Hsiang Yü had already been destroyed, [T'ien] Heng was afraid of being executed, [so] with his clients and guests he fled into the sea. The Emperor was afraid that if he stayed long he would create trouble, [so] sent a messenger to grant [T'ien] Heng amnesty, saying, "If [T'ien] Heng [and his party] come [and surrender], the great [person in his company will be made] a king and the lesser [persons] marquises. If [he and his following] do not come, I will immediately send out troops and punish [him and his followers] with death." [T'ien] Heng was dismayed, [so], riding a [four-horse] post-carriage,[3] he went to Lo-yang. When he was [still] thirty li away, he committed **7a**

[1] The Southern ed. (ca. x–xii cent.), the SC, the Han-chi (ii cent.), and the Tzu-chih T'ung-chien (1084) read, "in being sure of obtaining the victory in battle and being sure of taking and getting booty from whatever [place] one attacks."

[2] Cf. Mh II, p. 303f, HS 1A: 35b.

[3] Ju Shun comments, "According to the Code, [a carriage with] four horses having long limbs is a chih-chuan 置 傳 ("post carriage"); with four horses having medium limbs it is a ch'ih-chuan 馳 傳 ("galloping carriage"); with four horses having short limbs it is a sheng-chuan 乘 傳 ("riding carriage"); with one or two horses it is a yao-chuan 軺 傳 ("small carriage"). One who is in haste rides a sheng-chuan." The Shuo-wen explains 傳 as 遽 "post-carriage." Cf. also 12: n. 9.3.

suicide. The Emperor admired his faithfulness and wept for him. He sent out two thousand soldiers to bury him with the rites of a king.

A banished man, Lou Ching, begged for an interview and said to the Emperor, "Your Majesty has taken the empire differently from [the way the] Chou [dynasty did],[1] [so that] your capital in Lo-yang is not advantageous. It is better to enter the passes and occupy the stronghold of the Ch'in [dynasty]." The Emperor asked Chang Liang about it. [Chang] Liang therefore urged the Emperor [likewise]. On that day [the Emperor] mounted the imperial chariot and went westwards to fix his capital at Ch'ang-an. He installed Lou Ching as the Fung-ch'un Baronet and granted him the [imperial] surname, Liu.

June 26.　　In the sixth month, on the day *jen-ch'en*, a general amnesty for the world [was proclaimed].

July/Aug.　　In the autumn, the seventh month, the King of Yen, Tsang Tu, revolted.[2] The Emperor, himself [acting as] general, marched against him. In the

Sept./Oct.　　ninth month he captured [Tsang] Tu. An imperial edict [ordered] the vassal kings to look for a meritorious person to be made king of Yen. "The King of Ching, your servant, [Han] Hsin," and others, ten [in all], all replied, "The merits of the Grand Commadent and Marquis of Ch'ang-an, Lu Wan, are the greatest

[1] According to the Book of History, the Chou dynasty took the empire without a serious struggle; Kao-tsu had to fight for his position. Cf. *HS* 43: 10b–11b.

[2] On this date, cf. *Mh* II, 384, n. 5. Hsün Yüeh (lived 148–209) in the *Ch'ien-han-chi*, following *SC* 16: 29, dates this rebellion in the eighth month. The *SC* ch. 8 (*Mh* II, 384) mistakenly dates it in the tenth month. Tsang Tu had been set up as king by Hsiang Yü and moreover was guilty of murdering the previous king of Yen, so, fearing punishment, he revolted first.

侯王視有功者立以爲燕王荊王臣信等十人皆曰太尉長安侯盧

月壬辰大赦天下秋七月燕王臧荼反上自將征之九月虜荼詔諸

張良良因勸上是日車駕西都長安拜婁敬爲奉春君賜姓劉氏六

曰陛下取天下與周異而都雒陽不便不如入關據秦之固上以問

殺上壯其節爲流涕發卒二千人以王禮葬焉戍卒婁敬求見說上

縮功最多請立以爲燕王使丞相噲將兵平代地利幾反上自擊

破之利幾者項羽將羽敗利幾爲陳令降上侯之潁川上至雒陽

舉通侯籍召之而利幾恐反後九月徙諸侯子關中治長樂宮

六年冬十月令天下縣邑城人告楚王信謀反上問左右左右爭

欲擊之用陳平計乃僞游雲夢十二月會諸侯于陳楚王信迎謁

[of all]. We beg you to make him King of Yen." **7b**
[The Emperor] sent his Lieutenant Chancellor [Fan] K'uai with troops to subjugate the region of Tai.[1]

Li Chi rebelled; the Emperor personally [led the the army to] attack him and routed his [army]. Li Chi had been a general of Hsiang Yü; when [Hsiang] Yü was defeated, Li Chi was the magistrate of Ch'en₂. He had submitted [to Kao-tsu] and the Emperor had made him a Marquis in the Ying-ch'uan [Commandery]. When the Emperor had arrived at Lo-yang, he had summoned the whole of the marquises that were enregistered, hence Li Chi had been afraid and had rebelled.

In the intercalary ninth month, [the Emperor] removed the members of noble families to Kuan-chung. He repaired the Ch'ang-lo Palace. **Oct./Nov.**

In the sixth year, in the winter, the tenth month, the Emperor ordered the prefectural cities and towns of the empire to build themselves city walls.[2] **VI** **Nov./Dec.**

A man gave information that the King of Ch'u, [Han] Hsin, was planning to revolt. The Emperor asked those around him [about it]; those around him vied [with each other], wanting to attack [Han **8a** Hsin. But the Emperor] utilized the stratagem [suggested by] Ch'en P'ing. So he feigned to make a trip to Yün-meng. In the twelfth month he assembled the nobles at Ch'en₂, and the King of **201 B.C.** Ch'u, [Han] Hsin, went to pay his respects. There- **Jan./Feb.**

[1] The *SC* (*Mh* II, 384) tells that Tsang Tu had conquered Tai after revolting. The *HS* leaves this statement out and so leaves Fan K'uai's expedition motiveless.

[2] The First Emperor had destroyed the inner and outer walls of cities (*Mh* II, 165); Kao-tsu allowed them to be rebuilt. But this edict was probably merely legalizing what had been done previously, for we hear of fortified cities before this time, even in Ch'in times; cf. 1A: 16b.

upon [the Emperor] arrested him.[1]

An imperial edict read, "Since the world has been at peace, eminent and distinguished persons who have merit have been appointed marquises. I am but newly seated [on the throne, hence] have not been able to plan a complete [reward for] their meritorious actions. They themselves have lived with the army for nine years, [so that] whether because they are not yet accustomed to the laws and ordinances, or because they formerly violated the law, [those who have committed] great [crimes] have been killed or mutilated. I pity them greatly. Let there be an amnesty granted to all the world."[2]

T'ien K'en congratulated the Emperor, saying, "[Your Majesty's plans are] very good. Your Majesty has taken Han Hsin and also rules from [the region of] Ch'in. Ch'in is a country with an excellent geographical situation. It is girdled by the [Yellow] River, with mountains as barriers, separated [from the rest of the world] along a thousand *li* [of border] with a million lance-bearers—[the strength of] Ch'in is proportionate to double[3] that of a hundred **8b** [enemy]. Its geographical situation is convenient and favorable; when it sends down its troops [from the passes] upon the nobles, it is like [a person] on top of a high building upsetting water into a tile gutter.

----

[1] For this stratagem, cf. *Mh* II, 386, n. 3. A vassal must visit the emperor when he arrives in the vassal's territory; in this way Kao-tsu was able to capture Han Hsin without a battle.

[2] The *SC* merely says (*Mh* II, 386) that on the same day that Han Hsin was arrested a general amnesty was proclaimed; the *HS* quotes the proclamation, but leaves out its date.

[3] Reading 二 to mean 倍, as in *Analects* XII, ix, 3 and the 墨子經說. This sentence is far from clear; Chavannes translates quite differently.

因執之詔曰天下既安豪桀有功者封侯新立未能盡圖其
功身居軍九年或未習法令或以其故犯法大者死刑吾甚
憐之其赦天下田肯賀上曰甚善陛下得韓信又治秦中秦
形勝之國也帶河阻山縣隔千里持戟百萬秦得百二焉地
執便利其以下兵於諸侯譬猶居高屋之上建瓴水也夫齊

東有琅邪卽墨之饒南有泰山之固西有濁河之限

北有勃海之利地方二千里持戟百萬縣隔千里之

外齊得十二焉此東西秦也非親子弟莫可使王齊

者上曰善賜金五百斤上還至雒陽赦韓信封為淮

陰侯甲申始剖符封功臣曹參等為通侯詔曰齊古

Now Ch'i in the east has the richness of Lang-ya and Chi-mo; in the south are the fastnesses of Mount T'ai; in the west are the obstacles on the Muddy River; on the north it has the advantages of the P'o Sea. Its territory is two thousand *li* square and it has a million lance-bearers. It is marked off and separated [from the rest of the world] along more than a thousand *li* [of boundary—the strength of] Ch'i is proportionate to double[1] that of ten [enemy]. These are [then] 'an eastern and a western Ch'in.[2] **9a** Only your own son or your own brother may be sent to be king over Ch'i." The Emperor replied, "Good." He gave him [the equivalent of] five hundred catties of gold.[3]

The Emperor returned to Lo-yang and pardoned Han Hsin, appointing him as Marquis of Huai-yin. On the day *chia-shen*[4] [the Emperor] first split the **9b** tallies and appointed his meritorious subjects, Feb. 13 Ts'ao Ts'an and others, as marquises.

An imperial edict said, "Ch'i is an anciently

[1] Cf. p. 110, n. 3.

[2] I.e., Ch'i on the east is similar to Ch'in on the west.

[3] Gifts of this sort are sometimes said to be of 金 and sometimes of 黃金, "real gold." For the distinction, cf. p. 175, n. 2. Silver was not coined until 125 B.C. (Cf. *HS* 24B: 12b in the comment.) *HS* chap. 24B: 3b says, "When the Ch'in [dynasty] united the world, its money 幣 was of two sorts: actual gold made into *yi* 溢 [Meng K'ang, prob. ca. 180–260, says a *yi* was 20 ounces weight] was called the superior [kind of] money, and copper cash made like the Chou [dynasty] cash. [On them] is the inscription, 'Half ounce'; their weight is the same as the inscription. But pearls, jade, tortoise-shells, cowries, silver, tin, and the like were used for vessels, ornaments, and valuable treasures, not made into currency." Page 1b of the same chapter says, "Actual gold an inch square weighs a catty 斤. Cash 錢 are round with square holes; their weight is in terms of *shu* [1/24 of an ounce, cf. ch. IV, App. I]."

[4] *HS* 16: 4b to 9b records ten appointments on this date, including that of Ts'ao Ts'an.

founded state; but now it [has been broken into] commanderies [with their] prefectures. Let it again become [a state with] a nobility. General Liu Chia has several times performed great deeds; select him and some other persons who are large-hearted and kind, cultivated and pure, to rule over re-

Feb./Mar.

Mar. 7

gions in Ch'i and Ching." In the spring, the first month, on the day *ping-wu*, the King of Han_h, [Han_w] Hsin, and others memorialized [the throne], begging that Liu Chia be made King of Ching, [ruling over] the fifty-three prefectures of the former Tung-yang Commandery, the Chang Commandery, and the Wu Commandery, and that [the Emperor] set up his younger brother the *Wen-hsin* Baronet, [Liu] Chiao, as King of Ch'u, [ruling over] the thirty-six prefectures of the Tang Commandery, the Hsieh

10a

Mar. 13

Commandery, and the T'an Commandery. On [the day] *jen-tzu* [the Emperor] set up his older brother, the *Yi-hsin* Marquis, [Liu] Hsi, as King of Tai, [ruling over] the fifty-three prefectures of the Yün-chung, the Yen-men, and the Tai Commanderies. He set up his son, [Liu] Fei, as King of Ch'i, [ruling] over the seventy-three prefectures of the Chiao-tung, the Chiao-si, the Lin-tzu, the Chi-pei, the Po-yang, and the Ch'eng-yang[1] commanderies. [The Emperor] made the kingdom of Han_h out of the thirty-one prefectures of the T'ai-yüan Commandery, and removed the King of Han_h, [Han_w] Hsin, [to it], with his capital at Chin-yang.[2]

---

[1] Of the preceding commanderies, Tung-yang, Chang, Wu, T'an, Chiao-tung, Chiao-hsi, Lin-tzu, Chi-pei, Po-yang, and Ch'eng-yang were not among the thirty-six commanderies of Ch'in times. They were created in the period of Ch'u and Han, after the downfall of the Ch'in dynasty.

[2] The kingdom of Han_h had been in Honan; it was now moved to a new region, in Shansi. In this way a possibly

之建國也今爲郡縣其復以爲諸侯將軍劉賈數有大功及擇寬惠脩絜者王

齊荊地春正月丙午韓王信等奏請以故東陽郡鄣郡吳郡五十三縣立劉賈

爲荊王以碭郡薛郡郯郡三十六縣立弟文信君交爲楚王壬子以雲中鴈門

代郡五十三縣立兄宜信侯喜爲代王以膠東膠西臨淄濟北博陽城陽郡七

十三縣立子肥爲齊王以太原郡三十一縣爲韓國徙韓王信都晉陽上巳封

取上素所不快計羣臣所共知最甚者一人先封以示羣臣三月

足用徧封而恐以過失及誅故相聚謀反耳上曰爲之奈何良曰

而所封皆故人所愛所誅皆平生仇怨令軍吏計功以天下爲不

將往往耦語以問張良良曰陛下與此屬共取天下今已爲天子

大功臣三十餘人其餘爭功未得行封上居南宮從復道上見諸

When the Emperor had already appointed [to noble positions] twenty[1] odd men of great merit, the rest disputed over their [respective] merits, for **10b** which enfeoffments had not yet been made. When the Emperor was in the Southern Palace, from above on the double passageway,[2] he saw the generals often talking together privately. He asked Chang Liang [about it, and Chang] Liang said, "Your Majesty conquered the world together with these people. Now you are already the Son of Heaven, and those whom you have enfeoffed are all your old friends and those whom you love, while those whom you have punished with death were all enemies you have made in your life-time, against whom you held a grudge. Now the army officers are counting up those who have merits and think that the world is insufficient to enfeoff them all, so they fear that for a [trifling] fault they might meet with the punishment of death. Hence they meet and plan to rebel." The Emperor replied, "What can I do for that?" [Chang] Liang replied, "Take the persons whom your Majesty has always disliked, figuring out the one whom all your courtiers know [you dislike] the very most, and enfeoff him first in order to show your courtiers [that you really mean them well]." In the

rebellious noble was moved out of central China to the northern border.

[1] The present text says "thirty"; but the *Han-chi* says "twenty"; *HS* 40: 7b and the *Tzu-chih T'ung-chien* (1084) say the same; in the table in *HS* chap. 16, twenty-seven appointments are recorded before the first month of Kao-tsu's sixth year—the character 三 is plainly a copyist's error for 二.

[2] The "double passageways" 復 道 were covered eleva d passageways between the various palaces. The *T'ai-p'ing Yü-Lan*, ch. 181, p. 4b says that between the Northern and Southern Palaces there was a distance of 7 *li*; in between there was a "double passageway" with three lanes: the central one for the Emperor and the other two for the high officials. Cf. Glossary.

Apr./May third month the Emperor held a feast and enfeoffed Yüng Ch'ih. Thereupon he urged his Lieutenant Chancellor [Hsiao Ho] to hasten and determine the merits [of the officers] and make the [due] appointments. When the feast was over, the courtiers were all glad and said, "Even Yung Ch'ih [has been made] a marquis; we have no cause at all for anxiety."

The Emperor returned to Yüeh-yang. Once every five days he would pay homage to the *T'ai-kung* [his father]. The Household Steward of the *T'ai-kung* admonished the *T'ai-kung*, saying, "Heaven has not two suns; the land has not two sovereigns. Although the Emperor is your son, he is the lord of men. Although you, the *T'ai-kung*, are his father, you are his subject. Why should you be the cause of the lord of men making obeisance before one who

11a is his subject? In this way, his majesty and authority are then not exhibited." Afterwards when the Emperor [came to pay] homage, the *T'ai-kung*, holding a broom, welcomed him at the door and walked backwards.[1] The Emperor was greatly startled. He descended[2] and supported the *T'ai-kung*. The *T'ai-kung* said, "The Emperor is the lord of men, why should you overturn the principles of the world on my account?" On that account the Emperor in his heart approved the words of the Household Steward and granted him five hundred catties of actual gold.

---

[1] These actions: holding a broom, welcoming him at the door, and walking backwards, indicated that *T'ai-kung* was acting as a subject, paying respect to the Emperor. *SC* 74: 3a tells that when Tsou Yen "went to Yen, King Chao of Yen, holding a broom, ran before him [to clear the way]." In the *Chuang-tzu* it is said that "The duty of disciples is to shake [their master's] skirts and sweep his mat."

[2] The Emperor probably descended from his seat in his chariot and lifted up *T'ai-kung*, who was bending down, sweeping the path where the Emperor was to tread.

上置酒封雍齒因趣丞相急定功行封罷酒羣臣皆喜曰雍齒且侯吾屬

亡患矣上歸櫟陽五日一朝太公太公家令說太公曰天亡二日土亡二

王皇帝雖子人主也太公雖父人臣也奈何令人主拜人臣如此則威重

不行後上朝太公擁彗迎門郤行上大驚下扶太公太公曰帝人主奈何

以我亂天下法於是上心善家令言賜黃金五百斤夏五月丙午詔曰人

114

In the summer, the fifth month, on [the day] *ping-* June/July
wu, an imperial edict said, "Of all the close relation- July 5
ships, none is closer than that of father and son.
Therefore when a father possesses the world he hands
it down to his son, and when a son possesses the
world his dignity reverts to his father—this is the
highest perfection of human principles. In former
days the world was in great disturbance, armed
troops arose everywhere, and all the people suffered
calamities. We Ourself wore armor, wielded a
pointed [weapon], and Ourself led Our officers and
soldiers, braving danger and difficulty in order to
put down the tyrannous and rebellious. We have
set up a nobility, ended the war, and given the
people rest, [so that] the world [is enjoying] a great
peace. This is all [due to] the teaching and instruction of the *T'ai-kung* [Our father]. The kings, the
marquises, the generals, the many ministers, and the
Grandees have already honored Us [with the title
of] Emperor; but the *T'ai-kung* has not yet had any
title. Now We present to and honor the *T'ai-kung*
with the title of the Grand Emperor."

In the autumn, the ninth month, the Huns be- **11b**
sieged the King of Han_h, [Han_w] Hsin, at Ma-yi, and Oct./Nov.
[Han_w] Hsin surrendered to the Huns.

In the seventh year, in the winter, the tenth VII
month, the Emperor in person acting as general Nov./Dec.
attacked the King of Han_h, [Han_w] Hsin, at T'ung-ti,
and beheaded his general.[1] [But Han_w] Hsin
escaped and fled to the Huns. Together with[2]

---

[1] *HS* 33: 7b says that this general's name was Wang Hsi
王喜. For this event, cf. that passage.
[2] Chu Tzu-wen (before 1198) argues that in this passage
and in the parallel sentence in the biography of Han_w Hsin,
the word 與, which has been translated "together with," is not
in the original text, because it does not make sense to say that
these generals, together with their king, set up another person
as king and then collected their king's troops for this new king.

115

his generals, Man-ch'iu Ch'en and Wang Huang, they together set up a descendant of the former king of Chao, Chao Li, as King [of Chao], collected the scattered troops of [Han_w] Hsin [for him], and, together with the Huns, they resisted [the forces of] the Han_s [dynasty].[1] The Emperor, [starting] from Chin-yang, fought a succession of battles and took advantage of his victories to pursue the

12a defeated. He went to Lou-fan, [where] he met with a severe cold spell, [so that] two or three out of every ten officers and soldiers lost fingers [or toes]. Thereupon he went to P'ing-ch'eng, [where] he was besieged by the Huns for seven days. He used the secret plan of Ch'en P'ing and succeeded in getting out.[2] [Then] he ordered Fan K'uai to

後趙利爲王收信散兵與匈奴
共距漢上從晉陽連戰乘勝逐
北至樓煩會大寒士卒墮指者
什二三遂至平城爲匈奴所圍
七日用陳平祕計得出使樊噲

It is quite true that if we retain the word translated "together with," Han_w Hsin cannot be included in the subject of the sentence regarding the collection of the scattered troops. Chu Tzu-wen thinks that after Han_w Hsin had fled, his troops caused trouble, not knowing where their king was. His generals thereupon set up another king and gathered up the troops, then made a league with the Huns to resist the forces of Han_s. He may be right; Wang Hsien-ch'ien agrees with him.

However, on the principle that, other things being equal, a more difficult reading is to be preferred, the word translated "together with" has been retained in the translation, understanding that the construction is merely a loose one. Then Han_w Hsin, from his refuge with the Huns, gave his consent and aid in setting up Chao Li as king, but remained there, allowing the two generals to collect his scattered troops.

[1] In the time of the Chou dynasty, the state of Chao had occupied the region to which Han_w Hsin had been appointed. Kao-tsu had also appointed Chang Ao as King of Chao, but had given him only part of the territory of the former kingdom of Chao, dividing it with the new kingdom of Han_h. Now that Han_w Hsin had been driven out of this region, a scion of the former Chao kings was set up in his place, making two kings of Chao, with different territories, a rebellious and a legitimate kingdom. Possibly Chao Li had indifferent success as king, for on 1B:16b a Chao Li is mentioned as a general of Ch'en Hsi, but this may have been a different person.

[2] The SC ch. 110 says that he heavily bribed the Yen-chih 閼氏, who was the Empress, the wife of the Shan-yü, the Hun emperor; HS 40:16b says, "His plan is secret, the world has not succeeded in hearing [what it was]." But Huan T'an (prob. died 29 A.D.) in his Hsin-lun, writes, "Someone said, 'Ch'en P'ing dissolved the siege at P'ing-ch'eng for Kao-tsu, but it is said that this affair is secret, that the world has not succeeded in hearing [what it was]. He used workmanship that was marvellous

留定代地十二月上　還過趙不禮趙王是　月匈奴攻代王喜　棄國自歸雒陽敕爲　合陽侯辛卯立子如

stay in order to subjugate the region of Tai. In the twelfth month the Emperor returned. He passed through Chao but did not treat the King of Chao courteously.[1]

200 B.C. Jan.

In this month the Huns attacked Tai, and the King of Tai, [Liu] Hsi, abandoned his state and of his own accord returned to Lo-yang.[2] He was forgiven and made Marquis of Ho-yang. On [the day] hsin-mao[3] [the Emperor] made his son, [Liu]

Feb. 15

and surpassingly good, hence it was kept hidden and not transmitted. Have you been able, by considering the circumstances, to understand this affair?' I answered him [thus]: This stratagem was on the contrary shabby, mean, awkward, and evil, hence it was hidden and not reported. When Kao-tsu had been besieged for seven days, Ch'en P'ing went and pursuaded the Yen-chih. The Yen-chih spoke to the Shan-yü and [Kao-tsu] was let out. From this we can know what he used to persuade her. At that time Ch'en P'ing must have said, 'The Han [Emperor] has such fine and beautiful women that no one in the world can express [the beauty] of their forms and countenances. Now he is seriously distressed and has already sent a fast messenger to get and bring them, intending to present them to the Shan-yü. When the Shan-yü sees these women, he will certainly love and desire them greatly. If he loves and desires them, then you, the Yen-chih, will daily be [more and more] separated from him and [will see him] infrequently. It is better to take advantage of the fact that [these women] have not yet arrived and order that the Han [Emperor] should be allowed to escape and go. If he is gone, he will not bring [these] women here.' The Yen-chih was a woman who had a jealous disposition, which necessarily made her all the more hate [that such things should happen], so she mixed in [the affair and the Han Emperor was allowed] to go. This explanation is simple and necessary. When [this stratagem] was employed, [Ch'en P'ing] wanted to make [people think that it was] a supernatural marvel, hence it was kept hidden and secret and not divulged. Liu Tzu-chün [Liu Hsin, d. 23 B.C.] heard of my saying and at once called it good." P'ei Yin (fl. 465-472) adds the further detail that Ch'en P'ing had some painters first paint pictures of these women.

[1] This was Chang Ao, not Chao Li. This slight almost cost Kao-tsu his life. Cf. 1B: 13a and the Glossary, sub Chang Ao.

[2] The SC (Mh II, 393) reports this event in the next (eighth) year; its Table puts it in the ninth year, probably because of the confusion about the day. Cf. n. 3.

[3] According to Chavannes' calendar (T'oung Pao, vol. VII, p. 24) and that in Variétés Sinologiques vol. 29, there could have been no hsin-mao day in the twelfth month of Kao-tsu's seventh year. Chavannes' calendar puts such a day in the twelfth months of the eighth and ninth years; Variétés Sinologiques vol. 29 allows such a day only in the twelfth month of the ninth year. In view of the length of time required for Liu Hsi to travel to Lo-yang and have his successor appointed, it seems probable that this appointment occurred in the following (the first) month. The tenth day of the first month of Kao-tsu's seventh year—Feb. 15, 200 B.C.—was a hsin-mao day; this appointment was probably made on that date. But the next sentence mentions "the spring," which means the first month: either the HS believed that the appointment was made in the twelfth month (not noticing that then "hsin-mao" must be a mis-

Ju-yi, King of Tai.

In the spring [the Emperor] ordered that when a Gentleman-of-the-Palace commits a crime [deserving] a more [severe punishment] than that of shaving the whiskers,[1] [the officials] should ask [the throne's consent to the sentence], and that people who had sons born to them should be exempted from public service for two years. In the second month he went to Ch'ang-an. Hsiao Ho was building the Wei-yang Palace, and was erecting the Eastern Portal, the Northern Portal, the Front Hall, the Arsenal, and the Great Granary. The Emperor saw their greatness and elegance and was very angry. He said to [Hsiao] Ho, "The world is full of tumultuous cries; I have toiled and suffered for many years; my success or failure cannot yet be known—why are you building these palaces and halls beyond measure?" [Hsiao] Ho replied, "The world is not just yet subjugated—for that reason we should take this opportunity to complete the palaces and halls. Moreover the Son of Heaven has the four seas [and all within them] for his household. Without[2] great and elegant [buildings], you will not [be able to display] your authority and majesty. We should not moreover let it be that later generations should find anything to be despised." The Emperor was delighted, removed from Yüeh-yang, and established his capital at Ch'ang-an. He established the office[3] of the Superintendency over the Impe-

12b

Feb./Mar.

令壯麗亡以重威且亡令後世有以加也上說自櫟陽徙都長安
也何曰天下方未定故可因以就宮室且夫天子以四海爲家非
甚怒謂何曰天下匈匈勞苦數歲成敗未可知是何治宮室過度
至長安蕭何治未央宮立東闕北闕前殿武庫大倉上見其壯麗
意爲代王春令郞中有罪耐以上請之民產子復勿事二歲二月

---

take) or the historian is completing his account of a sequence of events that began in the twelfth month before he mentions another month, therefore omitting to say "first month" because he had trespassed into it.

[1] Since all punishments involved some mutilation, the lightest sentence was that of cutting off the beard. It carried a two year sentence of penal servitude. Cf. 8: 24b.

[2] Wang Hsien-ch'ien remarks that the word 介 is redundant; the *SC* and the *Han-chi* do not have it; it is a dittography for the next occurrence of this word.

[3] We read 官 for the 宮 of the text at the suggestion of

置宗正宮以序九族夏四月行如雒陽

八年冬上東擊韓信餘寇於東垣還過趙趙相貫高等恥上不禮

其王陰謀欲弒上上欲宿心動問縣名何曰柏人上曰柏人者迫

於人也去弗宿十一月令士卒從軍死者爲槥歸其縣縣給衣衾

棺葬其祠以少牢長吏視葬十二月行自東垣至春三月行如雒

rial House to arrange the precedence among his nine [classes of] relatives. In the summer, the fourth month, he went to Lo-yang.

13a
May

In his eighth year, in the winter, the Emperor went east to attack Han$_w$ Hsin's[1] remaining robbers[2] at Tung-yüan. On his return, he went thru [the state of] Chao. The Chancellor of Chao, Kuan Kao, and others [felt] humiliated [because] the Emperor did not extend any courtesy to their King, [and so] secretly plotted, wishing to assassinate the Emperor. The Emperor was going to pass the night [at a certain place, but] his spirit was moved, so he asked what the name of the prefecture was. He was answered, "Po-jen." The Emperor said, "A po-jen is a person harassed by someone."[3] He went away and did not spend the night [there].

VIII
Winter

In the eleventh month [the Emperor] ordered that the officers and soldiers who had died when with the army should be put in provisional coffins and returned to their [home] prefectures; their prefectures should supply their shrouds, their coverlets, their [permanent] coffins, their burials, their [mortuary] furnishings, and should sacrifice [to them] a ram and a pig. The chief officials should supervise their funerals.

Nov./Dec.

In the twelfth month [the Emperor] went from Tung-yüan to [the capital]. In the spring, the third month, he went to Lo-yang. He ordered that the

Dec./Jan.
199 B.C.
Mar./Apr.

Ch'ien Ta-chao (1744–1813); the Official ed. (1739) also reads thus.

[1] The *SC* in this passage and the *HS* in the preceding and following passages mentions Han$_w$ Hsin; the word "Wang" has evidently dropped out here.

[2] The orthodox historian calls the army of a rebel, "robbers."

[3] He is making a play on words. The name of the city, Po-jen 柏人, sounds the same as the words 迫人, which mean "a harassed person." This association saved him from assassination.

officials and soldiers who went with the army to P'ing-ch'eng,[1] those who defended the city and the walled towns, should all be exempt from public service for life. Those whose noble rank was not above that of Public Chariot shall not be allowed to wear the Hat of the House of Liu. Merchants are not to be permitted to wear brocade, embroidery,

13b flowered silk, crape linen, fine linen, sackcloth, or wool, carry weapons, or ride a quadriga or a horse.[2]

衣
錦
繡
綺
縠
絺
紵
罽
操

得
冠
劉
氏
冠
賈
人
毋
得

勿
事
爵
非
公
乘
以
上
毋

及
守
城
邑
者
皆
復
終
身

陽
令
吏
卒
從
軍
至
平
城

[1] Cf. 1B: 12a. At P'ing-ch'eng Kao-tsu was besieged at a neighboring walled hill.

[2] Hu San-hsing (1230–1287) defines 錦 as 織文 "with woven ornaments."

Hu San-hsing defines 繡 as 刺文而五絑備者也 "with pricked designs in all five colors."

Yen Shih-ku defines 綺 as 文繒也卽今之細綾也 "ornamented silk, the same as the present flowered silk." Fine satin is also called by this name.

Wang Hsien-ch'ien defines 縠 as 縐紗 "crape linen made out of *Pueraria phaseoloïdes*."

Yen Shih-ku defines 絺 as 細葛也 "fine linen made out of *Pueraria phaseoloïdes*."

Yen Shih-ku defines 紵 as 織紵爲布及疏也 "woven fibres of *Sida* or hemp *abutilon*, *Boehmeria nivea* or *Urtica nivea*, made into cloth and coarse."

Ch'ien Ta-chao (1744–1813) says that 罽 is defined in the *Shuo-wen* as a "fish-net." He says the word here should be 縰, which he defines as 西胡毳布也 "a cloth made of hair [imported from] the western [nomads of central Asia or Mongolia by the name of the] Hu." Yen Shih-ku says it is 織毛若今毾及氀毲之類 "woven hair, like the present rugs and the mat used by the Emperor in worshipping Shang-ti." This sumptuary law has become famous.

The indication of a person's position in society by his clothing was a common practice of the time. The word 褐 denoted not only a coarse woolen cloth, but also "clothes of the common people." The Emperor Ching ordered his officials to wear certain kinds of clothes and certain decorations on their carriages to indicate their rank. Cf. 5: 8a. The *Shang-shu Ta-chuan* (supposed to have been recited by Master Fu, who was 99 years old in 179–157 B.C.; the passage translated below is referred to in the *HHS*, Treatise 29: 2a, written by Ssu-ma Piao, prob. ca. 240–304, and in *HHS* 49: 5b, by Fan Yeh, 398–445) ch. 1, p. 2, says, "The ancient Emperors [referring to the time of Yao] had to [know how to] command the people. Those people who were able to respect their elders and take pity upon orphans, who knew what to take and what to reject, what to be attracted to and what to yield [to others] and who could perform their parts with all their might [were allowed to ask for] a commandment from their prince. If they secured the commandment, then only could they obtain [the privilege of] riding in an ornamented carriage with a pair of horses or wear a

兵乘騎馬秋八月更有罪未發覺者赦之九月行自雒

陽至淮南王梁王趙王楚王皆從

九年冬十月淮南王梁王趙王楚王朝未央宮置酒前

殿上奉玉卮爲太上皇壽曰始大人常以臣亡賴不能

治產業不如仲力今某之業所就孰與仲多殿上羣臣

In the autumn, the eighth month, there was a Aug./Sept. pardon granted to those officials who had committed crimes [but] had not yet been detected.

In the ninth month, [the Emperor] went from Sept./Oct. Lo-yang to [the capital]. The King of Huai-nan, [Ch'ing Pu], the King of Liang, [P'eng Yüeh], the King of Chao, [Chang Ao], and the King of Ch'u, [Liu Chiao], all accompanied him.

In the ninth year, in the winter, the tenth month, IX the King of Huai-nan, [Ch'ing Pu], the King of Nov./Dec. Liang, [P'eng Yüeh], the King of Chao, [Chang Ao], and the King of Ch'u, [Liu Chiao], came to court at the Wei-yang Palace [to pay their homage. The Emperor] held a feast in the Front Hall. The Emperor held up a jade wine-cup[1] and drank a toast to the health of the Grand Emperor, saying, "At first you, sire, continually thought of me, your servant, as a good-for-nothing, one who could not apply himself to any professional occupation,[2] who was not as industrious as [my brother] Chung. Now who has achieved the more, I or Chung?" The many courtiers in the Hall all called out, **14a**

pair of embroidered brocade [collars]. Those who did not secure [the prince's] commandment did not get to wear [such clothes] nor get to ride [in such carriages]. If they did ride [in such carriages] or wear [such clothes], they were fined. Common people had wooden carriages with a single horse and wore linen or plain silk." (Another ed. puts this passage in ch. 2, p. 27b.) While the above passage is probably rationalizing on the basis of Han practises, it shows that the sentiment underlying such sumptuary distinctions was ancient. The Li-chi gives detailed rules for a gentleman's clothing (cf. ch. x, xxxvi, Couvreur's trans. I, 620–2, II, 587–90; Legge, I, 449ff: II, 395f).

[1] Ying Shao says, "It is a ceremonial utensil for drinking wine. Anciently they were made of a horn and held four sheng 升." [Shen Ch'in-han says he was mistaken, anciently they held three sheng.] Han Fei-tzu 13: 7a, sect. 34 says, "Now if you have a jade wine-cup (chih) [worth] a thousand [catties] of gold, and it is open through, without a base, can it hold water?" Thus the chih 卮 was a vessel for pouring, with a base. The Po-ku T'u-lu has pictures of four of these chih dating from Han times. One (seemingly typical) is said to be 2.5 inches high, with a rounded square mouth, 3.9 inches in its longest diameter and 3.1 inches in its shorter diameter, weighing 12½ ounces, and holding 9/100 of a wine-ladle (tou).

[2] Cf. 1A: 3a.

"Long life," They laughed loudly and made merry.

Dec./Jan.　　In the eleventh month [the Emperor] removed to
198 B.C.　Kuan-chung five great clans of Ch'i and Ch'u: the Chao clan, the Chu clan, the Ching clan, the Huai clan, and the T'ien clan, and gave them the advantage of its fields and dwellings.[1]

Jan./Feb.　　In the twelfth month he went to Lo-yang. The rebellious conspiracy of Kuan Kao and his accomplices were discovered. [Kuan] Kao and his accomplices were arrested and captured;[2] the King of Chao, [Chang] Ao, was also captured and put in prison. An imperial edict [was issued to the effect that] anyone who dared to follow the king would be punished by [death and] the extermination of his three [sets of] relatives. [The king's] Gentlemen-of-the-Palace, T'ien Shu, Meng Shu, and others, ten persons [in all], themselves shaved their heads, put on iron collars,[3] made themselves slaves of the king's household, and followed the king to prison. The king did not really know of [Kuan Kao's]

---

[1] This transportation was at the advice of Lou Ching, to fill up the land, and to prevent their rebelling. They were the kingly clans of the feudal states, Ch'i, Ch'u, Yen, Chao, Han_h, and Wei_h. Cf. *HS* 43: 13b. More than 100,000 people were thus moved. Yen Shih-ku (581–645) says that the word 屈 should here be given the ancient pronounciation for *chu*[5].

[2] Liu Pin (1022–1088) distinguished these words: *tai* 逮 is directly going after and taking a man who does not run away 逮者其人存直追取之; *pu* 捕 is searching for and seizing a man who has run away 捕者其人亡當討捕也. Or *tai* is simply calling a person by name and summoning him; *pu* is to tie and bind him 逮徒呼名召之捕加束縛矣.

[3] This action consisted in giving themselves the treatment criminals and slaves received, in order to enable them to go to prison with their king. Cf. p. 118, n. 1. Chi Pu, a general of Hsiang Yü, was hunted, after Hsiang Yü was killed. A price was on his head. He similarily shaved his head, put an iron collar around his neck, and sold himself into slavery in order to escape. Cf. *HS* 37: 1.

自髡鉗爲王家奴從王就獄王實不知其謀春正

下獄詔敢有隨王罪三族郎中田叔孟舒等十人

如雒陽貫高等謀逆發覺逮捕高等并捕趙王敖

氏景氏懷氏田氏五姓關中與利田宅十二月行

皆稱萬歲大笑爲樂十一月徙齊楚大族昭氏屈

月廢趙王敖爲宣平侯徙代王
如意爲趙王趙國內寅前有
罪殊死已下皆赦之二月行自
雒陽至賢趙臣田叔孟舒等十
人召見與語漢廷臣無能出其

conspiracy. In the spring, the first month, [the Feb./**Mar.**
Emperor] dismissed the King of Chao, [Chang] Ao,
and made him the Marquis of Hsüan-p'ing.
He moved the King of Tai, [Liu] Ju-yi, to be the
King of Chao, ruling over the state of Chao. Those **14b**
who, before [the day] *ping-yin*, had committed Mar. 11
crimes not serious enough [to deserve] the punishment of an irrevocable death sentence were all pardoned. In the second month [the Emperor] went Mar./Apr.
from Lo-yang to [the capital]. [He esteemed as]
capable [men] the ten courtiers of Chao, T'ien Shu,
Meng Shu, and the others, summoned them to an
interview, and conversed with them. None of the
courtiers in the Han court were able to surpass the
best[1] [efforts] of these men. The Emperor was de-

---

[1] Lit. "surpass their right." Yen Shih-ku (581–645) says, "Anciently the right was considered the more honorable," contrary to the practice in the Ch'ing court. The Han dynasty regularly esteemed the right the more honorable. Cf. *Mh* II, 415, n. 1.

But such was not always the case in ancient times. Liu Pin (1022–1088) said, "Those who are at peace and at home consider the left more honorable, whereas those who are at war consider the right more honorable. Honoring the right was a custom of the time of the Warring Kingdoms (iii & iv cent. B.C.)." Wu Jen-chieh (ca. 1137–1199) said, "[The statement], 'Those who use weapons honor the right,' comes from the book of [the philosopher] Lao-tzu [sect. 31]. Anciently in inauspicious matters the right was esteemed; weapons are inauspicious instruments and so the right was esteemed, probably because they were treated with inauspicious ceremonies. In the *Li-chi* it says, 'In riding in a prince's chariot we dare not leave the left [place] empty,' and the commentator says that in a carriage the left is considered more honorable. In a traveling carriage the left is more honorable, [whereas] in a war chariot the right is more honorable. The Prince of Weiₕ left his chariot and rode a horse, emptying the left [place in the chariot], and himself invited Hou Sheng [to occupy that place]; hence at the time of the Warring Kingdoms at times the left was esteemed. The *Li-Chi*, chap. 35, in discussing carriages and war chariots, says, 'In the army the left is esteemed.' In the *Tso-chuan* it says, 'Han Chüeh 韓厥 acting as charioteer took his place in the middle,' and the commentator Tu [Yü, 222–284] said, 'Except for the commander-in-chief, the charioteer always was in the center [place in the chariot], the general was on the left.' [Hence we] know that according to the proprieties of the war chariot, only the prince and the commander-in-chief esteemed the right. Among the rest of the generals the left was esteemed. Yen Shih-ku, in a comment on chap. 14, wrote, 'The Han [dynasty] followed the principles of court procedure of the highest antiquity in honoring the right; hence those

lighted and appointed·every one of them as Administrators of commanderies or Chancellors of the nobles.

Aug. 7   In the summer, the sixth month, on [the day] yi-wei, the last day of the month, there was an eclipse of the sun.

X   In the tenth year, in the winter, the tenth month,
Nov./Dec. the King of Huai-nan, [Ch'ing Pu], the King of Yen, [Lu Wan], the King of Ching, [Liu Chia], the King of Liang, [P'eng Yüeh], the King of Ch'u, [Liu Chiao], the King of Ch'i, [Liu Fei], and the King of Ch'angsha, [Wu Ch'eng], came to court [to render their
197 B.C. homage.]

May/June   In the summer, the fifth month, the Grand
15a Emperor[1] died; in the autumn, the seventh month,

朝夏五月太上皇后崩秋七
王梁王楚王齊王長沙王來
十年冬十月淮南王燕王荆
相夏六月乙未晦日有蝕之
右者上說盡拜爲郡守諸侯

officials who were serving the nobles who held office were called "left officials." '
According to the saying of Szu Wei, 'Now we divide the land and establish officials for it; this is to "left" it,' then the name of 'left officials' was already in use in the Ch'unch'iu period (722–486 B.C.)" Ch'üan Tsu-wang (1705–1755 A.D.) said, "Chung Hui was the 'left' chancellor 左相 of T'ang, Yi-yin as 'right' chancellor preceded him; Ch'ing Feng was the 'left' chancellor of Ch'i, Ts'ui Shu as 'right' chancellor preceded him, not necessarily in accordance with military etiquette. In their military etiquette only the people of Ch'u esteemed the left; hence 'the king rode with the left cohorts.' [Tso-chuan, Legge, p. 319.] In the state of Lu [the most cultured in ancient China] the position in the center of the army was left vacant and Chi [the chancellor] commanded from the left division—then accordingly in Lu the left was also esteemed—it is difficult to explain away these contradictory facts. Probably in matters of precedence, those who esteemed the right were the more numerous." In popular usage today, the right is the more esteemed.

[1] The present text reads, "the Grand Empress" 太上皇后, who would be Kaotsu's mother. But this reading is certainly wrong. On 1B: 4a Kao-tsu's mother is spoken of as "deceased" and is given a posthumous title. Ju Shun quotes the comment in the Han-chiu-yi (supposedly by Wei Hung, fl. dur. 25–57) as saying, "The mother of the Emperor Kao-[tsu] died in the time of the wars at [a place] north of Hsiao-huang; later a funerary temple [for her] was made at Hsiao-huang." When Kao-tsu's father was given the title, "the Grand Emperor," his mother should also have been given a title, if she were living; and since the historian quotes the edict granting the title, the title would have been mentioned; its absence is proof that she was dead. The Tzu-chih T'ung-chien 12: 4a, written by one of China's keenest historians, reads, "In the fifth month the Grand Emperor died at the Yüeh-yang palace; in the seventh month on [the day] kuei-mao, the Grand Emperor was buried at Wan-

故封豨爲列侯以相國守代今乃與

曰豨嘗爲吾使甚有信代地吾所急

皇廟于國都九月代相國陳豨反上

死罪已下八月令諸侯王皆立太上

月癸卯太上皇崩葬萬年赦櫟陽囚

on [the day] *kuei-mao*, he was buried at Wan-nien. Aug. 9
[The Emperor] pardoned those imprisoned at Yüeh- **15b**
yang whose crimes were less than[1] those [deserving]
death. In the eighth month he ordered the vassal Aug./Sept.
kings all to set up temples to the Grand Emperor
at the capitals of their states.[2]

In the ninth month, the Chancellor of State in Sept./Oct.
Tai, Ch'en Hsi, revolted. The Emperor said,
"[Ch'en] Hsi has acted as my envoy; he has had my
entire confidence. I have been anxious about the
region of Tai, hence I appointed [Ch'en] Hsi to be a
marquis, and, as Chancellor of State, to guard Tai;
but now with Wang Huang and others he has

nien." The *Tzu-chih T'ung-chien Kao-yi* 1:3a (also by Szu-ma Kuang) says, "The *Han-chi* [4:2b] in the fifth month has not the word *hou* and in the seventh month has not the word 'died.'" We have adopted this reading and omit these two characters.

On the other hand, the *SC* (*Mh* II, 393) writes, "In the spring and summer nothing happened," from which it might be inferred that the *SC* puts both the death and the burial of Kao-tsu's father in the seventh month. *SCHC* 7:65; 8:48, 60 (*Mh* II, 313, 365, 377) say that Hsiang Yü returned to the King of Han₃ his father, his mother, his wife and children. But earlier, after the battle at P'eng-ch'eng, it says merely that he sent to seek for his father and his wife, and that these two were captured by Hsiang Yü (*Mh* II, 300, 301). Chao Yi (1727–1814), in his *Nien-erh Shih Ta-chi* 1:13b, 14a, argues that it is not exact to explain "father, mother, wife, and children" as merely a general term for "family." Kao-tsu's father had a concubine in addition to the wife who was Kao-tsu's mother, and Kao-tsu had children by concubines in addition to the two by his wife, so that Kao-tsu's step-mother and his children by concubines were among those captured and returned by Hsiang Yü.

Yen Shih-ku quotes the *San-fu Huang-t'u* (probably written iii to vi cent.) as saying (at present this passage is a note to 6: 4b), "Kao-tsu first lived in Yüeh-yang, hence the Grand Emperor also [lived] at Yüeh-yang. In the tenth year, the Grand Emperor died and was buried on the plain north [of that place] and there was established the town of Wan-nien." The *HHS*, Mem. 23: 10a says, Kuang-wu "travelled east and passed Hsiao-huang, where is the park and mound of the Emperor Kao-[tsu]'s mother, the Empress *Chao-ling*." Hence Kao-tsu's father and mother were not buried together, as they would undoubtedly have been if they had died at the same place or in close succession.

[1] The Official ed. (1739) writes 巳 for 㠯, and Sung Ch'i says the former should be corrected to the latter.

[2] These were temples to the Han dynastic house. Since a goodly number of the kings were already members of the Liu family and eventually all of them were to be members of that house, this act was quite appropriate, altho Ho Ch'uo (1661–1722) says that it was "the beginning of impropriety," and that Wei Hsüan-ch'eng and Kung Yü (q.v. in Glossary) first detected its wrongfulness.

seized and ravaged the region of Tai. The officials and people [of Tai] have committed no crime; those who can leave [Ch'en] Hsi and [Wang] Huang and come to return [to their allegiance to me] will all be pardoned." The Emperor reached Han-tan from the east. [Then] the Emperor was delighted and said, "[Ch'en] Hsi did not come south and hold Han-tan, in order to[1] bar [the passage up] the river Chang. I know that he is really incapable of doing anything." The Chancellor of Chao, Chou Ch'ang, memorialized [the throne to the effect that] of the twenty-five cities of Ch'ang-shan,[2] twenty cities had been lost. He begged that the Administrator and [Commandary] Commandant be sentenced to death. The Emperor said, "Have the Administrator and [Commandery] Commandant rebelled?" and was answered, "No." The Emperor [then] said, "Their strength was inadequate; they have committed no crime."

16a The Emperor ordered Chou Ch'ang to select some of the valiant gentlemen of Chao who could be commissioned as generals. He reported back, and [the Emperor] interviewed four men. The Emperor treated them with contempt and scolded them, saying, "You striplings, have you the stuff to be generals?" The four men blushed for shame, and all fell prostrate to the earth. The Emperor

---

[1] Sung Ch'i (998–1061) says, "The old text [before vi cent.] writes 北 for 而. The *Han-shu K'an-wu* [1034] has changed it in accordance with the *SC*. Moreover the Chang River is not to the north."

[2] *HS* 28 Ai: 53a enumerates only 18 prefectures in the Ch'ang-shan commandery; the territory of Ch'ang-shan was evidently later curtailed.

將者白見四人上嫚罵曰豎子能爲將乎四人慙皆伏地上封
尉反乎對曰不上曰是力不足亡罪上令周昌選趙壯士可令
矢趙相周昌奏常山二十五城亡其二十城請誅守尉上曰守
自東至邯鄲上喜曰豨不南據邯鄲而阻漳水吾知其亡能爲
王黃等劫掠代地吏民非有罪也能去豨黃來歸者皆赦之上

appointed for each [the income of] a thousand families and made them generals. His close associates remonstrated with him, saying, "From [the time that you] entered Shu and Han, and [made an expedition] to punish [the state of] Ch'u, you have never yet [given] indiscriminate [rewards].[1] For what deeds do you now appoint these [people]?" The Emperor replied, "This is not anything that you understand. Ch'en Hsi has rebelled, and the regions of Chao and Tai are all in [Ch'en] Hsi's possession. I used a feathered call-to-arms to summon the empire's troops, but none have yet arrived. Now I can only count on the troops in Han-tan alone. Why should I be parsimonious about [the income of] four thousand families and not use it to console the young men of Chao?" They all replied, "You are right." He also sought whether Yo Yi had any descendants [living], found his grandson, [Yo] Shu, and enfeoffed him at Yo-hsiang, entitling him the *Hua-ch'eng* Baronet.

[The Emperor] asked about[2] the generals of [Ch'en] Hsi, [and found that] they were all former merchants. The Emperor said, "Then I know how to deal with them." So he bribed the generals of [Ch'en] Hsi with much gold, and many of [Ch'en] Hsi's generals surrendered. **16b**

In the eleventh year, in the winter, the Emperor was at Han-tan. A general of [Ch'en] Hsi, Hou Ch'ang, scouted about, leading more than ten thousand men. Wang Huang, leading more than a thousand cavalry, encamped at Ch'ü-ni. Chang Ch'un, leading more than ten thousand foot-soldiers, **XI Winter**

---

[1] Lit. "acted universally"; i.e., rewards had always been given for some particular reason.

[2] The *SC* has 聞 "heard," instead of the *HS* 問 "asked about."

十一年冬上在邯鄲豨將侯敞將萬餘人游行王黃將騎千餘軍曲逆張春將卒萬餘人度

知與之矣乃多以金購豨將豨將多降

趙子弟皆曰善又求樂毅有後乎得其孫叔封之樂鄉號華成君問豨將皆故賈人上曰吾

代地皆豨有吾以羽檄徵天下兵未有至者今計唯獨邯鄲中兵耳吾何愛四千戶不以慰

各千戶以爲將左右諫曰從入蜀漢伐楚賞未徧行令封此何功上曰非汝所知陳豨反趙

crossed the [Yellow] River to attack Liao-ch'eng; a general of the Han [dynasty], Kuo Meng, together with a general of [the state of] Ch'i, attacked [Chang Ch'un] and routed his [troops] severely. The Grand Commandant[1], Chou P'o, went by way of the T'ai-yüan [Commandery], entered and subjugated the region of Tai. He went to Ma-yi, [but] Ma-yi would not submit, [so] he attacked and massacred its [people]. A general of [Ch'en] Hsi, Chao Li, was defending Tung-yüan. Kao-tsu attacked it, [but] did not take it. [Some of] the soldiers [of the town] cursed him. The Emperor became angry, and, when the city surrendered, those soldiers who had cursed him were beheaded.[2] Those prefectures which had been firmly defended and did not surrender to the rebellious robbers,[3] were exempted from the land tax and capitation taxes for three years.

196 B.C. Feb./Mar.

In the spring, the first month, the Marquis of Huai-yin, Han Hsin, plotted a revolt at Ch'ang-an. He was exterminated with his three [sets] of relatives.[4]

General Ch'ai Wu beheaded the King of Han_h, [Han_w] Hsin, at Ts'an-ho. The Emperor returned to Lo-yang. An imperial edict said, "The territory

17a

of Tai is north of [that of] Ch'ang-shan, and borders on [the regions of] the barbarians.[5] Consequently,

---

[1] He was given this title only for this campaign.

[2] The *SC* tells that only those who had cursed and insulted him were executed. Cf. *Mh* II, 395.

[3] Cf. p. 119, n. 2.

[4] He was accused of rebellion by a man of his suite whose brother had offended him and feared he would be executed. The Empress *nee* Lü (in the absence of Kao-tsu) tricked Han Hsin into coming to the court and had him executed in the palace. Cf. *HS* 34: 13a; Glossary, *sub* Han Hsin.

[5] Lit. "the Yi and Ti." The *SC*, dealing with the time

王信於參合上還雒陽詔曰代地居常山之北與夷狄邊界趙乃
賦三歲春正月淮陰侯韓信謀反長安夷三族將軍柴武斬韓
不下卒罵上怒城降卒罵者斬之諸縣堅守不降反寇者復租
定代地至馬邑馬邑不下攻殘之豨將趙利守東垣高祖攻之
河攻聊城漢將軍郭蒙與齊將擊大破之太尉周勃道太原入

從山南有之遠數有胡寇難以爲國頗取山南太原
之地益屬代代之雲中以西爲雲中郡則代受邊寇
益少矣王相國通侯吏二千石擇可立爲代王者燕
王縮相國何等三十三人皆曰子恒賢知溫良請立
以爲代王都晉陽大赦天下二月詔曰欲省賦甚今

[the state of] Chao has [to control this territory] from south of the mountains.[1] It is far away [from its administrative headquarters], frequently pillaged [by] the Hu, and has difficulty in being a state. We will take a bit of the territory of the T'ai-yüan [Commandery] south of the mountains and augment [with it the region] belonging to Tai.[2] [The part of] Tai west of Yün-chung shall become the Yün chung Commandery. Thus Tai will be suffering less from border raids. You, kings, chancellors of states, marquises, and officials who [have the rank of] two thousand piculs, should select someone who can be made King of Tai." The King of Yen, [Lu] Wan, the Chancellor of State [Hsiao] Ho, and others, [altogether] thirty-three persons, unanimously replied, "Your son, [Liu] Heng, is capable, wise, gentle, and good. We beg that he be made King of Tai, with his capital at Chin-yang."[3] A general amnesty for all the world [was proclaimed].

In the second month, an imperial edict said, Mar./Apr. "[We] wish very much to lessen the poll-taxes, [but] now the offerings [made to Us] have no regulations, [so that] the officials sometimes make

of the legendary emperor Shun, speaks of the *Yi* 夷 as the eastern barbarians (*Mh* I, 68 & n. 1), but the *SC* in chap. 116 and the *HS* in chap. 95 uses this same word to refer to the barbarians in the west and south (including the peoples of the Tarim basin). The word became a general term for barbarians, altho earlier it was restricted to those in the east. *Ti* 狄 was the word used in early times to refer to the barbarians to the north of China (*Mh* I, 68 & n. 1).

[1] Wang Hsien-ch'ien says, "Formerly when [Liu] Ju-yi was king of Tai and Chang Ao was king of Chao, each had their own [territory] as their state. But after [Chang] Ao was removed, [Liu] Ju-yi was moved to be king of Chao and then also governed the region of Tai. Moreover Ch'en Hsi, as the Chancellor of State in Tai, was ordered to superintend the borders of both Tai and Chao. When [Ch'en] Hsi rebelled, Chou Ch'ang was the Chancellor of [Liu] Ju-yi's state, but Ch'ang-shan lost twenty cities, [showing that] the state of Chao could not care for all [that territory]. Hence Chao and Tai were again divided to be two states."

[2] In the earlier part of the *HS*, T'ai-yüan is said to have 31 prefectures; 28 Bi: 38b however mentions only 18.

[3] It had been the capital of Han$_w$ Hsin's Shansi state of Han$_h$. *HS* 4: 1b states that Liu Heng's capital was at Chung-tu, so evidently he too, like Han$_w$ Hsin, moved his capital away from Chin-yang.

the poll-tax heavy in order to use it for offerings [to Us], and for the vassal kings [this tax] is even heavier, [with the result that] the people suffer from it. Henceforth the vassal kings and marquises shall regularly pay court and make offerings [to Us,
17b the Emperor], in the tenth month,[1] and each commandery shall [make an offering] in accordance with[2] the total number of its people; each person per year [shall be taxed] sixty-three cash in order to provide for the expense of making offerings [to the Emperor]."

[The edict][3] also said, "Verily [We] have heard that no [true] king was greater than [King] Wen of the Chou [dynasty] and no Lord Protector was greater than [Duke] Huan of Ch'i—both needed capable men in order to make a name for themselves.[4] At present in the world there are capable men who are wise and able; why should only men of ancient times [be capable]? The trouble is that the ruler of men does not meet them. By what means

而成名今天下賢者智能豈特古之人乎患在
王者莫高於周文伯者莫高於齊桓皆待賢人
其口數率人歲六十三錢以給獻費又曰蓋聞
之令諸侯王通侯常以十月朝獻及郡各以
獻未有程吏或多賦以爲獻而諸侯王尤多民

[1] Ch'u Shao-sun (fl. 47–7 B.C.) in his supplement to *SC* 58: 8b, writes, "When the vassal kings come to court and appear before the Son of Heaven, [according to] the regulations of the Han [dynasty], each one must attend only four audiences. When they first come they attend a semiformal reception 小見. At dawn on the first day of the first month they bring the formal congratulations of the New Year at the regular audience, offering furs [or leather 皮] and presenting jade circlets 璧 and jade to offer New Year's congratulations, which was a formal audience. The third day after, a feast was given for the kings and they were granted gold, cash, and valuables. The second day after they again attended a semi-formal audience, took their leave, and departed. The whole stay [of the nobles] at Ch'ang-an was no more than twenty days. The semi-formal audiences were semi-formal banquets 燕, audiences in the forbidden apartments 禁門内; the drinking was in the inner apartments 省中, where people who were not eunuchs were not allowed to enter." This practice then began with Kao-tsu; he celebrated the tenth month as New Year's; in the time of the Emperor Wu, New Year's day was changed to the first month; the court reception was possibly continued in the tenth month, another was added in the first month.

[2] Wang Nien-sun shows by the citation of parallel passages that 率 here means 計.

[3] The following part of this edict is translated in G. Margouliès, *Le Kou-wen Chinois*, p. 49f. This is one of the edicts leading up to the establishment of the examination system.

[4] King Wen had Chiang Tzu-ya as his chancellor, and Duke Huan had Kuan-chung as his.

could a gentleman have access [to me]? Now I, by the spiritual power of Heaven,[1] [and by my] capable gentlemen and high officials have subjugated and possess the empire and have made it one family. I wish it to be enduring, that generation after generation should worship at my ancestral temple without cessation. Capable persons have already shared with me in its pacification. Should it be that [any capable persons] are not to share together with me in its comfort and its benefits? If there are any capable gentlemen or sirs who are willing to follow and be friends with me, I can make them honorable and illustrious. Let [the foregoing] be published to [all] the world, to make plain Our intention. Let the Grandee Secretary[2] [Chao] Yao[3] transmit it to the Chancellor of State; let the Chancellor of State [Hsiao Ho], the Marquis of Tso, trans- **18a** mit it to the vassal kings; the Palace Secretary for Administrating the Laws shall transmit it to the Commandery Administrators. If any [among their people] have an excellent[4] reputation and manifest

---

[1] This phrase is more than a conventional expression of gratitude; it implies the theory that the Han dynasty attained the throne by supernatural means, which helped it greatly in continuing on the throne. Cf. *HS* 100A: 8b, 9a.

[2] According to Shen Ch'in-han, in Kao-tsu's time there was not yet a Master of Writing, hence all edicts and ordinances were drafted by the Secretaries, who transmitted them outside the palace; the Grandee Secretary was the chief of the Secretaries, hence he directly transmitted the edict to the Chancellor of State.

[3] The text writes, "[Chou] Ch'ang," but that name is mistaken, for at this time Chou Ch'ang was Chancellor of Chao. According to *HS* 19B: 3a, the Grandee Secretary at this time was Chao Yao. He had been Secretary of the Tallies and Imperial Seals and was appointed Grandee Secretary in 197. In 188, when Empress *née* Lü took the throne, he was dismissed. His biography is in *HS* ch. 42.

[4] Reading 懿 instead of the present 意 with a quotation of this passage in a comment by Li Shan (649–689) on the preface to Wang Yung's *Ch'ü-shui Shih* in the *Wen-hsüan*. In addition to the fact that this reading restores the parallelism of the sentence, there is ample evidence given by Ch'ien Ta-hsin that 懿, 抑, 意, and 噫 were interchanged. Yen Shih-ku, who commented on the whole *HS*, does not remark on this character; evidently in his time the true reading was still understood.

virtue, [the officials]·must personally urge [them to
18b come], provide them with a quadriga, and send
them to go to the courts of the Chancellor of State
to have written down their accomplishments, their
appearance,[1] and their age.[2] If there are [such
ones] and [any official] does not report them, when
[this fact] becomes known, he shall be dismissed.
Those who are aged, infirm, or ill should not be
sent."

Apr./May   In the third month, the King of Liang, P'eng
Yüeh, plotted a rebellion. He was exterminated
with his three [sets of] relatives.[3] The imperial
edict said, "Do you select [some persons] who can
be made the King of Liang and the King of Huai-
yang." The King of Yen, [Lu] Wan, the Chancellor
of State [Hsiao] Ho, and others begged [the Emperor]

[1] Reading 儀 with Liu Pin (1022–1088) and others for the 義
in the text.

[2] The *Ku-wen-yüan* 10: 3b (a collection of literature made in
T'ang or Sung times) tells that Tung Chung-shu (ii cent. B.C.)
sent a letter to the secretary of Kung-sun Hung (the Lieutenant
Chancellor in 128–123 B.C.) saying, "I wish that you, sir
marquis, would open wide the road [opened by] the Chancellor of State Hsiao [Ho for the purpose of] seeking for capable men, and would keep narrow the gate for their selection and presentation [to the Emperor]." Hence Hsiao Ho
probably urged and approved of the edict in the text. The
task of selecting capable and able officials was the duty of the
Chancellor, so that the persons recommended by the various
magistrates went to him. In *HS* chap. 58, p. 6a we find the
statement, Kung-sun Hung "opened the Tung-ko 東閣 [a
small eastern hall in the palace] for the reception of capable
men." Hsieh Hsüan said to Chu Yün (in *HS* 67: 7a), "Stay
a while longer at the Tung-ko in order to interview the strange
gentlemen [sent up] from all quarters." In this passage we
find the earliest stage of the Chinese examination system.

[3] The *SC* tells that P'eng Yüeh was first transferred to Shu
after it was heard that he planned to revolt; when he planned
to revolt a second time, he was exterminated. Cf. *Mh* II, 395.

擇可以爲梁王淮陽王者燕王綰相國何等請
老癃病勿遺三月梁王彭越謀反夷三族詔曰
之駕遺詣相國府署行義年有而弗言覺免年
史中執法下郡守其有意稱明德者必身勸爲

立子恢爲梁王子友爲淮陽王罷東郡頗益梁罷潁

川郡頗益淮陽夏四月行自雒陽至令豐人徙關中

者皆復終身五月詔曰粵人之俗好相攻擊前時秦

徙中縣之民南方三郡使與百粵雜處會天下誅秦

to establish his son, [Liu] K'uei, as the King of Liang, and his son, [Liu] Yu, as the King of Huai-yang. [The Emperor] reduced considerably the Tung Commandery and added a part of it to [the state of] Liang. He [also] reduced considerably[1] the Ying-ch'uan Commandery and added a part of it to [the state of] Huai-yang.

In the summer, the fourth month, [the Emperor] 19a went from Lo-yang to [the capital]. He ordered that May/June the people of Feng who had been moved to Kuan-chung should all be exempted [from taxes and service] for life.[2]

In the fifth month an imperial edict said, "Accord- June/July ing to the customs of the people of [Nan-] Yüeh, they like to attack each other. At a previous time, the Ch'in [dynasty] moved people from the central prefectures[3] to the three commanderies of the southern quarter, and sent them to live intermixed with the many [tribes of] the Yüeh. It happened that when the world punished the Ch'in [dynasty],

[1] Ch'ien Ta-hsin (1728–1804) remarks that the Tung and the Ying-ch'uan Commanderies were not disestablished; parts of them were merely given to Liang and to Huai-yang.

[2] Ying Shao (ca. 140–206) tells that Kao-tsu's father was homesick and wanted to return home to Feng, but Kao-tsu built another city with its walls, its official residences, its markets, and its wards like those of Feng, calling it Hsin-feng, lit. "the New Feng," and moved the people of Feng to fill it up. Yen Shih-ku says this was "the old city of Hsin-feng." It is natural that Kao-tsu should have given special privileges to people from his home town. A similar exemption was granted to the old Feng, cf 1B: 20b.

[3] I.e., the Chinese, the people of the Yellow and Yangtze river basins, which was then China proper. The *SC* (*Mh* II, 168) says that the First Emperor sent inveterate vagabonds, parasites, and shop-keepers to conquer the territory of Lu-liang (present Kuang-tung), and made out of it the commanderies of Kuei-lin, Hsiang, and Nan-hai.

the [Commandery] Commandant of Nan-hai, [Chao] T'o, was living in the southern quarter and ruling it as its chieftain. He has made an excellent arrangement [of his government, so that] the people from the central prefectures have hence not diminished [in number] and the custom of the people of Yüeh to attack each other is progressively ceasing. For all [the foregoing, the region] is in debt to his ability. Now We establish [Chao] T'o as King of Nan-yüeh and commission Lu Chia to transmit his kingly seal and [its] cord." [Chao] T'o made obeisance [to the Emperor's edict] and acknowledged himself as [Kao-tsu's] subject.

July/Aug.   In the sixth month [the Emperor] ordered that the officers and soldiers who had followed him into Shu, Han_s, and Kuan-chung should all be exempted [from taxes and military service] for life.[1]

Aug./Sept.   In the autumn, the seventh month, the King of Huai-nan, [Ch'ing] Pu, revolted. The Emperor

---

[1] Kao-tsu had previously granted other favors to his old soldiers. In 202 B.C. (1B: 4b) the members of the noble houses in Kuan-chung were exempted for twelve years and the soldiers were granted honorary titles and they and their households exempted from public service (no period specified). Officers were given a step in rank and high officers were granted pensions. In 200 B.C. (1B: 13a) those who were besieged with him in P'ing-ch'eng, on his ill-fated campaign against the Huns, were given life-long exemption from public service. Soldiers killed in battle were to be sent home and buried at public expense. Now (196 B.C.) those soldiers who had been with him thru his whole victorious campaign from the time he started as a mere King of Han_s and who helped him to conquer Kuan-chung were given life-long exemption. In 195 B.C. (1B: 22b) their descendants were also granted exemption. These last two grants seem to have been made in order to forestall possible rebellions and to tie their interests to those of the house of Liu.

南海尉它居南方長治之甚有文理中縣人以故不
耗減粵人相攻擊之俗益止俱賴其力今立它爲南
粵王使陸賈即授璽綬它稽首稱臣六月令士卒從
入蜀漢關中者皆復終身秋七月淮南王布反上間

諸將滕公言故楚令尹薛公有籌策上見公薛公言布形埶上善

王上乃發上郡北地隴西車騎巴蜀材官及中尉卒三萬人爲皇之封薛公千戶詔王相國擇可立爲淮南王者羣臣請立子長爲

太子衞軍霸上布果如薛公言東擊殺荊王劉賈劫其兵度淮擊

asked the generals [for a plan of campaign]. The
Lord of Teng [Hsia-hou Ying] said that the former Chief Administrator of Ch'u, his excellency   **19b**
Hsieh, had formed a plan, and the Emperor saw[1]
his excellency. His excellency Hsieh told about
[Ch'ing] Pu's circumstances, and the Emperor approved his [plan] and appointed his excellency
Hsieh [to the income of] a thousand families. [The
Emperor next issued] an edict that the kings and
the Chancellor of State should select [someone] who
could be made King of Huai-nan. His subjects
[the kings and chancellors] begged that he make his
son, [Liu] Ch'ang, its king. The Emperor thereupon
mobilized as the Imperial Heir-apparent's Guard,
chariots and cavalry from the Shang commandery,
from the Pei-ti [Commandery], and from the Lung-
hsi [Commandery], skilled soldiers from Pa and
Shu, together with thirty thousand of the soldiers
[belonging to] the Palace Military Commander, and
had them encamp at Pa-shang. [Ch'ing] Pu really
[did] as his excellency Hsieh had said: he went
eastwards, attacked and killed the King of Ching,
Liu Chia, seized his troops, crossed the Huai
[River], and attacked [the state of] Ch'u.[2] The

---

[1] The Southern Academy ed. (1528), the Fukien ed. (1549),
and the Official ed. (1739) read 召 instead of the text's 見,
thereby making the passage say that the Emperor "summoned"
him—a statement more in accordance with Chinese ideas of
propriety. I have retained the more difficult reading.

[2] Ch'ing Pu started from his capital at the present Shou-
hsien on the Huai River in northern Anhui and struck at Kao-
tsu's cousin, whose capital was at the present Wu-hsien (Soochow) in southern Kiangsu, then went north to attack the
Emperor's brother, whose capital was at the present T'ung-hsien
(Suchow) in northern Kiangsu. Liu Chiao fled north into the
present Shantung. Ch'ing Pu fled from Kao-tsu south thru
Anhui, probably past his capital, and was routed near the present Chao Hu in central Anhui. He turned west, was again
routed in central western Anhui on the Pi River, and fled towards

King of Ch'u, [Liu] ·Chiao, fled to Hsieh. The Emperor granted a pardon to [everyone in] the world except [those guilty of] capital crimes, and ordered them all to enlist in the army. He summoned the troops of the nobles, and, with the Emperor in person acting as general, attacked [Ch'ing] Pu.

XII
Nov./Dec.
In his twelfth year, in the winter, the tenth month, the Emperor routed [the army of Ch'ing] Pu at Kuei-chui. [Ch'ing] Pu fled. [The Emperor] ordered a detached general to pursue him.

The Emperor, on his return, passed thru P'ei,[1] and stopped to make a feast in the palace at P'ei. He summoned all his friends, elders and young people, to attend[2] the feast. He sent out for the children 20a of P'ei, secured a hundred and twenty persons, and taught them some songs. At the height of the drinking, the Emperor struck a five-stringed lute,[3] and himself sang as follows:[4]

"A great wind raged
　　And the clouds flew and rose.
When my authority had been imposed upon [all]
　　within the [four] seas,

Ch'ang-sha in Hunan. He was caught and killed at P'o-yang in Kiangsi.

[1] It was Kao-tsu's home.

[2] Lit. "to assist at the feast."

[3] Ying Shao says, "Its shape is like a sê 瑟 [ch'in 琴 is written in the text, but it is a mistake for sê. The SC Cheng-yi (737) quotes this remark with sê] with a large head. It is strung with strings and they are struck with a bamboo [plectrum]." Yen Shih-ku adds that it has a narrow neck.

[4] This poem became after his death a ritual chant, sung and danced in the imperial ancestral temple by young people from P'ei. Cf. Mh III, 234. This song has become famous. Parker says it is "among the most remarkable specimens of genuine ancient poetry." In addition to Chavannes' translation (Mh I, clxi and II, 397), this poem has been translated by E. H. Parker in the New China Review, I (1919), p. 630, and in E. von Zach, Übersetzungen aus dem Wen Hsüan, p. 74. It was written out in seal character by Ts'ai Yung (133–192) and engraved on a stone tablet at the Ko-feng-t'ai (lit. "the Terrace [where Kao-tsu] sang [about] the wind") and is still preserved at P'ei.

教之歌酒酣上擊筑自歌曰大風起兮雲飛揚威加海內兮歸
留置酒沛宮悉召故人父老子弟佐酒發沛中兒得百二十人
十二年冬十月上破布軍于會缶布走令別將追之上還過沛
自將以擊布
楚楚王交走入薛上赦天下死罪以下皆令從軍徵諸侯兵上

故鄉安得猛士兮守四方令兒皆和習之上乃起舞慷慨傷懷泣數行下謂

沛父兄曰游子悲故鄉吾雖都關中萬歲之後吾魂魄猶思樂沛且朕自沛

公以誅暴逆遂有天下其以沛為朕湯沐邑復其民世世無有所與沛父老

諸母故人日樂飲懷歡道舊故為笑樂十餘日上欲去沛父兄固請上曰吾

I returned to my native village.
How may I secure valiant men
To defend the four quarters [of my empire]?"

He ordered all the children to reiterate it in concert; then the Emperor arose and danced. In sadness of mind and grieving in spirit many tears rolled down [his cheeks], and he said to the elders of P'ei, "The wanderer is saddened in his native village. Altho I [make] my capital in Kuan-chung, after my life is over, my spirit will rejoice[1] as it thinks of P'ei. Moreover, [beginning] from [the humble rank of] the Lord of P'ei, We have punished with extermination the tyrannous and rebellious [dynasty of Ch'in] and thereafter possessed the empire. Let[2] P'ei become Our private town.[3] [We] exempt its people from generation to generation, not [requiring] them to provide anything [for the public treasury]."

The elders, the matrons, and his old friends at P'ei [spent their time for] days rejoicing and drinking, extremely pleased and telling of [his] former [doings] in order to laugh and rejoice. [After] more than ten days, the Emperor wished to leave, [but] the elders of P'ei insistently begged him [to stay].[4] The

[1] The Official ed. (1739) reads 家 "its home," and quotes a remark of Sung Ch'i that it should read *lo* 樂; the *SC* inverts to read *lo*-思.

[2] According to the *Feng-su T'ung-yi* (written by Ying Shao), 其 was an expletive in the region of Ch'u; that may be its meaning here. But this word is used constantly as a sign of the imperative mood, especially at the beginning of a phrase in edicts, so that it seems to be straining the passage to give it any other meaning here.

[3] Lit. "the town that provides hot water for washing the hair." On such estates the lords paid no taxes to the Emperor; revenues from them went for the private expenses of the lord. Cf. *Mh* I, 287, n. 1, *ad fin.*

[4] The *SC* adds the words 留高祖 "[they begged] Kao-tsu to stay."

Emperor said, "My people are quite numerous; you, Elders, are not able to provide [for them]." There- 20b upon he departed. Those who were in P'ei emptied the city and all came to the west of the town to make offerings.[1] The Emperor stopped and stayed [there], and banqueted them in a tent for three days. The elders of P'ei all knocked their heads to the ground [before Kao-tsu] and said, "P'ei has happily obtained exemption, but Feng has not obtained it—if only your Majesty would take pity upon it!" The Emperor replied, "Feng is where I was born and raised; I could never forget it. But I [cannot exempt it] because it formerly revolted against me for the sake of Yung Ch'ih [and gave its allegiance] to Wei_h."[2] The elders of P'ei insistently begged him, so he also exempted Feng like P'ei.

The detached general of the Han [dynasty] attacked the army of [Ch'ing] Pu north and south of the River Pi,[3] and at both places routed it severely. [Then] he caught up with and decapitated [Ch'ing] Pu at P'o-yang.

Chou P'o subjugated Tai and beheaded Ch'en Hsi at Tang-ch'eng.

---

[1] Ju Shun says, "They presented cattle and wine" to their departing guest.

[2] Cf. 1A: 10b, 11a, 12a, and 1B: 10b.

[3] At the suggestion of Ch'üan Tsu-wang (1705–1755) we read 沘 for the 洮 Chao in the text. The Chao River was in the Ling-liang Commandery (present Kuangsi), a place which does not fit in with the preceding and following locations. The Pi River was in the Chiu-chiang Commandery; the two characters look alike and could easily have been exchanged. This emendation makes Ch'ing Pu's course logical. Cf. p. 135, n. 2.

Ku Tsu-yü (ca. 1631–1693) says however that the "Chao Shui" was the Chao Hu 洮 湖 of the T'ai-hu (between Chekiang and Kiangsu), with which Wang Hsien-ch'ien agrees. His interpretation does not require any emendation of the text and may be correct.

擊布軍洮水南北皆大破之追斬布番陽周勃定代斬陳狶於當城詔曰
耳吾特以其爲雍齒故反我爲魏沛父兄固請之廼幷復豐比沛漢別將
兄皆頓首曰沛幸得復豐未得唯陛下哀矜上曰豐者吾所生長極不忘
人衆多父兄不能給乃去沛中空縣皆之邑西獻上留止張飮三日沛父

An imperial edict said, "Wu was an anciently established state. In the past, the King of Ching [Liu Chia] has also had its territory. Now that he has died without issue, We wish again to establish a king of Wu. Let it be discussed who is able [to occupy this position]." The King of Ch'ang-sha, [Wu] Ch'en,[1] and others said, "The Marquis of 21a P'ei, [Liu] P'i, is dignified and sincere; we beg that you establish him as King of Wu." When he had already been installed [as King], the Emperor summoned him and said to [Liu] P'i, "Your appearance has the look of a rebel." So he patted him on the back and said, "If, [within] the coming fifty years, the Han [dynasty] has a revolt in the southeast, would it be you? The world is however [now subservient to] one house and is all one family; you must be careful not to rebel." [Liu] P'i knocked his head on the ground and said, "I would not dare [to do so]."[2]

In the eleventh month, [the Emperor] travelled Dec./Jan. from Huai-nan and returned [to the capital]. He 195 B.C. passed thru Lu and sacrificed to Confucius, offering him a suevotaurilia.[3]

[1] Yen Shih-ku says, "Some of the present texts have 芮 after the 'Ch'en' [making it read, 'Your subject, [Wu] Jui']; the popular copies have corruptly interpolated it."

[2] Kao-tsu did have an uncanny ability to size up a person's character, and this statement may be merely logical reasoning on his part, but it looks like a prophecy *post factum*. Ying Shao says, "Kao-tsu was wise in planning [for the future]. 'The look of a rebel' could even be known. That there would be a revolt in the southeast and to be capable of fixing upon 'fifty years' is [however] what [only] a diviner would know." Thus even he does not think that Kao-tsu could have on the spur of the moment known the future except thru a previous divination. In 154 B.C. Liu P'i did lead a rebellion of six kingdoms, was defeated, trapped, killed, and his kingdom abolished. Cf. *HS* 5: 4a; ch. 35; Glossary, sub Liu P'i.

[3] In this sacrifice, Kao-tsu seems to have been following

Jan./Feb.　In the twelfth month an imperial edict said, "The [First] Emperor of the Ch'in [dynasty], King Yin of Ch'u [Ch'en Shê], King An-hsi of Wei_h, King Min of Ch'i, and King Tao-hsiang of Chao, all have had their lines of descent cut off, being without issue. Let there be twenty families as the grave-keepers of the First Emperor of Ch'in; [for] each of [these kings of] Ch'u, of Wei_h, and of Ch'i, [let there be] ten families; [for] each of [the king of] Chao and the Prince of Wei_h, Wu-chi, [let there be] five families. We order that [these families] should watch with care the tumuli [to the care of which they have been assigned] and that they should be exempted and not made to give any other service."[1]

A general of Ch'en Hsi who had surrendered told that when [Ch'en] Hsi rebelled, the King of Yen, Lu Wan, had sent men to the place where [Ch'en] Hsi was, to plot secretly. When the Emperor sent the Marquis of Pi-yang, Shen Yi-chi, to go to escort

使人之豨所陰謀上使辟陽侯審食其迎綰綰
家復亡與它事陳豨降將言豨反時燕王盧綰
魏齊各十家趙及魏公子亡忌各五家令視其
襄王皆絕亡後其與秦始皇帝守冢二十家楚
月詔曰秦皇帝楚隱王魏安釐王齊愍王趙悼

the same policy that he followed in ennobling Yo Yi's descendant (cf. 1B: 16a)—to conciliate his people by honoring their heroes. This was probably the first time Confucius had been sacrificed to by anyone outside his own descendants. Cf. J. K. Shryock, *The State Cult of Confucius*, ch. VI. This passage is very likely unhistorical, for (1) there were no other imperial sacrifices to Confucius until 29 A.D., when the Emperor Kuang-wu merely sent a minister to sacrifice, and Kao-tsu's precedent, if he really sacrificed in person, would have been followed by his successors, and (2) this tradition that Kao-tsu sacrificed to Confucius is based on a passage in *SC* ch. 47 which contains some other rather doubtful statements (cf. ibid. p. 95), while Kao-tsu's Annals in *SC* ch. 8 omit this tradition. Kao-tsu's wound (cf. 1B: 32b) might not have troubled him seriously at this time; he did not die until almost half a year later. Cf. Duyvendak in *Jour. of Am. Or. Soc'y*, Sept. 1935, 55: 333–6.

[1] The care of the tomb involved the making of regular offerings to the spirits of the deceased as well as cleaning the mound, etc. Such offerings were expensive, hence the provision of a number of families and their exemption from other taxes—the amount they would otherwise pay as rent or taxes was to go for the provision of offerings, etc. In ordering these sacrifices Kao-tsu was following his general policy of conciliating his people in order to prevent further rebellions.

稱疾食其言綰反有端春二月使樊噲周勃將兵擊綰詔曰燕王綰與吾有故愛之如子聞

與陳豨有謀吾以爲亡有故使人迎綰綰稱疾不來謀反明矣燕吏民非有罪也賜其吏六

百石以上爵各一級與綰居去來歸者赦之加爵亦一級詔諸侯王議可立爲燕王者長沙

王臣等請立子建爲燕王詔曰南武侯織亦粤之世也立以爲南海王三月詔曰吾立爲天

子帝有天下十二年于今矣與天下之豪士賢大夫共定天下同安輯之其有功者上致之

[Lu] Wan [to the capital, Lu] Wan feigned sickness, [so that Shen] Yi-chi reported that there were signs that [Lu] Wan had rebelled. In the spring, the second month, [the Emperor] sent Fan K'uai and Mar./Apr. Chou P'o, with troops, to attack [Lu] Wan. The imperial edict said, "The King of Yen, [Lu] Wan, was an old friend of mine, and I loved him like a son. **21b** When I heard that he had plotted with Ch'en Hsi, I thought there was no such thing, hence I sent an envoy to escort [Lu] Wan [to the capital. But Lu] Wan feigned sickness and did not come, [so that] it is evident he has planned to rebel. The officials and people of Yen have committed no crime. I grant to each of its officials who have the rank of six hundred piculs and above, one step [in noble rank]; to those who have been [in revolt] with [Lu] Wan [but] leave him and come to return [to their allegiance to me], I will grant pardon and also add one step in noble rank." An edict [ordered that] the vassal kings should discuss who should be made King of Yen. The King of Ch'ang-sha, [Wu] Ch'en, and others begged that [the Emperor] establish his son [Liu] Chien as King of Yen.

An imperial edict said, "The Marquis of Nan-wu, Chih, is also a descendent of Yüeh; We establish him as King of Nan-hai."

In the third month an imperial edict said, "I Apr./May have been made the Son of Heaven, and as Emperor have now possessed the world for twelve years until **22a** the present. Together with the brave officers and talented grandees of the empire I have subjugated the empire; together we have pacified and reunited it. Among those [of my followers] who have distinguished themselves, I have established the best as kings, the next [best] as marquises, and the least have moreover been given the income of towns.

Moreover some of the relatives of my important subjects have become marquises. All have been themselves authorized to establish their officials and levy taxes. Their daughters have become[1] Princesses. The marquises who have the income of

22b towns all wear seals; we have granted them large residences. The officials [of the rank of] two thousand piculs We moved to Ch'ang-an to receive small residences. Those who went to Shu and Han, and subjugated the three [parts of the state of] Ch'in are all exempted [from taxes and services] from generation to generation. Towards the worthy officers and meritorious officials of the empire I may be said not to have been ungrateful. Let those who unrighteously rebel against the Son of Heaven and arbitrarily raise troops be punished by the united military forces of the empire and be executed. Let this be published and announced to the world to let it clearly understand Our intention."

When the Emperor was fighting against [Ch'ing] Pu, he had been wounded by a stray arrow; as he was traveling along he became ill. When his illness became severe the Empress [née] Lü called a good physician. When the physician entered and saw him, the Emperor asked the physician, "Can my sickness be healed?" The physician replied, "It can be healed."[2] Thereupon the Emperor scolded him, [using] disrespectful [language], "I took possession of the world as a humble citizen wielding a sword[3]—was not this [achievement by] the Decree

[1] Wang Hsien-ch'ien thinks that the character 爲, which now follows the phrase 公主, should precede it. We have followed his suggestion. There is probably some mistake in the text at this point.

[2] The Sung Ch'i ed. tells that the old text (before vii cent.) and the Yüeh ed. (ca. xi–xii cent.) omit the reply of the physician. The Ching-yu ed. (1034) also omits it. The physician's reply is found in SC 8: 35b and is needed for the narrative.

[3] Lit. "[wearing] clothes of [plain] cloth, and wielding a

見上問醫曰疾可治不醫曰可治於是上嫚罵之曰吾以布衣提三尺取天下此非

誅之布告天下使明知朕意上擊布時爲流矢所中行道疾疾甚呂后迎良醫醫入

世世復吾於天下賢士功臣可謂亡負矣其有不義背天子擅起兵者與天下共伐

侯食邑者皆佩之印賜大第室吏二千石徙之長安受小第室入蜀漢定三秦者皆

王次爲列侯下乃食邑而重臣之親或爲列侯皆令自置吏得賦斂女子公主爲列

天命乎命乃在天雖扁鵲何益遂不使治疾賜黃金五十斤罷之呂后問曰陛下

百歲後蕭相國既死誰令代之上曰曹參可問其次曰王陵可然少戇陳平可以

助之陳平知有餘然難獨任周勃重厚少文然安劉氏者必勃也可令爲太尉呂

后復問其次上曰此後亦非乃所知也盧綰與數千人居塞下候伺幸上疾愈自

of Heaven?　My fate is then with Heaven; altho Pien Ch'io [were here], what use could he be?" Therefore he did not let him treat his sickness, but granted him fifty catties of actual gold and dismissed him.

The Empress [*née*] Lü asked, "After your Maj- **23a** esty's decease,[1] when the Chancellor of State Hsiao [Ho] has died,[2] whom should I order to take his place?" The Emperor said, "Ts'ao Ts'an can [be chosen.]" She [then] asked who next, and he replied, "Wang Ling can [be chosen]. However he is a little stupid, [so] Ch'en P'ing can [be chosen] to assist him. Ch'en P'ing has superabundent intelligence, but he would find it difficult to bear the responsibility alone. Chou P'o is dignified and sincere, [but] he is not very polished; yet the one who will assure the peace of the house of Liu must be [Chou] P'o. He could be made Grand Commandant." The Empress [*née*] Lü again asked who next, and the Emperor replied, "After that you[3] too will not know [things]."

Lu Wan with several thousand men stayed at the foot of the Barrier, waiting, if by good chance the Emperor's sickness should become better, to come in

three foot [sword]." Common persons were compelled to wear plain cloth; three feet was the common length of a two-edged sword. The *SC* has here the word 劍, "sword"; the *HS* has omitted it in condensing. Yen Shih-ku tells that the vulgar copies have this word. Three ancient Chinese feet was about 27 inches long, English measure.

[1] Lit. "after the 'hundred years' "; previously in speaking of his decease, Kao-tsu had said, "after my 'ten-thousand years,' " cf. 1B: 20a.

[2] Here there is used the word at present often tabooed: 死.

[3] Kao-tsu uses the pronoun *nai* 乃. Shen Ch'in-han says that "originally *nai* was the pronoun used by a husband in speaking to his wife," quoting the *Hsi-ching Tsa-chi* (vi cent.). Wang Hsien-ch'ien says that it is merely a word of familiar address.

person to beg for pardon. [But] in the summer, the
June 1 fourth month, on [the day] *chia-ch'en*, the Emperor
died in the Ch'ang-lo Palace.[1] When Lu Wan
heard of it, he thereupon fled to the Huns.

The Empress [*née*] Lü plotted with Shen Yi-chi,
saying, "The generals together with the Emperor
formerly came from families enregistered as common
people; when they faced north[2] as courtiers, in
their hearts they have always felt dissatisfied, and
23b now they [will] nevertheless [have to] serve the young
lord [his son]. If they are not all completely exterminated together with their families, the empire
will not be at peace." For this reason [the Empress]
did not [announce the death and] proclaim a mourning. Someone heard of it and spoke to Li Shang.
[Li] Shang saw Shen Yi-chi and said [to him], "I have
heard that the Emperor has already been dead for
four days, and that [the Empress] has not proclaimed
any mourning and wishes to kill the generals. If
[the situation] is really like this, the empire is certainly in danger. Ch'en P'ing and Kuan Ying,

[1] The *Han-chiu-yi* written by Wei Hung (fl. 25–57), says,
"When the Emperor Kao-[tsu] died, on the third day, the
first clothes were put on the corpse in his room below the
window. There was made of chestnut wood a spirit tablet,
eight inches long, square in front and round behind, a foot in
circumference, which was placed in the window, facing outwards
from inside [the room]. Silk floss was spread out as a screen.
In front of it were four sticks of white wood as thick as a finger
and three feet long, bound with white fur, set in the four directions in the window with the spirit tablet in their center. On
the seventh day the corpse was completely clothed, put into the
coffin, and sacrificed to in the window, [using] pap made of
glutinous millet and sheep tongues. When he had already
been buried, the spirit tablet was taken up, enclosed in a wooden
cover, and kept in the great hall of the temple, in a niche in the
western wall."

[2] Since the throne always faces south, courtiers always face
north.

入謝夏四月甲辰帝崩于長樂宮盧綰聞之逐亡入匈奴呂后與審食

其謀曰諸將故與帝為編戶民北面為臣心常鞅鞅今事少主非盡

族是天下不安以故不發喪人或聞以語酈商酈商見審食其曰聞帝

已崩四日不發喪欲誅諸將誠如此天下危矣陳平灌嬰將十萬守滎

144

起細微撥亂世之正平定天下為漢太祖功最高上尊號曰高皇帝初

赦天下五月丙寅葬長陵巳下皇太子羣臣皆反至太上皇廟羣臣曰帝

中大臣內畔諸將外反亡可蹻足待也審食其入言之乃以丁未發喪大

陽樊噲周勃將二一萬定燕代此聞帝崩諸將皆誅必連兵還鄉以攻關

leading a hundred thousand [men], defend Jung-yang; Fan K'uai and Chou P'o, leading two hundred **24a** thousand [men], are subjugating Yen and Tai—when these[1] [people] hear that the Emperor has died and the generals have all been killed, they will certainly turn about face with their troops in order to attack Kuan-chung. With the great ministers revolting inside [the passes] and the generals turning against [the dynasty] outside [the passes], it could await its destruction on tiptoe."[2] Shen Yi-chi **24b** entered and told these [words to the Empress]. So on [the day] *ting-wei* [the Empress] proclaimed a **June 4** mourning and granted a general amnesty to the world.

In the fifth month, on [the day] *ping-yin*, [the **June 23** Emperor] was buried in the Ch'ang Tomb. When [the coffin] had been put in place, the imperial heir-apparent and the courtiers all returned and went to the temple of the Grand Emperor.[3] The courtiers said, "The Emperor arose from humble [beginnings]; he established order in a troubled generation, and turned it back to the right [path]. He pacified and subjugated the world, and became the Grand Founder[4] of the Han [dynasty]. His achievements were very great.[5] We offer him the high title of Kao-huang-ti."[6]

---

[1] The Fukien ed. (1549) writes 比; the *SC*, the *Han-chi* (ii cent.) & other *HS* texts write 此.

[2] I.e., destruction would come in a moment.

[3] The ancestral temple of the imperial family.

[4] 太祖. The word became his temple name; cf. 5:2b.

[5] 高; this word is made his title.

[6] 高皇帝, lit. "the Great Emperor." This is his posthumous name. He is usually known as Han Kao-tsu, from the name of the dynasty and words taken partly from his posthumous title and partly from the phrase in note 4.

In his early life, Kao-tsu did not cultivate literary studies, but by nature he was intelligent and penetrating. He liked to make plans and was able to listen [to others]. From a superintendent of a gate or a man exiled to the frontier[1] [upwards, anyone] who came to see him [was treated] as an old [friend]. At the beginning [of his reign] he conformed to the people's wishes when he made an agreement [with them] in three articles;[2] when the empire had been subjugated, he commanded Hsiao Ho to set in order the [criminal] laws and orders,[3] Han Hsin to set forth the military methods,[4] Chang Ts'ang to fix the calendar and measures,[5] Shu-sun T'ung to establish the rites and etiquette,[6] and Lu Chia to compose

25a the *Hsin-yü*. With his meritorious followers he split tallies and made oaths, with red writing and an iron certificate, a golden box and a stone chest, and kept them in the ancestral temple.[7] Altho daily no leisure was afforded him, his designs and plans were vast and far-reaching.

In eulogy we say,[8] In 'Spring and Autumn' [times], the historian of [the state of] Chin, Ts'ai

---

[1] Referring to Li Yi-chi and Lou Ching. Cf. 1A: 15b; 1B: 7a.

[2] Regarding legal punishments. Cf. 1A: 20a, b.

[3] Cf. *HS* ch. 23; Glossary *sub* Hsiao Ho. The following clauses are taken from *SC* 130:28.

[4] *HS* 30: 60a lists "Han Hsin, in three chapters" among the books on war and strategy. 30: 65a reads, "When the Han [dynasty] arose, Chang Liang and Han Hsin arranged and ordered its military methods."

[5] Ju Shun interprets this phrase as referring to the calendar and to weights and measures; Yen Shih-ku says the second part of this phrase refers to the standard models [for weights and measures]. Cf. 42: 5a.

[6] He fixed the etiquette and laws of the Han ancestral temple and to some extent the general etiquette and laws of the Han dynasty. Cf. Glossary *sub* Shu-sun T'ung; Hu Shih's account in *Jour. N. C. Br. R. A. S.* 60: 24–5.

[7] The foregoing items are used in connection with the ceremonies of enfeoffing nobles. Cf. Glossary, *sub* Marquis.

[8] This stock phrase "in eulogy" introduces a summary by

高祖不脩文學而性明達好謀能聽自監門戍卒見之如舊初順

民心作三章之約天下既定命蕭何次律令韓信申軍法張蒼定

章程叔孫通制禮儀陸賈造新語又與功臣剖符作誓丹書鐵契

金匱石室藏之宗廟雖日不暇給規摹弘遠矣

贊曰春秋晉史蔡墨有言陶唐氏既衰其後有劉

累學擾龍事孔甲范氏其後也而大夫范宣子亦

曰祖自虞以上爲陶唐氏氏在夏爲御龍氏在商爲

豕韋氏在周爲唐杜氏晉主夏盟爲范氏范氏爲

晉士師魯文公世奔秦後歸于晉其處者爲劉氏

Mo, said, "When the T'ao and T'ang family[1] had lost its power, among its descendants there was a Liu Lei who learned to train dragons.[2] He served K'ung-chia. The Fan family were his descendants." Moreover the Grandee Fan Hsien-tzu also said, "My ancestors before [the time of] Yü [Shun] were surnamed T'ao and T'ang; in the [time of the] Hsia [dynasty], they were surnamed Yü-lung; in [the time of] the Shang [dynasty], they were surnamed Shih-wei; in [the time of] the Chou **25b** [dynasty], they were surnamed T'ang and Tu; when [the state of] Chin became the lord of China's oaths,[3] they were surnamed Fan. A [member of the] Fan [family] was the Supreme Judge of Chin. In the time of Duke Wen of Lu, [the family] fled to Ch'in.[4] Later they returned to Chin. Those [of the Fan family] who remained [in Ch'in] became

the author. The practise of introducing an opinion by the historian, as distinguished from the recital of facts, began with the *Tso-chuan*, which uses the phrase 君子曰 for that purpose. The *SC* uses the phrase 太史公曰 and the *HS* uses 贊曰—each marks a summary and expression of personal opinion.

The practise of introducing a quotation into the historian's summary is copied from the *SC*, which frequently does that, one famous quotation extending over many pages.

[1] The ancient distinction between the clan name 姓 and the family name 氏 is kept in the following passage in the text—family names changed from time to time, since they were based on incidental historical events, such as the possession of a particular fief; clan names were inherited and did not change. But in Han times that distinction was lost. Pan Ku seems to have known that distinction and to have realized that in his time it was no longer pertinent. Szu-ma Ch'ien does not even seem to know of this distinction, and confuses the two.

[2] Ying Shao says that he not only made them obey his will but also nourished and reared them. This passage is also quoted in the *SC* (*Mh* I, 168).

[3] This literary phrase refers to Duke Wen of Chin (reigned 636–628 B.C.), who became Lord Protector, the professed leader of the Chinese feudal states. The word here translated China is 夏.

[4] Yen Shih-ku, basing his account on the *Tso-chuan*, says that in 621 B.C. Duke Hsiang of Chin died and Szu Hui with Hsien-mieh 先蔑 travelled to the state of

the Liu family."[1] Liu Hsiang said, "In the time 劉 時 獲 魏
of the Contending States, [a member of] the Liu 向 劉 於 遷
family from Ch'in was made prisoner of war by 云 氏 魏 大
Wei_h.[2] When [the state of] Ch'in destroyed [the 戰 自 秦 梁
26a state of] Wei_h,[3] [the family] moved to Ta-liang 國 秦 滅 都

Ch'in where they went to meet the Prince Yung 公子雍, intending to make him the heir of Chin. In 620 B.C., using a Ch'in army, they brought Yung into Chin. But when Hsüan-tzu of Chao set up Duke Ling 靈公 and fought with the Ch'in army, defeating it at K'u-shou 剆首, Hsien-mieh fled to Ch'in and Szu Hui followed him. Cf. Legge, *Tso-chuan*, p. 243[5], 246[16].

[1] Yen Shih-ku continues that in 614 B.C. some people of Chin got Shou-yü of Wei_h to pretend to revolt against Wei_h, and lured Szu Hui to welcome him. The state of Ch'in returned to him his wife and children. The rest of his family remained in Ch'in, but, since they had no official rank or fief, they took again the family name previously used by Liu Lui.

The sentence in the text about the family again taking the Liu surname is quoted from the *Tso-chuan*, Duke Lu, 13th year (Legge's translation, vol. I, p. 264, par. 2). On that sentence Ch'i Shao-nan (1703–1768) quotes a remark of K'ung Ying-ta (574–648) in his *Tso-chuan Su*, doubting the authenticity of this sentence in the *Tso-chuan*. Szu Hui's family attained no prominence in the state of Ch'in in his lifetime nor did they later do anything worthy of remark. Hence there was no reason for the *Tso-chuan* to notice their surname. Moreover, the sentence about their surname does not fit in with the subject matter of the preceding or following. He thinks it was not originally in the *Tso-chuan*, but was added by some scholar when the Han dynasty arose, as a means of gaining their favor.

In the time of the Han Emperor Ming (58–75 A.D.), Chia K'uei petitioned the throne saying, "The five classics offer no proof or prophecy showing that the Liu family is the descendant of Yao; only Tso has any definite statement." The sentence about the Liu family was probably added to the *Tso-chuan* however before the time of Chia K'uei; in 78 B.C. Kuei Hung 眭弘 (*HS* 75: 1b) memorialized the throne, saying, "The house of Han carries on the line of Yao," so that in his time the *Tso-chuan* may have already contained this sentence. Later Liu Hsiang (76–6 B.C.) praised Kao-tsu saying that he had "descended from the Emperor T'ang [Yao]," and Wang Mang (ruled 6–23 A.D.) called the Han dynasty "the descendants of Yao." Pan Piao himself in his *Wang-ming-lun* (cf. *HS* 100A: 10b) said, "[They are the] descendants of the Emperor Yao." This spurious geneology had great political importance. Cf. *HS* 100A: 7a–11a.

[2] Wen Yin (fl. ca. 196–220) said that when, in the time of the Six States (468–246 B.C.), the state of Ch'in made an expedition against Wei_h, a Mr. Liu was with the army and was captured by Wei_h, so that the family was thus made to live in Wei_h.

[3] The state of Wei_h was destroyed by Ch'in in 225 B.C., but Yen Shih-ku thinks

祖即位置祠祀官則有秦晉梁荊之巫世祠天地綴之

豐公豐公蓋太上皇父其遷曰淺墳墓在豐鮮焉及高

帝本系出自唐帝降及于周在秦作劉涉魏而東遂爲

于豐故周市說雍齒曰豐故梁徙也是以頌高祖云漢

and dwelt at Feng.   Hence Chou Fu said to Yung
Ch'ih,[1] 'Feng was formerly a colony of Liang.'
Thus the eulogy of Kao-tsu said,[2]

'The line of descent of the Han Emperor
Is traced from the Emperor T'ang [Yao].
Coming on down to the Chou [dynasty],
In [the state of] Ch'in it became the Liu [family].
It crossed into Wei_h and went eastwards.
Thereupon [its head] became the Lord of Feng.' "[3]

The Lord of Feng was indeed the Grand Emperor's father.   The period since his moving [to
Feng] had been brief, [for] there are few mounds or
graves [of the family] at Feng.   When Kao-tsu took
the throne, he established officials for the worship
[of his ancestors], so there were shamans from Ch'in,
Chin, Liang, and Ching.[4]   For generations the

that this sentence refers to the time when King Chao of Ch'in
(306–266 B.C.) made an expedition against Wei_h and the King
of Wei_h left the city of An-yi 安邑 and moved eastwards to
Ta-liang, calling his state Liang.   Liu Ch'ang (1019–1068)
thinks Yen Shih-ku is mistaken.

[1] Cf. 1A: 11a.

[2] These six lines are of four words each and rime.

[3] 豐公.   This is the first occurrence of this title in the book.
It seems as if someone had thought that since Kao-tsu was at
first known as "the Lord of P'ei," his grandfather must have
been known as "the Lord of" at least the town he lived in.
Cf. p. 40, n. 1.

[4] The four regions in which Kao-tsu's supposed ancestors
had lived.   The Fan family had held office in Chin, hence Chin
shamans were necessary to worship their ancestral spirits; a
branch of Fan Hui's descendants were supposed to have remained in Ch'in, where they took the surname Liu, so that Ch'in
shamans were needed for them; the Liu family went to Wei_h
(which was also called Liang, from the name of its capital city),
hence Liang shamans were needed; later the family moved to
Feng, which was in Ching (Ch'u), so that Ching shamans were
also needed.   The principle was that ghosts need the sort of
worship peculiar to the region where they lived and were buried.

worship of Heaven and Earth has been accompanied by the worship [of these ancestors].[1]   How could [these facts] be untrustworthy?   From the foregoing [accounts] we infer that the Han [dynasty] succeeded to the fortunes of Yao; its virtues and the happiness recompensing it are already great.   The cutting in two of the snake,[2] the auspicious omens which appeared,[3] the banners and pennons which emphasized [the color] red[4] in harmony with the virtue of fire,[5] were responses which came of their own accord, [thereby showing that Kao-tsu] secured the [dynastic] rule from Heaven.

漢書一下
自然之應得天統矣
著符旗幟上赤協于火德
漢承堯運德祚已盛斷蛇
以祀豈不信哉由是推之

[1] The ancestors were taken as the surrogate or representative of Heaven or as those who introduce the worshipers to Heaven and so are worshiped simultaneously with Heaven. Cf. "The Works of Hsüntze," chap. xix, 20; H. H. Dubs, "Hsüntze," p. 114.

[2] Cf. 1A: 6b, 7a.

[3] The wonderful sights, the physiognomization, and the emanation. Cf. 1A: 3b, 5b, 7b.

[4] Cf. 1A: 9b.

[5] Cf. p. 35, n. 2. This last sentence condenses Pan Piao's essay on "The Discussion of the Destiny of Kings," found in HS 100A: 8a–11b.

APPENDIX I

THE CONJUNCTION OF THE FIVE PLANETS IN *TUNG-CHING*

HS 1A: 18b reads, "In the first year, in the winter, the tenth month [Nov. 14–Dec. 12, 207 B.C.] there was a conjunction of the five planets in [the constellation] *Tung-ching*."

Dr. J. K. Fotheringham of Oxford has very kindly calculated this conjunction. According to his results, this conjunction cannot have been correctly recorded for 207 B.C., inasmuch as at that time, although the planets were within about 41° of longitude of each other, "Mercury and Jupiter were on one side of the sun, visible as morning stars, and Venus, Mars, and Saturn were on the other side, visible as evening stars." In 206 B.C., Mars was far away from Jupiter.

The date of closest approach for these planets was on May 30, 205 B.C., when the planetary longitudes were as follows: Mercury and Jupiter at 88.3° right ascension, Saturn at 90.7°, Mars at 98.4°, and Venus at 111.3°. The total range in right ascension was thus 23°.

But at that time all the planets were not in the constellation *Tung-ching*. The right ascensions of the stars in that constellation are calculated for 205 B.C. by Dr. Fotheringham as follows: μ Gemini as 62.8°, ν as 64.9°, ϵ as 67.3°, γ as 67.8°, ξ as 70.5°, ζ as 73.3° and λ as 77.7°. *Tung-ching* is however stated by Chinese authorities to contain 33 Chinese degrees, which is about 32.5° in European measurement. The next constellation in the Chinese zodiac is *Kuei* 鬼, whose constituent stars ranged at that date from 95.3° to 98.8° R.A. This constellation is said to contain 4 Chinese degrees (about 3.9° in our measurement). Hence "it is clear from this that the space between one asterism in the list of zodiacal constellations and the next was reckoned to the preceding asterism. At least this was so with" *Tung-ching*. Then *Tung-ching* extended from 62.8° to 95.3° R.A. Even so, on May 30th, Mars was in *Kuei* and Venus in the next constellation, *Liu*.

Dr. Fotheringham has however calculated that on May 16th, 205 B.C., when Mercury was first opposite the first star in *Tung-ching*, being at 62.8°, the other planets were located as follows: Jupiter at 85.0°, Mars at 88.8°, Saturn at 88.9°, and Venus at 95.9°. They were thus spread over 33.1° of longitude. The first four planets were in *Tung-ching*, and Venus was just over in *Kuei*. Venus had last been seen in *Tung-ching*

151

on May 14th, two evenings previous. But *Kuei* is usually mentioned together with *Tung-ching* in the *HS*; the two were grouped together as the constellation *Shun-shou* 鶉 首 (lit., "the head of the quail"). Chinese astronomers thus had no difficulty in giving "the conjunction the benefit of any doubt." We may then take the middle of May 205 B.C. as the date of this conjunction.

How did this conjunction get dated in November 207 B.C. in the *HS*? That date was the result of a misunderstanding on the part of the author. The earliest extant statement about this conjunction is found in the *SC* 37: 40a, "When the Han dynasty triumphed, the five planets appeared in conjunction in [the constellation] *Tung-ching*." [Cf. *Mh* III, 407. Chavannes adds a note that this conjunction happened in 200 B.C., on the authority of Ssu-ma Cheng's *So-yin*. But the *So-yin* gives that date, not to this conjunction, but to the event mentioned next, the siege of Kao-tsu at P'ing-ch'eng, for the note comes after the sentence recounting the siege. Elsewhere the *SC* (*Mh*. II, 389, 390) gives this date for the siege.]

The date when "the Han dynasty triumphed" may be variously given. Kao-tsu dated his accession from the time he received the surrender of Tsu-ying in November 207 B.C., but Hsiang Yü was not killed until January 202 B.C., and Kao-tsu did not ascend the throne as emperor until Feb. 22, 202 B.C. It might also be said that the triumph occurred when Kao-tsu returned from Han and conquered the three Ch'in successor states—June 206 B.C. He however first actually assumed imperial prerogatives when he did away with the Ch'in dynasty's gods of the land and grains and substituted his own—on March 5, 205 B.C. About the time of the conjunction in May 205 B.C., Kao-tsu did triumph over Hsiang Yü, when he entered P'eng-ch'eng, Hsiang Yü's capital, but he was severely defeated immediately afterwards. Perhaps this conjunction actually helped to keep up his courage after that defeat (cf. 1A: 33b). It was thus quite natural that Kao-tsu's assumption of imperial prerogatives in March 205 should have been linked with the conjunction in May, and that the conjunction should have been said to have happened when the Han dynasty triumphed.

The astrological interpretation of this conjunction also assisted in bringing about the statement in the *HS*. The ancient Chinese allocated the various regions of the sky to various states, just as was the case in the ancient Mediterranean world. According to Cheng Chung (ca. 5 B.C.–83 A.D.), *Shun-shou*, which includes *Tung-ching* and *Kuei*, was allocated to Ch'in. Since Kao-tsu had possessed himself of this territory, it is natural that the conjunction should have been interpreted with reference to his dynasty. Ying Shao remarks that this conjunction indicated that a new emperor of a new dynasty would conquer by his righteousness.

Because of this astrological interpretation, when the exact date of the conjunction had been forgotten, it was natural to have put this conjunction at the beginning of the Han dynasty's reign. Liu Hsiang (80–9 B.C.) wrote, "When the Han [dynasty] entered [the region of] Ch'in, the five planets appeared in conjunction in [the constellation] *Tung-ching*." In *SC* 89: 9b (repeated in *HS* 23: 6b, 7a) we find a further detail: "The old gentleman Kan said, 'When the King of Han [Kao-tsu] entered the pass [Oct. 207 B.C.], the five planets appeared in conjunction in [the constellation] *Tung-ching*. *Tung-ching* is the portion [of the heavens allocated to] Ch'in. Whoever reached [that place] first should have been made its king.' "

With the foregoing statement before him, it is quite natural that Pan Ku should have written as he did and dated this conjunction at the official beginning of the Han dynasty in November 207 B.C. He evidently had no exact record of the conjunction except the foregoing passages and was not sorry, in his record, to glorify the dynasty under which he was writing. [Reproduced by permission from the *Jour. A. O. S.*, Sept. 1935, vol. 55, pp. 310–3.]

THE HAN DYNASTY'S EARLIER CALENDAR

In ancient times, several calendars were used in China. Months were always counted from new moon to new moon, a month occupying the time of a lunation, but the year did not always begin at the same period. For astronomical purposes, months were numbered by the twelve horary characters, beginning with the month which normally contains the winter solstice. The calendar anciently used in the feudal state of Chin, said to be that of the legendary Hsia dynasty, put the first month in the third 寅 astronomical month. The Yin calendar, used in the state of Sung, began the year one month earlier, putting New Year's day in the second 丑 astronomical month. The royal calendar of the Chou dynasty began the year one month earlier, New Year's day coming in the first astronomical 子 month. (Cf. H. Maspero, *La Chine antique*, pp. 222–223.) The Ch'in dynasty put New Year's day one month farther forward, into the twelfth 亥 astronomical month. The early Han rulers continued this practise, until, in 104 B.C., the Han Emperor Wu put New Year's day back to the period it occupied in the Hsia calendar, in the third 寅 astronomical month, where it stayed (with unimportant exceptions) until the time of the Chinese Republic. (For a fuller account, cf. Havret, in the *T'oung Pao*, vol. 8, p. 399.)

The *SC* and *HS* were both written after the Han calendar reform in 104 B.C., but they record events occurring at a time when the year began three months earlier than at the time they were writing. Which calendar did they use? What names did they give to the months, those in use in later Han or in Ch'in times?

The true answer to the above questions is a very peculiar one: the Ch'in dynasty kept the same names (numbers) for the months as those used in Hsia (and later Han) times, but merely shifted the date of New Year's day and the attendant official ceremonies. That is, the Ch'in dynasty made New Year's day occur in the month which they called the "tenth" month, so that the month which they called the "first month" was the fourth in order from the beginning of the official year! The Han Emperor Wu merely restored New Year's day to the beginning of what he *and his predecessors* had been calling the "first" 正 month, but which month had not previously begun the year.

The existence of such an anomalous calendar as one beginning with the "tenth" month is so unnatural that only quite conclusive evidence should make us accept it. This evidence is even more important because Yen Shih-ku (581–645 A.D.), the outstanding commentator on the *HS*, contradicts our view—he said that the Ch'in dynasty had really called the month with which their year began the "first" month, and numbered the months consecutively beginning with that one; and that the authors of the *SC* and *HS* had *changed* the names of the months to correspond to the different names given them in Han times after the calendrical reform. The evidence for the contrary view is presented below:

I. In the first place, there is ample evidence from the *SC*, *HS*, and other documents to show that in Ch'in and early Han times the year did actually begin with what the historians called the "tenth" month and that the "first" month was the fourth in the order of the months. Since exactly three months are reckoned to a season, the Ch'in calendar then made the year begin with the first month of autumn and made the "first" month begin the spring season. The pertinent points in the following passages are accordingly: the order of the months in the year, the seasons at which certain months come, and the month and season in which official ceremonies occurred. Italics are mine.

a. In chap. 5 of the *SC* we read (cf. *Mh.* II, 91): "In the 48th year of King Chao-hsiang, in the *tenth* month, [the state of] Han~h~ offered [to Ch'in the city of] Yüan-yung. The army of Ch'in was divided into three armies. . . . In the *first* month, the troops were disbanded." Note that in the same year, the "first" month comes *after* the "tenth" month.

b. In the monthly tables of the *SC* (chap. 16; cf. *Mh* III, 59) during the second year of the Second Emperor, the months are enumerated *beginning* with the *tenth* month, next the eleventh and twelfth months, and then only the first month. It is here called the 端月, for 正 was tabooed, since it was the personal name of the First Emperor.

c. In chap. 8 of the *SC* (cf. *Mh* II, 393) we read, "In the *tenth* month of the tenth year [of Kao-tsu], Ch'ing Pu, King of Huai-nan, P'eng Yüeh, King of Liang, Lu Wan, King of Yen, Liu Chia, King of Ching, Liu Chiao, King of Ch'u, Liu Fei, King of Ch'i, Wu Jei, King of Ch'ang-sha, all came to court at the Ch'ang-lo Palace. In the spring and summer, nothing [of note] happened. In the seventh month, the Grand Emperor died at the Yo-yang Palace." The great court reception at the beginning of the official year then occurred in the tenth month, which was in winter, for spring came afterwards.

d. In the *HS*, 4:15b f, we read, "In the spring of the fifteenth year, a yellow dragon appeared at Ch'eng-chi. The Emperor issued an edict ordering a discussion of a sacrifice in the suburbs. . . . In the *fourth* month, in the *summer*, the emperor visited Yung and then first sacrificed to the

Five Emperors." Since the *SC* says that in ancient times the sacrifice to the Five Emperors was always made in the summer, the fourth month came in summer; hence the first month came in the spring.

e. In *HS* 6: 6b we read, "In the fourth year [of the period Yüan-kuang (131 B.C.)] Tou-yin, the Marquis of Wei-chi, who had committed a crime, was executed publicly. In the *spring*, the *third* month, on the day *yi-mao*, the Lieutenant Chancellor [T'ien] Fen died." But the *SC* 107: 12b, says, "On the last days of the *twelfth* month, [the Marquis of Wei-chi] was sentenced to be publicly executed in the market-place in Wei-ch'eng. In that spring the Marquis of Wu-an [the chancellor] died of illness." Then the execution occurred before the spring, according to the *HS*, and in the twelfth month, according to the *SC*; the death occurred in the spring and in the third month.

f. In *SC* 16: 9b, 10a, b, 12a we read, "[In the first year of the state of Han₈], in the first month, Hsiang Yu divided Kuan-chung. . . . The second month was the beginning of the [reign of] the King of Han₈, the former Lord of P'ei. . . . In the third month he made Nan-cheng his capital." Now in 22: 1b we read, "In the first year of the Emperor Kao-tsu, in the Spring, the Lord of P'ei became the King of Han₈ and went to Nan-ch'eng." Thus the first, second, and third months came in spring.

g. In chap. 25 of the *SC*, the explanation of the twelve musical tubes begins with the tenth month (cf. *Mh* III, 303), "Among the sonorous tubes, [it, i.e. the tenth month, corresponds to] the Yin-chung." The explanation proceeds month by month, and ends with the ninth month (cf. ibid. 313), "Among the musical tubes, [it, i.e. the ninth month, corresponds to] the Wu-yi." Thus the order of the tubes follows that of the official year, from the tenth to the ninth month.

h. In *HS* 90: 7b, 8a, b we read, "When Wang Wen-shu . . . became the administrator of Ho-nei, . . . by the end of the *twelfth* month, in all the commandery there was not a thief to make any dogs bark. Those few [thieves] whom he did not catch and who fled to neighboring commanderies, he pursued. Meanwhile spring had come. [Wang] Wen-shu stamped his feet and sighed, 'Alas! If the *winter* months should be prolonged one more month, it would be sufficient [for my task].' . . . The Emperor considered him an able [person] and promoted him to be Palace Military Commander." Now according to *HS* 19B: 18b, he was appointed Palace Military Commander in 119 B.C., 15 years before the reform of the calendar. In his time, the twelfth month came in winter.

i. In the *Book of Rites*, chap. 17, p. 4a we find the following, "In the third month of *autumn* 季 秋 . . , it was [ordered] that the nobles should unify their practises and customs and that [the officials of] all the districts [should come] to receive [instructions for their government] at [the grand reception] on the first day of the month in the coming year." The commentary tells us that this passage refers to Ch'in practises. Since the great court reception was held on New Year's day, that festival came in winter.

j. In the *HS* 1B: 17a we read, "In the eleventh year . . . the second month, an imperial edict said, . . . 'The vassal kings and marquises shall regularily pay court and make offerings in the *tenth* month." The reference is again to the grand court reception on New Year's day, here stated to occur in the tenth month.

k. In *HS* 4: 6b we read, In the *third* month of the first year, "an edict said, 'Now it is the time of *spring*, when [nature is] harmonious, and the plants and trees are all growing, when things all have means of enjoying themselves." Then the third month was in spring. But cf. p. 236, n. 4.

l. In *HS* 6:26a we read, In the first year of the period Yüan-feng (110 B.C.) "an imperial edict read, 'Let the *tenth* month [begin] the first year of the [period] Yüan-feng.' " Hence the year began with the tenth month. (Altho the word 'begin' is not actually in the text, the passage plainly implies it.)

m. In chap. 15 of the *SC* we read, "In the thirty-seventh year, in the *tenth* month, on the day *kuei-ch'ou* [Nov. 1, 211 B.C.], the First Emperor went out on a trip. [cf. *Mh* II, 184] . . . [In the *seventh* month] . . . on the *ping-yin* day, the First Emperor died in the P'in terrace at Sha-ch'iu . . . In the *ninth* month the First Emperor was buried in Mt. Li" (cf. ibid. 193). In Chap. 15 of the *SC* (Chavannes did not translate this passage), it reads, "The first year of the Second Emperor. In the *tenth* month, on the day *wu-yin* [an edict was issued ordering] a general freeing of criminals. In the *eleventh* month, he made the Rabbit park. In the *twelfth* month, he went to the O-fang Palace. In the *ninth* month of that year the commanderies and districts all rebelled." Thus the historians began a year with the tenth month and ended it with the ninth month. There are many such passages.

n. In the *HS* 4: 9a (cf. *Mh* II, 461), we read, "In the *eleventh* month [of the second year], on the day *kuei-mao* [Jan. 2, 180 B.C.] the last day of the month, there was an eclipse [Oppolzer's no. 2447]. The imperial edict read: . . . 'Since on the last day of the eleventh month there was an eclipse—a reproach that was seen in the heavens—how great must the calamity be!' " In this passage too events in the tenth month are recorded as preceding this one and events in the first month follow it.

o. The *SC* 96: 5a (*HS* 42: 5a), tells that when Chang Ts'ang was

CHAPTER I

Lieutenant Chancellor, he advised that because Kao-tsu arrived at Pa-
shang (cf. *HS* 1A: 19b) in the tenth month, and was consequently considered to have overthrown the Ch'in dynasty in that month, the date
of New Year's day should not be changed from the date set by the Ch'in
dynasty. Thus the conquest of Ch'in was commemorated by continuing
New Year's day on the date of his conquest. In the same chapter we
read, "It was ordered that all the kings and marquises should always
appear at court and make presentations in the *tenth* month." The same
statement appears in *SC* chap. 99 and *HS* chap. 43. Hence the early
Han tenth month was the same as the Ch'in tenth month. An interesting confirmation is found in the *HHS*, chap. 14, where it says that
on the first day of each month and at the beginning of the year a
great court was held at which presents and congratulations were received
(from the nobles); the officials (however) congratulated (with presents)
in the first month. In chap. 16 of the *HHS* it says "The reason that
of all the first days of the months, only on the first day of the *tenth* month
did they follow the former custom, was because in that month Kao-tsu
subjugated the Ch'in dynasty and began the first year of his reign."

p. In the *SC* and the *HS* (before 104 B.C.) the intercalary month
is always called the "later ninth month" 後 九 月. (Since twelve lunations
do not make quite a solar year, every two or three years an extra, intercalary month was added). After the calendrical reform in 104 B.C.,
the intercalary month was inserted at various times of the year to keep
the seasons occurring in the proper months. The only adequate reason
for the intercalary month always previously coming after the *ninth*
month is that thus it was put at the *end* of the year.

II. The foregoing passages amply prove that in Ch'in and early Han
times the year began with what was later called the "tenth" month.
But did the historians change the names of the months, as Yen Shih-ku
said they did? We have already had evidence that such was not the
case: passages *j*, *k*, *l*, and *o* quote imperial edicts which fix the months in
the same seasons as those they later occurred in. The cyclical characters
in passages *e*, *m*, and *n* enable us to check the dates; for, with a sixty day
cycle, the same characters would not reappear in a month that came three
months later. There is also the evidence furnished by the following
passages:

q. In *HS* 6:31b we read, "In the fifth month, in the summer, [in the
first year of the (period) T'ai-ch'u (104 B.C.)], the calendar was corrected, making the first 正 month begin the year." If the months
had previously been numbered from the beginning of the official year,
the record should have been different, something like the following:

The calendar was corrected, making the fourth month the first month. The wording of the *HS* shows that previously the "first" month did not begin the year.

r. The great scholar Chia Yi, who lived 200–168 B.C. (before the calendrical reform) wrote a poem which is reproduced in his biography in the *SC* chap. 84 and *HS* chap. 48. In that poem the word for summer occurs in the rime, so that the historian could not have changed it, and it is coupled with the cyclical characters for the day: "In the year *Shan-o* 單閼 in the *fourth* month, in the first month of *summer*, on the day *keng-tzu*, when the sun was setting, an owl perched in my house." The naming of the year as the fourth in the twelve year cycle enables us to identify it as 174 B.C. If the months were numbered beginning with the astronomical twelfth month (in which New Year's day then occurred), the fourth month would have been the first month of spring, not summer. The cyclical character also enables us to identify the month, for we know the cyclical character for the day of the calendrical reform, 19 years later, and a simple calculation (cf. *Chinese Social and Political Science Review*, vol. 18, p. 166) enables us to determine the characters for the days of each month in the year the poem refers to. The day *keng-tzu* could not have come in the fourth month after New Year's day of that year; but it could have come in the seventh month after New Year's day, which Chia Yi called the "fourth" month. Then the "fourth" month occurred in summer and contemporary writers numbered the month in which New Year's day came as the "tenth" month.

s. Liu An, King of Huai-nan, committed suicide in 123–2 B.C., before the reform of the calendar. In his chapter on astronomy he writes (I confess that I do not altogether understand the passage), "The cycle of the universe begins with the first month 正月 which is the third astronomical month 建寅 when the sun and moon have both entered five degrees into the [constellation] Ying-shih [α, β Pegasus]." Here he says plainly that the "first" month is the third astronomical month, not the twelfth astronomical month, with which the Ch'in and early Han dynasty began the year.

t. In the same book he tells that Mercury appears near the constellations Andromeda and Aries at the spring equinox in the second month, near Gemini and Cancer at the summer solstice in the fifth month, near Virgo at the autumn equinox in the eighth month, and near Sagitarious and Capricornus at the winter solstice in the eleventh month. Elsewhere in the book he gives the positions of the sun among the constellations for the twelve months of the year. Allowing for the precession of the equinoxes, those positions are the same as for the months called by the same names in Ch'ing times, altho the book was written before the calendar reform.

u. A stone inscription known as 漢趙璱羣臣上醻刻石 found on a hill near Han-tan, has inscribed on it the date *ping-yin* in the eighth month of the twenty-second year of the kingdom of Chao (B.C. 158). This is a contemporary record made before the correction of the calendar. If the months had been counted beginning with New Year's day, the eighth month could not have contained a *ping-yin* day at all.

There is thus ample proof that the Ch'in and early Han dynasties used a curious calendar in which New Year's day and the official celebrations connected therewith came in what they called the "tenth" month, and that the reform in 104 B.C. did not change the names of the months, but merely shifted the date for New Year's day, altho a court celebration was continued to be held on the first days of the tenth month, because that date commemorated the founding of the dynasty. Hence the *SC* and the *HS* use the same names for the months as those used in Ch'in and Han times, which were the same as those in use in the time their authors wrote.

The foregoing evidence has been mostly collected by Wang Yin-chih (1766–1834; Giles no. 2252); his famous reply to Yen Shih-ku is transcribed in Wang Hsien-ch'ien's *Ch'ien-Han-shu Pu-chu*, chap. 1, pt. A, pp. 23–26. Wang Hsien-ch'ien himself added material; further significant material is found in a paper by Chen Chin-sien, "The Anomalous Calendars of the Ch'in and Han Dynasties" in the *Chinese Social and Political Science Review* for July 1934, vol. 18, p. 157 ff.

THE METHOD USED IN CHECKING RECORDED ECLIPSES

For the checking of the eclipses recorded in Chinese records with astronomical computations there is the monumental *Canon der Finsternisse*, by Th. von Oppolzer, published in Vienna, in 1887, in which are calculated all the eclipses from 1208 B.C. to A.D. 2161. This book of tables gives the day, hour, and minute when eclipses occurred, the longitude of the sun at the time of the conjunction, and charts the paths of the central eclipses. Since and during Oppolzer's time, improvements in astronomical computations have shown that his calculations may be slightly in error. In the case of some Chinese eclipses, corrections of Oppolzer may be found in F. K. Ginzel, *Spezieller Kanon der Sonnen- und Mondfinsternisse für das Ländergebiet der klassischen Altertumswissenschaften und den Zeitraum von 900 vor Chr. bis 600 nach Chr.*, Berlin, 1899. Ginzel has again been corrected. The most recent work is P. V. Neugebauer, *Astronomische Chronologie*, Berlin, 1929. For Han times, Oppolzer is correct to within about half an hour.[1] As no one since Oppolzer has produced a set of tables and charts covering Chinese territory, so that his book is the only one convenient to use, and as so little correction of his results is necessary, we may take Oppolzer's calculations as being as reliable now as ever, except at regions near the limit of visibility and when great exactness is necessary.

Oppolzer charts only the paths of umbral (i.e., total, annular, and annular-total) eclipses (more exactly, only central eclipses). In most cases, the Chinese however observed the sun as only partially eclipsed. The region in which an umbral eclipse may be viewed as partial extends in all directions from the umbral path. Oppolzer did not calculate this area. We have allowed, on Oppolzer's charts, $\frac{15}{16}$ to 1 inch at right angles to the path of an umbral eclipse and $\frac{3}{8}$ of an inch from the ends in the direction of that path, as the area in which an umbral eclipse may be seen as partial, remembering however that when we approach those limits, we may need to make allowance for Oppolzer's errors and also that the region of partiality may extend for much greater distances.[2]

---

[1] In my computations of Han eclipses by Neugebauer's method I have found Oppolzer's times for eclipses in error by varying amounts, from less than a minute to a maximum of 36 minutes.

[2] To determine approximately the region in which an umbral eclipse may be seen as partial, I transferred the plotted charts for some 35 recent eclipses from the nautical almanacs to polar coordinates, like those used by Oppolzer in his charts, and measured

CHAPTER I

More than one-third of the total number of solar eclipses—about 35.3 per cent—are nowhere umbral. These "partial eclipses" should be distinguished from umbral eclipses which are viewed from some points as

---

the areas of partial visibility. These eclipses belonged to 26 different saros series and included all the umbral eclipses of the 19 years preceding 1938, in order to include all the saros series now running which produce umbral eclipses. While this is only a small proportion of the 152 saros series in Oppolzer's *Kanon*, the uniformity of results makes them probably typical. The areas of visibility for 23 of these eclipses were conchoid and for 12 were cylindrical.

The curves for the areas in which an umbral eclipse is viewed as partial are of two sorts: cylindrical and conchoid. In those cases in which the moon's umbra reaches regions in the vicinity of the earth's equator, the limits of partial visibility for the eclipse are roughly parallel to the umbral path, so that the area of visibility swept by the moon's penumbra forms a sausage-shaped curve. I shall call such eclipses "cylindrical" in default of a better term. When the moon's umbra comes closer to the poles, its penumbra reaches beyond the northern (or southern) limits to which the sun is visible, so that the eclipse is visible only as far north (or south) as the sun is visible and the northern (or southern) border of the area of partial visibility is cut off. Then the area of visibility assumes a shell-like shape. I shall call such eclipses "conchoid." In the balance of this discussion, for simplicity's sake, I shall consider only the northern hemisphere, in which China is located. These results however apply equally well to the southern hemisphere, with directions reversed.

Conchoid curves are obtained for those eclipses in which the moon's penumbra reaches the northern limits to which the sun is visible; such eclipses are those near the ends of a saros or exeligmos series. Cylindrical curves are obtained for those eclipses in which the penumbra does not reach that far north. This limit depends, of course, upon the season of the year: at the summer solstice, the sun reaches "north" as far as the polar circle on the opposite side of the globe; at the winter solstice, it reaches only to the polar circle on this side; at the equinoxes, it reaches to the poles; in between, the northern limits of the sun depend upon the date in the year.

For cylindrical eclipses, the area of partial visibility, as measured on charts similar to and of the same dimensions as those of Oppolzer, extended for a distance of $\frac{15}{16}$ to 2 inches at right angles to the path of umbral eclipse, with a mode of $1\frac{1}{4}$ inches, and also extended from $\frac{3}{8}$ to 1 inch in the same direction as and beyond the ends of that path.

For conchoid eclipses, outside the polar regions, that area extended from 1 to $2\frac{5}{8}$ inches at right angles to the path of the umbral eclipse and from $\frac{3}{8}$ to 1 inch from the ends in the direction of that path. Within the polar regions, greater variations occurred. The area of visibility sometimes extended only for $\frac{3}{8}$ of an inch at right angles to the path of centrality or only $\frac{1}{16}$ inch from the ends in the direction of the path. Since however China does not extend that far north, we may neglect these limits.

The area of visibility reaches its greatest size when the line joining the ends of the umbral path lies north and south and the convex side of that path faces west; then the eclipse is visible for a distance of $1\frac{1}{2}$ to 2 inches south from the umbral path (except near the ends), for $1\frac{1}{2}$ to $1\frac{3}{4}$ inches westwards from the ends of that path, and from $\frac{1}{16}$ to $\frac{1}{2}$ inch in the direction opposite to south from the ends of that path (which direction may also be south but across the pole). In proportion as the umbral path is tilted away from a general east and west direction, these unusual conditions are likely to be realized.

partial. Since in partial eclipses the moon's umbra does not touch the earth, Oppolzer has not indicated them on his charts. Yet they figure among the eclipses recorded in Chinese history.

Astronomical chronology has sometimes neglected partial eclipses; J. Fr. Schroeter's *Spezieller Kanon der zentralen Sonnen- und Mondfinsternisse*, Kristiania, 1923, which claims to chart all eclipses visible in Europe from 600 to 1800 A.D., omits partial eclipses entirely, even though many such were visible within that region. Such eclipses are sometimes quite conspicuous, sometimes being visible even from the polar circle as far south as five degrees to the other side of the equator, so that historians have recorded them. In dealing with these partial eclipses, we are aided by certain empirical principles, known to the Greeks, but not much used in modern times. Eclipses recur at intervals of 6585.3 days (18 years and 10 or 11 days), which period is called a *saros*. At intervals of three saroi, 19,756 days (approximately 54 years 1 month), called by Ptolemy an *exeligmos*, solar eclipses recur at approximately the same place. If the eclipses occurring at intervals of an exeligmos are plotted on a map, it will be found that they form a series which has certain definite characteristics. Such a series invariably begins with a run of partial eclipses visible in the neighborhood of one of the earth's poles, followed by a long run of umbral eclipses, which gradually shift to the other pole of the earth, and ends with a run of partial eclipses.[3] A solar exeligmos series covers a period of from 1244 to 1532 years or 23 to 28 exeligmoi, with an initial and terminal run of 2 to 8 exeligmoi during which only partial eclipses occur. If the noon points of the umbral eclipses are plotted for such a series, the resulting curves[4] show periods of shifting and periods of quietude, in the latter of which the curve usually describes a loop. In periods of shifting, the noon points during a period of 6 exeligmoi may shift as much as 180 degrees of longitude and 90 degrees of latitude; whereas, in a period of quiescence, at a node, the noon points during as much as 8 exeligmoi may be located within an area of 60° of longitude and 30° of latitude or less.

Since partial eclipses are those in which the moon's umbra (or its prolongation) passes over one of the earth's poles, and since successive eclipses in the same exeligmos series are located close to each other, it is possible to determine definitely that a partial solar eclipse was not visible

[3] The data upon which this part of the discussion is based will be found in the papers of Dr. Alexander Pogo in *Popular Astronomy*, vol. 43, 1935.

[4] For such curves, cf. Neugebauer, *Astronomische Chronologie*, I, p. 24; Pogo, *Popular Astronomy*, Jan. 1935; W. Hartner, "Das Datum der Shih-ching-finsternisse," *T'oungpao*, 1935, diagram, p. 202–3.

in China by counting backwards or forwards by exeligmoi to the first umbral eclipse. If that umbral eclipse was visible in the south polar regions, the partial eclipse cannot have been visible in China. In this manner half of the partial eclipses may be disposed of. A simpler method of discovering whether a partial eclipse is visible in China is by noting Oppolzer's calculated value of γ for that eclipse. If it is negative and between -1.0 and -1.6, the eclipse was partial and visible only in the southern hemisphere. By the above methods the regions of visibility for about five-sixths of all eclipses may be approximated without calculation.

If the nearest umbral eclipse in the same exeligmos series was visible near the north pole, we cannot say with any certainty by this method whether the partial eclipses in that series were visible in China. Less than one-third of such partial eclipses are visible there, since only the eclipse at one of the three saroi in an exeligmos can usually be visible in China, and since the farther partial eclipses are from the nearest umbral eclipse in the same exeligmos series, the more they tend to move northwards, outside of Chinese latitudes. Because of the shifting in longitude shown by some series, a determination of the approximate circumstances of a partial eclipse from umbral eclipses in the same exeligmos series is not reliable.

The visibility of partial eclipses in the northern hemisphere and of umbral eclipses that lie near the limits of visibility must be calculated. For that purpose the method used in Neugebauer, *Astronomische Chronologie,* has been used. A useful preliminary step is to use the elements given by Oppolzer with Neugebauer's tables as the latter directs (Op. cit. I, p. 103). In this way little more than a mere inspection of Neugebauer's tables is necessary. But the results thus obtained are only approximate, and are useful only to eliminate eclipses that are plainly invisible in China. In all cases where exact results are required, the computation should be carried through as directed by Neugebauer. The elements given in Oppolzer furnish a useful check upon such computations.

THE ECLIPSES DURING THE REIGN OF THE EMPEROR KAO-TSU

During this period of twelve (or fifteen) years, only three eclipses are recorded. We discuss them in chronological order.

i. In the third year of Kao-tsu's reign, the tenth month, on the day *chiu-hsu*, a solar eclipse is recorded (1A: 35a). This date was, according to P. Hoang, *Concordance des chronologies néoméniques, chinoise et européenne*, ("Variétés sinologiques," no. 29), Shanghai, 1910, (which is used for dates throughout), December 20, 205 B.C. For that date Oppolzer calculated his solar eclipse no. 2387. It was merely partial; calculation according to the method in P. V. Neugebauer, *Astronomische Chronologie* (which is used for such calculations throughout), shows that the eclipse reached a magnitude of 0.51 (the diameter of the sun being 1.00) at Ch'ang-an at 10:44 a.m., local time.

HS 27 Cb: 13a adds, "It was 20 degrees in [the constellation] Tou," whose stars were then in R.A. 241.1° to 253.3°. The sun was in long. 266.0° = 265.6° R.A.[1] There is thus good agreement in both the date and location of the sun.

ii. In the third year, the eleventh month, the day *kuei-mao*, the last day of the month, a second solar eclipse is listed (1A: 35a). *HS* 27 Cb: 13a adds, "It was three degrees in [the constellation] Hsü," whose two stars, α Equulei and β Aquarii, were then in R.A. 291.1° and 293.2°. This date was Jan. 18, 204 B.C., but there was no eclipse on that date, for Oppolzer gives none.

The *Han-chi* (written by Hsün Yüeh, lived 148–209) records the preceding and the next eclipse (2: 11b, 4: 2a), copying the recording in the *HS*, but omits this one, which, in view of the fact that the *Han-chi* takes its material mostly from the *HS*, makes it look as though this eclipse was not in the text of the *HS* during the second century A.D. If so, it was interpolated both into chapters 1 and 27. In view of the fact that Hsün Yüeh noted all the other eclipses that are in the *HS* for the first half century of the Han period, even the one only found in *HS* ch. 27 (cf. ch. 4, App. IV, vi), it is difficult to explain otherwise his omission of this eclipse.

During the seven years between the proceeding recorded eclipse and the next one, there occurred 14 solar eclipses, of which only one was

---

[1]Since Chinese astronomical data were always referred to the equator, not the ecliptic, celestial positions must be reduced to right ascension for purposes of comparison.

visible in China.[1] Oppolzer numbers this one 2396, and dates it on Oct. 8, 201 B.C., which was in the sixth year, eighth month, on the last day, *kuei-wei* (if Hoang's calendar is one day in error). Oppolzer calculates the sun in long. 191.6° = 190.7° R.A. The magnitude of this eclipse was calculated for Ch'ang-an and was found to have reached only 0.02, at 7:44 a.m. local time, so that it was practically invisible there; at the present Pei-p'ing its magnitude however reached 0.28 at 8:26 a.m., local time, so that this eclipse might have been reported from the east. Oppolzer's solar eclipse no. 2400, on Aug. 18, 199 B.C. seemed also visible in China, but calculation showed that it was invisible in any part of China and even in the present Canton.

The eclipse of 201 B.C. might have been the one intended by this recording, although it is not easy to explain the discrepancy of the cyclical day. The *SC* does not record any of the three eclipses that the *HS* lists in the reign of Kao-tsu. Pan Ku thus inserted them into the account of events given in the *SC* from some other source. Some astronomer who edited the list of eclipses thus used by Pan Ku might have given an illegibly dated eclipse the next possible date for an eclipse after the first and legibly dated solar eclipse. But two solar eclipses at successive new moons can happen only when two small eclipses occur in different (northern and southern) hemispheres.

Since however the *Han-chi* does not have this eclipse, it seems more likely that some person of the third or later centuries interpolated this eclipse for a time when he knew that an eclipse might have happened, in order to emphasize the gravity of the period. In June/July of this year, Kao-tsu barely escaped with his life from the siege of Jung-yang.

The location in the heavens given for this eclipse does not agree with anything we can calculate. It must have been calculated from the date of the year given to this eclipse, for it is about 28 Chinese degrees after the preceding one.

iii. In the ninth year, the sixth month, on the day *yi-wei*, the last day of the month, a third solar eclipse is recorded (1B: 14b). This date was Aug. 7, 198 B.C.; Oppolzer calculates his solar eclipse no. 2402 for that date. *HS* 27 Cb: 13a adds, "It was 13 degrees in [the constellation] Chang," whose stars then ranged from 118.6° to 133° R.A. Oppolzer calculates the sun as at long. 129.4° = 131.9° R.A. There is thus a very close checking between observation and calculation here.

[1] Besides those whose location Oppolzer charts, the following three partial eclipses were invisible because they belong to initial (i.) or terminal (t.) runs in exeligmos series whose nearest umbral eclipse was located near the south pole: no. 2389 (i.); no. 2390 (t.); and no. 2398 (t.). In addition two partial eclipses were visible in the northern hemisphere, both of which were invisible in China: (1) no. 2388, on May 17, 204 B.C.; calculation shows that this eclipse was invisible; (2) no. 2397, on Mar. 4, 200 B.C.; calculation shows that at lat. 40°N it was visible only in the Atlantic Ocean and Europe.

CHAPTERS II AND III

INTRODUCTION

These two chapters give an account of the chief events during the time that the government was in control of the Empress *née* Lü, the wife of Emperor Kao-tsu. Chapter II treats of the period when her son, Emperor Hsiao-hui, was on the throne and chapter III of the period after his death when she openly took control. These chapters, like chapter I, are largely based on the corresponding chapter in the *SC*, chapter IX. Pan Ku, however, added some new material; he seems to have had available a collection of imperial edicts and possibly an official annalistic chronicle, upon which he drew.

The *SC* puts this material into one chapter; Pan Ku divides it into two because there were two rulers. Pan Ku furthermore has transferred into his "Memoirs" the more sensational stories given in the *SC*, seemingly because he felt that these accounts concerned the private lives of the actors, rather than their public acts. Thus he has left in these "Annals" only the bare mention of Liu Ju-yi's death and that of Liu Yu, and has said nothing about the Empress's treatment of the Lady *née* Ch'i. Concerning the attempted assassination of Liu Fei, he mentions only its administrative result. He gives those accounts in full in his "Memoir of the Imperial Relatives by Marriage" and the "Memoir of the Five Kings who were Sons of Kao-tsu." Thus Pan Ku seems to have conceived of the "Annals" as chronicles properly devoted to the official acts of the ruler and the important events of the reign, rather than as an attempt to give in full an account of the period. Such an account must be gathered from the mine of material in the remainder of this encyclopedic history.

This period of fifteen years constituted a period of rest and recuperation after the fighting and destruction preceding the reign of Kao-tsu and the civil war during it. The only serious conflict was an internal one, which did not come to a head until the very end of the period. Kao-tsu had eliminated all his important feudal kings except those of his own family, so that during this period there were no revolts, such as had plagued him. Peace was made with the only important external enemy, the Huns, and it was cemented by sending a girl of the imperial family

167

to be a bride of the Hun emperor, the *Shan-yü*. There was only one war—with the state of Nan-yüeh, located at the present Canton; but the mountains proved such a barrier that the war was confined to border forays, and the Chinese generals did not even try to cross the mountains. Thus the people secured a rest, the population could increase, and the country became prosperous.

The Chancellor of State, Hsiao Ho, who had administered Kao-tsu's empire, died in the second year of this period. He nominated Kao-tsu's greatest fighter, Ts'ao Ts'an, as his successor, thus emphasizing the tradition that since the empire had been conquered by Kao-tsu's personal followers, it should be ruled by them. This tradition was followed as long as any capable followers of Kao-tsu remained alive and was the factor that prevented the overturn of the state.

Liu Ying, known as Emperor Hsiao-hui, proved a kindly but weak young man. He was only in his sixteenth year when he came to the throne, and the real power went to his mother, then entitled the Empress Dowager *née* Lü. She had taken an active part in the conquest of the empire, had suffered severely in that contest, and had gathered around her a faction, chiefly composed of members of the Lü family (including two of her older brothers who had been generals of Kao-tsu and had been ennobled by him as marquises) and of her relatives by marriage, especially the valiant Fan K'uai, who had married her younger sister, the able and determined Lü Hsü. This faction ennabled the Empress Dowager to enthrone her son, although he was not the oldest nor the favorite son of Kao-tsu. The oldest son was Liu Fei, who had been made King of Ch'i, the most important part of the empire next to Kuan-chung. But Liu Fei was not the son of Kao-tsu's wife, and so could be passed over.

Since the Empress Dowager had only barely succeeded in enthroning her son, she felt driven to cultivate the interests of the people in order to bolster up her power. Hence, although she committed grave crimes, she proved a good ruler. She could not afford the unpopularity of misrule and was too intelligent to indulge in it. She lightened the taxes and removed some of the severe punishments that had been inherited from the Ch'in dynasty, repealing, for example, the Ch'in law against the possession of proscribed books. She allowed the commutation of punishments, even of capital punishment, for money payment, which, in those days of severe and harsh punishments, was a lightening of penalties rather than an invitation to the wealthy to commit crime. The most serious crimes were not commuted.

But she came into conflict with her son the Emperor when she attempted to take vengeance upon her rival. She imprisoned closely in the Palace the favorites of her husband, especially the Lady *née* Ch'i, who had almost succeeded in displacing her as Empress. The Empress Dowager wanted a keener revenge, but dared do nothing more as long as the Lady's son was alive. This ten-year-old boy, Liu Ju-yi, Kao-tsu's favorite child, had been made King of Chao with a capable and brave Chancellor to guard him. When this Chancellor would not send the boy to the capital, the Empress Dowager removed the Chancellor and had the boy brought. But he was a favorite of the Emperor too, so the sixteen year old Emperor met his half-brother at a village ten miles from the capital and carefully conducted him to his own apartments, where he guarded him by always keeping him by his side. After several months, one morning early the Emperor went out hunting, leaving Ju-yi sleeping. The Empress Dowager immediately had her step-son poisoned. The Emperor could do nothing to his own mother, not even for murder.

Then the Empress Dowager had the dead boy's mother, the Lady *née* Ch'i, terribly mutilated and thrown out into the gully through which ran the sewer, naming her "the Human Swine." She took her son to see her mutilated rival; he did not recognize the poor lady; when an attendant informed him of her identity, the Emperor wept himself into a nervous breakdown. For a year he could not leave his bed. When he recovered, he sent this message to his mother: "Your deed was utterly inhuman. I am your son, so I cannot again govern the country." Then he gave himself over to drinking, to women, and to pleasure.

The next year Liu Fei came to court. At a family dinner the Emperor seated Fei above himself, as befitted the oldest brother. The Empress Dowager became angry and ordered two goblets of poisoned wine for Fei. Then she commanded him to drink a toast. But the Emperor took one of the goblets to drink; without a descendant on the throne the Empress Dowager would have been helpless; she hastily arose and upset her son's goblet. Then Fei took alarm and left. He feared for his life, but found that the Empress Dowager had merely acted in a fit of anger; so he made his peace with her by presenting her daughter, Kao-tsu's oldest child, the Princess Yüan of Lu, with a commandery and appointing this step-sister as his Queen Dowager.

Emperor Hui died in the seventh year of his rule. The Empress Dowager had married him to the daughter of Princess Yüan. Such a union was quite proper, since the girl had a surname different from that of her husband. But she had no child. The Emperor had however had a son by a lady of his harem; the Empress Dowager named this babe the son of the Empress and killed his mother. The babe was made Heir-apparent and was enthroned as Emperor. Since he was her grandson, and the Empress was her granddaughter, the Empress Dowager herself boldly took the Emperor's place in court and issued imperial decrees and edicts in her own name.

Then she strengthened her position by appointing four of her nephews from the Lü family as kings, and, to forestall trouble over the succession, if anything should happen to the babe, she took six babes of the Lü family and named them marquises, asserting that they were children of Emperor Hui.

This action brought her into conflict with one of the established practises of the dynasty, which was after her death to prove stronger than she. Kao-tsu had gathered his immediate followers and made them swear a solemn oath in a ceremony in which a white horse had been killed and the lips of each had been smeared with the blood. This oath was to the effect that no one except members of the imperial Liu family should be made king and no one should be made marquis except for deeds of valor. Kao-tsu had taken this step when he was plagued by the rebellions of those vassal kings not members of the imperial clan; but he had himself violated this oath in the appointment of his boyhood and close friend, Lu Wan, as King of Yen. The Empress Dowager's important officials had all been followers of Kao-tsu and had taken this oath; yet they respected her ability and recognized that she had materially assisted in winning the empire, so that she also was one of the followers of Kao-tsu; these facts and the power of the Lü faction kept the officials from making any overt move against her. The Senior Lieutenant Chancellor, Wang Ling, protested in private, but he was promoted to an advisory post which left him powerless. The Empress Dowager thus succeeded in establishing herself firmly in control. She had a committee of the high officials and nobles arrange the precedence of the nobles in the court, thus increasing the prestige of her faction.

In 184 B.C. the child emperor learned of his real mother. Boy-like he boasted, "The Empress could have killed my mother and pass me as her son. I am not yet grown up, but when I am grown up, I will change things." Such a threat to the Empress Dowager's power could not be tolerated; the child was pronounced insane, imprisoned to death in the palace prison, and the ministers were ordered to suggest his successor.

They knew that he was the only natural son of Emperor Hui; in seeming deference to the Empress Dowager but in real unwillingness to be a party to her action they replied merely that they accepted her orders. She then selected one of the six babes she had previously named as marquises and sons of Emperor Hui and appointed him Emperor. The ministers said nothing; this appointment was not their work; they consequently felt free to overturn it later.

In order to consolidate her power, the Empress Dowager had married some of Kao-tsu's sons to girls of her family, the Lü. One of them, Yu, did not love his wife and favored a concubine; he was slandered to the Empress Dowager as having said that after her death he would attack the Lü family. She summoned him to the capital and starved him to death in his lodgings. Another son, K'uei, was so oppressed by his wife, a Lü girl, who poisoned his beloved concubine, that he committed suicide. A third, Chien, died; the Empress Dowager sent to have his son killed and end his kingdom. There were left now only two out of the eight sons of Kao-tsu, only three of whom had died a natural death.

The Empress Dowager knew she could not live much longer; to perpetuate her clan's power she appointed her two nephews, Lü Ch'an and Lü Lu, the first as Chancellor of State, in charge of the civil government, and the second as First Ranking General, in charge of the military. To placate the Liu faction, she appointed its head, Liu Tse, a venerable cousin of Kao-tsu, as King of Lang-ya, and gave royal posthumous titles to Kao-tsu's mother, older brother, and older sister. Thus she prepared for the inevitable.

In March/April 181, as the Empress Dowager was returning to the capital from a religious ceremony in the suburbs, she was bitten in the side by a dog, which immediately disappeared. When she was brought back to the Palace, the diviner brought the response, "It is the ghost of Ju-yi, become an evil spirit." The wound probably became infected; she died on August 18. By a testamentary edict she made grants to the nobles, generals, and officials, leaving the government in charge of her two nephews.

Revolution arose immediately. There had been much criticism of the Empress Dowager; one portent after another had been noted. Twelve days after the death of Liu Yu there had been an eclipse total at the capital, and the Empress Dowager was said to have declared, "This is on my account." Those of Kao-tsu's personal followers, such as the famous Lu Chia, who had been unable to stomach the Empress Dowager's rule and had retired to their estates, returned to the capital to readjust matters. The Lieutenant Chancellor Ch'en P'ing and the Grand Commandant Chou P'o were both old friends of Lu Chia. They had all been companions of Kao-tsu and had taken the oath. They were ready to eliminate the Lü faction, for they owed their positions to having been followers of Kao-tsu even more than to the favor of the Empress Dowager.

They were actively aided by the Liu faction, composed of the Liu family and its adherents.

Overt action was taken by the King of Ch'i, who was the eldest son of Liu Fei, the eldest son of Kao-tsu. He mobilized his army and tricked Liu Tse into aiding him. Kuan Ying, one of Kao-tsu's best generals, was sent against the rebels; but Kuan Ying had also taken the oath. He went half-way and encamped, sending word to the King of Ch'i that he would later join him. Thus the Lü power crumbled.

Kao-tsu's followers in the capital meanwhile conspired to overthrow the Lü, with Chou P'o and Ch'en P'ing at their head. They had a friend of Lü Lu point out to him that the appointment of nine kings from the Liu family and three kings from the Lü family had been quite legal, since it had been done after deliberation by the high officials and with the concurrence of the kings—that thus the imperial power was not absolute, but was limited by the consent of the high ministers and the highest nobles. He was told that if the Lü promptly surrendered their power and retired to their estates, they would not be molested; but if not, they would be suspected of rebellion and proceeded against. Lü Lu saw the correctness of this reasoning and agreed, but he had to submit the matter to his clan, and so action was postponed.

On September 26 the defection of Kuan Ying was reported to Lü Ch'an. The bureaucracy was so honeycombed with conspirators that word of this news was immediately taken to Chou P'o. Lü Lu was promptly tricked into giving up control of the army; the troops unanimously declared for the Liu faction, and Lü Ch'an, seemingly the only able man among the Lü faction, was killed. The next day the whole Lü clan was massacred. Thus the power of the Empress Dowager collapsed like a house of cards within six weeks after her death. Then the high officials and heads of the Liu clan met and chose as the next emperor the oldest surviving son of Kao-tsu, whose reputation and that of his wife's family were better than that of the King of Ch'i.

In this manner the first threat to the House of Liu from members of clans allied by marriage was removed by the action of Kao-tsu's loyal followers. The House of Liu was securely fixed on the throne and its continuation secured. It is interesting that this House was finally overthrown by another clan whose power likewise came from inter-marriage with the royal house.

Chapter II

THE SECOND [IMPERIAL ANNALS]

The Annals of [Emperor Hsiao-]Hui[1]

漢書二　惠紀第二

孝惠皇帝高祖太子也母曰呂皇

后帝年五歲高祖初為漢王二年

立為太子十二年四月高祖崩五

月丙寅太子即皇帝位尊皇后曰

Emperor Hsiao-hui was the Heir-apparent of [Emperor] Kao-tsu. His mother was called the Empress [*née*] Lü.[2] When Emperor [Hsiao-hui] was in his fifth year, Kao-tsu first became King of Han₈. In [Kao-tsu's] second year [the future Emperor Hsiao-hui] was established as Heir-apparent; in the twelfth year, the fourth month, Kao-tsu died.

In the fifth month, on [the day] *ping-yin*,[3] the Heir-apparent took the imperial throne. He honored the Empress, entitling her, the Empress Dowager. He granted to the common people one step in noble rank.[4]

(marginal dates:) 206 B.C. — 205 B.C. — 195 B.C. — June 1[5] — June 23

---

[1] The *SC* includes the events of this emperor's reign in its chapter devoted to the Empress Lü, whereas the *HS* pursues the more logical course of giving each emperor a separate chapter. Ch'i Shao-nan (1703–1768), referring to this difference, says of the *HS*, "In rectitude and in [its] principles it is most correct."

[2] For names of persons, places, and official titles, cf. the "Glossary of Names".

[3] This date was June 23, 195 B.C., 22 days after his predecessor's death, the same day as that on which his predecessor was buried.

[4] At the accession of an emperor, favors were generously bestowed. This was not the first time, as Shen Ch'in-han thought, that aristocratic ranks were given to the common people, for they had previously been bestowed in 206 B.C. Cf. 1A: 30b. These ranks were probably awarded to the heads of families. In 262 B.C., when Chao Shêng received his territory, according to the *Chan-kuo Ts'e* (iii cent. B.C.), section on Chao, chap. 21, he granted to all the officials an increase of three steps in rank and to the common people who could gather together, to each family he granted six catties of gold. (But *SC* 43: 35a, in repeating this story, tells that he granted to the officials and people three steps in rank and to the officials and people who were able to maintain peace among themselves six catties of gold. Cf. *Mh* V, 118.) Kao-tsu had given to all his soldiers at least the fifth rank (cf. 1B: 5a). The first rank was Official Patrician 公 士, cf. *Mh* II, 528, 1°; Duyvendak, *Book of Lord Shang*, p. 62.

[5] *HS* 1 B; 23a.

173

The Gentlemen-of-the-Household and the Gentlemen-of-the-Palace [who had served] six full years
[were granted] three steps in noble rank; [those
who had served] four years [were granted] two steps.
The Gentlemen-outside-the-Household [who had
served] six full years [were granted] two steps.

1b Gentlemen-of-the-Household who had not [served]
a full year [were granted] one step. Gentlemen-outside-the-Household who had not [served] two full

2a years were granted ten thousand cash.[1] Enunchs[2]
and Masters of the Food [were treated] the same
as Gentlemen-of-the-Palace.[3] Palace Internuncios,
Guards, Spear-bearers, Men of War, and Grooms [were
treated] the same as Gentlemen-outside-the-Household. The Heir-apparent's [Chariot-]driver and his
Chariot-companion were granted the aristocratic rank
of Fifth [Rank] Grandee; the members of his suite
[who had served] five full years were given two steps.
There were granted to those who had provided for the
[imperial] burial ceremonies and [had positions ranking as] two thousand piculs, twenty thousand cash;
[to those who had positions ranking as] six hundred
piculs and over, ten thousand [cash]; to [those who
had positions ranking as] five hundred piculs, two

皇太后賜民爵一級中郎郎中滿六歲爵三級四歲二級外郎滿

六歲二級中郎不滿一歲一級外郎不滿二歲賜錢萬宦官尚食

比郎中謁者執楯執戟武士騶比外郎太子御驂乘賜爵五大夫

舍人滿五歲二級賜給喪事者二千石錢二萬六百石以上萬五

---

[1] Very possibly the edict went on to award proportionate
advancements in rank for other periods of service. At this
time, according to this edict, 10,000 cash is counted as worth
less than one step in rank, whereas in 18 B.C. a step in rank
could be purchased for 1000 cash. Cf. *HS* 10: 10a.

[2] Ying Shao (ca. 140–206) says that these eunuchs 宦官
were *hun-szu* 閽寺, door-keepers and eunuchs. The *Chou-li*
(Biot. trans. I, 150–153) tells that the *hun-jen* 人 were door-
keepers and the *szu-jen* were eunuchs in charge of the imperial
women. Cf. 19A: 16b, 17a.

[3] In view of the high dignity of these two officials and of the
fact that they served in the inner apartments, Su Yü (fl. 1913)
suggests that the words, "Gentlemen-of-the-Palace, *lang-chung*"
should be interchanged and we should read, "Gentlemen-of-the-
Household, *chung-lang*."

史二金減田租復十五稅一爵五大

六百石以上六金五百石以下至佐

斥土者將軍四十金二千石二十金

百石二百石以下至佐史五千視作

hundred piculs, and under, [down] to the Accessory Officials, five thousand [cash]. Of those who had superintended digging [the late Emperor's] grave,[1] the generals [were granted the equivalent[2] of] forty [catties] of gold, [those who had the rank of] two **2b** thousand piculs [were granted the equivalent of] twenty [catties of] gold, [those who had the rank of] six hundred piculs and above [were granted the equivalent of] six [catties of] gold, those [who had the rank of] five hundred piculs and less, down to the Accessory Officials [were granted the equivalent of] two [catties of] gold.

[The Emperor] reduced the tax on arable ground and revived it [at the rate of] one part in fifteen.[3] Those who had the aristocratic rank of Fifth [Rank]

[1] Fu Ch'ien (ca. 125–195) and Ju Shun (fl. dur. 221–265) say that 斥上 means to open up the earth for a tomb.

The Official ed. (1739) emends *shang* 上 to *t'u* 土; but Chang Chao (d. 1745) says that the Academy ed. (1124) and Sung Ch'i's ed. (xi or xii cent.) read *shang*. He says that Fu Ch'ien's and Ju Shun's comments show that the text originally read *t'u*. Chou Shou-ch'ang (1814–1884) however argues that probably at that time there was a current expression using *shang*.

[2] Mr. Cheng (fl. dur. 265–317) says that 四十金 means 四十斤金. Cf. p. 111, n. 3. Chin Shao (fl. ca. 275) remarks, "This speaks of . . . the equivalent of gold. In later [passages], whenever it says *huang-chin* 黃金, [it means] actual gold. When it does not say *huang*, it means cash. *HS* ch. 24 says that a catty of actual gold was worth 10,000 cash." Then a gift of *huang-chin* means actual gold, whereas a gift of *chin* means so many times 10,000 cash. Yen Shih-ku (581–645) agrees with the foregoing interpretation, but Liu Pin (1022–1088) says, "I say that whenever any book says so much *chin*, one *chin* is 10,000 cash; when there is [made] a grant of so many *catties* of *chin*, it is entirely of [actual] gold." We have adopted the earlier interpretation.

[3] Teng Chan (fl. ca. 208) writes, "In the beginning, the Han dynasty taxed [at the rate of] one-fifteenth [cf. 24A: 9b], less than the Chou [dynasty's] tax of one-tenth; in the mean time [the land tax] had been abolished, now it was revived."

Grandee, and officials [ranking as] six hundred piculs and above, together with those who had served the [young] emperor so that he knew their names, if they had committed crimes, and should justly be shackled like robbers, they were all to be put in honorable detention.[1] Those of [the aristocratic

3a rank of] Superior Accomplished and above,[2] together with the great-grandsons[3] of marquises or kings belonging to the imperial house by male or female descent who had committed crimes and should justly [suffer] mutilating punishment, to-

上及內外公孫耳孫有
盜械者皆頌繫上造以
皇帝而知名者有罪當
夫吏六百石以上及宦

[1] The shackles 械 were boards which held together the hands and feet of prisoners. Ju Shun says, "頌繫 means that they should be treated leniently and should be merely made to live in the residences of Division Heads and not enter the goal." Shen Ch'in-han however says, "This 'honorable detention' is the T'ang [dynastic] Code's 散禁, it does not mean that they do not have to go to prison." According to 23: 19b, in 145 B. C., Emperor Ching ordered that people over the eightieth and under the eighth year of age, together with pregnant women, blind musicians, and dwarfs, who must be held for criminal examination, should also be given "honorable detention." In 97 A. D. Emperor Ho established a special office for the criminal examination of Lieutenant Chancellors and high ministers. In a note to 23: 19b, Yen Shih-ku interprets "honorable detention" as "without the boards that hold together [a criminal's] hands and his feet 桎梏."

[2] Superior Accomplished 上造 was the second rank in the honorary hierarchy, next to the lowest; the fifteenth rank (from the bottom) was called the Somewhat Superior Accomplished 少上造 and the sixteenth the Greatly Superior Accomplished 大上造; Ying Shao (ca. 140-206) thinks the sixteenth rank is meant here; Yen Shih-ku (581-645) thinks the second rank is meant.

[3] Chang Yen says that 公孫 are descendants of marquises or kings of the imperial house. 耳孫 is pronounced, according to Yen Shih-ku, *jen₁-sun*, the first word being pronounced *jen₂* 仍. Chin Shao (fl. 275) says that it is the great-grandson of the great-great-grandson, i.e., the eighth generation of descent (counting the person from whom descent is counted as the first generation). In *HS* 12: 10a, however, Liu Yin is said to have been made King of Liang because he was a *jen₁-sun* of a great-great-grandson of King Hsiao of Liang whereas 14: 12a and 47: 11a both say he was a great-grandson of a great-great-grandson of King Hsiao. *HS* 12:2b speaks of the appointment of Emperor Hsüan's *jen₁-sun* and 99 A: 19b says plainly that they were his great-grandsons. The ancestry of Liu Hsin in 15 A: 5a confirms this statement. Yen Shih-ku says that in every instance the *HS* means great-grandson by *jen-sun*. The term is also used in *HS* 94 A: 32b. According to the *Erh-ya* (written before Han times, added to in Han times), the *jen₂-sun* is however the eighth generation in descent. Yen Shih-ku thinks that because the pronunciation of these two words *jen* is similar, the two phrases *jen-sun* mean the same. But others disagree. Ying Shao (ca. 140-206) says that *jen₁-sun* is the sixth generation. Li Fei (prob. iii cent.) says it was the fourth generation.

罪　者　年　歲　又
當　皆　七　有　曰
刑　耐　十　罪　吏
及　爲　以　當　所
當　鬼　上　刑　以
爲　薪　若　者　治
城　白　不　皆　民
旦　粲　滿　完　也
春　民　十　之　能

gether with those who should justly be made
to [build] the fortifications or [patrol from] the
break of day or pound [rice], were all to have
their whiskers shaved and be made to [cut] firewood
for the spirits or [prepare] pure rice.[1] Common
people who are in their seventieth year or over or
not fully ten years old, who had committed crimes
and should justly [suffer] mutilating punishment,
were not to be mutilated.[2]   3b

[1] The five "mutilating punishments" were: tatooing on the face, amputation of the
nose, amputation of the feet, castration, and capital punishment.

The punishment of [building] the fortifications or [patrolling from] the break of day
城旦 consisted, according to Ying Shao, in "rising early in the morning and patrolling
or building the fortifications. . . . It was a four year punishment." *Cf.* Chavannes,
Documents chinois decouverts, p. 63.

According to Ying Shao, "Females were not employed in outside work, but were
made to pound 春 [the husks off of] rice. It was a four year punishment." Cf.
Chavannes, ibid.

For the punishment of shaving the whiskers, cf. p. 118, n. 1.

Ying Shao tells that the punishment of "spiritual firewood" 鬼薪 consisted in
"gathering firewood for the ancestral temple. . . . It was a three year punishment."

Ying Shao also says, "Sitting and selecting rice to make it pure white [for use in
offerings at the ancestral temple] is [preparing] pure rice 白粲. It is a three
year punishment." Evidently it was for women, just as "spiritual firewood" was for
men.

The *Han-chiu-yi*, written by Wei Hung (fl. 25–57) B:9b contains the following: "All
who have committeed crimes, if male, have their heads shaved, wear an iron collar,
and are made to [work on] the fortifications in the morning—to [work on] the fortifications or [patrol] from the break of day is to build the fortifications. Females are
made to pound—to pound is to prepare [unhulled] rice; both serve for five years;
those who are not mutilated [serve] four years. [Cutting] firewood for the spirits is
for three years. Of those who [are sentenced to cut] firewood for the spirits, the
males cut down the firewood and twigs on the mountains for the sacrifices to the
spirits and divinities; the females who are [sentenced] to [make] pure rice, pick over
the rice for the sacrifices; both serve for three years. When the punishment is to
work as a robber guard, the robber guard, if male, stands on guard; if female, she works.
As a robber guard, both serve for two years. Males are [also] made to serve in frontier
garrisons at hard labor and females are made to do labor in the official buildings; both
serve for one year."

[2] Mutilating punishments (cf. above) all involved some bodily mutilation; the aged
and children were not to be punished thus. Cheng Chung (ca. 5 B.C. to A.D. 83) in a
note on the *Chou-li* 35: 33a, Autumn, Chang-lu, says, "Not to be mutilated 完 says
nevertheless that they should be held and work for three years, [but] not to have

[The edict] also said, "Officials [exist] for the sake of governing the people. If [the officials] are able to fulfil their [duties in] government, then the people [can] rely upon them. Hence [We] make their salaries large, the reason for doing which is [for the sake of] the people. Now the fathers and mothers, the wives and children, and the other members of the families[1] of officials who have [the rank] of six hundred piculs or above, together with the former officials who have in the past worn the seal of a General or of a Chief Commandant[2] and have led troops, or have worn the seal of an official [with the rank of] two thousand piculs—their families shall pay only the military tax and shall not be required to pay any other [taxes]."

[The Emperor] ordered the commanderies and the vassal kings to establish temples to Kao-[tsu].[3]

I　　In the first year,[4] in the winter, the twelfth
194 B.C. month, King Yin of Chao, [Liu] Ju-yi, died.[5]

盡其治則民賴之故重其祿所以為民也令
吏六百石以上父母妻子與同居及故吏嘗
佩將軍都尉印將兵及佩二千石官印者家
唯給軍賦他無有所與令郡諸侯王立高廟
元年冬十二月趙隱王如意薨民有罪得買

their bodies damaged." The *Han-chi* (ii cent.) misunderstands the text and says they should "escape" punishment. Stein found in the desert tablets indicating that certain persons were sentenced to forced labor and escaped mutilation. Cf. Chavannes, *Documents chinois*, p. 63.

[1] Yen Shih-ku says "The 同 居 are, besides father, mother, and wives, [those persons] like older and younger brothers, together with the older and younger brothers' children."

[2] According to *HS* 5: 6a, only in 148 B.C. was the title of Chief Commandant used for the previous Commandery Commandant. In the *SC*, Chief Commandant is found used of a Ch'in dynasty high military official as early as 207 B.C. (cf. *Mh* II, 273), and it is used in the *HS* under the date of 167 B.C. (cf. 4: 15a) as well as here. Possibly these early uses are anachronisms. Cf. *Mh* II, 524, xxv. More probably Chief Commandant was the title of an army officer lower than a General and higher than a Colonel, as well as being the title of a regular official in the commandery hierarchy.

[3] Previously the vassal kings had been ordered to establish temples to Kao-tsu's father (1B: 15b). Now the Han dynasty was attempting to unify the empire by giving it a common religion. The commanderies and kingdoms likewise established temples for the other emperors of the dynasty; we hear of a temple to the Emperor Wen in Lin-chiang; cf. 5: 6a.

[4] Years are counted from the first New Year's day after the emperor takes his throne. The remainder of the preceding year is counted as still belonging to his predecessor. Cf. 9: n. 1.1.

[5] He was poisoned by his step-mother. The *HS* relegates this story to the "Memoir

爵　爵　二　朝　主
三　戶　年　獻　邑
十　一　冬　城　尊
級　級　十　陽　公
以　春　月　郡　主
免　正　齊　以　爲
死　月　悼　益　太
罪　城　惠　魯　后
賜　長　王　元　春
民　安　來　公　正

[The Emperor ordered[1] that] when the common Jan. people commit crime, they are to be allowed to purchase thirty steps in noble rank in order to avoid capital punishment.[2] He granted to the common 4a people noble ranks, in each household one step [in rank].

In the spring, the first month, the city wall of Feb. Ch'ang-an was [partly] built.[3]

In the second year, in the winter, the tenth month, II King Tao-hui of Ch'i, [Liu Fei₂], came to court [to Nov./Dec. pay his respects]. He presented the Ch'eng-yang Commandery to be added to the estate of the Princess Yüan of Lu, and honored the Princess, appoint-

of the Imperial Relatives by Marriage," 97 A: 4a, and is here content to chronicle the bare fact of his death. Cf. *Mh* II, 409 f. The *HS* does not seem to have any fixed practise about referring to persons by their names or by their posthumous titles, sometimes using one and sometimes the other. In this translation, a posthumous name (such as Yin) will be preceded by the title of the person's rank (such as King); a personal name (such as Ju-yi) will be preceded by the person's surname.

[1] Wang Nien-sun (1744–1832) argues that this sentence should be preceded by the word *ling* 令, just as in the similar passage in 1B: 12a. For the meaning of *ling*, cf. 8: n. 11.2. Yen Shih-ku's comment contains this word, showing that it was in his text. The *T'ai-p'ing Yü-lan* (978–983), "Feng-chien," section 1, quotes this imperial order but without the *ling*. The old ed. (prob. Sung period) of the *Pei-t'ang Shu-ts'ao* (ca. 618), "Feng-chio," last section, quotes this order with the *ling*, although Ch'en Yü-mo's ed. (1600) deletes it.

[2] Ying Shao writes, "Each step cost 2000 cash, [so that capital punishment could be ransomed by paying] altogether 60,000 cash, like the present ransoming of crime by paying 30 bolts of fine close-woven silk." Possibly this value for noble ranks was only for the purpose of ransoming crime, for in the previous year a single step was worth more than 10,000 cash. Cf. p. 174, n. 1; also 10: n. 10. 2. Or else Ying Shao is guessing. This order does not allow the actual purchase of aristocratic ranks, but merely the commutation of capital punishment for a large money payment.

[3] Hu San-hsing (1230–1287) says, "The Han [dynasty] made its capital at Ch'ang-an. Altho Hsiao Ho had built the palaces and halls there, there had not yet been leisure to build a city wall. Emperor [Hui] began building it, and it was only finished in his fifth year [190 B.C.]." The *Tzu-chih T'ung-chien* (1084) says, "At first the northeast quarter of the wall was built." It is interesting that the edict allowing the building of city walls was issued in 202 B.C. (cf. 1B: 7b), but the city wall of the capital was not begun until 194 B.C. *HS* 16: 62a says that the Privy Treasurer Yang-ch'eng Yen built the Ch'ang-lo and Wei-yang palaces and the Ch'ang-an city wall.

193 B.C. ing her as his Queen Dowager.[1]

4b In the spring, the first month, on [the day] *kuei-yu*,
Feb. 20 there were two dragons seen at Lan-ling in the well
of a common citizen.[2] On the evening of [the day]
Feb. 22 *yi-hai*, they disappeared. In the Lung-hsi [Com-
Summer mandery] there was an earthquake.[3] In the summer
there was a drought.

The Marquis of Ho-yang, [Liu] Chung, died. In
the autumn, the seventh month, on [the day] *hsin-*
Aug. 16 *wei*, the Chancellor of State, [Hsiao] Ho, died.

III In the third year, in the spring, there were sent

月癸酉有兩龍見蘭陵
家人井中乙亥夕而不
見隴西地震夏旱邰陽
侯仲薨秋七月辛未相
國何薨

[1] She was the step-sister of King Tao-hui, and was older than he. The Empress
Dowager Lü had tried to poison her step-son, King Tao-hui. His Prefect of the Capital
had advised him to placate her by presenting some territory and this title to her
daughter, the Princess Yüan. Since a Dowager practically controls her son, King
Tao-hui was thus putting himself and his property largely under the control of the
Empress Dowager Lü's daughter as well as flattering her. According to 32: 9a, b, "In
187 B.C., the Dowager Queen Yüan of Lu died and the sixth year after the Marquis of
Hsüan-p'ing, [Chang] Ao, [her husband], also died. The Empress Dowager [*nee*] Lü
made the son of [Chang] Ao, [Chang] Yen, the King of Lu, [instead of merely making
him a marquis], because his mother had been a Dowager Queen [of Ch'i]."

The account of these intrigues is given in the *SC* (cf. *Mh* II, 411) and in *HS* 38: 1b,
hence the *HS* does not feel it necessary to do more here than merely mention its
administrative result. According to later Chinese conceptions, it was quite improper
for a king to make his half-sister his Queen Dowager, for that meant he was treating
her as his mother, whereas she was of the same generation as he. Emperor Hsiao-hui
was married by his mother to the daughter of his own full sister (cf. 2: 5a), which
is also improper, according to those conceptions, for this girl was also of a different
generation (cf. *Mh* II, 413, n. 1). But in ancient times, while a man normally married
only girls of the same generation as himself, it was the custom among the highest
classes of the nobility to marry also one niece, who was the daughter of one's oldest
maternal first cousin, and hence was of the generation following that of her husband.
Cf. Granet, *Chinese Civilization*, p. 339. The rule of generations was regularly disregarded in the Han period; Emperors Hsüan and Ch'eng both married cousins of a
different generation than they, so that King Tao-hui's appointment of his older half-
sister as his mother may have also been in accord with the conceptions of his time,
altho it was out of accord with conceptions current later.

[2] The text writes 家人; Ch'ien Ta-chao (1744–1813) says the words should be
interchanged, to read as they are written in the *Han-chi* (ii cent.). *HS* 27 Ca: 16a
writes, "There were two dragons seen at Lan-ling, in the T'ing-tung hamlet, in the
[family] well of Wan Ling."

[3] *HS* 27 Ca: 9a says it crushed more than 400 people.

萬人城長安秋七月都厩災南越王趙佗稱臣奉貢

立閩越君搖爲東海王六月發諸侯王列侯徒隷二

安三十日罷以宗室女爲公主嫁匈奴單于夏五月

三年春發長安六百里內男女十四萬六千人城長

from [the region] within six hundred *li* of Ch'ang-an, 146,000 [persons], male and female, to build the city wall of Ch'ang-an. In thirty days they were dismissed.[1]

A girl of the imperial house was made a Princess and given in marriage to the *Shan-yü* of the Huns.

In the summer, the fifth month, [the Emperor] made the Baronet of Min-yüeh, [Tsou] Yao, the King of Tung-hai.[2]

In the sixth month, from the [states of] the vassal kings and marquises, 20,000 criminals and retainers were sent to build the city wall of Ch'ang-an.[3]

In the autumn, the seventh month, there was a visitation [of fire] in the [imperial] stables at the capital.[4]

The King of Nan-yüeh, Chao T'o, pronounced himself a subject [of the Emperor] and presented tribute.[5]

In the fourth year, in the winter, the tenth month, IV

192 B.C.
Spring

June

5a
July

Aug.

[1] Mr. Cheng (fl. dur. 265–317) says they finished one side of the city wall.

[2] In 1B: 4a, b, Tsou Wu-chu is made *King* of Min-yüeh.

[3] Ho Ch'uo (1661–1722) remarks, "The distances of the vassal kingdoms [from the capital] were different, hence beforehand in the sixth month, these [people] were mobilized, causing each [group] to arrive at the [appointed] time. The building of the city wall was done in the spring, the first month, as previously."

[4] The text uses 災. The *Shuo-wen* (ca. 100) defines it as 天火, "a fire [started by] Heaven." *HS* 27A: 6b writes, "A fire [started by] human agencies is called a fire; a fire [started by] natural [or spiritual] means is called a visitation. 人火爲火, 天火爲災." Fires, floods, droughts, and sickness are now all called visitations 災. Etymologically this word means "fire."

The *San-fu Huang-t'u* (iii to vi cent.) says, "The stables at the capital were the places where the emperor's carriages and horses [were kept]."

[5] He had been enfeoffed by Kao-tsu; now that Kao-tsu was dead, he renewed his allegiance to the new emperor. He revolted soon after the death of Hsiao-hui. Cf. 95: 10a, b.

Nov. 10 on [the day] *jen-yin*, [the Emperor] established the
191 B.C. Empress *nee* Chang [as Empress].[1]

Jan./Feb.   In the spring, the first month, common people who were filially pious, fraternally respectful and [diligent] cultivators of the fields were recommended and their persons exempted [from taxes and forced service].

Apr. 1   In the third month, on [the day] *chia-tzu*, the Emperor was capped and [an amnesty was granted] to the world.[2] In reducing the laws and orders which annoyed the officials and people, there was abrogated the criminal law against possessing books.[3]

There was a visitation [of fire] in the Wild Goose Terrace in the Ch'ang-lo Palace. In Yi-yang it rained

5b blood.[4] In the autumn, the seventh month, on [the

Aug. 10 day] *yi-hai*,[5] there was a visitation [of fire] in the Ice Chamber of the Wei-yang Palace. On [the day]

Aug. 11 *ping-tzu*, there was a visitation [of fire] in the Weaving Chamber.

V   In the fifth year, in the winter, the tenth month,

四年冬十月壬寅立皇后張氏春正月
舉民孝弟力田者復其身三月甲子皇
帝冠赦天下省法令妨吏民者除挾書
律長樂宮鴻臺災宜陽雨血秋七月乙
亥未央宮凌室災丙子織室災

---

[1] For Liu Hsiang's reaction, cf. 27 A: 10b.

[2] Hsiao-hui was then in his twentieth year. Capping was a ceremony performed when a youth came of age. Wang Ming-sheng (1722–1797) notes that in 141 B.C. the boy who became Emperor Wu was capped in his 16th year; in 77 B.C. Emperor Chao was capped in his 18th year; *HS* 11: 1b records that Emperor Ai was capped in his 17th year; according to 12: 10a Emperor P'ing died in his 14th year and was capped when being dressed for burial. Wang Ming-sheng adds, "In ancient times emperors and nobles were all capped in their 12th year. After they had been capped they begot children. At the beginning of the Han [period] the classics were lost and incomplete, and there was no plain passage about the rites for the capping of the Son of Heaven, hence [that ceremony] had no definite time." However, after the classics were recovered, the Han emperors seem to have been just as irregular as formerly in performing this ceremony. Probably in Han times there was no definite age for capping the heirs apparent.

[3] The criminal law now abrogated was the famous decree of the Ch'in First Emperor which ordered that anyone concealing books should be executed together with his three sets of relatives.

[4] *HS* 27 Bb: 10b says that this event happened in the second year.

[5] This date is Aug. 10, 191 B.C., but 27 A: 10b, in narrating this event, dates it in the tenth month, which is impossible because there was no *yi-hai* day in that month; the *Han-chi* (ii cent.) puts it in the third month.

六年冬十月辛丑齊王肥薨令民得賣爵女子年

爵戶一級

大旱秋八月己丑相國參薨九月長安城成賜民

百里內男女十四萬五千人城長安三十日罷夏

五年冬十月雷桃李華棗實春正月復發長安六

it thundered.   The peach and plum [trees] flowered **Nov./Dec.** and the jujubes [produced] fruit.[1]

190 B.C.

In the spring, the first month, there were again **Feb./Mar.** sent from [the region] within six hundred *li* of Ch'ang-an 145,000 men and women to build the city wall of Ch'ang-an.   In thirty days they were dismissed.

In the summer there was a great drought.[2]   In **Summer** the autumn, the eighth month, on [the day] *chi-ch'ou,* **Sept. 24** the Chancellor of State, [Ts'ao] Ts'an, died.[3]

In the ninth month, the city wall of Ch'ang-an **Oct./Nov.** was completed.   [The Emperor] granted aristocratic ranks to the people, to each household one step.[4]

In the sixth year, in the winter, the tenth month, **VI** on [the day] *hsin-ch'ou,*[5] the King of Ch'i, [Liu] **Aug. 25,** Fei₂, died.

189.

It was ordered that the people were to be allowed to sell[6] noble ranks.   Girls who were in their fifteenth **6a**

[1] *HS* 27: Bb 1a says that laxity is punished by an unseasonably long warm spell at which time there may be plant anomalies.

[2] *HS* 27 Ba: 23b says that the water in the Yangtze and Yellow rivers was low and the gorges and valleys were dry.

[3] There was no *chi-ch'ou* day in that month.   There was such a day in the 8th month of the preceding year and in the 7th and 9th months of the same year.   His biographies in *SC* ch. 54 and *HS* ch. 39 do not date his death.   *HS* 39: 12b says, "[Ts'ao] Ts'an was Chancellor of State to the third year and died."   Hsiao Ho, the previous Chancellor of State, died in Hsiao-hui's second year (2: 4b), whereupon Ts'ao Ts'an was installed; three years later would be the fifth year; so that the year is corroborated.   *SC* 22: 5a (*Mh* III, 189) notes the death of Ts'ao Ts'an in the 8th month on the day *yi-ch'ou,* which would give a date possible in the 8th month, viz. Sept. 24, 190 B.C. Chavannes (*T'oung Pao,* vol. 7, p. 525) approves this reading.   The error of transcription involved in writing 己 for 乙 is quite likely.

[4] Yen Shih-ku remarks, "The head of the family received it."

[5] There was no *hsin-ch'ou* day in that month; *SC* 22: 5a (*Mh* III, 189) notes this death in the seventh month of the sixth year, the *hsin-ch'ou* day of which was Aug. 25, 189 B.C.   I find no evidence that this was anything but a natural death.   His son succeeded him; the Empress Dowager after his death merely took away some of his territory.

[6] The Official ed. (1739) writes "purchase 買" for the text's "sell 賣."

Nov./Dec. year and over, up to their thirtieth [year] and who
190   were not married were [ordered to pay as a tax] five
[times the] poll-tax.[1]

189 B.C.   In the summer, the sixth month, the Marquis of
July   Wu-yang, [Fan] K'uai, died.[2]

The Western Market of Ch'ang-an was built and
the Ao Granary was repaired.

VII   In the seventh year, in the winter, the tenth
Nov./Dec. month, chariots, cavalry,[3] and skilled soldiers were
sent to go to Jung-yang, led by the Grand Comman-
Sept. 29, dant,[4] Kuan Ying.

192   In the spring, the first month, on [the day] *hsin-*

十五以上至三十不嫁五算
夏六月舞陽侯噲薨起長安
西市修敖倉
七年冬十月發車騎材官詣
滎陽太尉灌嬰將春正月辛

---

[1] Ying Shao (ca. 140–206) writes, "The *Kuo-yü* (iii cent. B.C.) [says], 'The King of Yüeh, Kou-chien, ordered that if in his state a girl was in her seventeenth year and unmarried, her parents had committed a crime, for he wished that his people would multiply abundantly.' According to the Han Code, each person paid one poll-tax—a poll-tax was 120 cash; only merchants with male or female slaves [paid] two poll-taxes. Now they were caused [to pay] five [times] the poll-tax, it was a punishment for crime." Fu Ch'ien (ca. 125–195) however says, "A poll-tax is 127 [cash]." Liu Pin (1022–1088) remarks, "I say that 'girls [being taxed] five [times] the poll-tax' does not however [imply] that they were punished all at once with this [amount]. From 15 to 30 there are five stages [of five years each]. Each stage added one poll-tax."

The amount of the poll-tax in the above statements, about 120 cash, seems to have been the amount to which this tax was stabilized at the close of the Former Han and during the Later Han period; S. Kato, "A Study on the *Suan-fu*, the Poll-tax of the Han Dynasty," in *Mem. of the Research Department of the Toyo Bunko*, No. 1 (1926), 51–68, comes to the conclusion that this poll-tax was 190 cash under Emperor Wu; the evidence that it was 40 cash under Emperor Wen is not of the best.

[2] The death of a mere noble is not usually mentioned in the Imperial Annals. But Fan K'uai's wife was the younger sister of the Empress Dowager, and he belonged to her faction, that of the Lü family. Hence his death was a piece of good fortune for the Liu family.

[3] Yen Shih-ku (581–645) says, "Chariots are usually those who have been sentenced to military service and take arms, like the present frontier garrison chariots 車常擬軍興者, 若近代之戍車也. Cavalry are usually horses which have been kept, together with the persons [who have kept them], who have been ordered to be sent [away] and sentenced to cavalry service, like the present horses for war and their [former] owners who care for them. 騎常所養馬幷其人使行充騎, 若今武馬及所養者主也."

[4] According to ch. 19 and his biography, he did not secure this title until the time of Emperor Wen.

丑　蝕　宮　贊　寵
朝　之　九　曰　齊
日　既　月　孝　悼
有　秋　辛　惠　趙
蝕　八　丑　內　隱
之　月　葬　修　恩
夏　戊　安　親　敬
五　寅　陵　親　篤
月　帝　　　外　矣
丁　崩　　　禮　聞
卯　于　　　宰　叔
日　未　　　相　孫
有　央　　　優　通

ch'ou, the first day of the month, there was an
eclipse of the sun.[1] In the summer, the fifth month, 188 B.C.
on [the day] *ting-mao*, there was an eclipse of the sun July 17
and it was total.[2] In the autumn, the eighth month,
on [the day] *mou-yin*, the Emperor died in the Wei- Sept. 26
yang Palace. In the ninth month, on [the day]
hsin-ch'ou, he was buried at the An Tomb.   Oct. 19

In eulogy we say:[3] [Emperor] Hsiao-hui, in his **6b**
family, cultivated the love of his relatives; in the
state, he honored his Ruling Chancellors. He loved
[King] Tao-[hui] of Ch'i, [Liu Fei₂], and [King] Yin
of Chao, [Liu Ju-yi], most dearly.[4] His kindness
and his sense of respect were both deep indeed.
When he heard the admonition of Shu-sun T'ung,
he was greatly dismayed.[5] When he accepted the

---

[1] For eclipses, cf. App. I.

[2] According to Shen Ch'in-han (1775–1831), the *Hsi-Ching Tsa-chi* (prob. vi cent.)
says, "In the seventh year of Emperor Hui, in the summer, it thundered and there
was an earthquake. Several thousand of the great trees on the Southern Mountains
[near the capital] were all on fire, but [the fire] did not reach below them; on several
tens of *mou* of land the grass was all scorched and yellow. More than a hundred
days afterwards, people went there and got one set of dragon bones and two sets of
alligator bones [fossils?]."
Emperor Hui was in his twenty-third year when he died and he was buried 23 days
after his death.

[3] Cf. p. 146, n. 8.

[4] These two boys were his half-brothers. He tried to protect the second by always
keeping him with himself; the Empress Dowager had to wait to kill Ju-yi until Hsiao-hui
was out shooting and Ju-yi was sleeping alone. When the Empress Dowager tried
to poison Liu Fei by giving him two cups of poison at a feast, Hsiao-hui took one
cup; the Empress Dowager upset it and thus revealed her plan. These stories are told
in the *SC* and in *HS* 97A: 4a; 38: 1b. Cf. *Mh* II, 409 ff.

[5] *HS* 43: 17a, b, 18a says, "When they were building the double passageways [which
seem to have been elevated roofed passageways, cf. p. 113, n. 2] just south of the arsenal
[which was near the Wei-yang Palace], as [Shu-sun] T'ung was reporting to [the Em-
peror] on business, he took the opportunity to ask for a word in private and said,
'Why does your Majesty yourself build this double passageway? The robes and hat
of Emperor Kao-[tsu, which are preserved in] the funerary chamber [at his tomb], are
carried monthly [in procession] to the Temple of Kao-[tsu]. Why should his descendants climb up and travel above the [sacred] road of the ancestral temple?' Emperor Hui
was dismayed and replied, 'I shall quickly destroy it.' [But Shu-sun] T'ung said,
'The lord of men can manifest no faults. Now it is already made and the people all
know about it. I hope that your Majesty will make the Second Temple 原廟 north

response of the Chancellor of State Ts'ao [Ts'an], he was glad at heart.[1]   He may be called a [most] generous and kindly ruler.   He happened [upon a time when the state was ruled by] the Empress Dowager

寬仁之主
心說可謂
國之對而
然納曹相
之諫則懼

of the Wei [River, by the tomb of Kao-tsu], and that [Kao-tsu's] robes and hat will be carried monthly [in procession] to it, thus increasing and broadening the fundamental [conception] of filial piety [underlying] the ancestral temple.' Then the Emperor promulgated an imperial edict that the [high] officials should erect the Second Temple." The point was that a gallery of the "double passageways" (q. v. in Glossary) was carried above the sacred road.

[1] When the famous Chancellor of State, Hsiao Ho, died, he recommended Ts'ao Ts'an as his successor, even though there had been jealousy between the two. *HS* 39:11b ff. says, "When [Ts'ao] Ts'an took the place of [Hsiao] Ho as Chancellor of State, in all matters there was no change or alteration; he entirely followed the agreements and regulations of [Hsiao] Ho." But he gave himself to drinking day and night. When anyone would come to talk with him, he would give them to drink before they could get started, and give them more drink whenever they showed any signs of re-opening the subject, so that they went away drunk without having had a chance to speak. His subordinates in the office behind his residence likewise fell to drinking and singing and shouting daily. Someone invited him to visit this office, but when he visited it, he too took wine, sat down, and drank, singing and shouting louder than they! He shielded those who had committed small crimes, so that there was no business done in his office. Emperor Hui was much younger than Ts'ao Ts'an, so when he wondered at his Chancellor's behavior, he sent Ts'ao Ts'an's son to remonstrate with him. But Ts'ao Ts'an became angry and had his son beaten 200 stripes for doing so. "When the time came [for him to go] to court, [the Emperor] reproved [Ts'ao] Ts'an, saying, 'What sort of treatment have you given [your son], K'u? Formerly I sent him to remonstrate with you, sir.' [Ts'ao] Ts'an doffed his hat, begged [the Emperor's] pardon, and said, 'When your Majesty yourself considers the deeds of the Sage Hero [Kao-tsu], how do you compare with Emperor Kao-[tsu]?' Emperor [Hsiao-hui] replied, 'But how would We dare to hope [to compare Ourself with] the late Emperor?' [Ts'ao] Ts'an said, 'When your Majesty considers me, [Ts'ao] Ts'an, which [of us] is the more capable, I or Hsiao Ho?' The Emperor

漢書二
損至德悲夫
遭呂太后虧

[née] Lü, who damaged and injured his perfect virtue.[1]   It was sad indeed.

replied, 'You, sir, do not appear to be his equal.'   [Ts'ao] Ts'an replied, 'What your Majesty says is right.   [Since] moreover Emperor Kao-[tsu] and Hsiao Ho have subjugated the world and the laws and ordinances have all been made plain, is it not right that your Majesty [sits] with unruffled garments and with folded hands while I, [Ts'ao] Ts'an, and my colleagues [merely] guard our charges, following in the way [of Kao-tsu and Hsiao Ho, taking care that we] make no slips?'   Emperor Hui replied, 'Good.   You, sir, need not say anything more about it.' "

Ts'ao Ts'an was a devotee of Lao-tzu's doctrine that the best government is the one that governs least (cf. *Tao-te-ching*, ch. 60, 80); he tried to give the people a relief from the over-exacting government that characterized the Ch'in dynasty with its numerous laws and the period of Kao-tsu with its continual wars.

[1] The historian is thinking of the murder of the Emperor's beloved half-brother, Liu Ju-yi, and the terrible revenge wreaked upon Ju-yi's mother, the Lady *née* Ch'i, by the Dowager Empress *née* Lü.   When the Emperor's mother called him to see his mutilated step-mother, he did not recognize her; when he was informed who she was, he wept abundantly and became ill for more than a year (possibly he had a "nervous breakdown"), and sent people to say to his mother, the Empress Dowager, "This is an inhuman deed.   I am your son, [but, because of you] I am not able to rule the empire [rightly]."   Then he gave himself up to drinking and debauchery and did not pay any attention to government.   Cf. *Mh* II, 410.   This story is told in 97A: 4b; it was perhaps the worst deed of the Empress Dowager.

THE ECLIPSES DURING THE REIGN OF EMPEROR HUI

i. During these seven years, two eclipses were recorded. In the seventh year, the first month, on the day *hsin-ch'ou*, the first day of the month, the first of these eclipses is recorded (2: 6a). This date corresponds to Feb. 21, 188 B.C. *HS* 27 Cb: 13a adds, "It was 13 degrees in [the constellation] Wei₁'" whose stars were then in R.A. 299°–305°. The *Han-chi* (5: 14b) gives the cyclical day as *hsin-yu*, which was not the first day of that month. There was no eclipse on that date, for Oppolzer lists none.

Of the 22 eclipses in the 10 years since the last previously recorded eclipse in 198 B.C. and the 4 months before the next eclipse, only 4 were visible in China.[1] In this period five umbral eclipses were visible or seemingly visible in China: (1) no. 2404, on July 26, 197 B.C., 12 days before a *hsin-ch'ou* day, sun in long. 118.8°, visible in north China; (2) no. 2408, on June 6, 195 B.C., 52 days before such a day, sun in long. 70.4°; (3) no. 2410, on May 26, 194 B.C., 2 days after such a day, sun in long. 60.3°; (4) no. 2417, on Sept. 29, 192 B.C., 41 days before such a day, sun in long. 182.1° = 181.9° R.A.; (5), no. 2420, on Mar. 14, 190 B.C.; the magnitude of this eclipse was calculated and it was found invisible in China, visible only in western and central Siberia.

The fourth umbral eclipse, that of Sept. 29, 192 B.C., was very likely the one referred to in the text. This eclipse was not recorded in the *SC*, which was Pan Ku's chief source, so that he must have copied it from some list of eclipses. If that list was partly illegible, it is natural that Pan Ku or an editor of the list of eclipses might have misplaced this eclipse, especially as two eclipses coming close together might be understood to predict the Emperor's death. Thus this eclipse was put about one eclipse season before the next eclipse. Then the *hsin-ch'ou* 丑 of the text is an error for *hsin-yu* 酉 (a quite natural mistake), and Hoang's

---

[1] Besides those whose location Oppolzer charts, the following 3 partial eclipses were invisible because they belong to initial (i.) or terminal (t.) runs in an exeligmos series whose nearest umbral eclipse was located near the south pole: no. 2412 (t.); no. 2415 (i.); and no. 2422 (i.). In addition four partial eclipses were visible in the northern hemisphere, three of which were calculated and found invisible in the China of that date: no. 2405, no. 2413, and no. 2423. The other partial eclipse, no. 2414, on Oct. 9, 193 B. C. (24 days after a *hsin-ch'ou* day) was just invisible in Ch'ang-an, but visible at points north and west at sunset.

calendar is one day in error. *Hsin-yu* may indeed have been the original reading in the *HS* Annals, for the *Han-chi* today has that reading, although *hsin-yu* was not the first day of the month in which the eclipse is dated. *HS* 27 Cb: 16a says that this eclipse was on the same month and day as that of Feb. 15, 2 B.C., so that ch. 27 certainly read *hsin-ch'ou*. Conflation of the day in the Annals with that in ch. 27 probably came later. If we adopt this assumption, the eclipse happened in the third year, the ninth month, the first day. The location of the eclipse in the heavens is however greatly in error.

ii. In the seventh year, the fifth month, on the day *ting-mao*, a second eclipse, which is said in the "Annals" to have been total, is recorded (2: 6a). This date was July 17, 188 B.C., on which Oppolzer calculates his solar eclipse no. 2425. He charts the path of totality as passing through Ning-hsia, northern Shensi, a little north of K'ai-feng, and the present Shanghai. Calculation shows that at Ch'ang-an the eclipse reached a magnitude of 0.92 (sun's diameter = 1.00), at 3:12 p.m., local time. Hence the statement of the text in the "Annals" that the eclipse was total must have been taken from reports of places outside the capital. *HS* ch. 27 however says it was "almost total."

HS 27 Cb: 13a adds that the eclipse was "in the beginning of [the constellation], the Seven Stars," whose stars τ^2 and α Hydrae were then in 114.6° and 114.8° R.A. respectively. The longitude calculated for the sun is 110.1° = 111.8° R.A.

HS ch. 27 dates the eclipse on the day before the last day of the month. Hoang's calendar dates it on the last day of the month, whereas Chavannes' calendar (*T'oung pao*, VII, p. 25, cf. also p. 520) is a day in error in the other direction.

Chapter III

THE THIRD [IMPERIAL ANNALS]

The Annals of the Empress of Kao-[Tsu]

The Empress *née* Lü of [Emperor] Kao-[tsu] gave **1a, 1b** birth to Emperor Hui and assisted Kao-tsu in subjugating the empire. Her father and two older brothers[1] were enfeoffed by Kao-tsu as marquises. When Emperor Hui took the throne, he honored the Empress [*née*] Lü by making her Empress Dowager.

The Empress Dowager had made the daughter of the Emperor [Hui's] older sister, the Princess Yüan of Lu, the Empress, [but] she had no issue. [So the Empress Dowager] took the son of a Beauty from the [imperial] harem, pronounced him [the son of the Empress] and made him Heir-apparent.[2] When Emperor Hui died, the Heir-apparent was made Emperor.[3] He was young, [hence] the Empress **2a**

[1] Yen Shih-ku (581–645) says, "Her father was the old gentleman Lü, the Marquis of Lin-szu; her brothers were [Lü] Tse, the Marquis of Chou-lü, and [Lü] Shih-chih, the Chien-ch'eng Marquis." For names of persons, places, and official titles, cf. Glossary.

[2] Ho Ch'uo (1661–1722) says," 名之 [means] to name him as a son born to the Empress."

HS 27 A: 10b says, "The Empress had no issue, [but] a Beauty in the [imperial] harem had a male [child]. The Empress Dowager had the Empress name him [as her son] and killed his mother. After Emperor Hui had died and his heir had been established [as Emperor, he spoke] some resentful words, [so] the Empress Dowager dismissed him [cf. 3: 3b], and replaced him, establishing a scion of the Lü family, [Lü] Hung, as the Young Emperor." The similar phrasing used in recounting the killing of a son and his mother, a concubine, which happened after King Ling of Yen died (cf. 38: 3b), proves that the first Young Emperor was the son of Emperor Hui.

[3] In other cases, the day of an emperor's accession is given.

子取後宮美人子名之以爲太子惠帝崩太子立爲皇帝年幼

惠帝卽位尊呂后爲太后太后立帝姊魯元公主女爲皇后無

高皇后呂氏生惠帝佐高祖定天下父兄及高祖而侯者三人

高后紀第三

漢書三

191

Dowager appeared in court and pronounced [that she issued] the [imperial] decrees.[1] A general amnesty [was granted] to the world. Moreover she established [some] sons of her older brothers, Lü T'ai, [Lü] Ch'an, [Lü] Lu, and [Lü] T'ai's son, [Lü] T'ung, four persons [in all], as kings. She enfeoffed six persons of the Lü [clan] as marquises.[2] An account is in the "Memoir of the Relatives [of the Imperial House] by Marriage."

97A: 4b, 5a

I
187 B.C.
Feb./Mar.

In the first year, in the spring, the first month, an imperial edict said, "At a previous time Emperor Hsiao-hui said that he wanted to abolish the punishment of [death together with] the three [sets of]

元年春正月詔日前日孝惠皇
戚傳
王封諸呂六人爲列侯語在外
兄子呂台產祿台子通四人爲
太后臨朝稱制大赦天下廼立

Ch'ien Ta-chao (1744–1813) thinks that the reason that date is not given here is because the Empress Dowager's actions were tantamount to herself ascending the throne, and because the child did not himself rule, but was soon after degraded and imprisoned.

[1] Ever since, when an Empress has assumed the Emperor's power, her act has been called by this phrase, so that it has become an idiom. The *SC* says at this point, "In the first year all the proclamations and decrees emanated from the Empress Dowager." Yen Shih-ku says, "The words of the Son of Heaven are called (1) 'decrees 制書' and (2) 'edicts 詔書.' 'Decrees' means that they are commands for decreeing and regulating 制度之命. [These] were not what an Empress Dowager is permitted to pronounce. Now the Empress Dowager [*née*] Lü appeared in court and performed the duties of the Son of Heaven, making decisions about the many [affairs of the governmental] mechanism, hence she styled [her orders imperial] decrees and edicts." An empress could issue edicts, but the issuing of decrees was the sole prerogative of the Emperor. Cf. *T'ai-p'ing Yü-lan*, ch. 593, for a quotation from the *Han Chih-tu* (by Hu Kuang, 91–172) enumerating the four kinds of imperial orders. Cf. *Mh* II, 126, n. 2; 99 A: 4a.

[2] These four appointments were not all made at the same time. Lü T'ai was enfeoffed as King in 186, Lü Ch'an in 182, Lü Lu and Lü Tung in 180. According to *SC* ch. 9 (*Mh* II, 417), in the first year the Empress Dowager appointed Lü P'ing as Marquis of Fu-liu and Lü Chung, the son of Lü Shih-chih, as the Marquis of P'ei; in the fourth year (*Mh* II, 418), she appointed Lü T'a as Marquis of Yü (cf. 16: 65a), Lü Keng-shih, her nephew, as Marquis of T'eng, and Lü Fen, another nephew, as Marquis of Lü-ch'eng; in the eighth year (*Mh* II, 425), she appointed Lü Chuang, a younger son of Lü T'ai, as Marquis of T'ung-p'ing—these are the six marquises referred to. In addition there were other marquisates in her family: Lü Lu became Marquis of Hu-ling, later succeeding Lü Shih-chih as Chien-ch'eng Marquis; in 184, Lü Hsü, the younger sister of the Dowager Empress, was ennobled as the Marquis of Lin-kuang. The *HS* evidently did not count women in the enumeration of the six marquises.

山王弘為襄城侯朝為軹侯武為壺關侯

災立孝惠後宮子強為淮陽王不疑為恒

二千石者一人夏五月丙申趙王宮叢臺

除之二月賜民爵戶一級初置孝弟力田

帝言欲除三族皐妖言令議未決而崩今

relatives[1] and the ordinance against monstrous talk-ing,[2] [but] his deliberations had not yet been con-cluded when he died. Now We abolish these [punish-ments]." In the second month she granted noble Mar./Apr. ranks to the common people, one step to each house-hold. For the first time there were established Filially Pious, Fraternally Respectful, and [Diligent] Cultivators of the Soil—[each official ranking as] two thousand piculs [recommended] one [such] person [for appointment].[3] In the summer, the fifth month, on [the day] *ping-shen*, in the palace of June 11 the King of Chao, there was a visitation [of fire] in the Ts'ung-t'ai.[4]

[The Empress Dowager] appointed some sons of [Emperor] Hsiao-hui by [women of] his harem: [Lü] Ch'iang as King of Huai-yang, [Lü] Pu-yi as King of 2b Heng-shan, [Lü] Hung as Marquis of Hsiang-ch'eng, [Lü] Ch'ao as Marquis of Chih, and [Lü] Wu as

[1] Cf. Glossary, *sub* Three Sets.

[2] This law was probably directed against lese-majesty and libellious complaint against the government, such as charging it with tyranny or talk that would start a rebellion. This crime was again abolished in 178 B.C. Cf. 4: 10b. Yen Shih-ku says, "Outrageously erroneous talk 過誤之言 is considered 'monstrous talking.'" In 78 B.C. Kuei Hung interpreted some omens as implying that a commoner, descended from some ancient prince, would take the throne. Hence he advised the Han dynasty to resign and search for a sage. Ho Kuang, who controlled the government, had Kuei Hung executed for "falsely bringing forward monstrous talk, treason, and inhuman con-duct." Cf. 75: 1b, 2a.

[3] Yen Shih-ku says, "She specially appointed as officials [some] Filially Pious, Fraternally Respectful, and Diligent Cultivators of the Fields, and honored them [with an official] rank, wishing thereby to encourage the world, ordering that each one should perfect his conduct and devote himself to the fundamental, [agriculture]." Ch'ien Ta-chao points out that those ranking as two thousand piculs were Adminis-trators of commanderies and Chancellors of kingdoms, and says that this passage means that each of these officials were to recommend one person, and that it is im-possible that the position of Filially Pious, Fraternally Respectful, and Diligent Culti-vator of the Soil should be ranked as two thousand piculs. The Filially Pious and the Fraternally Respectful are distinguished in 4: 14b.

[4] In 27 A: 10b Liu Hsiang says that this fire occurred because King Yu of Chao, Liu Yu, was to be slandered and imprisoned to death. Cf. 3: 4b.

Autumn Marquis of Hu-kuan.[1] In the autumn, the peach and plum [trees] blossomed.

II   In the second year,[2] an imperial edict said, "The Emperor Kao-[tsu] reformed and ordered the world.[3] All those who distinguished themselves received a share of its territory and were made marquises. All the people [are enjoying] great peace; not one but has received of his bountiful virtue. We have been thinking and reflecting [on this matter]. If, down to the distant future, their merits and names have not been made manifest, there will be nothing to honor their great conceptions and exhibit them [for the benefit of] later generations. Now [We] wish to classify and rank the merits of the

於久遠而功名不著亡以尊大
民大安莫不受休德朕思念至
諸有功者皆受分地爲列侯萬
二年春詔曰高皇帝匡飭天下
秋桃李華

---

[1] *HS* ch. 13: 19b notes that Ch'iang was made King of Huai-yang on June 6, 187 B.C. Chin Shao (fl. ca. 275) says, "The Han commentator [gives] his name as Chang 長." Ju Shun (fl. dur. 221–265) tells that *HS* ch. 18 says, "All were sons of the Lü family and were made marquises because they were sons of Hsiao-hui," but this statement is not in the present text of that chapter. [Lü] Ch'iang was furthermore never a marquis, but was directly made a king. Possibly this latter saying is displaced, and should be after the last of these supposed sons.

HS 13: 21a says of the two of these five who are recorded in the date 180 B.C., "Because he was not [the Emperor Hui's] son he was killed." The *Tzu-chih T'ung-chien* (1084) thinks that all of these five were not really sons of Hsiao-hui because they are not mentioned in *HS* ch. 14, where are listed the vassals of the Liu surname, but are only mentioned in ch. 13, in which are listed vassals of other surnames and in ch. 18, in which are listed nobles related by marriage to the royal family. *SC* 9: 10b (*Mh* II, 432) says of two of these five: "Who had been pronounced the younger brothers of the Young Emperor" (who was a natural son of Hsiao-hui). *HS* 13: 19b says of Ch'iang and Pu-yi, "The Empress of Kao-[tsu] falsely set him up as a son of [Emperor] Hsiao-hui."

The *HS* thus clearly implies that these five children were not really sons of Hsiao-hui. It records their appointment in the terms in which that appointment was made, but indicates their true descent by listing them in the appropriate tables, and by the statement on 3: 8a.

HS 18: 4b also lists another supposed son of the Emperor Hsiao-hui by the name of [Lü] T'ai 大, who was made Marquis of Ch'ang-p'ing 昌平, and who in 181 became King of Lü 呂王. Cf. 13: 20b; *SC* 17: 12a. *SC* 9:10 groups him with the other spurious sons, so that he too was a scion of the Lü family. Cf. p. 209, n. 3.

[2] Following the mention of the year, the present text reads, "in the spring," but the next date is also "in the spring, the first month" (3a); since the chapter proceeds chronologically, this word "spring" should be "winter," according to Su Yü (xx cent.). *HS* 16: 2a recounts this matter, dating it merely "in the second year of the Empress of Kao-[tsu]." We have deleted "spring," following ch. 16.

[3] This sentence is a loose quotation from Analects XIV, xviii, 2.

誼施後世今欲差次列侯功以定朝位臧于

高廟世世勿絕嗣子各襲其功位其與列侯

議定奏之丞相臣平言謹與絳侯臣勃曲周

侯臣商潁陰侯臣嬰安國侯臣陵等議列侯

幸得賜餐錢奉邑陛下加惠以功次定朝位

marquises, so as to determine upon their positions in the court and preserve them in the Temple of Kao-[tsu] from generation to generation without end, so that their heirs may each inherit their merits and positions. Let [this matter] be discussed with the marquises, settled, and memorialized [to Us]."

[The reply was,] "The Lieutenant Chancellor your 3a subject [Ch'en] P'ing [says that] together with the Marquis of Chiang your subject [Chou] P'o, the Marquis of Ch'ü-chou your subject [Li] Shang, the Marquis of Ying-yin your subject [Kuan] Ying, the the Marquis of An-kuo your subject [Wang] Ling, [I have] carefully discussed [this matter].[1] The marquises have been fortunate [enough] to obtain grants of money for food and to have been appointed to [the income of] towns.[2] Your Majesty is increas- your favors to them by fixing their positions in the

---

[1] According to 16: 1b, Kao-tsu had fixed the relative ranking of 18 marquises, including Hsiao Ho and Ts'ao Ts'an; now the Empress Dowager ordered the relative ranking of the others. She was probably planning to win adherents and strengthen her clique thereby. These ranks are recorded in ch. 16. Ch'en P'ing was ranked by this committee as number 47; the other three had previously been ranked as numbers 4, 6, and 9 respectively in order of court precedence. Thus a committee of marquises who had previously been ranked among the first, together with the Lieutenant Chancellor, did the ranking.

[2] Ying Shao (ca. 140–206) says, "The nobles at the four seasons all get grants of money for food." Wen Ying (fl. ca. 196–220) says, "Food 飧 is the towns [from the income of which] they live. In the meantime [this phrase] was changed to be called 'poll-tax money 算錢,' [cf. p. 184, n. 1], like the present chief officials' salary 食奉, which they themselves report as wine-money 媵錢. It is the land tax 租奉 [perhaps this last phrase should be, "the (marquises') poll-tax"]. Yen Shih-ku says, "Food-money 餐錢 is grants of money for cooking and food 賜廚膳錢; 奉邑 was originally 食邑 'live [from the income] of towns' " Wei Chao (197–273/4) interprets differently: "Cooked food 孰食 is called 飧; wine and meat dishes are called 錢; grain and rice 粟米 are called 奉. The [marquises'] poll-tax and their [official] salary really constitute their income; at the four seasons they obtain [imperial grants at intervals—this is their food money." Shen Ch'in-han (1778–1831) adds, "In the T'ang [period], each [high] official, in addition to his monthly salary, had money for food and fodder. [This practise] probably began with the Han [period]."

195

court in accordance with their merit.   Your subjects
beg that [this record] be stored in the Temple of
Kao-[tsu]."   The memorial was allowed.

186 B.C.   In the spring, the first month, on]the day] *yi-*
Feb. 25   *mao*, there was an earthquake in Ch'iang-tao.   In
the Wu-tu [Commandery][1] a mountain fell down.
In the summer, in the sixth month, on the [day]
ping-hsü, the last day of the month, there was an
eclipse of the sun.[2]   In the autumn, the seventh
July/Aug.   month, the King of Heng-shan, [Lü] Pu-yi, died.[3]
The "eight *shu*" cash were put into circulation.[4]

3b   In the third year, in the summer, the Yangtze
III   River [and the Han River][5] overflowed, carrying

---

[1] Wang Hsien-ch'ien says that "道 March" is superfluous and should be omitted;
the former Han dynasty had only a Wu-tu Commandery and *Hsien*; the later Han
dynasty first had a Wu-tu March.

[2] For eclipses, cf. App. I.

[3] The *SC* at this point adds the statement, "His younger brother, the Marquis of
Hsiang-ch'eng, [Lü] Shan [cf. Glossary, *sub voce*], was made King of Ch'ang-shan and
his given name was changed to Yi."   Cf. *Mh* II, 418.   Hsün Yüeh's (148–209) *Han-chi*
says the same.   Shen Ch'in-han (1775–1831) thinks that the above sentence has dropped
out of the text of the *HS* at this point.

[4] Ying Shao says, "Originally the Ch'in [dynasty] cash were in substance like the
cash of the Chou [dynasty].   Their inscription was 'Half ounce,' and their weight was
the same as the inscription.   [These were] the 'eight *shu*' cash.   [But a *shu* is 1/24
of an ounce, (cf. 4: app. I), so that 8 *shu* is only one-third of an ounce.]   Because they
were too heavy, the Han [dynasty] changed and coined the 'leaf' 莢 cash.   Today
among the people, the 'elm leaf' 榆莢 cash are those.   The people suffered because
they were too light.   [So] at this time there were again put into circulation the 'eight
shu' cash."   The *HS* however mentions the 'leaf' cash later.   Cf. 3: 4b and p. 199, n. 2.
According to the *Ku-chin-chu*, attributed to Ts'ui Pao and probably written about 300,
"The 'leaf' cash weigh three *shu*."   But *HS* 24B: 3b says of cash, "Moreover each
at different times may be lighter or heavier; they are not the same [in weight]," so
that uniformity had not been secured in coinage.   Yeh Tê-hui (d. 1927) says that of
the Ch'in dynasty 'half-ounce' cash that have been preserved, the lightest weigh 15/100
of a tael and the heaviest 20/100 of a tael; the 'eight *shu*' cash would then correspond
to the lightest Ch'in cash.   Cf. p. 111, n. 3; p. 280.

[5] The words 漢水, "the Han River," have dropped out of the present text.   Ch'ien
Ta-chao reports that they are in the Southern Academy ed. (1528) and the Fukien
ed. (1549), and that the *Han-chi* reads, "The Yangtze River and the Han River overflowed."   Chou Shou-ch'ang (1818–1884) reports that Ho Ch'uo collated a small

秋星晝見

四年夏少帝自知非皇后子出怨言皇太后幽之

永巷詔曰凡有天下治萬民者蓋之如天容之如

地上有驪心目使百姓百姓欣然目事其上驪欣

交通而天下治今皇帝疾久不已廼失惑昏亂不

away more than four thousand families of common 185 B.C. people. In the autumn, a star appeared in day-time.[1]

In the fourth year, in the summer, the Young IV Emperor himself knew that he was not the son of the 184 B.C. Empress, and emitted some resentful words, [so] the Summer Empress Dowager shut him up in the Yung-hsiang.[2] The imperial edict said,[3] "Whoever possesses the world and rules all its people covers them like Heaven and supports them like Earth.. When the superior has a joyous heart in employing his subjects, the subjects rejoice in serving their superior; when the joy and the rejoicing meet each other, the world is in peace and good order. Now the Emperor has been ill for a long time and has not recovered; conse-quently [his mind] is lost and wandering, [and he has become] demented and confused; he is not able to succeed as an heir [to his ancestors], to perform [his duty] in the ancestral temples, nor to continue its sacrifices. He is not able to be entrusted with

character Sung text (prob. 1178) and says that after "Yangtze River" it had "the Han River." *HS* 27A: 21b says, "In the third year of the Empress of Kao-tsu, in the summer, in the Han-chung and Nan Commanderies there was high water. The rivers overflowed, carrying away more than 4000 families." Corresponding to the statement on 3: 5a that in the summer of the eighth year the Yangtze and Han Rivers overflowed, 27A: 21b says, "The rivers *again* overflowed." Hence the earlier passage should mention the Han as well as the Yangtze River. Wang Hsien-ch'ien reports that the Wang ed. (1546) and the Official ed. (1739) have "the Han River" at this point.

[1] This "star" might have been a nova, a comet, or the planet Venus, which is some-times visible in daytime.

[2] The *SC* at this point and *HS* 97A: 5a tell that the Empress Dowager's grand-daughter, the Empress, had had no children, so she simulated pregnancy. A child of a concubine was passed off as her son, then the child's mother was killed—this child then was made the Heir-apparent and became the Young Emperor. When he grew up he said, "How could the Empress Dowager kill my mother and name me [as her son]? I am not yet grown; when I am grown I will do what I will do." The Em-press Dowager heard of it and imprisoned him until he died. Cf. *Mh* II, 418 ff.

[3] The *SC* quotes this edict (with a few verbal changes) as a speech of the Empress Dowager. Cf. *Mh* II, 419.

the empire. Let it be discussed who should take his place."

The ministers all said, "The plans the Empress Dowager [has made] for the world whereby to maintain the [dynasty's] ancestral temples and the [dynasty's] gods of the soils and grains are very profound. We knock our heads on the ground [in respect] as we accept [your Majesty's] edict."[1]   In June 15 the fifth month, on [the day] *ping-ch'en*, [the Empress Dowager] made the King of Heng-shan, [Lü] Hung, the Emperor.[2]

4a   In the fifth year, in the spring, the King of V   Nan-yüeh, Commandant [Chao] T'o, called himself Emperor Wu of Nan-[yüeh].[3]   In the autumn, Aug./Sept.   the eighth month, the King of Huai-nan, [Lü] Sept./Oct.   Ch'iang, died.   In the ninth month, [the Empress Dowager] sent cavalry from the Ho-tung and the Shang-tang [Commanderies] to garrison the Pei-ti [Commandery].

VI   In the sixth year, in the spring, a star was visible 182 B.C.   in daytime.   In the summer, the fourth month, an May/June   amnesty was granted to the world and [the Empress Dowager] ranked the prefect of Ch'ang₂-ling

彊戇九月發河東上黨騎屯北地
五年春南粵王尉佗自稱南武帝秋八月淮陽王
頓首奉詔五月丙辰立恆山王弘爲皇帝
臣皆曰皇太后爲天下計所以安宗廟社稷甚深
能繼嗣奉宗廟守祭祀不可屬天下其議代之羣

---

[1] The Empress Dowager had dismissed the last heir of the Emperor Hui; they tell her they do not know what to do.

[2] *HS* 27A: 21b adds that in the autumn of this year there was high water in the Yellow River basin.

[3] This act constituted a rebellion against the dynasty. Chao T'o was commonly known as "尉佗 Commandant T'o," even after he had become king and emperor. The *SC* uses this name as the title of his biography.

The use of a title name, like Wu, by a ruler while he was living was contrary to the usual Chinese practise, although many ancient kings used a title while living. According to the *SC*, before Chao T'o was enfeoffed by Kao-tsu, he had called himself "King Wu of Nan-yüeh." Now he usurped the Emperor's title and called himself "Emperor Wu of Nan-yüeh." Wei Chao (197–273/4) understands the text in this sense. Then the word "Yüeh" has dropped out of the text at this point. The *Han-chi* and the *Tzu-chih T'ung-chien* (1084) both have that word. It has been suggested however that he changed the name of his kingdom from Nan-yüeh to Nan-wu, since there is mentioned a Chih, the Marquis of Nan-wu (cf. 1B: 21b), but there is no evidence to support this conjecture. An emperor would hardly change the name of his state to that borne by an unimportant marquisate.

at two thousand piculs.[1]   In the sixth month a wall **4b**
was built [around] Ch'ang₂-ling.   The Huns pillaged   July/Aug.
Ti-tao and attacked O-yang.   The "five *fen*" cash
were put into circulation.[2]

In the seventh year, in the winter, the twelfth   VII
month, the Huns pillaged Ti-tao and abducted more   181 B.C.
than two thousand people.   In the spring, the first   Jan./Feb.
month, on [the day] *ting-ch'ou*, the King of Chao,   Feb. 21
[Liu] Yu, died from being imprisoned in the princes'
lodgings at the capital,[3] and on [the day] *chi-ch'ou*,   Mar. 4
the last day of the month, there was an eclipse and
it was total.

[The Empress Dowager] made the King of Liang,
Lü Ch'an, the Chancellor of State, and the King of
Chao, [Lü] Lu, the First [Ranking] General.   She
established the Marquis of Ying-ling, Liu Tse, as the
King of Lang-ya.

In the summer, the fifth month, on [the day]
hsin-wei, an imperial edict said, "Lady Chao-ling   June 14
was the wife of the Grand Emperor.   The Wu-ai
Marquis, [Liu Po], and Lady Hsüan were the   **5a**
Emperor Kao-[tsu's] older brother and older sister.

[1] The tomb of Kao-tsu was at Ch'ang-ling; its magistrate
was raised to rank with Commandery Administrators.   Thus
Kao-tsu was honored.

[2] A *fen* 分 is one tenth of an inch, so that this name would
imply that they were one-half inch (0.45 Eng. meas.) in diameter.   Ying Shao says that these were the 'leaf' cash (cf.
p. 196, n. 4).   Sung Ch'i (998–1061) says that some other texts
write *shu* for *fen*, which is an error, for the five-*shu* cash were
not minted until the time of the Emperor Wu.   Ch'ien Ta-chao
notes that the Southern Academy ed. (1528) and the Fukien
ed. (1549) read thus.

[3] He was the sixth son of Kao-tsu.   He had married a lady
of the Lü family, but loved a concubine.   His wife slandered
him to the Empress Dowager, accusing him of having said that
he would attack that family after the death of the Empress
Dowager.   She sent for him and starved him to death in his
lodgings, then buried him as a commoner.   Cf. Glossary *sub*
Liu Yu.

阿陽行五分錢

六年春星晝見夏四月赦天下秩長陵令二千石六月城長陵匈奴寇狄道攻

七年冬十二月匈奴寇狄道略二千餘人春正月丁丑趙王友幽死于邸己丑

晦日有蝕之既以梁王呂產爲相國趙王祿爲上將軍立營陵侯劉澤爲琅邪

王夏五月辛未詔曰昭靈夫人太上皇妃也哀侯宣夫人高皇帝兄姊也號

Their titles and posthumous names are not adequate [to their stations].   Let it be discussed [what] titles [they should be] honored [with."   The reply was,] "The Lieutenant Chancellor, your subject, [Ch'en] P'ing, and others beg that you honor the Lady Chao-ling with the title, the Empress Chao-ling, the Wu-ai Marquis with the title King Wu-ai, and Lady Hsüan with the title Queen Chao-ai."

July   In the sixth month, the King of Chao, [Liu] K'uei, committed suicide.[1]   In the autumn, the ninth Oct. month, the King of Yen, [Liu] Chien, died.[2]   [The state of] Nan-yüeh invaded and pillaged the [king-dom of] Ch'ang-sha.   [The Empress Dowager] sent the Marquis of Lung-lu, [Chou] Tsao, with troops, to attack [the invaders].

VIII   In the eighth year, in the spring, the Palace Inter-180 B.C. nuncio Chang Shih-ch'ing was appointed a marquis. Spring. The officials in the eunuch's offices in the [palace] inner [courts] who were chiefs or assistants were all granted the rank of Kuan-nei Marquis with [the income of] estates, and in the summer, the Yangtze Summer and Han Rivers overflowed, carrying away more than ten thousand families.[3]

謚不稱其議尊號丞相臣平等請尊昭靈夫人曰昭靈

后武哀侯曰武哀王宣夫人曰昭哀后六月趙王恢自

殺秋九月燕王建薨南越侵盜長沙遣隆慮侯竈將兵

擊之

八年春封中謁者張釋卿爲列侯諸中官宦者令丞皆

---

[1] He was the fifth son of Kao-tsu.   He had been married to a grand-niece of the Empress Dowager; his wife surrounded herself with her people, spying upon him so that he could not do what he liked.   His queen poisoned the concubine whom he loved, and so, in sorrow for her, he committed suicide.   The Empress Dowager thereupon punished him by taking his title from his descendants, so that his ghost could not receive princely worship.   Cf. Glossary, sub Liu K'uei.

[2] Liu Chien was the eighth son of Kao-tsu.   He had one son, by a concubine; after his death the Empress Dowager sent men to kill this son, then disestablished his kingdom.   The SC and the Tzu-chih T'ung-chien date this death in the 9th month; the Han-chi wrongly dates it in the 8th month.

By this time, of the eight sons of Kao-tsu, only two were alive: Heng, who later became the Emperor Hsiao-wen, and Ch'ang, King of Huai-nan.   Three had died seemingly natural deaths, one was poisoned by the Empress Dowager, one had been starved to death by her, and one was driven by her grandniece to commit suicide. Princess Yüan of Lu, Kao-tsu's daughter and oldest child, had also died.

[3] HS 27A: 21b says, "In the Han-chung and Nan Commanderies the rivers again ran out [of their banks], carrying away more than 6000 families; in the Nan-yang [Com-

產頡兵秉政自知背高皇帝約恐爲大
郎吏各有差大赦天下上將軍祿相國
遺詔賜諸侯王各千金將相列侯下至
餘家秋七月辛巳皇太后崩于未央宮
賜爵關內侯食邑夏江水漢水溢流萬

In the autumn, the seventh month, on [the day] Aug. 18 *hsin-szu*,[1] the Empress Dowager died at the Wei- 5b yang Palace. By her testamentary edict she granted to each of the vassal kings [the equivalent of] a thousand [catties of] gold, to the generals, the chancellors, the marquises, and those of lower [rank], down to the Gentlemen and the officials, to each proportionately. A general amnesty was granted to the world.

The First [Ranking] General, [Lü] Lu, and the Chancellor of State, [Lü] Ch'an, had sole command of the troops and controlled the government.[2] They themselves knew [that they were acting] contrary to the covenant [made by] of Emperor Kao- [tsu and his associates],[3] and were fearful that they would be executed by the great officials and the vassal

mandery] the Mien River [a tributary of the Han] carried away more than ten thousand families." Evidently the population was much denser in Shensi than along the banks of the Yangtse River, or else events in the Yangtze valley received little notice from the court historians.

[1] Aug. 18, 180 B.C., which P. Hoang makes the first day of the 8th month; Chavannes (*Mh* II, 426 & n. 3; *T'oung Pao* 7: 26) puts an intercalary month in the 7th year instead of in the 8th year, as Hoang does, and dates this death on the last day of the 6th month, making it July 21. We have followed P. Hoang, for his calendar (which in this month seems to be one day in error) requires a smaller number of emendations in the text of the histories.

The *SC* states that while the Empress Dowager was out of the palace she was bit in the side by something that appeared to be like a blue dog and suddenly disappeared. When it was divined about, the diviner's reply was, "It was the King of Chao, [Liu] Ju-yi, [whom she had murdered], become an evil spirit." She fell sick of her wound and died of it four months later. Cf. *Mh* II, 425; *HS* 27 Ba: 27b.

[2] According to the *SC* and *HS* 97A: 5a, the Empress Dowager, before her death, had feared a revolution, and so ordered these two nephews to be made First Ranking General and Chancellor of State, respectively, and to reside in the Northern and Southern Armies to guard the capital for her family. Cf. *Mh* II, 426.

[3] According to the *SC*, Kao-tsu had made his generals and associates swear an oath made with the most solemn ceremony—a white horse was sacrificed and its blood smeared on the lips of those who took the oath—to the effect that all the empire should unite to combat those who were kings and did not belong to the Liu (the imperial) family. Cf. *Mh* II, 414. The Empress Dowager, by naming kings from members of her own family, that of Lü, had compelled the breaking of this oath.

kings. Hence they plotted sedition. At that time the Marquis of Chu-hsü, [Liu] Chang, the son of King Tao-hui of Ch'i, [Liu Fei₂],[1] was at the capital. Because the daughter of [Lü] Lu was his wife, he knew of their plot, so sent people to inform his older brother, the King of Ch'i, [Liu Hsiang], and induce him to mobilize his troops and come westwards.[2] [Liu] Chang, with the Grand Commandant, [Chou] P'o, and the Lieutenant Chancellor, [Ch'en] P'ing, intended to cooperate from within

Sept. [the capital] to execute the Lü [clan]. The King of Ch'i thereupon mobilized his troops and also tricked the King of Lang-ya, [Liu] Tse, into mobilizing the troops of his kingdom; [the King of Ch'i] united the [troops of Lang-ya with his own troops] and led them westwards.[3] [Lü] Ch'an, [Lü] Lu

臣諸侯王所誅因謀作亂時齊悼惠王
子朱虛侯章在京師以祿女爲婦知其
謀廼使人告兄齊王令發兵西章欲與
太尉勃丞相平爲內應以誅諸呂齊王
遂發兵又詐琅邪王澤發其國兵幷將

[1] Kao-tsu's oldest son.

[2] The SC (Mh II, 429) tells that the King of Ch'i's Chancellor opposed the King. (The Chancellors were appointed by the emperor to watch the vassal kings.) On Sept. 12 the King tried to have his Chancellor assassinated; the Chancellor raised his troops and tried to take the King captive, but the King then killed the Chancellor.

[3] The "trick" is expounded in SC 52: 3a, b, which reads, "He sent forth all the troops of his state and sent Chu Wu east to trick the King of Lang-ya [Liu Tse], by saying, 'The Lü clan is rebelling and the King of Ch'i, [Liu Hsiang], is mobilizing his troops, wishing to go west and execute [the Lü clan]. The King of Ch'i considers that his son is young in years, and inexperienced in warlike matters, [so] prefers to entrust his kingdom to you, great King. You, great King, were yourself a general of Emperor Kao-[tsu] and are experienced in warlike matters. The King of Ch'i dares not leave his troops, [so] he sends me, your servant, to beg you, great King, to favor him by coming to Lin-tzu [his capital] to visit the King of Ch'i, plan matters, and lead the troops of Ch'i together with yours westwards to subjugate the rebellion in Kuan-chung.' The King of Lang-ya believed him, thought [his suggestion] right, and galloped west to see the King of Ch'i. The King of Ch'i with Wei P'o and others thereupon detained the King of Lang-ya and sent Chu Wu to mobilize all [the troops] of the kingdom of Lang-ya; then [the King of Ch'i] united [them with his own troops and] led its troops [together with his own].

"When the King of Lang-ya, Liu Tse, saw that he had been deceived and could not return to his kingdom, he said to the King of Ch'i, 'King Tao-hui of Ch'i, [your father], was the oldest son of the Emperor Kao-[tsu]; by rights then you, great King, are the

而西產祿等遣大將軍灌嬰將兵擊之嬰至滎陽使人諭齊王與連

和待呂氏變而共誅之太尉勃與丞相平謀以曲周侯酈商子寄與

祿善使人劫商令寄給說祿曰高帝與呂后共定天下劉氏所立九

王呂氏所立三王皆大臣之議事已布告諸侯王諸侯王以爲宜今

太后崩帝少足下不急之國守藩廼爲上將將兵留此爲大臣諸侯

and the others sent the General-in-chief, Kuan Ying, with troops, to attack him. When [Kuan] Ying reached Jung-yang, he sent people to inform the King of Ch'i that he was going to ally himself with him, waiting until the Lü clan made a move, and then they would all together execute them.

The Grand Commandant, [Chou] P'o, together with the Lieutenant Chancellor, [Ch'en] P'ing, plotted, making use [of the fact that Li] Chi, the son of the Marquis of Ch'ü-chou, Li Shang, was on good terms with [Lü] Lu, and sent people who kidnapped [Li] Shang and ordered [Li] Chi to speak falsely to [Lü] Lu, saying, "Emperor Kao-[tsu] and the Empress [née] Lü together subjugated the world. The establishing of the nine kings from the Liu clan and of the three kings from the Lü clan was a matter all [done as a result of] deliberation by the great officials; when announcement and information [was made] to the vassal kings, the vassal kings considered it suitable.[1] Now the Empress Dowager is dead, and the Emperor is young. If your honor 6a does not quickly go [away] to your kingdom and act as a feudatory, but remain here as First [Ranking] General directing your troops, you will be suspected by the great officials and the nobles. Why do you not quickly return your general's seal, turn over your troops to the Grand Commandant, ask the King of

heir and the first grandson of Emperor Kao-[tsu]. You ought to be seated [on the throne]. Now the great officials are hesitating in their discussions [concerning the succession] and have not yet reached a decision, while I, Tse, am the oldest of the Liu family. The great officials will of course wait for me, Tse, before coming to a decision in their deliberations. Now you, great King, are detaining me, your servant, uselessly. It would be better to send me through the Pass to deliberate on this matter.' The King of Ch'i thought he was right, so prepared for him the necessities and chariots and sent off the King of Lang-ya. When the King of Lang-ya had gone, [the kingdom of] Ch'i thereupon set in motion its troops, went westwards, and attacked the Chi-nan [Commandery] of the kingdom of Lü."

[1] I.e., the government was not an absolute monarchy; the emperor acts only with the approval of his important subordinates.

Liang, [Lü Ch'an], also to return the Chancellor of State's seal, make a solemn oath with the great officials, and then go to your kingdoms? [Then] the troops of Ch'i will certainly be disbanded, the great officials will be at rest, your honor will sleep soundly, and you will rule as king over [a region of] a thousand *li*. This [act] would be a benefit for ten thousand generations."

[Lü] Lu agreed to his plan and sent people to inform [Lü] Ch'an together with the elders of the Lü [clan]. Some thought it disadvantageous. While they deliberated and hesitated and had not resolved upon anything, [Lü] Lu, who had confidence in [Li] Chi, went out on a trip[1] together with him, and passed by [the house of] his paternal aunt, Lü Hsü. [Lü] Hsü became angry and said, "You have been made a general, yet you abandon your army. The

6b Lü clan will now have no [place] to dwell." Then she took out all her pearls, jade, and precious objects, and scattered them around below the [main] hall, saying, "I will not keep them for others [to enjoy]."

Sept. 26　In the eighth month, on [the day] *keng-shen*,[2] the Marquis of P'ing-yang, [Ts'ao] Cho, who was

所疑何不速歸將軍印以兵屬太尉請梁王亦歸相國印與大臣盟

而之國齊兵必罷大臣得安足下高枕而王千里此萬世之利也祿

然其計使人報產及諸呂老人或以爲不便計猶豫未有所決祿信

寄與俱出游過其姑呂嬃嬃怒曰汝爲將而棄軍呂氏今無處矣迺

悉出珠玉寶器散堂下曰無爲它人守也八月庚申平陽侯窋行御

---

[1] The *SC* says that they went hunting; the *Tzu-chih T'ung-chien* follows it, while the *Han-chi* follows the *HS*.

[2] There was no *keng-shen* day in the eighth month; the *Tzu-chih T'ung-chien K'ao-yi*, by Ssu-ma Kuang (1019–1036), 1 : 5b, says that the text should read, "the ninth month," for although *SC* 9 : 11a (*Mh* II, 434) also reads "the eighth month *keng-shen*," yet previously (*Mh* II, 429) it reads "the eighth month *ping-wu*," and the days *keng-shen* and *ping-wu* cannot be in the same month here. Then this date is Sept. 26, 180 B.C. Chavannes reached the same Julian date (*Mh* II, 434), but by emending the previous date, not this one. The *SC* says in addition that it happened "in the morning." It also gives the impression that Ts'ao Cho overheard part of a conversation not intended for his ears.

史大夫事見相國產計事郎中令賈壽使從齊來

因數產曰王不早之國今雖欲行尚可得邪具以

灌嬰與齊楚合從狀告產平陽侯窋聞其語馳告

丞相平太尉勃勃欲入北軍不得入襄平侯紀通

尚符節廼令持節矯內勃北軍勃復令酈寄典客

performing the duties of the Grandee Secretary,[1] visited the Chancellor of State, [Lü] Ch'an, concerning the [yearly] accounts. The Chief of the Gentlemen-at-the-Palace, Chia Shou, had come from Ch'i, [to which he had been sent as] an envoy, and took advantage [of the opportunity] to reprove [Lü] Ch'an, saying, "You, King, have not quickly gone to your kingdom; now even though you should want to go, would it be still possible?" [Then] he described and told [Lü] Ch'an all about Kuan Ying uniting as an accomplice with [the kingdoms of] Ch'i and Ch'u.[2] When the Marquis of P'ing-yang, [Ts'ao] Cho, heard his speech, he galloped[3] [off] and informed the Lieutenant Chancellor, [Ch'en] P'ing, and the Grand Commandant, Chou P'o.

[Chou] P'o wanted to enter [the camp of] the Northern Army, but was not permitted to enter. The Marquis of Hsiang-p'ing, Chi T'ung-[chia], was Master of the Credentials, so [Chou P'o] ordered **7a** him to [get and] bear a credential which would fraudulently admit[4] [Chou] P'o to the Northern Army. [Chou] P'o next ordered Li Chi and the

---

[1] According to 19B: 5b, Ts'ao Cho became Grandee Secretary in 184 B.C. and was dismissed in 180 B.C. In that year an edict commanded the Lieutenant Chancellor of Huai-nan, Chang Ts'ang, to take his place; probably at this time Ts'ao Cho was merely acting for his successor who had been appointed, but had not yet taken up his duties. HS 42: 4b says that he was dismissed after the killing of the Lü clan, which Wang Hsien-ch'ien thinks is an erroneous statement, because at the time of Liu Heng's arrival in the capital on Nov. 14, Chang Ts'ang is already mentioned as Grandee Secretary (cf. 4: 3a).

[2] The SC (Mh II, 434) adds at this point, "He urged [Lü] Ch'an to hasten into the palace."

[3] The Sung Ch'i ed. says that the Shao ed. (xi or xii cent.) reads 以 for 馳.

[4] Reading 納 for 內, as in the passages on p. 7b, at the suggestion of Ch'ien Ta-chao.

Director of Guests, Liu Chieh, to say to [Lü] Lu, "The Emperor has sent the Grand Commandant to take charge of the Northern Army.   He intends to order your honor to go to your state.   Hasten to return your general's seal, resign,[1] and leave.   If you do not do so, misfortune will immediately come of it." [Lü] Lu thereupon took off his seal,[2] confided it to the Director of Guests, and thus handed his troops over to the Grand Commandant, [Chou] P'o.

[Chou] P'o entered the gate of the Army's [encampment] and issued his orders in the Army, saying, "Those who are for the Lü clan bare the right [arm]; those who are for the Liu clan bare the left [arm]."   In the Army [the soldiers] all bared their left [arms].[3]   Thereupon [Chou] P'o took control of the Northern Army.

However there was still the Southern Army.[4]

---

[1] The Sung Ch'i ed. says that the Southern ed. (ca. x-xii cent.) reads 綬 for the present 辭 and omits the words for "general".

[2] The SC (Mh II, 435) adds that Lü Lu did not think that Li Chi would deceive him.

[3] This phrase "bare the left arm" has become an idiom.

[4] Wu Jen-chieh (ca. 1137–1199) writes, "According to ch. 23, [at] the capital there were the encampments of the Southern and Northern Armies.   Although the Southern and Northern Armies of Han [times] were called two comparable armies, really the Southern Army was not the equal of the Northern Army.   Emperor Kao-[tsu] sent forth 30,000 troops of the Palace Military Commander.   When Wang Wen-shu was Palace Military Commander, he begged permission to replace the soldiers who had been lost, and secured several tens of thousands of men.   The roster of the Northern Army then must be said to have been large.   But when Kai K'uan-jao was Major of the Guard, the soldiers of the guard [the patrol inside the capital, cf. 19 A: 22b; 77: 1a] numbered not more than several thousand men.   Hence the military policy of the Han [dynasty] always stressed the Northern Army.   When Chou P'o had once entered the Northern Army, Lü Ch'an and his confederates could only fold their hands and meet death.   When the Heir-apparent Li [of Emperor Wu] did not secure help from the Northern Army, he was finally defeated by the Lieutenant Chancellor's troops.   [Cf. Glossary sub Liu Chü].   The general nature of the power of the two armies can thus be seen."

Wang Hsien-ch'ien (1842–1918) adds, "Hu [San-hsing, 1230-1287], in his comment on the [Tzu-chih] T'ung-chien, [says that] according to Pan [Ku's] Table [19A: 22b] the Colonel of the Capital Encampment [cf. Mh II, 521, XVIII, 1°] takes charge of

南軍丞相平召朱虛侯章
佐勃勃令章監軍門令平
陽侯告衞尉毋內相國產
殿門產不知祿已去北軍
入未央宮欲爲亂殿門弗

The Lieutenant Chancellor, [Ch'en] P'ing, sum- **7b**
moned the Marquis of Chu-hsü, [Liu] Chang, to
assist [Chou] P'o. [Chou] P'o ordered [Liu] Chang
to superintend the gates of the army's [encampment]
and ordered the Marquis of P'ing-yang, [Ts'ao Cho],
to inform the Commandant of the [Palace] Guards
not to admit[1] the Chancellor of State [Lü] Ch'an
at the gate of the [Front] Hall.[2] [Lü] Ch'an did
not know that [Lü] Lu had already given up the
Northern Army, [so] entered the Wei-yang Palace,
intending to create a sedition, [but the guards at]

[everything] inside the gates of the encampment of the Northern Army. There was
also a Palace Military Commander who took charge of patrolling the capital. His
subordinates were [the Colonel] of the Capital Encampment, the Pretors of the
Waters, and others, both chiefs and assistants. At the time of the Later Han [dynasty],
there were first established the Palace Captains at the Northern Army, having charge
of the five encampments. The commentator Liu [Chao, (fl. dur. 502–556), in a note
to *HHS*, Tr. 27: 7b] says that formerly there was the Colonel of the Capital Encampment commanding affairs within the encampment of the Northern Army. After
the Revival [23–25], the [Colonel of] the Capital Encampment was abolished, [but]
there were however established Palace Captains to superintend the five encampments. [Each palace had its encampment]. In addition, according to Pan [K'u's]
Table [19 A: 23a], after [the discussion of the Colonel of] the Capital Encampment
there [are mentioned] eight Colonels, all of whom were first established by the Emperor
Wu. According to my notion, before [the time of] the Emperor Wu, the Northern
Army was under the Palace Military Commander, hence he commanded the Chief of
the Capital Encampment, his assistants and other officers.

"The Southern Army was probably governed by the Commandant of the [Palace]
Guards [cf. Glossary *sub voce*]. According to Pan [Ku's] Table, the Commandant of
the [Palace] Guards had charge of the soldiers encamped as a guard to the palace
gates. When Chou P'o had entered the Northern Army, 'there was still the Southern
Army.' So he first sent Ts'ao Cho to inform the Commandant of the [Palace] Guards
not to admit Lü Ch'an at the gate of the [Front] Hall [in the Wei-yang Palace], and
afterwards sent the Marquis of Chu-hsü, [Liu Chang], to pursue [Lü] Ch'an and kill
him in the official's privy of the Gentlemen-of-the-Palace's quarters in the Wei-yang
Palace. According to this [account], we know that the Southern Army was under the
Commandant of the [Palace] Guards."

[1] Cf. p. 205, n. 4.

[2] This Front Hall was the hall of audience in the Wei-yang Palace; the imperial
apartments were there.

the gate of the [Front] Hall would not admit him. As he walked back and forth irresolutely, the Marquis of P'ing-yang, [Ts'ao Cho], galloped [off] and told the Grand Commandant, [Chou] P'o. [Chou] P'o still feared that [his party] would not be victorious, [so] dared not yet make a public announcement[1] to execute him, but spoke to the Marquis of Chu-hsü, [Liu] Chang, saying, "Hasten into the Palace to guard the Emperor." [Liu] Chang asked [Chou] P'o for a thousand soldiers, and entered the Wei-yang Palace by a side gate. He met [Lü] Ch'an in the court. It was late afternoon.[2] Thereupon he attacked [Lü] Ch'an, and [Lü] Ch'an fled. [There came] a great wind from Heaven and his retinue became panic-stricken, [so that] none of them dared to fight, [with the result that Liu Chang] pursued [Lü] Ch'an and killed him in the privy of the official's house connected with the office of the Gentlemen-of-the-Palace.[3]

When [Liu] Chang had killed [Lü] Ch'an, the Emperor ordered an Internuncio, bearing a credential, to congratulate [Liu] Chang.[4] [Liu] Chang

[1] The *SC* writes 訟 言; the *HS* reads the first word as 誦, which Wei Chao (197–273/4) and Teng Chan (fl. ca. 208) interpret as 公. Cf. *Mh* II, 436, n. 1.

[2] The Sung Ch'i ed. reports that the Yüeh ed. (prob. xi or xii cent.) and the Shao ed. (xi or xii cent.) omit 日. The fact that the sun was declining was probably taken as an approval by Heaven of this destruction.

[3] Ju Shun (fl. dur. 221–265) says that according to 19 A: 5a the Chief of the Gentleman-at-the-Palace controlled the gates and doors to the Palace in general and the Hall, hence his office was inside the Palace. *HS* 50: 5b speaks of a "chief in the office 署 of the Gentlemen-of-the-Palace," which Wang Hsien-ch'ien thinks was this place. The Han dynasty's palace as a whole was called a 宮; within it was the Front Hall 前 殿, the Forbidden Apartments 禁 中, the *Tung-ko* 東 閣 (p. 132, n. 2), the Harem 後 宮, etc.

[4] Yen Shih-ku says that he wanted to make kind inquiries.

中府吏舍廁中章已殺產帝令謁者持節勞章章
擊產產走天大風從官亂莫敢鬬者逐產殺之郎
勃請卒千人入未央宮掖門見產廷中日餔時遂
敢誦言誅之廼謂朱虛侯章曰急入宮衞帝章從
俳個往來平陽侯馳語太尉勃勃尚恐不勝未

欲奪節謁者不肯章廼從與載因節信馳斬長
樂衞尉呂更始還入北軍復報太尉勃勃起拜
賀章日所患獨産令已誅天下定矣辛酉殺呂
祿荅殺呂頾分部悉捕諸呂男女無少長皆斬
之大臣相與陰謀以爲少帝及三弟爲王者皆

wished to take his credential [from him, but] the Internuncio was unwilling [to part with it]. Then [Liu] Chang went with him in his carriage. By using his credential [as] a passport [allowing him entrance], he galloped [to the Ch'ang-lo Palace] and beheaded the Commandant of the [Palace] Guard at the Chang-lo [Palace], Lü Keng-shih. He returned, **8a** entered the Northern Army, and reported back to the Grand Commandant, [Chou] P'o. [Chou] P'o arose, bowed to [Liu] Chang in congratulation, and said, "The only one I was worried about was [Lü] Ch'an. Now that he has been executed the empire has been made stable [again]."

On [the day] *hsin-yu*,[1] they killed[2] Lü Lu and **Sept. 27** beat to death Lü Hsü. Dividing themselves into detachments, they arrested all the Lü clan, male and female, without [making any distinction of] youth or age, and beheaded them all. The great officials and chancellors planned together secretly; because they considered that the Young Emperor and the kings his three younger brothers[3] were all [in reality]

[1] The day after the one in which the preceding events, including the murder of Lü Ch'an, happened. According to p. 204 n. 2, this was Sept. 27, 180 B.C.

[2] The Official ed. (1739) writes "beheaded 斬" for the 殺 in the text.

[3] This was the second "Young Emperor"; the first one was Hsiao-hui's natural child and had been imprisoned to death by the Empress Dowager in 184 B.C.; the second Young Emperor was Lü Hung. His three supposed younger brothers were (1) the Marquis of Chih, Lü Chao, who had succeeded Lü Heng as King of Heng-shan, (2) the Marquis of Hu-kuan, Lü Wu, who had become the King of Huai-yang, and (3) the Marquis of Chang-p'ing, Lü T'ai, who had become King of Lü. (The *SC* [cf. *Mh* II, 441] speaks of the King of Liang, but Liang is a mistake for Lü. At that time the King of Liang had been Lü Ch'an.) The name of the place, Lü, was changed to Chi-ch'uan 濟川, so that Lü T'ai is also called the King of Chi-ch'uan.

not sons of [the Emperor] Hsiao-hui, [the great officials and chancellors] together executed them and honored and established Emperor Wen [upon the throne]. An account [of all the foregoing] is in the "Memoir of Chou P'o" and the "[Memoir of] the Five Kings [who were Sons of] Kao-[tsu]."

40 : 23 b
38 : 6a, b

In eulogy we say: During the times of [Emperor] Hsiao-hui and the Empress of Kao-[tsu], the world had succeeded in putting behind it the sufferings [during the period of] Contending States. Both ruler and subjects sought for effortlessness.[1] Hence although Emperor Hui folded his hands[2] and the Empress of Kao-[tsu], a female lord, assumed the rule and governed without going out of the doors to her apartments, yet the world was quiet, [mutilating] punishments and [other] penalties were seldom used, the people were busy in sowing and harvesting, and clothing and food multiplied and were abundant.

[1] Cf. p. 186 n. 1, *ad fin.*
[2] Possibly alluding to Ts'ao Ts'an's phrase, "Your Majesty sits with unruffled garments and folded hands." Cf. p. 186 n. 1, *ad fin.* Much of this eulogy is taken from the corresponding passage in *SCHC* 9 : 37f; cf. *Mh* II, 442.

CHAPTER III

THE ECLIPSES DURING THE REIGN OF THE EMPRESS OF KAO-TSU

i. Two eclipses are recorded during this period of eight years. In the second year, the sixth month, on the day *ping-hsü*, the last day of the month, a solar eclipse is recorded (3: 3a). The *Han-chi* (6: 2a) notes this eclipse in the sixth month without giving any day. The date in the *HS* corresponds to July 26, 186 B.C., but there was no eclipse at that time.

In the seven years from the last total eclipse in the reign of Emperor Hui, in 188 B.C., to the next total eclipse of 181 B.C., 15 eclipses occurred, of which only one was visible in China.[1] This umbral eclipse is Oppolzer's number 2434, on May 6, 184 B.C., 15 days before a *ping-hsü* day; calculation of its circumstances shows that it merely reached a magnitude of 0.08 in the present Soochow at 8:48 a.m., local time, a magnitude of 0.05 at the present Changsha at 8:08 a.m., and was invisible in northern China, including Ch'ang-an.

The explanation of this eclipse recording is not easy. It is possible that the eclipse of 184 B.C. was observed at Wu (present Soochow) or Lin-hsiang (present Changsha). But at both of those places the eclipse was little more than a mere contact. At Wu it began at 8:12 and ended at 9:04, lasting 48 minutes; at Lin-hsiang it lasted from 7:48 to 8:16, only 28 minutes. It was unobservable except by special means, such as watching the reflection of the sun in water or in a mirror in order to reduce its glare. A patient astronomer who knew that the eclipse was expected or some farmer accidentally seeing the sun reflected in a flooded rice-field might have seen the eclipse. The Administrator of the Commandery might have then considered it important and have reported

---

[1] Besides those whose location Oppolzer gives, the following 4 partial eclipses were invisible in China because they belong to initial or terminal runs of exeligmos series whose nearest umbral eclipse was located near the south pole: no. 2430 (i.), no. 2431 (t.), no. 2439 (i.), and no. 2440 (t.). In addition, 4 partial eclipses were visible in the northern hemisphere, but calculation shows that all were invisible in China: no. 2428, on Dec. 31, 187 B.C. was far outside of Chinese territory. No. 2429, on May 28, 186 B.C. was invisible south of 60° lat. No. 2437, on Oct. 19, 183 B.C. was visible only as far east as European Russia and western Siberia. No. 2438, on Mar. 15, 182 B.C., was located far outside of Chinese territory.

the eclipse to the capital. The cyclical day of the eclipse, *ping-tzu*, might have been mistaken for *ping-hsü*. The whole procedure however involves so many hardly probable events that it seems better to reject this eclipse as unobservable.

Then how did this listing of an eclipse come to be made? It is not found in the *SC*; the *SC* likewise does not record the total eclipse of 188 B.C., which the *HS* has recorded correctly. It is possible that some eclipse outside of this period of seven years was mistaken for this one; if so, the order of the listed eclipses has somehow been disarranged. Thus it might have been the eclipse of Sept. 29, 192 B.C.; indeed, if that is the case, we can say that all the eclipses from 194 to 175 B.C. were recorded. There is however no other reason for adopting this date.

The juxtaposition of this eclipse in the "Annals" with an earthquake, the death of a pretended child of Emperor Hui, Pu-yi, a flood, and a star seen in daytime (3: 3a, b) make it look as though someone thought that an eclipse was due because of the Empress Dowager's actions, and inserted it into the annals Pan Ku was using to supplement the *SC*. The latter does not have any of these five calamities, although it elsewhere records the death (with a different month) in its "Tables" (17: 8b). If this listing is an insertion, I do not think that we can blame it upon Pan Ku; the great exactness of the *HS*'s list of eclipses in the latter half of Former Han times and his rejection of the eclipse listed in 157 B.C. just before the death of Emperor Wen (cf. ch. 4: App. III, vi), shows that Pan Ku did not unwarrantly insert eclipses into his *History*.

Possibly some particularly bold government official manufactured this eclipse to express his dislike of the Empress Dowager's rule and reported it. If so, his deed, if detected, would have brought him capital punishment; during the reign of Emperor P'ing, Kung-sun Hung was accused of having falsely reported a lesser calamity—that a fire had damaged government buildings—and was imprisoned and executed (cf. 100A: 5b). The report of a calamitous visitation was felt as a reflection upon the government, and was dangerous. Since at that time there was much criticism of the Empress Dowager's actions, some official might however have ventured to memorialize an eclipse. At that time the Han officials did not lack bravery. The foregoing seems the best explanation of this eclipse.

ii. In the seventh year, the first month, on the day *chi-ch'ou*, the last day of the month, a total eclipse is recorded (3: 4b). *HS* 27 Cb: 13b adds, "It was 9 degrees in [the constellation] Ying-shih [whose stars were then in 319.3° and 320.2° R.A.], [which constellation] is [taken to represent] the interior of the Palace chambers. At that time the

APPENDIX

Empress of Kao-[tsu] showed aversion from it and said, 'This is for me.' The next year it was fulfilled," when the Empress Dowager died in the next year. It was indeed dramatic that the only solar eclipse total in Ch'ang-an for centuries should have come just before the death of the Empress Dowager.

Hoang's calendar gives this date as March 4th, 181 B.C., for which Oppolzer lists his solar eclipse no. 2441. Computation of this eclipse shows that it was total in Ch'ang-an at 2:52 p.m., local time, although Oppolzer and Ginzel calculate the umbral path as passing through central China. The SC 9: 7b says, "In daytime it became dark." The sun was in longitude 340.7° = 342.3° R.A.

CHAPTER IV

INTRODUCTION

Pan Ku, in writing these annals of Emperor Wen's reign, was very conscious of the fact that he was also writing many Treatises and Memoirs which deal with the same period. He wished to avoid undue repetition, so put much of the material dealing with this period into those Treatises and Memoirs that naturally required it. He makes cross-references to the most important of those accounts. These Annals are accordingly not a complete account of the reign, but rather the annalistic background to a much longer history, together with an account of those events that do not fit better into the Treatises or Memoirs. Thus the great raid of the Huns in 166 B.C. is barely mentioned, for a full account is given in the "Memoir on the Huns." For a reader who has an adequate knowledge about the period, such as that to be gained from the Treatises and the Memoirs, this chapter sums up the period very well, since it sets every important event in its chronological relations, even though it does not always point out the significance of each event. This chapter should accordingly be read, not as an attempt at writing a modern history of the period, but for what it was intended to be—an account of Emperor Wen together with a mention of the important events in the reign, which account is part of a much longer history that treats elsewhere of special subjects and of the important personages mentioned therein. For a partial summary of those events and personages, the reader is referred to the notes and the Glossary.

* * *

The chief source for this chapter was chapter X of the *SC*, which deals similarily with Emperor Wen's reign. That chapter has not however come down to us without changes. Into it there has been interpolated the eulogy from this chapter of the *HS* (cf. p. 272, n. 1); other changes may also have been made. Pan Ku however had the original of that chapter. He did not follow it slavishly; some material in it has been transferred to the relevant Treatises in the *HS*, for example the account of the circumstances leading up to the abrogation of the law considering wives and children as accomplices to a crime (cf. 4: 5b) and to the abolition of mutilating punishments (cf. 4: 14b). In other cases, material

214

has been added. The *SC* omits altogether any mention of years *Ch'ien* IV, V, VII, VIII, IX, X, XI, XII, and *Hou* III, IV, V; the *HS* chronicles events in each of these years. Some interesting edicts have also been added, as for instance the ones on 4: 7a, b, and on 16b, 17a. Sometimes deliberate corrections have been made in the *SC* account. The long discussion concerning the appointment of an heir-apparent (4: 5b–6b) is given in the *SC* as a *conversation* between the Emperor and his officials; the *HS* quotes it as an exchange of *written* memorials and edicts. We know that the imperial court kept in its files duplicates of all imperial edicts, in order to check any forged edicts; cf. Glossary, *sub* Tou Ying. Pan Ku had access to the imperial records and probably compared the *SC* versions of these imperial edicts with the copies in the court files. Thus from them he added the statement that this discussion was taken from written, not oral documents. This change thus shows his care and faithfulness to his sources.

Pan Ku probably also had available some sort of annals kept at the imperial court, which listed such events as the Emperor's travels in and out of the Palace and also portents, eclipses, drouths, earthquakes, deaths of emperors, empresses, vassal kings, lieutenant chancellors, etc. The material in the *HS* annals for the years omitted in the *SC* account can be traced to such annals and to what would be found in the imperial edicts of those years. These palace annals were probably distinct from the source from which was taken the chronological record of officials in part B of chapter 19, for this record and the rest of the *HS* partly duplicate, usually supplement, and occasionally contradict each other. Pan Ku's chapter on Emperor Wen is thus not a copy of the chapter in the *SC*, but an independent composition, which took that chapter of the *SC* as its principal source, copying it verbatim where it did not need correction, because that was the best means of securing an accurate record, just as the *SC* had previously copied its source material. Sources were not mentioned by either author, for history was not written to credit sources, but to give facts.

* * *

Emperor Wen came to the throne under exceptionally favorable circumstances, for he was *chosen* for the place by the most influential persons in the empire, who consequently took the responsibility for him. Hsiao-hui, Kao-tsu's heir, together with Hsiao-hui's descendants, had all died; the attempt of the Empress Dowager *née* Lü to continue her family's influence by enthroning spurious sons of Hsiao-hui had been frustrated by the action of Kao-tsu's immediate followers, who were her high officials. After the massacre of the Lü clan, the high officials and the leaders of the imperial clan gathered in conclave at the capital. Liu Chiao, Kao-tsu's sole surviving brother, was old and possibly ill, for he died the next year. He remained in his kingdom of Ch'u. The other leaders of the clan were all there: the wife of Liu Po, Kao-tsu's oldest brother, who was the chief priestess in the ancestral worship, the wife of Liu Chung, Kao-tsu's next oldest brother, and Kao-tsu's cousin, Liu Tse, the oldest active male member of the clan. The choice lay between Liu Hsiang, King of Ch'i, the oldest son of Kao-tsu's oldest son, and Liu Heng, King of Tai, Kao-tsu's oldest living son. The latter was chosen, because his mother's family had not the unpleasant reputation possessed by that of Liu Hsiang. Primogeniture was thus considered as merely an important, but not a necessary requirement for the succession.

Liu Heng showed the proper reluctance to accept the throne and was duly installed. He was personally a modest and unaffected young man in his twenty-second year, who had already reigned as King of Tai to the seventeenth year.

His character is perhaps best shown in his edicts, which deserve to rank among the greatest official pronouncements of all time. Pan Ku esteemed them highly, for he quoted them extensively. The edict ordering the cessation of prayers for the Emperor's personal happiness (4: 15b), that on the peace with the Huns (4: 17a, b), and the very remarkable testimentary edict (4: 19a–21a) are especially noteworthy.

Emperor Wen accepted whole-heartedly the Confucian doctrine that the ruler exists for the welfare of his subjects and put that doctrine into practise. He reduced the taxes and lightened the burdens of the people, economizing in his personal expenses and avoiding any grand displays. One later story is that he even attended court wearing straw sandals! He asked the people for criticism of his rule (in his case this request was sincerely meant) and he sought for capable commoners to assist in the administration. He ordered the various divisions of the empire to recommend their best men to the imperial court, and selected amongst them by a written examination. These recommendations and examinations seem not however to have occurred regularly, but only when there was a special imperial call. Emperor Wen stressed agriculture by his personal example in the sacred field and by his edicts, and was much worried by famine and scarcity, even going so far as to abolish the land tax on cultivated fields (soon revived by his successor). While he was thus personally a Confucian in his belief and government, he was no bigot. He established Erudits for the non-Confucian philosophies; candidates studied these philosophies as well as the Confucian teachings; Chia Yi was at first the only Confucian Erudit at his court (cf. 36: 32b). Yet as a result of Emperor Wen's personal influence, Confucianism was given such a preponderant influence that the prohibition by Emperor Wu in 141 B.C. of non-Confucian philosophies was a natural consequence.

During this reign, the Huns began making serious inroads after having been quiescant during the preceding two short reigns. Kao-tsu had had trouble with them, and had made peace with them, cementing it by sending a princess of the imperial family to be a wife of the Hun emperor, the *Shan-yü*. In 177 B.C. the Huns invaded the Chinese borders and occupied Ordos. After the death of Mao-tun, the greatest *Shan-yü*, which happened soon after 174 B.C., the Huns, in the winter of 167/6 B.C., made their greatest raid. Hsiao-wen's pacifistic policy of economizing seems to have left him without adequate defense or they found a lightly defended road around his defenses; led by the *Shan-yü*, thousands of Hun horsemen came south through the passes in the present eastern Kansuh, down the Chien and Wei River valleys, where they burnt the Hui-chung Palace, and rode to Kan-ch'üan, in sight of Ch'ang-an. Emperor Wen immediately made strenuous efforts for defence, and the Huns left. In 162 B.C. peace was made with them, but in the winter of 159/8 they raided again. During this period there were thus begun the sporadic invasions by the Huns which were to lead to the military expeditions of Emperor Wu.

The only rebellion during this period was that of Liu Hsing-chü, King of Chi-pei, who believed himself inadequately rewarded for having previously taken the lead in eliminating the power of the Lü clan. This rebellion was quickly put down. It made Chia Yi realize the danger of vassal kingdoms, and he advised the Emperor to divide up the great fiefs in order to weaken their power. Emperor Wen rejected his advice, but in 164 B.C. he quietly began putting it into effect, dividing up two kingdoms among nine scions of their kingly families. This policy was continued, urged by Chao Ts'o, and led to the rebellion of the Seven States in the next reign. Eventually this policy so enfeebled the power of the imperial clan that Emperor Wu could at one stroke dismiss with impunity half of the marquises who were members of the imperial clan.

The superstitious practises which were to deface Emperor Wu's reign likewise began with Emperor Wen. He was doubtless a personally devout man who accepted the universal belief that the gods could be influenced by certain practises. The periodic famines natural to north China were thought to come from the anger of the gods; Emperor Wen, in his efforts to aid his people, was thus drawn into special religious practises for the cultivation of the divine favor upon his people. In

166 B.C. he increased the sacrifices. Adventurers took advantage of this religious propensity: Kung-sun Ch'en and Hsin-yüan P'ing encouraged him to extend the imperial worship and formulated the new rites required. The latter person led the Emperor into other superstitious practises, making a yellow dragon appear, hiding and dramatically finding a jade cup inscribed, "Prolongued life to the Lord of Men," and also hiding a three-legged cauldron at Fen-yin, which, when found, would appear to be a lost cauldron of the Chou dynasty. He conducted an unsuccessful search for it; it came to light only much later, in 113 B.C., when it made a great stir. He is said to have seen the sun twice at its zenith on the same day, and as a consequence to have induced Emperor Wen to begin again the numbering of the years of his reign. Although Hsin-yüan P'ing's deceits were discovered and he was executed in 164 B.C., the precedent had been set of an emperor favoring those who could bring special favors from the gods or spirits. Emperor Wu brought it to fruition.

Emperor Wen's reign was thus a period of beginnings: of the Confucian influence, of trouble with the Huns, of the division of fiefs, and of important imperial superstition. It was the first really long reign in the dynasty and it established many of the practises of the dynasty. It was thus natural that this Emperor should have been posthumously entitled the Great Exemplar of Emperors.

Personally Liu Heng was an admirable, though not entirely perfect character. He is generally considered to have been one of the best rulers of China. He showed genuine statesmanship. Thus he ended the desultory war and rebellion of the kingdom of Nan-yüeh without any fighting: he found in north China the cousins of its ruler, Chao T'o, made large gifts to them and cared splendidly for the tomb of Chao T'o's parents, then, in a tactful letter, he set forth satisfactory boundaries for Nan-yüeh and told its ruler that there could not be two emperors in the world. Chao T'o promptly changed his own title from that of Emperor to King and acknowledged himself a subject of Emperor Wen. The latter had so arranged matters that by so doing Chao T'o would gain much and lose nothing except an empty title and a tribute which was repaid by gifts from the imperial court. Thus Liu Heng strove by all means to maintain peace.

He honestly worked for the best interests of his people and set their advantage above his own. He sought for and accepted even the severest criticism. He discouraged corruption and restrained the severity of his officials, so that capital punishment became a rare thing. He ameliorated the severities of the law, abolishing mutilating punishments and other unnecessary cruelties. He established old-age pensions. Hence the country became prosperous and there were made the accumulations of wealth and population which enabled Emperor Wu to conquer the surrounding world. Emperor Wen tried to maintain an even-handed justice, even getting his mother's younger brother, Po Chao, who had been responsible for the murder of an imperial attendant, to commit suicide. Yet he does not seem to have punished his own Heir-apparent, Liu Ch'i, when the latter killed his cousin, Liu Hsien, in a drunken dispute over precedence while gambling. While Liu Heng seems to have been a morally admirable, yet slightly weak character, it is only his due that he has been extravagently admired ever since.

CHAPTER IV

THE FOURTH [IMPERIAL ANNALS]

THE ANNALS OF [EMPEROR HSIAO-]WEN

爺定代地立爲代王都中
曰薄姬高祖十一年誅陳
孝文皇帝高祖中子也母
文紀第四
漢書四

Emperor Hsiao-wen was a son of Kao-tsu, nei-ther the oldest nor the youngest. His mother was called the Concubine[1] [*née*] Po. In the eleventh 196 B.C. year of Kao-tsu,[2] [Emperor Kao-tsu] executed Ch'en Hsi, pacified the region of Tai, and made [his 1b son Heng[3]] the King of Tai, with his capital at

---

[1] She is entitled here a *yi* 姬. Fu Tsan (fl. ca. 285) writes, "The *Han Ch'ih-lu Ling* [prob. written in Han times, now lost] and the *Mao-ling-shu* [lost before 312] both [say that the *yi* was] an official in the court, ranking as equivalent to a position of two thousand piculs, in position next below the Favorite Beauty [cf. Glossary *sub voce*] and above the Eighth [Rank] Ladies 八子 [fourth rank concubines]." Yen Shih-ku (581–645) says that *yi* is merely a complimentary term for 'concubine', not an official title, for *HS* 97A: 2a enumerates the ranks in the imperial harem, but does not mention any rank *yi*. Ju Shun (fl. dur. 189–265) says, "姬 is pronounced 怡 *yi²* and is a common term for the ordinary concubines," on which statement Ch'ien Ta-chao (1744–1813) remarks, "At the time of the Six Dynasties [265–618], people called their fathers' concubines *yi²*, which is this word. But they did not know that 姬 had the pronunciation *yi²*, hence they changed the writing [of the word] to 姨." Li Tz'u-ming (1829–1894) adds, "姬 meaning concubine has one signification; [the same word] meaning a surname is a different signi-fication. These two significations have the different pronunciations [*yi* and *chi*]. [Fu] Tsan's explanation was based upon the official documents of his [own] time; how could he have imaginatively fabricated it?" Ch. 97 also uses *yi* as a title; the mother of Em-peror Ching's heir was at first styled the *Yi née* Wang. For names of persons, places, and official titles, cf. the Glossary.

[2] Cf. 1B: 17a. Ch'en Hsi was not killed until the end of 196 B.C., in the twelfth year, but Liu Heng was made King of Tai in Feb./Mar. 196 B.C., in the eleventh year.

[3] The Sung Ch'i ed. reports that the Yüeh ed. (xi–xii cent.) contains the words 子恒, which have been translated in brackets. Ch'i Shao-nan (1703–1768) says that the Academy ed. (1124) also contains these words, but that the Sung Ch'i ed. (xi or xii cent.) does not. He says that these words are not original, because the annals of an emperor do not use his given name, since it became taboo when he ascended the throne.

180 B.C. Chung-tu. In the seventeenth year [of Liu Heng's
Aug. 18 reign as King of Tai], in the autumn, the Empress of
Kao-[tsu] died. The [members of] the Lü [clan]
plotted to make a rebellion, wishing to endanger the
Liu clan, [but] the Lieutenant Chancellor, Ch'en
P'ing, the Grand Commandant, Chou P'o, the Marquis
of Chu-hsü, Liu Chang, and others together executed
them, [then] planned to set up the King of Tai, [Liu
Heng, as the next emperor]. A discussion [of the
3:5b-8a foregoing matters] is found in the "Annals of the
Empress of Kao-[tsu]" and in the "Memoirs of the
38:3b-6b Five Kings [Who Were Sons of] Kao-[tsu]."

The great officials thereupon sent some people to
invite the King of Tai to come. His Chief of the
Gentlemen-at-the-Palace, Chang Wu,[1] and others
discussed [the matter] and all said, "The great officials of the Han [court] were all generals of the time
of the deceased Emperor Kao-[tsu], are experienced
in military affairs, and [use] many stratagems and
deceits. Their intentions [may] not stop with this
[proposal]. They feared only the majesty of the
Emperor Kao-[tsu] and the Empress Dowager [*née*]
Lü. Now they have executed the [members of the
Lü [clan] and have newly tasted blood[2] in the

都
十
七
年
秋
高
后
崩
諸
呂
謀
爲
亂
欲
危
劉
氏
丞
相
陳
平

太
尉
周
勃
朱
虛
侯
劉
章
等
共
誅
之
謀
立
代
王
語
在
高
后

紀
高
五
王
傳
大
臣
遂
使
人
迎
代
王
郎
中
令
張
武
等
議
皆

曰
漢
大
臣
皆
故
高
帝
時
將
習
兵
事
多
謀
詐
其
屬
意
非
止

此
也
特
畏
高
帝
呂
太
后
威
耳
今
已
誅
諸
呂
新
喋
血
京
師

---

[1] Chang Wu later became a general against the Huns. Chief of the Gentlemen-at-
the-Palace was the title given him after Liu Heng had ascended the throne as Emperor (cf. 4:4b), but the vassal courts had functionaries with the same titles as those
used in the imperial court, so that Chang Wu might possibly have had this title in the
state of Tai before he went to the capital.

[2] Those bound together by an oath sealed the oath by annointing their lips with the
blood of a victim. Cf. *Mh* II, 414, n. 1; *SC* ch. 76. The *SC* ch. 10 writes *ch'ieh-hsüeh* 啑血
and the *HS* writes *tieh-hsüeh* 喋血. The two phrases have the same meaning. There are
however two interpretations of this phrase. (1) Chavannes (*Mh* II, 414 & n. 1), following
Yen Shih-ku, translates the phrase "march in blood." Fu Ch'ien (ca. 125–195) says, "喋
should be pronounced *tieh*, the *tieh* meaning 'to trample on,'" and Ju Shun says, "When,
in killing people, a vast amount of blood is shed it is *tieh-hsüeh*," so that Yen Shih-ku
seemingly has grounds for his statement. (2) Nevertheless Chou Shou-ch'ang (1814–
1884) writes, "In my opinion, *tieh* is itself the *tieh* [in the phrase] *ch'ieh-tieh* 唪喋. It
is used in *HS* ch. 57 and the commentator says, 'It means the noise made by fowl when

以迎大王爲名實不可信願稱疾無往以觀其變中尉

宋昌進曰羣臣之議皆非也夫秦失其政豪桀並起人

人自以爲得之者以萬數然卒踐天子位者劉氏也天

下絕望一矣高帝王子弟地犬牙相制所謂盤石之宗

也天下服其彊二矣漢與除秦煩苛約法令施德惠人

capital. They use [this] invitation to you, great King, as a pretext; in reality they cannot be trusted. We hope that you will announce yourself ill and not go [to the capital], in order to watch their moves."

The Palace Military Commander [of Tai], Sung 2a· Ch'ang, stepped forward and said, "The opinion of the courtiers is wrong. When the Ch'in [dynasty] lost its control, braves and heroes arose together, each one [of whom] thought he would obtain [the imperial throne]—they could be counted by the ten thousands. Nevertheless the person who finally mounted the throne of the Son of Heaven was of the Liu clan. [These ambitious people of] the world have given up any hopes [of attaining that throne. The foregoing is] the first point.

"The Emperor Kao-[tsu] made kings of his sons and kinsmen. Their territories interlock like the teeth of a dog;[1] they are what may be called, 'being founded on a rock.'[2] The world has submitted to their power. [The foregoing is] the second point.

"When the Han [dynasty] arose, it did away with the vexatiousness and harshness of the Ch'in [dynasty], reduced [the number of] their laws and ordinances,[3] and showed its virtue and bounty.[4]

---

eating.' Its derived meaning is *tieh-hsüeh*, and it is interpreted 'to taste with the mouth.' *SC* ch. 90 says *tieh-hsüeh* and the *Shih-chi Chi-chieh* [written by P'ei Yin, fl. 465–472] quotes Hsu Kuang (352–425) [as saying], '*Tieh* is also written *ch'ieh*,' which is sufficient proof that these two characters were originally interchanged. But 蹀 [which Fu Ch'ien used to give the pronunciation of *tieh*, and which Yen Shih-ku and Chavannes misunderstood to give the meaning of *tieh*] has the radical 足, and Hsü Shen [fl. 100] interprets it as 'trample.' So 蹀 cannot be written as 喋." Then *tieh-hsüeh* does not mean "to march in blood." Wang Hsien-ch'ien (1842–1918) approves of Chou Shou-ch'ang's interpretation.

[1] I.e., irregularily interlocking. Cf. *Mh* II, 445, n. 2.

[2] The Chinese figure of speech is quite parallel to the Jewish figure used in the translation. The figure implies that the establishment of the dynasty is as secure as if it were held down by a large mill-stone. Cf. *Mh* II, 445, n. 3.

[3] Cf. 1A : 20a, b.

[4] A quotation from 1A : 30b, which passage explains it.

Everyone is satisfied, and it would be hard to move or shake [them from their allegiance to the Han dynasty. The foregoing is] the third point.

"Moreover, although, by means of her power, the Empress Dowager [*née*] Lü established three kings from the Lü [clan] and arrogated to herself the [imperial] power, [issuing imperial] decrees on her own authority, yet when the Grand Commandant [Chou P'o] by means of one credential entered the Northern Army and once gave a call, the soldiers all bared their left arms[1] [to show that they were] for the Liu clan, rebelled against the Lü [clan], and finally, for this reason, exterminated [the Lü clan]. This [triumph] then was bestowed by Heaven, it was not [achieved] by human power. Although the great officials should now wish to do something else [than seat as emperor a scion of the Liu clan], the people would not permit themselves to be used by them; how could their faction [seize] the sole power? Inside [the capital] there are your relatives, [the Marquis of] Chu-hsü, [Liu Chang], and [the Marquis of] Tung-mou, [Liu Hsing-chü]; outside [the capital they would have to] fear the power of [the kingdoms of] Wu, Ch'u, Huai-nan, Lang-ya, Ch'i, and Tai.[2] Just now of the sons of the Emperor Kao-[tsu], there are only the King of Huai-nan [Liu Ch'ang] and yourself, great King. You, great King, are moreover the elder [of the two]. Your ability, your sageness, your paternal love, and your filial piety are known all over the world; hence the great officials are following the hopes of the world in desiring to welcome and establish you, great King, [on the imperial throne]. You, great King, should not have any doubts."

大王大王又長賢聖仁孝聞於天下故大臣因天下之心而欲迎立大
盧東牟之親外畏吳楚淮南琅邪齊代之彊方今高帝子獨淮南王與
授非人力也今大臣雖欲爲變百姓弗爲使其黨寧能專一邪內有朱
太尉以一節入北軍一呼士皆袒左爲劉氏畔諸呂卒以滅之此乃天
人自安難動搖三矣夫以呂太后之嚴立諸呂爲三王擅權專制然而

---

[1] Cf. 3: 7a.

[2] The King of Wu was Liu P'i, a first cousin of Liu Heng; the King of Ch'u was Liu Chiao, his uncle; the King of Huai-nan was Liu Ch'ang, his half-brother; the King of Lang-ya was Liu Tse, a cousin; the King of Ch'i was Liu Hsiang, a nephew; Tai was his own kingdom.

王大王勿疑也代王報太后計
猶豫未定卜之兆得大橫占曰
大橫庚庚余爲天王夏啓以光
代王曰寡人固已爲王又何王
平卜人曰所謂天王者乃天子

The King of Tai reported [the matter] to his Queen Dowager. They discussed it, [but] hesitated and did not reach a decision. [Then] they divined about it by means of the tortoise-shell. The lines obtained[1] were the 'great transversal.' The interpretation was:

> "The 'great transversal' [means] a great change. **2b**
> I [the recipient of the oracle] will be the Heavenly King.
> [Emperor] Ch'i of the Hsia [dynasty] thereby [likewise] glorified [his ancestors by continuing the dynasty]."[2]

The King of Tai said, "I am of course already a king; how could I again be made a king?" The diviner replied, "By this phrase, 'the Heavenly King,' is [meant] however the Son of Heaven."

---

[1] Ying Shao (fl. ca. 140–206) says, "When a tortoise [is used], [divination] is called 兆; when stalks of plants [are used], it is called 卦. In divination by the tortoise one uses a rod to make the tortoise-[shell] glow; the lines were exactly transversal."

[2] These three lines rime and are each of four characters. They seem to be a passage quoted from an ancient and lost book of divination in which this response is mentioned as having been given to King Ch'i of the Hsia dynasty. That there were other books of divination using the hexagrams besides the ones that have come down to us is shown by a tablet of the first cent. B.C., containing an interpretation of one of the hexagrams, which interpretation is not found in *Book of Changes* (cf. Chavannes, *Documents chinois decouverts par Aurel Stein*, p. 25). The last word of the first line should be pronounced *kang* to complete the rime. Karlgren, *Analytic Dictionary*, 316, gives the T'ang pronunciation *kang*. The meaning of the first line is obscure. Fu Ch'ien (ca. 125–195) says that the last two characters mean "crosswise." Chang Yen (prob. iii cent.) says, "Transversal lines [mean] 'there was not a thought but did him homage' [*Book of Odes* III, 1, x, 6, (Legge, p. 463)]. *Keng* 庚 is 更 to change. It says that he should leave [the condition of] a noble and ascend the imperial throne. Before this time, when the Five Emperors ruled the world and [became] aged, they resigned [the throne] to a capable [person]. In the time of [Emperor] Ch'i of the Hsia [dynasty], [the son of the great Yü], for the first time [a father] passed on his title [to his son, Emperor Ch'i], and was moreover able to rule gloriously over the patrimony founded by his deceased lord. Emperor Wen also succeeded to the heritage of his father. It says that he is one like [Emperor] Ch'i." Cf. *Mh* II, 447, n. 1.

Chavannes remarks that in the *Tso-chuan*, the phrase "the Heavenly King 天王" always refers to the son of Heaven of the Chou dynasty. Cf. *Mh* II, 447, n. 2.

Thereupon the King of Tai then sent Po Chao, the younger brother of his Queen Dowager, to see the Grand Commandant, [Chou] P'o. [Chou] P'o and the others told him all their reasons for inviting and seating the King [of Tai on the imperial throne.[1] Po] Chao returned and reported, "They are indeed trustworthy. There is nothing suspicious." The King of Tai laughingly said to Sung Ch'ang, "It is really as you, sir, said." Then he ordered Sung Ch'ang to be his Chariot Companion, Chang Wu and others, six persons in all, to ride in six 'riding chariots,'[2] and went to Ch'ang-an.

When he came to Kao-ling, he stopped and sent Sung Ch'ang ahead to Ch'ang-an to observe how things had turned. When [Sung] Ch'ang reached the Wei [River] Bridge, all [the officials, including] the Lieutenant Chancellor and [those ranking] below [him], welcomed [Sung] Ch'ang. He returned and 3a reported; then the King of Tai advanced to the Wei [River] Bridge. [There] the officials bowed and paid their respects to him, calling themselves his subjects. The King of Tai got down [from his carriage] and bowed to them. The Grand Commandant, [Chou] P'o, advanced and said, "I wish to beg for a word in private." Sung Ch'ang replied, "If what you have to say is of public [interest], say it publicly; if what you have to say is of private [concern], a [true] king has no private [interests]." The Grand Commandant [Chou] P'o then knelt and offered the imperial seal [and credentials[3]] of the Son of Heaven. The

間宋昌曰所言公公言之所言私王者無私太尉勃乃跪上天子璽代王謝
皆迎昌還報代王乃進至渭橋羣臣拜謁稱臣代王下拜太尉勃進曰願請
乘六乘傳詣長安至高陵止而使宋昌先之長安觀變昌至渭橋丞相已下
曰信矣無可疑者代王笑謂宋昌曰果如公言乃令宋昌驂乘張武等六人
也於是代王乃遣太后弟薄昭見太尉勃勃等具言所以迎立王者昭還報

[1] We have emended 者 to 意 in accordance with the suggestion of Wang Hsien-shen (1859–1922), for the SC reads the latter character and Yen Shih-ku uses it in his explanation, so that it was in his text. The reason the great ministers had for selecting Kao-tsu's younger son rather than his eldest grandson, the King of Ch'i, was that they feared the family of the wife of the King of Ch'i would cause such trouble as the Lü family had caused. Cf. Mh II, 439.

[2] Cf. p. 107, n. 3.

[3] The SC and the Tzu-chih T'ung-chien (1084) at this point adds the word 符; later

曰至邸而議之閏月己酉入代邸羣臣從至

上議曰丞相臣平太尉臣勃大將軍臣武御

史大夫臣蒼宗正臣郢朱盧侯臣章東牟侯

臣與居典客臣揭再拜言大王足下子弘等

皆非孝惠皇帝子不當奉宗廟臣謹請陰安

King of Tai refused them and said, "Let us go to the prince's lodge[1] and discuss this matter."

In the intercalary month on [the day] *chi-yu*,[2] [the Nov. 14 King of Tai, Liu Heng,] entered the prince's lodge of Tai. The courtiers followed him to [the lodge]. Thoy presented [the results of] their discussion, saying, "The Lieutenant Chancellor your subject [Ch'en] P'ing, the Grand Commandant your subject [Chou] P'o, the General-in-chief your subject [Kuan Ying[3]], the Grandee Secretary your subject [Chang] Ts'ang, the Superintendent of the Imperial House your subject [Liu] Ying-[k'o], the Marquis of Chu- **3b** hsü your subject [Liu] Chang, the Marquis of Tung-mou your subject [Liu] Hsing-chü, and the Director of Guests your subject [Liu] Chieh, making repeated obeisances, say to your Highness the great King: the [Imperial] Sons [Lü] Hung and the others are all not sons of Emperor Hsiao-hui and have no right to have charge of [the worship in] the [imperial] ancestral temples. Your subjects have

in this passage (p. 4a) the *HS* also has it; hence it was originally in the text here, according to Wang Hsien-ch'ien.

[1] Yen Shih-ku says, "The sojourning quarters at the capital for those at court from commanderies or kingdoms are usually named 邸 [the princes' lodges]. This word [means] to arrive, meaning the place to which one comes." Cf. *Mh* II, 412, n. 1.

[2] This was 48 days after the Lü family had been exterminated.

[3] The text writes at this point Wu. The *SC* 10: 3b writes Ch'en Wu 陳武. Fu Ch'ien (ca. 125–195) says this is Ch'ai Wu 柴武, for on p. 12a, Ch'ai Wu is said to have been made Commander-in-chief in 177 B.C. In the passage corresponding to p. 12a, the *SC* and the *Han-ti Nien-chi* (before 275) both write Ch'en Wu; Fu Tsan (fl. ca. 285) says that he had two surnames.

But Ch'en (or Ch'ai) Wu did not become General-in-chief until three years after this time. Lü Ch'an had made Kuan Ying General-in-chief and sent him to attack the army of Ch'i; he however revolted against the Lü family and joined the Liu cabal; cf. 3: 5b. Hence he is the person who had this title at this time and should be mentioned here. Because he was appointed by the Lü family, who were usurpers, he is not mentioned in the table of officials in 19B: 6b. In the distribution of rewards (cf. 4: 5a, b) "General Kuan Ying" was awarded a territory of 3000 families and the equivalent of 2000 catties of gold. Hence we are fairly safe in following Ch'ien Ta-chao in saying that the *HS* has made a slip here.

respectfully begged the Marquise of Yin-an, the Queen of King Ch'ing,[1] the King of Lang-ya [Liu Tse], the marquises, and the officials [ranking at] two thousand piculs to discuss [this matter, and we all say]: You, great King, are the son of the Emperor Kao-[tsu] and are the proper [person] to be his successor. We hope that you, great King, will take the throne of the Son of Heaven."

The King of Tai replied, "The upholding [of the worship] in the Temple of Emperor Kao-[tsu] and the [imperial] ancestral temples is a weighty matter.

4a I am lacking in ability and am not the person suitable [for this task]. I hope that you will ask the King of Ch'u [Liu Chiao][2] to consider who is suitable. I personally do not dare to undertake [this task]."

侯頃王后琅邪王列侯吏二千
石議大王高皇帝子宜爲嗣願
大王卽天子位代王曰奉高帝
宗廟重事也寡人不佞不足以
稱願請楚王計宜者寡人弗敢

---

[1] The SC So-yin (by Szu-ma Cheng, fl. 713–742) says that Su Ling (fl. 196–227), Hsü Kuang (352–425) and Wei Chao (197–273/4) think that the Marquise of Yin-an and the Queen of King Ch'ing were different persons; Ho Ch'uo (1661–1722) and Wang Hsien-ch'ien (1842–1918) agree, because the SC, by adding the words "the Marquis" before the name of King Ch'ing makes it plain that they were two persons. Szu-ma Cheng explains that King Ch'ing, Liu Chung, was, at his death, merely a marquis, since he had resigned his kingdom. (Cf. Mh II, 449, n. 2.) Su Ling says that the Marquise of Yin-an was "the wife of Kao-tsu's eldest brother, Liu Po, and the mother of [Liu Hsin, who was] the Marquis of Keng-chieh," and that the Queen of King Ch'ing was "the wife of Kao-tsu's elder brother, Liu Chung." HS 36: 2a also tells that the mother of Liu Hsin, the Marquis of Keng-chieh, was the wife of Liu Po. Ju Shun however identifies this Marquise and the Queen as the same person. He says, "When the Queen of King Ch'ing was appointed as the Marquise of Yin-an, Lü Hsü was the Marquise of Lin-kuang and the wife of Hsiao Ho was also the Marquise of Tso. Moreover the Table of marquises of the imperial family [ch. 15] has no Marquis [or Marquise] of Yin-an for this period, so that we can thereby know that she was the Queen of King Ch'ing. In my opinion the chief priestess [in the ancestral sacrifices] at the Han [temple] was the Marquise of Yin-an, the wife of Emperor Kao-[tsu's] older brother." It is however possible that the absence of this marquise's name from the table of marquises is because of her sex; we have followed the majority of the commentators in considering them as two persons. Chavannes disagrees.

[2] Liu Chiao, a younger brother of Kao-tsu, was the then oldest male member of the imperial family. Cf. Mh II, 450, n. 1. He was not mentioned in the memorial asking Liu Heng to take the throne, probably because he was ill and not in the capital. Ho Ch'uo says that this request to consult Liu Chiao is according to the proprieties, for "the Marquise of Yin-an [the wife of Kao-tsu's oldest brother] and the Queen of King Ch'ing [the wife of Kao-tsu's second older brother] were both women and the King of Lang-ya, [Lin Tse], was a distant relative."

當羣臣皆伏固請代王西鄉讓者三南鄉讓者再丞

相平等皆曰臣伏計之大王奉高祖宗廟最宜稱雖

天下諸侯萬民皆以爲宜臣等爲宗廟社稷計不敢

忽願大王幸聽臣等臣謹奉天子璽符再拜上代王

曰宗室將相王列侯以爲其宜寡人寡人不敢辭遂

While all the courtiers prostrated themselves and insistently begged him, the King of Tai, [Liu Heng, then] facing the west, refused thrice, and, when facing the south, refused twice.[1] The Lieutenant Chancellor, [Ch'en] P'ing, and the others all said, "Your subjects have humbly deliberated over this [matter]. You, great King, are the most suitable and capable [person] to receive [charge of] the Temple of Kao-tsu and the [imperial] ancestral temples. Even though the nobles and the people of the world all consider you suitable, we, your servants, who have been planning for the sake of the [dynasty's] ancestral temples and the [dynasty's] gods of the soils and grains, have not dared to be careless. We hope that you, great King, will favor us by listening to your servants. Your servant, respectfully holding the seals and the credentials of the Son of Heaven, making repeated obeisances, presents them [to you]."

The King of Tai said, "If the imperial house, the generals, the chancellors, the kings, and the marquises consider that there is no one[2] more suitable than myself, I would not dare to refuse." Thereupon he took the throne of the son of Heaven.

[1] Ju Shun says, "Someone says that the seats of guest and host face east and west; the seats of prince and minister face south and north." Hu San-hsing (1230–1287) contradicts the opinion of Ju Shun (which Chavannes adopted, cf. *Mh* II, 450, n. 2) to the effect that Liu Heng, by turning towards the south, was showing himself more complaisant to his subject's wishes. He says, "Probably when the King entered the prince's lodge of Tai, the courtiers of the Han court followed and came to the King, and he treated them in accordance with the proprieties of guest and host, hence he faced west, and when the courtiers urged him to take a higher position, he refused thrice. The courtiers thereupon supported the King to a seat facing due south, [south is the direction the emperor's throne always faces], and the King again refused twice. Therefore the turning to the south was not what the King could help, but the courtiers, supporting him, made him face south. If we assume that he eagerly seated himself facing the south, would that have been possible?"

[2] Reading 莫 for 其 in accordance with the *SC* and the suggestion of Wang Nien-sun (1744–1832).

The courtiers arranged themselves by him in accordance with their rank. They sent the Chief of the Stud, [Hsia-hou] Ying, and the Marquis of Tung-mou, [Liu] Hsing-chü, first to clear[1] the

4b palace. [Then] they presented the prescribed equipage for the Son of Heaven[2] and went to meet [the new Emperor] at the Prince's Lodge of Tai. The

Nov. 14 Emperor, on the same day, at sundown, entered the Wei-yang Palace.

That night he installed Sung Ch'ang as General of the Guards, commanding the Southern and Northern Armies, and Chang Wu as Chief of the Gentlemen-at-the-Palace. [The Emperor] walked through the [Palace] Halls, [then] returned and seated himself [on the throne] in the Front Hall, and issued an edict, which said, "An imperial edict of decree[3] to the Lieutenant Chancellor [Ch'en P'ing], the Grand Commandant [Chou P'o], and the Grandee Secretary [Chang Ts'ang]. In the interval [since the last legitimate ruler], the Lü [clan] has been directing affairs, arbitrarily assuming the [imperial] authority, and plotting to commit treason, [thereby] seeking to

丞相太尉御史大夫間者諸呂用事擅權謀
武爲郎中令行殿中還坐前殿下詔曰制詔
入未央宮夜拜宋昌爲衞將軍領南北軍張
居先清宮奉天子法駕迎代邸皇帝卽日夕
卽天子位羣臣以次侍使太僕嬰東牟侯興

---

[1] According to 38:7a, Liu Hsing-chü especially asked to go with Hsia-hou Ying and clear the palace. Ying Shao says, "According to the old code, to whatever place the Son of Heaven is to go and favor by visiting it, there must first be sent the Chief Forerunner 靜室令 [cf. *Han-kuan Ta-wen*, 3: 11b] to go and investigate, to clear and pacify the [Palace] Hall in order to take precautions against untoward events." According to the SC (cf. *Mh* II, 440 f), the Young Emperor was still living in the forbidden apartments of the palace, and had to be ejected. He was moved to the apartments of the Privy Treasurer and killed later in the night after Emperor Wen had taken the throne.

[2] Ju Shun says, "The prescribed equipage is with the Palace Attendants, the [imperial] Chariot Companion, and the [Chief Commandant] Custodian of the [Imperial] Equipages and the Gentlemen driving 36 auxiliary carriages."

[3] The Sung Ch'i ed. reports that the Ching-te ed. (1004–1005) does not have the words 制詔. The SC also does not have them nor the three titles following them. These titles have probably the same significance as the titles in the edict on 1B: 17b, 18a.

為大逆欲危劉氏宗廟賴將相列侯宗室大臣

誅之皆伏其辜朕初卽位其赦天下賜民爵一

級女子百戶牛酒酺五日

元年冬十月辛亥皇帝見于高廟遣車騎將軍

薄昭迎皇太后于代詔曰前呂產自置爲相國

endanger the ancestral temples of the Liu clan. Thanks to the generals, the chancellors, the marquises, the imperial house, and the great ministers, [the Lü clan] have been executed and have all suffered for their crimes.[1] We have newly ascended the throne. Let there be an amnesty [granted] to the world and let there be granted to the common people one step in [noble] rank and to the women of a hundred households an ox and wine, and [let there be universal] drinking for five days."[2]

5a

In his first year, in the winter, the tenth month, on [the day] *hsin-hai*, the Emperor was presented in the temple of Kao-[tsu].[3] He sent the General of Chariots and Cavalry Po Chao to go to the Empress Dowager at Tai and invite her [to come to the capital].

I
Nov. 16

An imperial edict said, "Formerly Lü Ch'an set himself up as Chancellor of State, [set up] Lü Lu

---

[1] Cf. *Mh* II, 124, n. 1.

[2] It has been debated just who these women were. Yao Ts'a (533–606) thinks that they were the wives of those who were granted ranks. Li Hsien (651–684) thinks they were families of women which had no male members: in those families which had males, the head of the family was given a rank; to those families which had no males, meat and wine were given. But Shen Ch'in-han (1775–1831) replies that there would be few families without male members, so that it would be difficult to divide an ox among them. No amount of meat and wine is specified; in *SC* 28: 32b it is said, "To a hundred families, one ox and 10 piculs of wine." Cf. *Mh* II, 503. Possibly the emperor wanted everyone to enjoy himself, so, as Su Lin (fl. 196–227) said, "To the men were granted noble ranks [Yen Shih-ku explains that the head of the household received the step; 2: 4a says that one step in rank was given to a family] and to the women were granted an ox and wine [for the families to enjoy]." This practise was later common, cf. 6: 27a, 32a, 36a, etc. Cf. *Mh* II, 452, n. 1.

Wen Ying (fl. ca. 196–220) says, "[According to] the Han Code, when three or more people gather to drink wine without [adequate] motive, they shall be fined [the equivalent of] four taels of gold." The Emperor's edict permitting drinking was then an extraordinary privilege. Cf. *Mh* II, 452, n. 2. The Sung Ch'i ed. reports that the Nan ed. (ca. x–xii cent.) and the Chekiang ed. (xi–xii cent.) read 餔 instead of 酺.

[3] This was the second day after the emperor had entered the capital and taken the throne. The presentation in the imperial ancestral temple was an important feature of the coronation.

as First [Ranking] General and unauthorizedly sent General Kuan Ying with troops to attack [the army of] Ch'i, wishing to substitute [the Lü clan] for the Liu clan.　[Kuan] Ying remained at Jung-yang and planned in unison with the nobles to execute the Lü clan. Lü[1] Ch'an wished to do evil things, [but] the Lieutenant Chancellor [Ch'en] P'ing together with the Grand Commandant [Chou] P'o and others planned to snatch away the army of [Lü] Ch'an and the others.　The Marquis of Chu-hsü,

5b [Liu] Chang, was at the head [of the cabal] and first arrested and beheaded [Lü] Ch'an; the Grand Commandant [Chou] P'o in person led the Marquis of Hsiang-p'ing, [Chi] T'ung, who held a credential and bore a [false] imperial edict [ordering Chou P'o] to enter [and take command of] the Northern Army.[2]　The Director of Guests [Liu] Chieh took away Lü[3] Lu's seal.　Let there be added to the estate of the Grand Commandant [Chou] P'o ten thousand households and [let him be] granted [the equivalent of] five thousand catties of gold; to the estate of the Lieutenant Chancellor [Ch'en] P'ing and of General [Kuan] Ying each [let there be added] three thousand households and [let them be granted the equivalent of] two thousand catties of gold; to the estates of the Marquis of Chu-hsü, [Liu] Chang, the Marquis of Hsiang-p'ing, [Chi] T'ung, [and the Marquis of Tung-mou, Liu Hsing-chü],[4] to each [let there be added] two thousand households and [let them be granted the equivalent of] a

諸侯合謀以誅呂氏呂產欲爲不善丞相平與太尉勃等謀奪產

呂祿爲上將軍擅遣將軍灌嬰將兵擊齊欲代劉氏嬰留滎陽與

等軍朱虛侯章首先捕斬產太尉勃身率襄平侯通持節承詔入

北軍典客揭奪呂祿印其益封太尉勃邑萬戶賜金五千斤丞相

平將軍嬰邑各三千戶金二千斤朱虛侯章襄平侯通邑各二千

[1] The Sung Ch'i ed. reports that the Nan ed. (x–xii cent.) and the Chekiang ed. (xi–xii cent.) omit the surname here.

[2] For these events, cf. 3: 5b ff.

[3] The Sung Ch'i ed. reports that the Nan ed. and the Chekiang ed. omit the surname here.

[4] The *SC* at this point adds "of the Marquis of Tung-mou, Liu Hsing-chü." *HS* 38: 6b also states that Liu Hsing-chü was made the same grant as Liu Chang; those six words seem to have dropped out of the *HS* text.

下人民未有厭志今縱不能博求天下賢聖有德之人

所以尊宗廟也詔曰朕既不德上帝神明未歆饗也天

地皆歸之盡除收帑相坐律令正月有司請蚤建太子

幽王子遂為趙王徙琅邪王澤為燕王呂氏所奪齊楚

戶金千斤封典客揭為陽信侯賜金千斤十二月立趙

thousand catties of gold. Let the Director of Guests [Liu] Chieh be appointed as the Marquis of Yang-hsin and be granted [the equivalent of] a thousand catties of gold."

In the twelfth month, [the Emperor] made [Liu] Sui, the son of King Yu of Chao [Liu Yu], the King of Chao. He had shifted the King of Lang-ya, [Liu] Tse, to be the King of Yen.[1] The territory that the Lü clan had taken away from [the kingdoms of] Ch'i and Ch'u was all returned to [those kingdoms].[2]

[The Emperor] completely abrogated all the statutes and orders for the arresting of wives and children and punishing them with [the criminal].[3]

In the first month the [high] officials begged [the Emperor] to name his Heir-apparent soon, so as to honor the ancestral temples. His imperial edict read, "Since We are without virtue, the Lords on High and the gods have not enjoyed Our sacrifices[4] [to them] and the people of the empire have not satisfied their desires. Now even if I cannot search through the empire thoroughly for the [most] capable, sage, and virtuous man [to whom I might] resign the empire,[5]

179 B.C. Jan./Feb.

Feb./Mar.

6a

---

[1] The *SC* dates this appointment on Nov. 15, two months previously. Possibly the *HS* mentions it now because of its importance in connection with the enlarging of Ch'i and Ch'u. Cf. n. 2.

[2] Wang Ch'i-yüan (xix cent.) says, "Liu Tse's kingdom, Lang-ya, was a commandery taken from Ch'i; when Lü T'ai was made King of Lü with P'eng-ch'eng as his kingdom, [his territory] was taken from Ch'u. Now the Lü family had been executed, the kingdom of Lü ended, and the appointment of [Liu] Tse shifted too, hence this territory was returned to Ch'i and Ch'u, to which it had previously [belonged]." Cf. 38: 6b.

[3] Cf. *Mh* II, 454–455. The long edict in the *SC* accompanying this abrogation has been transferred in the *HS* to ch. 23. Ying Shao says, "帑 [means] children 子. According to the Ch'in [dynasty] laws, when a person committed a crime they joined with him [in punishment] his house and family. Now [the Emperor] abrogated this law." Cf. 5: n. 2.1. The practise nevertheless continued; cf. 5: 4a.

[4] The Sung Ch'i ed. reports that the Nan ed. and the Chekiang ed. do not have the character 也 at this point; Wang Hsien-ch'ien adds that these editions are correct, for the *SC* is also without this character.

[5] The Emperor was thinking of the example given by Yao and Shun, who each passed

yet, to speak of appointing my Heir-apparent beforehand is to double my lack of virtue.   What shall I
say to the empire [in justification of such an act]?
Be satisfied [with the present situation]."

The [high] officials replied, "To appoint an heir-apparent beforehand is the means whereby to be mind-
ful of the ancestral temples and the gods of the soils
and grains and not neglect the empire."   The Emperor
said, "The King of Ch'u [Liu Chiao] is my youngest
uncle; since he is advanced in years, he has seen much
of the justice and natural law of the world and has a
clear understanding of the constitution of the state.
The King of Wu [Liu P'i] is to Us as an older
brother.[1]   The King of Huai-nan [Liu Chang] is
[Our] younger brother.   All of them are embracing
virtue.   [If one of these three men] were made to
reinforce Us, would not that be adequate [provision
for upholding the ancestral temples and the gods]?
Among the vassal kings, the imperial house, my
older and younger brothers [and cousins], and my
meritorious subjects, there are many who are capable
and also virtuous and just; if you select one who is
virtuous to reinforce [Us] in doing what We cannot
accomplish, that would be a blessing from the gods
of the soils and grains and a [piece of] good fortune
for the empire.   Now you do not select and present
[one of them], but say that [the heir] must be [Our]
son, [so that] people will think that We have neglected the capable and virtuous, think only[2] of [Our]

而　建　太　之　豈　朕
嬗　太　子　義　爲　之
天　子　所　理　不　不
下　所　以　多　豫　能
焉　以　重　矣　哉　終
而　重　宗　明　諸　是
曰　宗　廟　於　侯　社
豫　廟　社　國　王　稷
建　社　稷　家　宗　之
太　稷　不　之　室　靈
子　不　忘　體　昆　天
是　忘　天　吳　弟　下
重　天　下　王　有　之
吾　下　也　於　功　福
不　也　上　朕　臣　也
德　曰　曰　兄　多　今
也　楚　季　也　賢　不
謂　王　父　淮　及　選
天　季　也　南　有　舉
下　父　春　王　德　焉
何　也　秋　弟　義　而
其　高　也　者　曰
安　閥　皆　若　必
之　天　秉　舉　子
有　下　德　有　人
司　　　以　德　其
曰　　　陪　以　以
豫　　　朕　陪　朕

---

over their children and appointed an able person from outside their family as their
successor.   But cf. *Mh* II, 455, n. 1.   The *SC* does not have the word 詔, so that
this passage appears there as a speech of the Emperor.   Probably this passage is taken
from an exchange of edicts and memorials.   It is then illuminating in that it shows the
manner of intercourse between the officials and the emperor.

[1] Liu P'i was actually a cousin of the Emperor.   He was the son of Liu Chung, an
older brother of Kao-tsu.

[2] The Sung Ch'i ed. reports that the Yüeh ed. reads 傳 for 專; Wang Hsien-ch'ien
adds that that edition is wrong, for the *SC* reads as the text does here.

爲忘賢有德者而專於子非所以憂天下也朕甚不取有司固請曰
古者殷周有國治安皆且千歲有天下者莫長焉用此道也立嗣必
子所從來遠矣高帝始平天下建諸侯爲帝者太祖諸侯王列侯始
受國者亦皆爲其國祖子孫繼嗣世世不絕天下之大義也故高帝
設之以撫海內今釋宜建而更選於諸侯宗室非高帝之志也更議

sons, which is not the way to care about the empire. We will certainly not adopt [this procedure]."

The [high] officials insistently begged [the Emperor], saying, "In ancient times, when the Yin and Chou [dynasties] possessed their states, good order and peace [reigned], and they both [lasted] for almost a thousand years. [The reason that] none of [the dynasties] who possessed the empire [lasted] as long [as they][1] is because they used this method. The source [of the practise] of always making one's successor a son is already very distant. Emperor Kao-[tsu], who first pacified the empire and established the nobles, is the Great Founder of emperors. The vassal kings and marquises who first received their kingdoms are also the founders for their kingdoms. Their sons and grandsons will succeed them from generation to generation without end. This is the greatest moral and political principle in the world. Hence Emperor Kao-[tsu] established [this principle] in order that they might [continue] to govern the whole world. Now to pass by one who is suitable to be appointed and select someone else from the nobles or the imperial house is not the will of Emperor Kao-[tsu]. To deliberate over a change [of the heir] is inappropriate. Your son Ch'i[2] is your eldest; he is sincere,[3] liberal, kind, and benevolent.

6b

---

[1] Cf. *Mh* II, 456, n. 2.

[2] Liu Ch'i was not the eldest son of the Emperor, for his first wife had had three sons, but she and her sons had all died before this time. Cf. *Mh* II, 496. Liu Ch'i later became the Emperor Ching. *SC* 10: 7a uses 某 for his given name, because of the taboo on it; the *HS* mentions the name here and uses the same word again on p. 9a. Yet in the chapter on the Emperor Ching and in its later annals the *HS* rarely uses this word. Cf. 6: 24a, 8: 13a. Su Yü (fl. 1913) remarks that in Pan Ku's time the emperor was only distantly related to the emperors of the Former Han period, hence taboos were no longer stressed. The foregoing is typical of the way Szu-ma Ch'ien and Pan Ku regarded the taboo on the personal names of emperors.

[3] The *SC* and the *Tzu-chih T'ung-chien* (1084) write 純厚; the *HS* and the *Han-chi* (ii cent.) write the first character of this phrase 敦.

We beg that you appoint him as your Heir-apparent." The Emperor thereupon consented [to do so]. Then he granted one step in noble rank to those people in the empire who would be the successors of their fathers. He appointed General Po Chao as Marquis of Chih.

Apr./May   In the third month, the [high] officials begged [the Emperor] to appoint the Empress. The Empress Dowager said, "[The Emperor] should make the mother of the Heir-apparent, [the lady] née Tou,[1] the Empress."

An imperial edict said, "Just now it is spring, when [nature] is harmonious, and the plants and trees and all living beings have means of enjoying themselves, yet [among] my subjects there are widowers, widows,

7a orphans, and childless, distressed and suffering people, and some at the point of death, but no one goes to look after their suffering. What should those who are the fathers and mothers of the common people[2] do [about this situation]? Let it be discussed what are the means to aid and lend to them."

[The edict] also said, "Unless the aged have silk,[3] they will not be warm; unless they have meat, they will not be well-nourished. Now at the beginning of the year,[4] if [We] do not at the right moment send

母將何如其議所以振貸之又曰老者非帛不煖非肉不飽今歲首
樂而吾百姓鰥寡孤獨窮困之人或阽於死亡而莫之省憂爲民父
曰立太子母竇氏爲皇后詔曰方春和時草木羣生之物皆有以自
爲父後者爵一級封將軍薄昭爲軹侯三月有司請立皇后皇太后
不宜子啓最長敦厚慈仁請建以爲太子上乃許之因賜天下民當

---

[1] In Chou times the Empress was chosen for different reasons; cf. *Mh* II, 458 & n. 1.

[2] The emperor and officials were supposed to be the fathers and mothers of the people. This phrase is used as early as the *Book of History*, V, iv, 16 (Legge, p. 333). This edict is merely summarized in the *SC*. Cf. *Mh* II, 458.

This edict of an emperor the Chinese have considered "truly virtuous" deserves to be contrasted with the legendary reaction of Gautama the Buddha to his "four encounters" (sickness, age, death, and the hermit). Hsiao-wen tried to relieve suffering; Gautama concluded it was inevitable. This edict probably initiated the practise of government loans to poor people.

[3] Cotton was not brought to China until later. Silk and linen (including hemp) were used for clothing.

[4] This sentence might seem to contradict the conclusion arrived at in 1: App. II.

不時使人存問長老又無布帛酒肉之賜將何以佐天下子孫孝養

其親今聞吏稟當受鬻者或以陳粟豈稱養老之意哉具為令有司

請令縣道年八十已上賜米八月一石肉二十斤酒五斗其九十已

上又賜帛人二疋絮三斤賜物及當稟鬻米者長吏閱視丞若尉致

不滿九十嗇夫令史致二千石遣都吏循行不稱者督之刑者及有

people to visit and ask about [the health of] the elders and aged, nor make grants of [linen] cloth, [plain] silk, wine, or meat [to these people], in what way can [We] assist the children and grandchildren of the empire in filial piety to care for their relatives?

"Now [We] have heard that officials when giving grain to those who should receive gruel[1] sometimes use stale millet. How can this befit the intention of caring for the aged? For all these matters [you should prepare] ordinances." The [high] officials begged that [the Emperor] order that [in the] prefectures and marches[2] those in their eightieth [year] and above should be granted per person per month one picul of rice, twenty catties of meat, five *tou*[3] of wine, and that those in their ninetieth [year] and above should also be granted per person two bolts of silk and three catties of silk wadding. For those to whom should be given goods or a grain allowance of gruel or rice, the chief officials[4] [of the prefecture] should supervise it and the Assistant [Prefect] or Chief of Police should transmit it. For those who are not fully ninety [years of age], the Inspector of Fields, the Prefect, or an official should transmit it. The [officials whose positions rank at] two thousand piculs should send their Director of Officials to travel about [inspecting]; those who are unworthy should be beaten.[5] To those who have suffered mutilating punishments together

7b

But the emperor is not here thinking of the calendar year, since the edict was issued in the "third month." He is thinking of the seasons, which were thought to begin with the spring.

[1] Yen Shih-ku says that 鬻 is thin congee 淖麋.

[2] Cf. Glossary, *sub* Ch'iang-tao.

[3] Cf. App. I.

[4] Cf. p. 88, n. 1.

[5] Wu Jen-chieh (ca. 1137–1199) writes that 督 has two meanings: in addition to its usual meaning "to examine" it is also used to mean "beat" and is interchanged with 殺. This beating was performed without baring the body. *HS* 76: 7b, col. 8 definitely establishes this meaning.

with those who have committed crimes [deserving
the punishment of] shaving the whiskers or more
serious [crimes],[1] this order should not apply.

8a
May/June [In this month] King Yüan of Ch'u, [Liu] Chiao,
died. In the fourth month there was an earthquake
in Ch'i and Ch'u. Twenty-nine mountains[2] collapsed on the same day and floods came out from
their sides or welled up.[3] In the sixth month [the
July/Aug. Emperor] ordered that the commanderies and kingdoms should not come [to the capital] to make offerings [of tribute]. He showed his grace to the world
and the nobles and the barbarians [of the] four
[quarters], both far and near, rejoiced and were
agreeable.

Then [the Emperor] provided for those meritorious
persons who came [with him] from [the kingdom of]
Tai. His imperial edict said, "At the time when the
great officials had executed the Lü [clan] and invited Us [to take the throne], We were hesitant and
suspicious like a fox.[4] All [Our officials] stopped
Us. Only [Our] Palace Military Commander, Sung
Ch'ang, urged Us [to go]. We have therefore[5]
been able to protect the [imperial] ancestral temples.
We have already elevated [Sung] Ch'ang to be General of the Guards. Let [Sung] Ch'ang be appointed

罪耐以上不用此令楚元王交薨四月齊楚地震
二十九山同日崩大水潰出六月令郡國無來獻
施惠天下諸侯四夷遠近驩洽乃脩代來功詔曰
方大臣誅諸呂迎朕朕狐疑皆止朕唯中尉宋昌
勸朕朕已得保宗廟已尊昌爲衛將軍其封昌爲

---

[1] Cf. p. 118, n. 1. Those aged who had committed more serious crimes than this
were not to receive any pension. The *SC* (*Mh* II, 458) states that orphans under their
ninth year were also to receive grants.

[2] HS 27Ca: 10a says, "In Ch'i and Ch'u there was an earthquake and mountains fell
in 29 places on the same day. All [of them] sent out high water which broke through
the sides up or welled up."

[3] Yen Shih-ku remarks, "To break through the side is 潰; to well up is 出."

[4] Yen Shih-ku says, "The fox in his character as an animal is by nature very suspicious. Every time he crosses a river on ice he listens as he crosses. Hence we talk of a
suspicious person and call him 'as suspicious as a fox.'" Cf. *Mh* II, 458, n. 2.

[5] Reading 以 for 已 with the *SC*, at the suggestion of Su Yü (xx cent.). He says
that these two characters were interchanged.

相蔡兼爲樊侯
戶封淮南王舅趙兼爲周陽侯齊王舅駟鈞爲靖郭侯故常山丞
食邑六百戶淮陽守申屠嘉等十八五百戶衛尉足等十八四百
十八人益邑各三百戶吏二千石以上從高帝潁川守尊等十八
壯武侯諸從朕六人官皆至九卿又曰列侯從高帝入蜀漢者六

as Marquis of Chuang-wu" and let the six officials who came with Us [be elevated] to [the rank of] the nine great ministers.[1]

[The edict] also said, "The marquises who followed the Emperor Kao-[tsu] into Shu and Han[2] were sixty-eight persons; for each [one of them let there be] added to their estates three hundred families. [Among] the officials [of positions ranking as worth] two thousand piculs and above who followed the Emperor Kao-[tsu, let there be given to] the Administrator of Ying-ch'uan, Tsun, and others, ten persons [in all], the income of six hundred families; to the Administrator of Huai-yang, Shen-t'u Chia, and others, ten persons [in all, the income of] five hundred families; to the Commandant of the [Palace] Guard, Tsu, and others, ten persons [in all, the income of] four hundred families." [The Emperor] appointed Chao Chien, the maternal uncle of the King of Huai-nan [Liu Ch'ang], as Marquis of Chou-yang, Szu Chün, the maternal uncle of the King of Ch'i [Liu Hsiang], as Marquis of Ching-kuo,[3] and **8b** Ts'ai Chien, the former Lieutenant Chancellor of the [former kingdom of] Ch'ang-shan, as Marquis of Fan.

In the second year, in the winter, the tenth month, II the Lieutenant Chancellor, Ch'en P'ing, died.[4] An Nov./Dec.

---

[1] Wang Hsien-ch'ien says that, because of the phrasing, the last clause of this sentence is not given in the original wording of the edict, but is a summary made by the historian. The *SC* has the same wording. For a list of the "nine great ministers" under the Han dynasty, cf. *Mh* II, 459, n. 2.

[2] Cf. 1A: 28a.

[3] Chavannes explains that because Emperor Wen had given his own maternal uncle, Po Chao, an appointment, he also appointed these other maternal uncles to avoid jealousy. Cf. *Mh* II, 460, n. 1. In spite of all his care, Liu Hsing-chü finally revolted.

[4] Ch'ien Ta-chao writes, "In [recording] the death of a Lieutenant Chancellor, the general rule is to record the day but not write his surname. Only for Ch'en P'ing and Kuan Ying the surname is written but the day is not written. For Shen-t'u Chia the day is not recorded. For Ti Fang-chin, both surname and day are written." *SC* 10: 8a adds that the Marquis of Chiang, Chou P'o, was made Lieutenant Chancellor.

imperial edict said, "We have heard that anciently the nobles, for whom there were established more than a thousand states,[1] each [actually] governed his own territory and at the [proper] time paid tribute [to the sovereign. Then] the people were not harassed or made to suffer; the superior and inferiors were content and rejoiced; there was no one who transgressed against[2] virtue. [But] now the marquises mostly live in Ch'ang-an, far from their estates,[3] [so that] their officials and retainers who transport [to them their taxes and provisions] are put to expense and suffering. Moreover the marquises have thus no means of instructing and teaching their people. Let it be ordered that the marquises are to go to their states. As to [those who are imperial] officials, together with those who are retained [at the court] by an imperial edict, they shall send their heirs-apparent [to their states]."[4]

178 B.C.   In the eleventh month, on [the day] *kuei-mao,*
9a the last day of the month, there was an eclipse of the
Jan. 2   sun.[5] The imperial edict said, "We have heard that when Heaven gave birth to the common people, it established princes for them to take care of and govern them. When the lord of men is not virtuous and his dispositions in his government are not equable, Heaven then informs him [of that fact] by a

聞之天生民爲之置君以養治之人主不德布政不均則天示
國爲吏及詔所止者遣太子十一月癸卯晦日有食之詔曰朕
安邑遠吏卒給輸費苦而列侯亦無繇教訓其民其令列侯之
其地以時入貢民不勞苦上下驩欣靡有違德令列侯多居長
二年冬十月丞相陳平薨詔曰朕聞古者諸侯建國千餘各守

---

[1] *SC* 10: 8a says instead that they "established their states for more than a thousand years." Cf. *Mh* II, 460.

[2] Cf. *Mh* II, 460, n. 3.

[3] Wang Ch'i-yüan (xix cent.) says, "The three imperial commanderies [the capital commandery, Tso-p'ing-yi, Yu-fu-feng] were not used for enfeoffing marquises. The nearest estates of the marquises were several hundred *li* from Ch'ang-an; the distant ones were then a thousand *li* or several thousand *li* [away]. Only the Kuan-nei Marquises had the income of towns in Kuan-chung."

[4] Chou Shou-ch'ang says, "[According to] the Han [dynastic] Code, the oldest sons of kings and marquises were all called 'Heirs-apparent' 太子; the mothers of the kings were called 'Dowager Queens' 太后; [these titles were] not necessarily [held only by the oldest son and mother] of the Son of Heaven."

[5] Cf. App. III.

方正能直言極諫者以匡朕之不逮因各敕以職任務省繇費以便

矣令至其悉思朕之過失及知見之所不及匄以啓告朕及舉賢良

執政猶吾股肱也朕下不能治育羣生上以累三光之明其不德大

宗廟以微眇之身託于士民君王之上天下治亂在予一人唯二三

之災以戒不治乃十一月晦日有食之適見于天災執大焉朕獲保

calamitous visitation, in order to forewarn him that he is not governing [rightly]. Now on the last day of the eleventh month there was an eclipse of the sun—a reproach[1] visible in the sky—what visitation could be greater?

"We have secured [the position as] guardian of the [imperial] ancestral temples; with a feeble and insignificant person [We] have been entrusted with a place above the educated[2] and common people and the princes and kings. The good or bad government of the world depends upon Ourself.[3] Even the two or three [persons] administering the government are like my legs and arms. Below Us, [We] have not been able to govern well and nurture the multitude of beings; above [Us, We] have thereby affected the brilliance of the three luminaries.[4] This lack of virtue has been great indeed.

"Wherever this order arrives, let all think what are Our faults and errors together with the inadequacies of Our knowledge and discernment. We beg that you will inform and tell Us of it and also present [to Us] those capable and good persons who are four-square and upright and are able to speak frankly and unflinchingly admonish [Us], so as to correct Our inadequacies. [Let] everyone be therefore diligent in his office and duties. Take care to lessen [the amount of] forced service[5] and expense in order to benefit the people.

[1] Yen Shih-ku says, "適 should be read as 謫, i.e., 'a reproach.'" Ho Ch'uo (1661–1722) remarks, "Ever since the Ch'in dynasty no awe had been felt at [events in] the sky; at the time of the Emperor Wen we first hear of this sort of speech." However the Empress née Lü was very much worried by a total eclipse; cf. 3: App., ii; *Mh* II, 423.

[2] Instead of 士 'educated people,' the *SC* has 兆 'million [people]'; 士民 may however be a compound noun, meaning merely 'people.'

[3] The phrase 予一人 was used by the Emperor of himself; its connotation was not that of praising the Emperor, as in the translation "I, the Unique Man," but "humble. He wants to say that the [Emperor's] own ability is equivalent to that of one person." *Po-hu-t'ung* (i or iii cent.), A:7b.

[4] Yen Shih-ku says, "The three luminaries are the sun, the moon, and the stars."

[5] Yen Shih-ku says that 繇 should be read as 傜.

"Since We are unable to [spread the influence of Our] virtue to distant [regions], with anxiety [We] reflect on the iniquitous conduct of foreigners,[1]
9b against whom, therefore, [We] have made preparations without ceasing. Now although [We] are unable to dismiss the encampments and garrison soldiers at the border, [need We] also be attentive to [Our personal] troops and make Our guard large?[2] Let the army of the General of the Guard[3] be abolished. Of the horses which the Chief of the Stud has now, [let] there remain just[4] enough; [let] all the remainder be given for the posts and post-horses."[5]

In the spring, the first month, on [the day] *ting-*
Feb. 15 *hai*,[6] an imperial edict said, "Now agriculture is the foundation of the world. Let the sacred field
10a be opened. We Ourself lead in plowing in order to provide millet and grain offerings for the [imperial] ancestral temple. Those people who are punished [and made to] work in the prefectural offices, together with those who have borrowed seed and food, and have not paid it back, and those who have not

以給宗廟粢盛民謫作縣官及貸種食未入入未
丁亥詔曰夫農天下之本也其開籍田朕親率耕
將軍軍太僕見馬遺財足餘皆以給傳置春正月
備未息今縱不能罷邊屯戍又飭兵厚衞其罷衞
民朕既不能遠德故惘然念外人之有非是以設

---

[1] Wang Hsien-ch'ien (1842–1918) says that 'foreigners' here refers to the Hu and Yüeh peoples, to the northwest and southeast of Central China respectively.

[2] Wang Hsien-ch'ien says that the last clause in this sentence refers to the troops and guard at the capital.

[3] The army at the capital, over which Sung Ch'ang had been appointed. But that army was not altogether disbanded; it is mentioned again on p. 11b.

[4] Yen Shih-ku (581–645) says that 遺 means 留, and that 財 is the same as 纔, which means 少 'a little.'

[5] The *Kuang-ya* (by Chang Yi, fl. 227–233) says that 置 is 驛. Cf. *Mh* II, 462, n. 4.

[6] Shen Ch'in-han notes that the *History of the Southern Ch'i Dynasty*, ch. 9, p. 27b says that the Emperor Wu of that dynasty (483–494) was advised to and did plow the sacred field on the day *ting-hai* Feb. 14, 485. Wang Chien (452–489) says that in the classics there is no mention of a *hai* day. Ho T'ung-chih (449–503) replies, "[Emperor] Wen of the Han [dynasty] used this day to till the sacred [field] and worship the God of Agriculture. Later kings, following his example, used it. There is no further meaning [to the day *ting-hai*]." For a discussion of the Sacred Field, cf. App. II.

王參爲太原王揖爲梁王五月詔曰古之治天下朝有進

爲河間王章爲城陽王興居爲濟北王因立皇子武爲代

悼惠王子朱虛侯章東牟侯興居有功可王乃遂立辟彊

王幽死朕甚憐之已立其太子遂爲趙王遂弟辟彊及齊

備者皆赦之二月有司請立皇子爲諸侯王詔曰前趙幽

paid in full, [let] them all be pardoned."[1]

In the second month,[2] some [high] officials begged [the Emperor] to establish his Imperial Sons as vassal kings. His imperial edict said, "Previously when King Yu of Chao, [Liu Yu], died from being imprisoned, We deeply sympathized with him. [We] have already made his Heir-apparent, [Liu] Sui, the King of Chao. The younger brother of [Liu] Sui, [Liu] Pi-ch'iang, together with the sons of King Taohui of Ch'i, [Liu Fei₂], the Marquis of Chu-hsü, [Liu] Chang, and the Marquis of Tung-mou, [Liu] Hsing-chü, are meritorious [persons] and worthy to be made kings." So [the Emperor] thereupon[3] established [Liu] Pi-ch'iang as the King of Ho-chien, [Liu] Chang as the King of Ch'eng-yang, and [Liu] Hsing-chü as the King of Chi-pei. Because of [those appointments], he established his Imperial Sons, [Liu] Wu as the King of Tai, [Liu] Ts'an as the King of T'ai-yüan, and [Liu] Yi₅ as the King of Liang. **March**

In the fifth month an imperial edict said, "According to the ancient [mode of] governing the world, in the court there was the banner for initiating improvements,[4] and the post for speaking ill and **June** **10b**

---

[1] They were not to be punished for the crime committed when they failed to repay and were forgiven the repayment.

[2] The text writes "third month," but HS 14: 6b, 7b, 10b, 13a lists all these appointments in the *second* month on the day yi-mao, Mar. 15. We have accordingly emended 三 to 二. Cf. Mh II, 464, n. 2.

[3] Wang Hsien-ch'ien says that 遂 (which we have translated "thereupon") is an interpolation from the preceding sentence. The SC does not have it.

[4] This banner was supposed to have hung where five roads met at the court of Yao; anyone who had an improvement to propose stood under it. Cf. Mh II, 465, n. 1. In the Wen-yüan Ying-hua (written ca. 978, by Li Fang) ch. 362, p. 6b, Lu Shih (fl. dur. 48–33 B.C.) in his own comment on his Hua-chien [Painted Admonishments], is quoted as saying, "[According to] the stories of the two Han dynasties, in the third year of the Emperor Wen [177 B.C.] there were painted at the Yung-ming Hall [his text says it was inside the Wei-yang Palace, but, according to the San-fu Huang-t'u, (iii to vi cent.) in the Wei-yang Palace there was a Hsien-ming Hall, but no Yung-ming Hall] the five colored objects: the plant that curbs negligence [which grew in the court of Yao and

criticizing,[1] whereby there was kept open the way for [good] government and [whereby] remonstrances were caused to come [to the Emperor]. Now in the law there are the crimes of speaking evil and criticizing and of monstrous speech.[2] These [laws] keep the courtiers from daring to express their whole feelings so that the sovereign has no means of hearing about his mistakes and errors. By what means then [can we make] capable and good [people] from distant quarters come [to Us]? Let [these laws] be abrogated.

"If it happens that people make imprecations against the sovereign and have made pledges to each other, but later give each other the lie, the officials consider it treason, and, whatever else they may say, the officials nevertheless consider it speaking evil and criticizing. These [acts] are from the stupidity of unimportant people, who do

善之旌誹謗之木所以通治道而來諫者也
今法有誹謗訞言之罪是使衆臣不敢盡情
而上無由聞過失也將何以來遠方之賢良
其除之民或祝詛上以相約而後相謾吏以
爲大逆其有他言吏又以爲誹謗此細民之

bent its head each time a slanderous flatterer entered the palace], the banner for initiating improvement, the post for speaking ill and criticizing [cf. below], the drum for daring to admonish [the prince]; and the single horned monster [which gores wicked people when it sees them]."

[1] This legend seems to have originated in the *Shih-tzu*. Szu-ma Cheng quotes the *Shih-tzu* (iii cent. B.C.) as saying "Yao established the post for speaking ill and criticizing." The *Lü-shih Ch'un-ch'iu* (possibly forged by Kao Yu, fl. 205–212, according to Maspero, *TP* 20: 231) 24: 31 (Wilhelm's trans. p. 422) however says that this post belonged to Shun. Fu Ch'ien (ca. 125–195) says, "Yao made them. [They were] posts with a cross-piece [on the] bridges." Ying Shao says, "They were boards at the side of the bridges on which to write the errors and faults of the government. At [the time of] the Ch'in [dynasty], they were done away with; now they were reestablished." Yen Shih-ku approves of the latter explanation. Shen Ch'in-han says, "Ts'ui Pao (fl. dur. 265–420) in his *Ku-chin-chu* [C: 7a, b, makes] Ch'en Ya ask, 'What [likeness] had the posts for speaking ill and criticizing that Yao erected?' He answered, '[Like] the present ornamental pillars, with a cross-piece on the post like a flower and shaped like a well-sweep. On the large roads where thoroughfares meet they were everywhere placed. Some people call them "sign-posts 表木." They are a sign that the kings receive admonition and also to point out the roads. The Ch'in [dynasty] however abolished them and the Han [dynasty] first reestablished them. Now in the Western Capital [Ch'ang-an] they are called "posts with cross-pieces 交午"'柱."

[2] The Empress *née* Lü had abolished this latter crime; evidently it had been revived. Cf. 3: 2a and p. 193, n. 2, also 11: 3a. Yen Shih-ku says that 訞 and 妖 are synonymous.

愚者符而然故今親率羣臣農以勸之其賜天下

無勿詔民故親率羣臣農以勸之其賜天下

知聽曰或茲

抵治農不親率羣臣農以勸之其賜天下

死九天務率

胅月下本臣

甚初之而農

不與大事以

取郡本末勸

自守也故之

令爲民生其

以銅所不賜

來虎恃遂天

有符以胅下

犯竹生憂

此使也其

not know [what they are doing] and run into death.
[Such punishments are what] We very much do not
want.   From the present time on, whenever there
are those who transgress in this manner, do not admit
them to trial."[1]

In the ninth month, there were first made for the Sept./Oct.
Administrators of Commanderies bronze tiger cre
dentials and envoy's bamboo credentials.[2]

An imperial edict said, "Agriculture is the great 11a
foundation of the world; it is what the people depend
on for their [very] life.   Nevertheless the people
sometimes do not apply themselves to the fundamental but occupy themselves with what is least
[important].   As a result their livelihood is deficient.
We are anxious about this state of affairs, hence We
now at this time Ourselves lead [Our] ministers in
agricultural [pursuits] in order to exhort them [to

[1] Cf. *Mh* II, 465, n. 2.

[2] Ying Shao says, "Bronze [or copper] tiger credentials were of the first to the fifth
[in number].   When the state must mobilize its troops, [the Emperor] sent a messenger
to the commanderies who matched his [half of] the credential [with the other half held
by the commandery official].   If the credential matched, then [the official in charge]
listened to and accepted [the envoy].   The bamboo envoy's credentials all use five stalks
of arrow-bamboo [a small species of bamboo].   They are five inches long and are engraved in seal characters number one to number five."   The *Han-chiu-yi* (i cent.) says,
"A commandery or a state was given three bronze tiger credentials and five bamboo
envoy credentials."   Chang Yen (prob. iii cent.) says, "The credentials were substituted
for the ancient *kuei* 圭 [a long narrow jade used as insignia] and *chang* 璋 [the length-
wise half of a *kuei*], because they were simpler and easier."   Yen Shih-ku says, " 'To
make credentials for the commandery administrators' means: each one was divided into
two halves [lengthwise].   The right [half] was left in the capital; the left [half] was used
to give to him [the commandery administrator]."   Ch'ien Ta-chao says, "The *Shuo-wen*
[ca. 100, says] 琥 is an auspicious jade [tablet used for] mobilizing forth troops.   [On it]
is the carving of a tiger.   He who employs troops uses his majesty and bravery, hence
[he uses] jade.   Bronze [ones] always use [the character] 虎."   Cf. 3 : 7a.   In *Mh* II,
466, n. 1, there is a picture of one with Chavannes' account of them.   He must be wrong
when he says that "la partie gauche était remise à celui qu'on voulait charger d'une
mission;" the inscription he prints says that it was given to the commandery Administrator.   The *SC* (*Mh* II, 465) writes that these credentials were made for "the Administrators or Chancellors of commanderies or kingdoms."

stress agriculture in their government]. Let there be granted to the people of the empire this year half of the land tax on the cultivated fields.''[1]

III   In the third year, in the winter, the tenth month, Dec. 22 on [the day] *ting-yu*, the last day of the month, there was an eclipse of the sun.[2]   In the eleventh month, June 6, on [the day] *ting-mao*, the last day of the month, 176 B.C. there was an eclipse of the sun. The imperial edict said, "Sometime ago an imperial edict ordered the marquises to go to their states. [But they asked] to be excused and have not gone. The Lieutenant Chancellor is [the person] whom We honor [most]. Let him lead the marquises to their states for Us.''[3] Thereupon the Lieutenant Chancellor, [Chou] P'o, was dismissed and sent to go to his state.

177 B.C.   In the twelfth month, the Grand Commandant, the Jan./Feb. Marquis of Ying-yin, Kuan Ying, was made Lieuten-
11b ant Chancellor[4] and the office of Grand Commandant was abolished; [his duties] were taken care of by the Lieutenant Chancellor. In the summer, the May/June fourth month, the King of Ch'eng-yang, [Liu] Chang, died. The King of Huai-nan, [Liu] Ch'ang, killed the Marquis of Pi-yang, Shen Yi-chi.[5]

June/July   In the fifth month, the Huns entered and occupied the Pei-ti [Commandery], south of the [Yellow] River,[6] whence they marauded. The Emperor

---

[1] Yen Shih-ku says, "They were excused from it and it should not be collected.''

[2] Cf. App. III.

[3] The Southern Academy ed. (1528–30), the Fukien ed. (1549), the Official ed. (1739) and the *SC* all write 朕 instead of 遂. We have adopted this reading.

[4] Usually appointments and dismissals of even the highest officials were not recorded in the Annals; in this case, because the Grand Commandant's office was abolished in consequence, an appointment was recorded.

[5] He murdered him in his house. For details, cf. ch. 44 and Glossary *sub* Liu Ch'ang.

[6] This was the Ordos region in the north of the present Shensi, south of the great northern bend of the Yellow River. It had been conquered by Meng T'ien, a general of the First Emperor (cf. *Mh* II, 167) and was taken away from the Huns again by Wei Ch'ing in 127 B.C.; cf. 6:10b.

入居北地河南爲寇上幸甘泉遣丞相灌嬰
擊匈奴匈奴去發中尉材官屬衛將軍軍長
安上自甘泉之高奴因幸太原見故羣臣皆
賜之舉功行賞諸民里賜牛酒復晉陽中都
民三歲租留游太原十餘日濟北王興居聞

favored the Kan-ch'üen [Palace by visiting it.[1] The Emperor] sent the Lieutenant Chancellor Kuan Ying to attack the Huns,[2] and the Huns left. [The Emperor] sent[3] the Palace Military Commander, with skilled soldiers[4] belonging to [the army of] the General of the Guard, to encamp at Ch'ang-an. The Emperor went from the Kan-ch'uan [Palace] to Kao-nu, and, availing himself of the opportunity, he favored [the kingdom of] T'ai-yüan [by visiting it] and saw his former officials.[5] He granted [favors] to them all, promoting those who had distinguished themselves. He gave favors to the common people, granting them by hamlets an ox and wine. He exempted the people of Chin-yang and Chung-tu from the land tax for three years.[6] He stayed and amused himself in [the kingdom of] T'ai-yüan for more than ten days.

When the King of Chi-pei, [Liu] Hsing-chü, heard

[1] Ju Shun quotes Ts'ai Yung (133–192) as saying, "Where the chariots and equipage of the Son of Heaven go, the people and the officials consider it an unhoped for piece of good fortune, hence it is called 'the favor of a visit 幸見.' The chief magistrate [of the prefecture], the San-lao, and their official subordinates themselves visit [the emperor's] coach. Music is played and they are granted wine, food, silk, bonnets of linen or of linen woven with white nettle [the Sung Ch'i ed. says that the words for 'wine' and 'linen' were not in the Yüeh ed (xi–xii cent.)], ornaments worn at the girdle, girdles, and the like. The common people [are granted by the emperor] steps in noble rank by number or the half of the land tax on the fields. Hence they therefore call it 'a favor 幸.' "

[2] HS 94A: 10a says that he ordered out border officers, chariots, and cavalry, [altogether] 80,000 [in number] to go to Kao-nu. HS 27Ba: 23b says there were ordered out chariots, cavalry, and soldiers, [altogether] 85,000 [in number]. Cf. de Groot, Die Hunnen, pp. 74–76.

[3] Chavannes (Mh II, 469, n. 3) suggests emending 發 to 廢. The word for "abolish" in this sense (cf. above) is however 罷. In the "Treatise on Offices" (ch. 19) there is no record of this office having been abolished at this time; the text's reading is preferable.

[4] For "skilled soldiers", who were cavalry and cross-bowmen handling the heaviest cross-bows, cf. p. 80, n. 2; SC 57: 1b; HS 42: 6a; 49: 11a; Mh II, 469, n. 4.

[5] T'ai-yüen had been part of Emperor Wen's former Kingdom of Tai. At this time the Emperor's son Liu Ts'an had been made its King.

[6] Chin-yang and Chung-tu had been the capitals of the kingdom of Tai when Emperor Wen had been its King.

that the Emperor had gone to Tai and that he him-
12a self intended to attack the Huns, [the king] rebelled
and mobilized his troops, wishing to surprise Jung-
yang.[1]　Thereupon an imperial edict abolished the
troops of the Lieutenant Chancellor[2] and made the
Marquis of Chi-p'u, Ch'ai Wu, the General-in-chief,
leading four generals[3] [with] a multitude [number-
ing] a hundred thousand to attack [Liu Hsing-chü].
The Marquis of Ch'i, Tseng Ho, was made a General
and encamped at Jung-yang.　In the autumn, the
Aug. Sept. seventh month,[4] the Emperor [went] from T'ai-
yüan to Ch'ang-an.　His edict read, "The King of
Chi-pei [Liu Hsing-chü] has been ungrateful for [Our]
goodness, rebelled against his sovereign, deceived and
led into error his officials and people, and committed
treason.　Those among the officials and people of Chi-
pei who stopped [rebelling] of their own accord before
the troops arrived and those who submitted together
with their army, their cities, or their towns, are all
to be pardoned and restored to their official [posi-
tions] and their [aristocratic] ranks.　Those who
have been with the King, [Liu] Hsing-chü, leave
him, and come [to Us] will also be pardoned."　In
ept./Oct. the eighth month the King of Chi-pei, [Liu] Hsing-
chü, was captured and committed suicide.[5]　[The

赦之復官爵與王興居去來者亦赦之八月虜濟北王興居自
誤吏民為大逆濟北吏民兵未至先自定及旦軍城邑降者皆
軍軍滎陽秋七月上自太原至長安詔曰濟北王背德反上詿
棘蒲侯柴武為大將軍將四將軍十萬眾擊之祁侯繪賀為將
之代欲自擊創奴乃反發兵欲襲滎陽於是詔罷丞相兵以
帝

---

[1] He felt that he had not been adequately rewarded by the Emperor Wen, for,
although he had done more than anyone else in overthrowing the Lü faction, he had
been given only a small territory.　He belonged to the party that wished to enthrone
the King of Ch'i, Liu Hsiang, and took the opportunity given by the Emperor's absence
from the capital to start a rebellion.

[2] He had been commanding the troops formerly under the control of the Grand
Commandant.　Cf. 4: 11b.

[3] Ch'i Shao-nan (1703–1768) says that these four generals were (1) the Marquis
of Ch'ang, Lu Ch'ing (cf. *Mh* III, 141, no. 107), (2) the Marquis of Kung, Lu Pa-shih
(cf. *Mh* III, 133, no. 52), (3) the Marquis of Ning, Wei Su (cf. *Mh* III, 137, no. 75),
and (4) the Marquis of Shen-tse, Chao Chiang-yeh (*Mh* III, 127, no. 4).　Cf. *SC* 22:7b.

[4] *HS* 27Ba: 23b says that this autumn there was a drought all over the empire.

[5] The *Hsi-ching Tsa-chi* (prob. vi cent.) says, "When [Liu] Hsing-chü first raised his

殺　四　劉　千　絳
赦　年　有　戶　侯
諸　冬　屬　秋　周
與　十　籍　九　勃
興　二　家　月　有
居　月　無　封　罪
反　丞　所　齊　逮
者　相　與　悼　詣
　　　灌　賜　惠　廷
　　　嬰　諸　王　尉
　　　薨　侯　子　詔
　　　夏　王　七　獄
　　　五　子　人　作
　　　月　邑　爲　顧
　　　復　各　列　成
　　　諸　二　侯　廟

Emperor] pardoned those who had rebelled with [Liu] Hsing-chü.

In the fourth year,[1] in the winter, the twelfth month, the Lieutenant Chancellor Kuan Ying died. In the summer, the fifth month, [the Emperor] exempted from all taxes the families of the [members of the] Liu [house] who had members enregistered [as belonging to the imperial house]. He granted estates to the sons of the vassal kings, to each [the income of] two thousand households.[2] In the autumn, the ninth month, [the Emperor] appointed ten[3] sons of King Tao-hui of Ch'i, [Liu Fei2], as marquises. The Marquis of Chiang, Chou P'o, committed crime; he was arrested and brought to the Imperial Prison of the Commandant of Justice.[4] The Ku-ch'eng Temple was built.[5]

IV
12b
176 B.C.
Jan./Feb.
June/July

Oct.

troops, a great wind came blowing straight from the east. It blew straight his banners and flags right up in the sky into a cloud and [a flag] dropped into a well in the western part of his [capital] city. His horses all neighed sorrowfully and would not advance. [His followers] on the left and right, [including] Li K'uo and others, admonished him, but he would not listen. Therefore he later committed suicide."

[1] The SC mentions no events in the fourth or fifth years.

[2] HS 27Bb: 13a says, "In the sixth month (July) there was a great fall of snow."

[3] The text reads, "seven sons," but HS 15 A: 3b–5b enumerates ten sons of King Tao-hui as all appointed in the fifth month on the day chia-yin (July 1, 176 B.C.). Sun Yüeh's Han-chi follows ch. 15. HS 38:7b also says "seven sons." In their ancient form, "seven" and "ten" are easily confused.

[4] Chou P'o was arrested on the report that he planned to rebel. At the intercession of the Empress Dowager née Po, the Emperor Wen finally freed Chou P'o. He returned to his state and died in 169 B.C.

[5] The Ku-ch'eng Temple was the temple for Emperor Wen's posthumous worship. Ju Shun says, "He made his temple while he was alive. [The meaning of its name] is like [the phrase] in the Book of History [IV, V, i, 2; Legge, p. 199] 'he regarded (Ku) [continually the bright] requirements [of Heaven,' implying that Ku-ch'eng means, 'he regards the performance of Heaven's requirements']. The temple of the Emperor Ching was called Te-yang 德陽, that of the Emperor Wu was called Lung-yüan 龍淵, that of the Emperor Chao was called P'ai-hui 徘徊, that of the Emperor Hsüan was called Lo-yu 樂淤, that of the Emperor Yüan was called Ch'ang-shou 長壽, that of the Emperor Ch'eng was called Yang-ch'ih 陽池." After the burning of these temples in the period between the two Han dynasties, the first emperor of the Later Han Dynasty built one temple for all these emperors, with

V   In the fifth year, in the spring, the second month,
175 B.C. there was an earthquake.   In the summer, the fourth
Feb./Mar. month, the order [against] casting counterfeit cash
Apr./May was abrogated.   [The coinage] was changed and four
shu cash were made.[1]

13a   In the sixth year, in the winter, the tenth month,
VI the peach and plum [trees] blossomed.   In the elev-
Nov./Dec. enth month, the King of Huai-nan, [Liu] Ch'ang,
Dec./Jan. plotted a rebellion, was dismissed, exiled to Yen-tao
174 B.C. in the Shu [Commandery], and died [on the way[2]] at
Yung.

VII   In the seventh year, in the winter, the tenth
Nov./Dec. month, [the Emperor] ordered that Dowager Mar-
chionesses, wives of marquises, sons of vassal kings,
together with officials [with positions ranking as
worth] two thousand piculs, were not arbitrarily to
173 B.C. make levies nor arrests.   In the summer, the fourth
May month, an amnesty was granted to the world.   In
July 4 the sixth month, on [the day] *kuei-yu*, there was a
visitation [of fire] in the towers[3] screening the
Eastern Portal of the Wei-yang Palace.

五年春二月地震夏四月除盜鑄錢令更造四
銖錢

六年冬十月桃李華十一月淮南王長謀反廢
遷蜀嚴道死雍

七年冬十月令列侯太夫人夫人諸侯王子及

separate compartments (called "temples") for each emperor.   Fu Ch'ien (ca. 125–195)
says, "The [Ku-ch'eng] Temple was south of the city of Ch'ang-an, and was built by
Emperor Wen.   By turning round one can see the city wall, hence it is named [*ku-ch'eng*, lit. 'looking back on the city wall']."   Yen Shih-ku replies that this interpretation is senseless and does not do justice to the words.   He prefers Ying Shao's inter-
pretation, which is that Emperor Wen, "when he made a temple for himself, made it
humble and low, so it could be completed while watching it," (i.e., in a short time).
Chia Yi (198–165 B.C.) said, "Through the Ku-ch'eng Temple he became the Great
Exemplar of the empire, as unsurpassed as the Han [dynasty]."

  [1] Four *shu* was ⅙ of an ounce.   These cash then weighed ⅓ of what the Ch'in dynasty's
cash did.   Chia Yi and Chia Shan both protested against this coinage; cf. ch. 24 and 51.

  [2] Adding the word 道, at the suggestion of Wang Nien-sun (1744–1832), to
correspond with the wording in *HS* 27Bb: 13a and *SC* 22: 8a.   Yen Shih-ku's comment
implies that it was in his text.   The *HS* in this sentence condenses a page of the *SC*
and adds the name of the place where Liu Ch'ang died.   The omitted material is put
in the *HS* into the "Memoir of Liu Ch'ang."   He starved himself to death in his sealed
prisoner's cart.   To clear himself of the suspicion of fratricide, the Emperor executed
the chiefs of the prefectures on the road who had not attended to Liu Ch'ang and buried
him with the honors of a marquis.   Cf. *SC* ch. 18, *HS* ch. 44; Glossary *sub voce*.

  The *SC* does not record anything after the sixth year down to the thirteenth year.

  [3] Ju Shun says, "The eastern [palace] portal with the towers on both sides of it

吏　捕　月　罘　八
二　夏　癸　罳　年
千　四　酉　災　夏
石　月　未　　　封
無　赦　央　　　淮
得　天　宮　　　南
擅　下　東　　　厲
徵　六　闕　　　王

In the eighth year, in the summer, [the Emperor] enfeoffed as marquises the four sons of King Li of Huai-nan, [Liu] Ch'ang.[1] A long comet appeared in the eastern quarter [of the sky].[2]

In the ninth year, in the spring, there was a great drought.

In the tenth year, in the winter, [the Emperor] travelled and favored [by a visit] the Kan-ch'üan [Palace]. General Po Chao died.[3]

13b
VIII
172 B.C.
Summer
IX
171 B.C.
X
Winter
170 B.C.

all burnt." Chin Shao (fl. ca. 275) says, "Only the towers of the eastern gate burnt." Yen Shih-ku says, "The screen towers are small towers connecting the portals 罘 罳 謂連闕曲閣也. They are used to cover places where there are double openings in the walls. [Because of] their shape, they are called *fou-szu* (net) like. They are also called screens 屏. [The first word of this name] is pronounced [the same as] 浮." Sung Ch'i says that the Chiang-nan ed. (before 976) writes the second word of this name as 思. Wang Nien-sun says that this edition is correct, for the *Shuo-wen* has not the word *szu* 罳. In various places the name of this screening wall is written 罘思 (as in ch. 27), 浮思, 桴思, or 復思. In modern times the 'net' radical has been added to the second character. Yen Shih-ku's comment gives no pronunciation for the second character, showing that in his time it was written without the 'net' radical. Cheng Hsüan, in a note to *Chou-li* 41:34a, sub *Chiang-jen*, says, "The corner of a city wall is called a 角浮思." Wang Hsien-ch'ien concludes, "Then the *fou-szu* is a small building with an upper storey 小樓, for on the corners of city walls and above the portals there always are such [buildings]. Then above this screening wall there was also a building to cover and screen the wall."

[1] These four were Liu An, made Marquis of Fou-ling, Liu P'o, Marquis of An-yang, Liu T'zu, Marquis of Yang-chou, and Liu Liang, Marquis of Tung-ch'eng. These appointments were all made on June 2. Cf. 15A: 6a, b. This appointment was the cause of a fruitless admonition by Chia Yi; cf. ch. 48.

[2] Wen Ying (fl. ca 196–220) says, "The three [kinds of special] stars [i.e. comets] are the bushy ones 孛 [lit. 'shooting out,' like vegetation], the brooms 彗, and the long 長 ones. In their prognostications they are somewhat alike, however in their shape they are slightly different. The light rays of bushy comets are short; their light goes out in [all] four [directions], [it is] bushy and shooting out. The light rays of broom comets are long and tufted like a broom. With long comets there is one straight light ray, which points sometimes to the end of the sky, sometimes a hundred feet [long], sometimes thirty feet, sometimes twenty feet, without any regularity. [According to the] *Ta-fa* 大法 [seemingly the name of an unknown book], bushy and broom comets are mostly [signs of] doing away with the old and spreading the new, [or] of fire visitations; long comets are mostly [signs of] war."

[3] *HS* 18: 6a says, "He was sentenced for killing a messenger [of the Han emperor] and committed suicide." Cheng Te (fl. dur. 265–317) says, "[Po] Chao killed a messenger of the Han [emperor]. The Emperor Wen could not bear to execute him,

XI   In the eleventh year, in the winter, the eleventh
Dec./Jan. month, [the Emperor] travelled and favored [the
169 B.C.   kingdom of] Tai [with a visit]. In the spring, the
Feb./Mar. first month, the Emperor returned from [the king-
July/Aug. dom of] Tai [to the capital]. In the summer, the
sixth month, the King of Liang, [Liu] Yi₅, died.
The Huns pillaged Ti-tao.

XII   In the twelfth year, in the winter, the twelfth
168 B.C.   month, the [Yellow] River broke [its dykes] in the
Jan./Feb. Tung Commandery.[1] In the spring, the first
Feb./Mar. month, [the Emperor] granted estates of two thous-
14a   and families to each of the daughters of the vassal
Mar./Apr. kings. In the second month, the Beauties in the
Emperor Hsiao-hui's harem were sent [home] and
it was ordered that they might be married. In the
Apr./May third month, the [customs] barriers were done away
with and passports were no [longer] used.[2]

還夏六月梁王揖薨匈奴寇狄道
十一年冬十一月行幸代春正月上自代
十年冬行幸甘泉將軍薄昭死
九年春大旱
長子四人爲列侯有長星出于東方

[so] sent the high ministers to drink wine with him, wishing to cause him to commit
suicide. [Po] Chao was not willing [to do so. Hence the Emperor] sent officials
wearing mourning garments to go and weep for him; then he committed suicide. He
had committed a crime, hence it is said that he 'died' 死," instead of the word ordinarily
used for the death of a marquis, 薨 (cf. 2: 6a for an example of the latter). Ju Shun
adds, "It is also said that when [Po] Chao lost while gaming with the Emperor Wen
and had to drink wine [as a punishment for losing], a Gentleman-in-attendance poured
out [too] little [wine] for [Po] Chao while another Gentleman-in-attendance reprimanded
and roared at him, and that while this Gentleman was gone down to wash [his hair, Po]
Chao sent a man to kill him [because of his lack of manners]. For this reason Emperor Wen caused him to commit suicide."

[1] For details, cf. ch. 29. Levies from the Tung Commandery rebuilt the dykes.

[2] Chang Yen (prob. iii cent.) says, "Passports (chuan⁴ 傳) are credentials 信,
like the present 'passport' (ko-so 過所)." Ju Shun says, "Two columns of writing
on silk are divided; by holding one of them, when you go in or out of the [customs]
barrier, if it matches [with the other of the pair], then you are permitted to pass. It is
called a chuan." Li Ch'i (fl. dur. 221–265) says, "A passport (chuan) is a ch'i 棨"
[a wooden staff with a little flag, divided like a tally]. Yen Shih-ku adds, "Chang
[Yen's] explanation is correct. Anciently some used a ch'i and some used silk. The
ch'i was an engraved stick [the halves of which] matched and made a credential." She
Ch'in-han says, "In the Chou-li [15:11a, sub] the Szu-kuan [cf. Biot's trans. I, p. 330], the
commentator, [Cheng Hsüan, says], 'A chuan is like the present ko-so documents

An imperial edict said, "The road along which to guide the people is [to make them] devote themselves to fundamentals. We Ourselves have led the world in agriculture for ten years down to the present, yet to the countryside there has not been added any newly broken land, and [as soon as] one year has not a good harvest,[1] the people have hungry looks. This [shows that] those who apply themselves to [agriculture] are still too few, and that moreover the officials have not especially put their attention on it. I have many times put forth edicts, and yearly have urged the people to plant and sow,[2] but the results [of my action] have not yet appeared. This is [because] the officials have not been diligent in upholding my edicts or [because] they have not been intelligent in urging the people [to agriculture]. Forsooth, my farmers [have suffered] very bitterly, and yet the officials have perceived none of it; how then can [the officials effectively] encourage [agriculture]? Let there be granted to the farmers this year half of the land tax and tax on produce."

[The edict] also said, "The Filially Pious and the Fraternally Respectful are the most advantageous [persons] in the world. The Cultivators of the Fields are the fundamental sources of life. The *San-*

which are transmitted.' The *Shih-ming* [written by Liu Hsi (Han period), 6:3a, *sub*] 示 [says], 'To show. With a *ko-so*, when you come to a barrier or ford, it is used to show to them.' The saying of Ju [Shun], 'Two columns of writing on silk are divided,' comes from a comment of Cheng [Hsüan on the *Chou-li* 3:6b, *sub*] the *Hsiao-tsai* [cf. Biot's trans. of *Chou-li*, I, p. 42 who also says], '*Chih-chi* means 'two similar writings on one tablet which are separated.' [The latter] is the present contract 券書 [which is also divided]. The *Shih-ming* [6:2b], says, '莉 is to divide. A large writing on a tablet is broken in the middle and divided.' This [article] is also like the *chuan* of the *Chou-li*. They are divided and written on silk, hence *HS* 64B:7b calls them hsü 繻 ['passports']. Today they are called *lu-yin* 路引]."

[1] Yen Shih-ku says that 登 means 成.

[2] The word in the text 樹 is interpreted by Yen Shih-ku as 蓺 殖, 'to sow and plant'.

十二年冬十二月河決東郡春正月賜諸侯王女邑各二千戶二

月出孝惠皇帝後宮美人令得嫁三月除關無用傳詔曰道民之

路在於務本朕親率天下農十年于今而野不加辟歲一不登民

有飢色是從事焉尚寡而吏未加務也吾詔書數下歲勸民種樹

而功未與是吏奉吾詔不勤而勸民不明也且吾農民甚苦而吏

lao are the teachers of the people.   Honest officials are an example to the people.   We greatly approve of the conduct of these few [kinds of] grandees.[1]

"Now in prefectures of ten thousand families it is said, 'There are none who [are able to] conform to
14b   [the Emperor's] order.'[2]   How can peoples' natures be really [so inadequate]?   This is because the way the officials have of recommending the capable is not adequate.   Let Internuncios be sent to recompense and make grants: to the *San-lao* and the Filially Pious, five pieces of silk per person, to the Fraternally Respectful and the Cultivators of the Fields, two pieces, to the honest officials of [the rank of] two thousand piculs and above, for every hundred piculs, three pieces.   When [the Internuncio] arrives, [let him] ask the people if there is anything inconvenient or discontenting, and let him establish the regular number of *San-lao*, Filially Pious, Fraternally Respectful, and Cultivators of the Fields in accordance with the number of households and people, and order each to apply himself with all his mind in order to guide the people [aright]."

XIII   In the thirteenth year, in the spring, the second
167 B.C.   month, on [the day] *chia-yin*, an imperial edict said,
Mar. 16   "We Ourself lead the world in farming and plowing in order to offer millet and sacrificial grain [in sacrifice].   The Empress herself raises silk-worms in order to provide sacrificial clothing.   Let ceremonies and rites be established [for these procedures]."[3]

匹及問民所不便安而以戶口率置三老孝悌力田常員令各率其意以
勞賜三老孝者帛人五匹悌者力田二匹廉吏二百石以上率百石者三
之行令萬家之縣云無應令豈實人情是吏舉賢之道未備也其遣謁者
力田爲生之本也三老衆民之師也廉吏民之表也朕甚嘉此二三大夫
莫之省將何以勸焉其賜農民今年租稅之半又曰孝悌天下之大順也

---

[1] "Grandees", denoting the Filially Pious, the Fraternally Respectful, the Cultivators of the Fields, the *San-lao* and honest officials, is here merely a term of respect.

[2] Yen Shih-ku says, "There were no Filially Pious, Fraternally Respectful, or Cultivators of the Fields who deserved to be sought out and recommended in conformity with [the Emperor's] order."

[3] It looks as if Emperor Wen began these imperial ceremonies.

道　十　皇　五　莫
民　三　后　月　大
焉　年　親　除　焉
　　春　桑　肉　今
　　二　以　刑　厪
　　月　奉　法　身
　　甲　祭　語　從
　　寅　服　在　事
　　詔　其　刑　而
　　曰　具　法　有
　　朕　禮　志　租
　　親　儀　六　稅
　　率　夏　月　之
　　天　除　詔　賦
　　下　祕　曰　是
　　農　祝　農　謂
　　耕　語　天　本
　　以　在　下　末
　　供　郊　之　者
　　粢　祀　本　無
　　盛　志　務　以

In the summer, [the Emperor] abolished the secret Summer
invocator.[1] A discussion is in the "Treatise on the
Suburban Sacrifice and Offerings to the Spirits."   25A:19a

In the fifth month, [the Emperor] abolished the May/June
law providing for mutilating punishments. A discussion is in the "Treatise on Punishments and
Laws."[2]   23:12b–14b

In the sixth month, an imperial edict said, "Agri- June/July
culture is the foundation of the world. No duty is
greater. Now if [anyone] personally follows this
pursuit diligently, he has yet [to pay] the impositions
of the land tax and tax on produce. This is making[3] no distinction between [the treatment of what
is] fundamental and [what is] least important.[4]
This is not appropriate to [Our] way of encouraging
agriculture. Let there be abolished the land tax and
tax on produce [levied] upon the [cultivated] fields,
and let there be granted to the orphans and widows
of the empire [linen] cloth, silk, and silk wadding, to
each person a definite amount."

In the fourteenth year, in the winter, the Huns 15a
pillaged at the frontier and killed the Chief Com- XIV

---

[1] *HS* 25A:19a reads, "When the Emperor Wen had been on the throne to the thirteenth
year, he gave an edict saying, 'The Office of secret invocator is to bear away [the
Emperor's] faults to someone below [the Emperor]. We very much disapprove of [this
sort of thing]. Let [this office] be abolished.'" For this official, cf. *Mh* III, 448; II,
473, n. 7. Ying Shao says, "The state tabooed him, hence he was called 'secret.'"
Hung Liang-chi (1746–1809) says, "He is probably the *Tien-shih* 甸師 of the *Chou-li*,"
who takes the responsibility for faults and misfortunes upon himself instead of the
Emperor. Cf. Biot's trans., I, 85; *HS* 25A:17a.

[2] The *HS* has shifted the explanatory material which is in the *SC* at this point to
ch. 23. Cf. *Mh* II, 474 ff.

[3] Liu Pin (1022–1088) says, "I suspect that 謂 should be 爲"; Wang Hsien-ch'ien
remarks that the *SC* writes the second character, and that anciently these two characters
were interchanged.

[4] Li Ch'i (fl. dur. 220–265) says, "The fundamental is agriculture. The least important is merchandizing. It says that agriculture and merchandizing both pay the
land tax and are not different. Hence he did away with the land tax on the [cultivated]
fields." The land tax on cultivated fields was reëstablished in 156 B.C. Cf. 5:3a.

Winter mandant of the Pei-ti [Commandery], [Sun] Ang.[1] [The Emperor] sent three generals to encamp in the Lung-hsi, the Pei-ti, and the Shang Commanderies.[2] The Palace Military Commander Chou Shê was made General of the Guard; the Chief of the Gentlemen-at-the-Palace Chang Wu was made General of Chariots and Cavalry to encamp north of the Wei [River] with a thousand chariots and a hundred thousand cavalry and foot-soldiers. The Emperor himself inquired about the army's welfare and aroused the troops by reiterated instructions and orders and by making grants to the officers and soldiers. He himself wanted to make the expedition against the Huns. When the courtiers remonstrated, he would not listen, [but] when the Empress Dowager earnestly besought him, the Emperor however stopped. Thereupon [the Emperor] made the Marquis of Tung-yang, Chang Hsiang-ju, the General-in-chief. The Marquis of Ch'eng, Tung Ch'ih,[3] the Prefect

15b of the Capital, and Luan Pu were both made generals

166 B.C. to attack the Huns. The Huns fled.

騎將軍軍渭北車千乘騎卒十萬人上親勞軍勒兵

西北地上郡中尉周舍爲衞將軍郎中令張武爲車

十四年冬匈奴寇邊殺北地都尉卬遣三將軍軍隴

寡布帛絮各有數

異也其於勸農之道未備其除田之租稅賜天下孤

---

[1] *HS* 94A: 13a, b says that the Shan-yü with 140,000 horsemen entered Chao, Pa, and the Hsiao Pass as far as P'eng-yang, burnt the Hui-chung Palace, and rode to Kan-ch'üan, in sight of Ch'ang-an. This was the greatest of the Hun raids.

[2] According to 94 A: 13b, the Marquis of Ch'ang, Lu Ch'ing, was the general sent to the Shang Commandery; the Marquis of Ning, Wei Su, was the general sent to Pei-ti; the Marquis of Lung-lü, Chou Tsao, was the general sent to Lung-hsi.

[3] According to 16: 16b, Tung Ch'ih was Marquis of Ch'eng 成; the *SC* in this passage also says "Marquis of Ch'eng"; *HS* 94: i, 13b writes the same. The text at this point however writes 建成; the first character is then an interpolation. We have omitted it.

HS 16: 16b says that Tung Ch'ih 董赤 was the son of Tung Tieh and was appointed Marquis of Ch'eng. The *SC* at this point also writes Ch'ih; *HS* 19B: 8b writes that in this year the Prefect of the Capital was Tung Ch'ih. *HS* 94A: 13b also writes Tung Ch'ih. The text here however writes his given name as Ho 赫. In ancient times, according to Ch'ien Ta-chao (1744–1813) Ho and Ch'ih were interchanged. Since Ch'ih is written more frequently, we read it here.

SC 10: 13b says that the Marquis of Ch'eng, Ch'ih, was made the Prefect of the Capital and that Luan Pu was made general. *HS* 19B: 8b notes that in this year

申教令賜吏卒自欲征匈奴羣臣諫不聽皇太后固要

上乃止於是以束陽侯張相如爲大將軍建成侯董赫

內史欒布皆爲將軍擊匈奴匈奴走春詔曰朕獲執犧

牲珪幣以事上帝宗廟十四年于今歷日彌長以不敏

不明而久撫臨天下朕甚自媿其廣增諸祀壇場珪幣

In the spring, an imperial edict said, "It is now the Spring fourteenth year that We have had [the opportunity] to present the sacrificial oxen, the jade tablets, and the pieces of silk for the service of the Lords on High and the [imperial] ancestral temples. As the elapsed time has become longer and longer, and [We] have been neither intelligent nor brilliant, yet have controlled and governed the world for a long time, We Ourselves are very much ashamed [because We are unworthy]. Let there be extended and augmented the mounds on which sacrifices are made, the level places for sacrifice,[1] the jade tablets, and the pieces of silk at the various sacrifices.

"Formerly the ancient Kings extended [their benefits] far and wide and did not seek for any recompense; they performed the sacrifice from a distance [to the great mountains and rivers],[2] but did not pray for their own happiness.

> In the place of honor were the sages, in the less
>   honorable place were their relatives;[3]
>   The people [came] first, they put themselves last;

[this was] the extreme of the utmost wisdom. Now

the Prefect of the Capital was Tung Ch'ih. According to *SC* ch. 100, Luan Pu was never Prefect of the Capital, and *HS* ch. 19 does not record it. According to *HS* 94A: 13b, the Marquis of Ch'eng, Tung Ch'ih, was made General, and his being Prefect of the Capital is not mentioned. The statement that anyone was made Prefect of the Capital is quite irrelevant to the military campaign. Wang Hsien-ch'ien suspects that the mention of Tung Ch'ih being Prefect of the Capital is an interpolation in the *SC*. The natural translation of the *HS* at this point would seem to be, "The Chien-ch'eng Marquis, Tung Ho, and the Prefect of the Capital, Luan Pu, were both made generals." We have adapted our translation to the facts.

[1] Yen Shih-ku says, "Heaping up earth makes a 壇; to sweep clean the ground makes a 場; 幣 is silk for worshipping the spirits." For Chavannes' interpretation of this passage, cf. *Mh* II, 478, n. 2.

[2] This sacrifice to the illustrious mountains and the great rivers, called 望, was supposedly very ancient. Its ceremony is described in *Mh* I, 62, n. 3.

[3] Lit. "on the right" and "on the left." The right was usually the place of honor. Cf. p. 123, n. 1.

These two lines are of four characters each and rime.

I have heard that when the sacrificial officials pray for happy omens,[1] they all [endeavor to make] happiness revert upon Our private person, and do not [pray] for [Our] subjects. We are very much ashamed at this. If now, in spite of Our lack of virtue, [We] nevertheless specially and solely enjoy the good [coming] from their [prayers for] happiness, and my subjects have no share in it, that will double my lack of virtue. Let it be ordered that the sacricial officials, in presenting their respectful [offerings], should not beg for anything."

XV 16a 165 B.C. Spring In the fifteenth year, in the spring, a yellow dragon appeared at Ch'eng-chi.[2] The Emperor thereupon issued an edict [ordering] the discussion of the sacrifice in the suburbs and [other] sacrifices. Kungsun Ch'en made clear the colors of the [sacrificial] robes; Hsin-yüan P'ing established the five temples.[3] A discussion [of the foregoing matters]

25A:19b 20a is in the "Treatise on the Suburban Sacrifice and Offerings to the Spirits."

May/June In the summer, the fourth month, the Emperor favored Yung [by a visit] and for the first time was presented to the Five Lords [on High] by means of a suburban sacrifice. An amnesty [was granted] to the world. [The Emperor] renewed the sacrifices to the famous mountains and the great rivers, which had

十五年春黃龍見於成紀上乃下詔議郊祀公孫臣明服色新垣

祠官致敬無有所祈

以朕之不德而專鄉獨美其福百姓不與焉是重吾不德也其令

之極也今吾聞祠官祝釐皆歸福於朕躬不爲百姓朕甚媿之夫

昔先王遠施不求其報望祀不祈其福右賢左戚先民後已至明

---

[1] Ju Shung says, "釐 [means] happiness 福." Yen Shih-ku says that this character's "original form is 禧; this is a borrowed use. Both are pronounced hsi[1]." Cf. Mh II, 479, n. 2.

[2] Shen Ch'in-han tells that the Ts'ê-fu Yüan-kuei (completed 1013) adds that the character wang 王 appeared in the sun. The Yü-hai (compiled by Wang Ying-lin, 1223–1296), ch. 195, p. 2a quotes the Wang-Ch'i-ch'ing (existed dur. 502–556), "In the time of the Emperor Wen, in the sun there was the word wang."

[3] The SC (Mh II, 481) says that these five altars were the Temples to the Five Lords [on High] north of the River Wei. Ch. 25 tells that they were northeast of Ch'ang-an, north of the road, at the Ch'ang-men T'ing. Cf. Mh III, 458. Kung-sun Ch'en had told the Emperor that northeast of Ch'ang-an (where these temples were later located) there was a supernatural emanation in five colors.

平設五廟語在郊祀志夏四月上幸雍始郊見五帝赦

天下脩名山大川嘗祀而絕者有司以歲時致禮九月

詔諸侯王公卿郡守舉賢良能直言極諫者上親策之

傅納以言語在鼂錯傳

十六年夏四月上郊祀五帝于渭陽五月立齊悼惠王

been worshipped and whose [sacrifices] had been stopped. The officers charged therewith [were ordered to] perform the [proper] rites [at the right time of] the year and season.

In the ninth month, an imperial edict [ordered] Oct. the vassal kings, the ministers, and the commandery administrators to present [to the Emperor] those who were capable and good, and could speak frankly and admonish [their superiors] unflinchingly. The Emperor in person questioned them [by setting a literary exercise]. They set forth in [written] words their ideas for adoption.[1] A discussion is in the "Memoir of Ch'ao Ts'o."   49 : 17a-22a

In the sixteenth year, in the summer, the fourth XVI month, the Emperor made a suburban sacrifice to the 164 B.C. Five Lords [on High] at [the altars] to the north of the Apr./May Wei [River]. In the fifth month, [the Emperor] ap- May/June pointed six sons of King Tao-hui of Ch'i [Liu Fei₂], and three sons of King Li of Huai-nan [Liu Ch'ang], as kings.[2] In the autumn, the ninth month, there Sept./Oct. was found a jade cup with the inscription, "Prolonged life to the Lord of Men."[3] [The Emperor]

---

[1] This event seems to have been one of the beginnings of the examination system. Chou Shou-ch'ang says, "This was the first time the Han court set literary exercises for the [prospective] officials. Before this, in the second year that he was on the throne, an imperial edict [ordered] the presentation of the capable and good persons, who were four-square and upright, able to speak frankly and admonish unflinchingly [cf. p. 9a], [but] we do not hear who was presented. At the [present] time [the authorities] for the first time [set] literary exercises for the [prospective] officials, using the three sets of virtues, [filial piety and brotherly respect, sageness and goodness, perfect virtue and uprightness], and Ch'ao Ts'o [who later became Grandee Secretary], because he had the highest grade, was promoted from [the position of] the Heir-apparent's Household Steward to Palace Grandee." HS 49: 17a ff. records Emperor Wen's questions and Ch'ao Ts'o's reply. The Emperor invited the capable and good persons to advise him about the state of the government, human relations, and to give frank admonitions.

[2] The state of Ch'i was divided into six parts for these six kingdoms. Cf. 14: 7–9. It became the imperial policy to enfeeble its nobles by dividing their fiefs among their children.

[3] Hsin-yüan P'ing feigned it was found and ordered it presented to the Emperor,

ordered that universal drinking [should be permitted all over] the empire. The next year [the Emperor] changed the beginning [of the count for the years of his rule].

Hou I　In the latter [part of his reign],[1] the first year,
16b　in the winter, the tenth month, the deceits of Hsin-
Nov./Dec.　yüan P'ing were discovered; he plotted rebellion, and was exterminated with his three [sets of] relatives.[2]
163 B.C.　In the spring, the third month, the Empress *née* Chang
Apr./May　of [Emperor] Hsiao-hui died.[3]

後元年冬十月新垣平
下大酺明年改元
杯刻曰人主延壽令天
人皆爲王秋九月得玉
子六人淮南屬王子三

according to Ying Shao. Hsin-yüen P'ing also said that the tripods of the Chou dynasty, which had been lost in the Szu River, were in the Yellow River at Fen-yin, because he had seen the emanation of precious metals there. Search was made, but nothing was found. So the Emperor built a temple on the southern bank of the River there with the intent of praying them out. Cf. *Mh* II, 481, n. 3; III, 460.

[1] Chang Yen (prob. iii cent.) says, "Hsin-yüen P'ing observed the sun twice at its meridian [on the same day] and considered it a good omen, hence [the Emperor] changed the beginning [of the count of the] years [of the imperial rule] in order to obtain the blessing of lengthened years." Cf. *Mh* III, 459. The *SC* (*Mh* II, 481) records a "seventeenth" year, and says that the Son of Heaven changed this year to be the first year of his reign. It says nothing about a "Ch'ien" or "Hou" year-period in his reign, merely mentioning "the second year in the latter [part of the reign] 後二年," etc. Then Emperor Wen merely had two "first" years; the historians were the first to speak of the "Hou" years in his reign. This was not the first time, according to the histories, that the numbering of years in a ruler's reign was changed: in 334 B.C., according to the *Bamboo Books* (composed about the end of iv cent. B.C., buried until found in 281 A.D., but altered later; cf. Legge, *Shoo-king*, I, p. 174) King Hui-ch'eng of Wei_h changed the beginning [of his reign] and called his thirty-sixth year his first year; in 324 B.C. King Hui-wen of Ch'in changed his fourteenth year to the first year. The *SC* (*Mh* II, 70) also records the latter change. Wang Hsien-ch'ien (1842–1918) thinks that these changes were modelled by the historians after the one made by Emperor Wen, although they may have been made when these rulers adopted the title of "king" in those years. The reason for this change seems to have been that the number of years being thus decreased, the ruler would live longer—King Hui-ch'eng is recorded as having ruled sixteen years after he changed the numbering of his years!

[2] Information concerning his deceits was given the emperor. Yen Shih-ku says, "Because his false acts were discovered, he was afraid he would be executed; hence he plotted a rebellion."

[3] The word used for her death here is *hung* 薨, not the word appropriate for an Empress's death, which is *peng* 崩. Chang Yen (prob. iii cent.) said, "The Empress leagued with the Lü clan, was dismissed, and lived in the Northern Palace [outside the Wei-yang Palace, a mark of disgrace; the Empress Dowager usually lived in the Wei-yang Palace], hence it is not said that she *peng*." Cf. 97A: 5b. Ho Ch'uo (1661–1722)

詐覺謀反夷三族春三月孝惠皇后張氏薨詔曰間
者數年比不登又有水旱疾疫之災朕甚憂之愚而
不明未達其咎意者朕之政有所失而行有過與乃
天道有不順地利或不得人事多失和鬼神廢不享
何以致此將百官之奉養或費無用之事或多與
與

An imperial edict said, "Recently for many years there have continually been no good harvests. Moreover there have been visitations of floods, droughts, sickness, and epidemics. We have been very much worried because of them. We are ignorant and not perspicacious and do not yet understand just what is to blame. We have been thinking: is there some fault in Our [way of] government or is there some defect in [Our] conduct? Or is it that [We] have not obeyed the Way of Heaven or have perhaps not obtained the advantages of Earth, or are the affairs of men in great discord,[1] or have the spirits and divinities been neglected [so that] they have not enjoyed [Our offerings]? How has this been brought about? Or is it that the salaries of the officials are perhaps too lavish, or that useless activities are perhaps too many? How is it that the people's food is scarce and lacking?

"Now when the fields are measured, they have not

replies, "She was not mourned and buried in accordance with the rites for an Empress, hence it is not said that she *peng*. She is recorded as 'Empress,' hence although she had nevertheless retired and lived alone, she had not been dismissed. Chang [Yen] is following ch. 97." Chou Shou-ch'ang (1814–1884) says, "A dismissed Empress's death is not recorded. Of the Empress [*née*] Po of the Emperor Ching [but cf. 5: n. 6.6] and of the Empress [*née*] Hsü of the Emperor Ch'eng it is recorded that they were dismissed, but not recorded that they died. This was the [set] practise of the historians. Although the Empress of Hsiao-hui was dismissed and established in a separate palace, as a matter of fact there was no known imperial edict ordering her dismissal, hence it was nevertheless recorded that she *hung*."

Cowell and Crommelin calculate that Halley's comet passed perihelion in May of this year; it is interesting that it was not recorded. Cf. *Monthly Notices* of the *Royal Astronomical Society*, 68: 670. Since eclipses are also not mentioned during this decade, it looks as though the recorders of phenomena deliberately refused to record eclipses or comets, for the good reign of Emperor Wen made them think that Heaven was sending no admonitions, hence they concluded that there were no "visitations."

[1] Perhaps the Emperor had *Mencius* II, ii, i, 1 in mind. Cf. Legge, p. 208.

decreased, and when the population is counted, it has not increased, [so that] the amount of land per person is greater than in ancient times. Yet there is very much too little food; where does the blame for it lie? Is it that Our subjects devote themselves to what is least important,[1] whereby those [persons] who injure agriculture are multiplied? [Is it due to the fact that] they make wine and lees, thereby wasting much grain and that masses of food are given to the six [kinds of] domestic animals? I have not yet been able to attain the proper mean between what is immaterial and what is important. Let [this matter] be discussed with the Lieutenant Chancellor, the marquises, the officials [of ranks worth] two thousand piculs, and the Erudites. Should there be anything that might be of assistance to Our subjects, let them apply themselves with all their minds[2] and think deeply [about the matter]. Let them not hide anything [from Us]."[3]

II   In the second year, in the summer, [the Emperor]
162 B.C. traveled and favored [by a visit] the Yü-yang Summer Palace at Yung. In the sixth month, the King of July Tai, [Liu] Ts'an, died.

The Huns [asked for] peace and friendship.[4]

---

[1] I.e., merchandizing.

[2] Interpreting *shuai* 率 by *hsi* 悉, in accordance with the suggestion of Wang Hsien-ch'ien, who says that these two words are alliterative, hence the second was changed to the first. [In Hunan both words are pronounced with an initial *s*; Karlgren gives the T'ang pronunciations siĕt and shiuĕt.] The phrase *shuai-yi* 率意 was previously used in 4: 14b; ch. 9 and 10 frequently use *hsi-yi*. *Shuai* has the meaning of *hsi*.

[3] Sung Ch'i (998–1061) says that the word 也 follows the last word of this clause in one ed.; Ch'ien Ta-chao reports that this word is in the Fukien ed. (1594).

[4] *HS* 94A: 13b, 14a says, "Yearly they entered the border, killed and captured very many people, most of all in the Yün-chung and Liao-tung [Commanderies], more than 10,000 people in a commandery. The Chinese [Emperor] was much worried about them, so he sent an envoy to bear and transmit a letter to the Huns. The *Shan-yu* also . . . replied saying [that he wanted] peace and friendship." Ch. 94 thereupon cites the Emperor Wen's edict, but not the portion in this chapter. The agreement was that the Great Wall should separate the two countries; neither should overpass it.

二年夏行幸雍棫陽宮六月代王參薨匈奴和親詔曰朕既

不明不能遠德使方外之國或不寧息夫四荒之外不安其

生封圻之內勤勞不處二者之咎皆自於朕之德薄而不能

達遠也間者累年匈奴並暴邊境多殺吏民邊臣兵吏入不

能諭其內志以重吾不德夫久結難連兵中外之國將何以

The imperial edict said, "Since We are not perspicacious, We have been unable to [extend the influence of Our] virtue to distant [regions]. This has caused states outside the borders sometimes to be disquiet and discontented. Now when [the people] outside the four wildernesses [at the borders][1] do not live quietly, [the people] within the fiefs and the imperial domain[2] toil, suffer, and are not in repose. The responsibility for [trouble] both [inside and outside the borders] lies altogether in the scantiness of Our virtue and its inability to penetrate to distant [regions].

"In recent times, for many years in succession, the Huns have simultaneously ravaged the border regions; they have killed many of the officials and people. Our subjects at the border, the soldiers and officers, have moreover[3] not been able to enlighten them[4] concerning [Our] inner intentions, thereby aggravating my lack of virtue. Since thus for a long time the Central [Empire] and the outer kingdoms[5] have been tied up in difficulties and continued hostilities, how can they themselves be contented [with this situation]?

"Now We 'have risen early and gone to sleep

---

[1] According to the *Book of History*, Yu divided the world into five concentric domains, the outermost of which was the wilderness domain 荒服. Yen Shih-ku says, "The Jung and Ti [occupied] the wilderness domain, hence it is said, 'The four wildernesses.' It says that it is a wilderness, [where] they suddenly go and come without any regularity. The *Erh-ya* says that Ku-chu [in the north], Pei-hu [in the south], Hsi-wang-mu [a place in the west], and Jih-hsia [in the east] are called the four wildernesses."

[2] Yen Shih-ku says, "The region which the emperor governs by himself [extends] for a thousand *li* [from the capital]; 'not being in repose' [means] not to secure a peaceful dwelling-place."

[3] Wang Hsien-ch'ien says that the Official ed. writes *yu* 又 for 入, which is the correct emendation. The *SC* also reads *yu*.

[4] The *SC* has 吾 instead of the *HS*'s 其. Cf. *Mh* II, 482, n. 2.

[5] The Han empire and the Hun and other nations. The Han dynasty did not consider itself as a kingdom, but as the empire which included all the kingdoms.

late';[1] [We] have toiled and suffered for the world; [We] have been solicitous and unhappy about all the people; for them We have been compassionate, sad,
17b and disquieted; not for one day has [this matter] left [Our] mind. Hence [We] have sent envoys [in rapid succession, so that] the caps and [carriage] coverings [of one caravan] were in sight [of the second], and their wheel tracks[2] were uninterrupted [on the road], in order to enlighten the *Shan-yü* concerning Our intentions.

"Now the *Shan-yü* has returned[3] to the path of the ancients; he has sought for the peace of [Our] gods of the soils and grains; [his proposal] is advantageous for the interests of all the people. Recently, [together] with Us, we have [both] given up altogether the slight wrongs [we have done to each other]; hand in hand we are marching upon the road of high [principle]. We have bound ourselves together in the relationship of brotherhood in order to conserve the good[4] people of the world. The peace and friendship has been fixed upon to begin from the present year."[5]

III   In the third year, in the spring, the second month,
161 B.C. [the Emperor] travelled and favored [the kingdom
Mar./Apr. of] Tai [by a visit].[6]

年
偕之大道結兄弟之義以全天下元元之民和親以定始于今
今單于反古之道計社稷之安便萬民之利新與朕俱棄細過
一日忘於心故遣使者冠蓋相望結轍於道以諭朕志於單于
自寧今朕夙與夜寐勤勞天下憂苦萬民爲之惻怛不安未嘗

---

[1] A commonly used quotation from the *Book of Odes*, Pt. I, Bk. V, iv, 5 (Legge, I, p. 100).

[2] Ch'ien Ta-chao says that 徹 is the ancient 轍, and that the Southern Academy ed. (1528) and the Fukien ed. (1549) write the second character. The Official ed. also writes the second character; the *SC* has 軼.

[3] Cf. *Mh* II, 483, n. 2. Yen Shih-ku's note seems to indicate that his text had 返 instead of the present 反.

[4] Cf. *Mh* II, 483, n. 4. Yao Ch'a lived 533–606.

[5] In the correspondence between Emperor Wen and the Shan-yü (translated in de Groot, *Die Hunnen*, pp. 86 ff.) there is no evidence of any marriage to cement this peace; a girl of the imperial house had previously been sent to be married to the *Shan-yü* when *Shan-yü* Lao-chang came to the throne.

[6] The *SC* records nothing from this year to the sixth year. *HS* 27A: 21b adds, "In the autumn there was a great rain day and night, which did not end until the thirty-fifth day. In the Lan-t'ien [prefecture] the rivers from the mountains carried away more

三年春二月行幸代

四年夏四月丙寅晦日有食之五月赦天下免官

奴婢爲庶人行幸雍

五年春正月行幸隴西三月行幸雍秋七月行幸

代

In the fourth year, in the summer, the fourth
month, on [the day] *ping-yin*, the last day of the
month, there was an eclipse of the sun.[1]   In the
fifth month, an amnesty was granted to the world.
[The Emperor] freed the government male and
female slaves and made them ordinary people.   [The
Emperor] travelled and favored Yung [by a visit].

    IV

    Aug. 16,
161 B.C.
160 B.C.
June/July

In the fifth year, in the spring, the first month,
[the Emperor] travelled and favored the Lung-hsi
[Commandery with a visit].   In the third month,
he travelled and favored Yung [with a visit].   In the
autumn, the seventh month, he travelled and favored
[the kingdom of] Tai [with a visit].

    V
159 B.C.
Feb.
Apr.
July/Aug.

In the sixth year, in the winter, thirty thousand
Hun horsemen entered the Shang Commandery and
thirty thousand [Hun] horsemen entered the
Yün-chung [Commandery].   The Chief of the
Palace Grandees, Mien,[2] was made General of
Chariots and Cavalry, and stationed at Fei-hu; the
former Chancellor of [the kingdom of] Ch'u, Su Yi,

    VI
Winter

    18a

than nine hundred families and the Han [River] destroyed the houses of more than eight
thousand common people.   More than three hundred people were killed."

[1] Cf. App. III, v.

[2] Yen Shih-ku says that this man's title is Palace Grandee, and his surname is Ling.
Hsü Kuang (352–425) had however said that the title was Chief of the Palace Grandees; Yen Shih-ku replies that the surnames of all the officials are given in this passage
and that there was not at this time any Chief of the Palace Grandees, for the title was
not instituted until 156 B.C.   Chavannes follows Yen Shih-ku; cf. *Mh* II, 484, n. 2.
But Chou Shou-ch'ang (1814–1884) replies that 19B: 4b says that in 188 B.C. a Mien
was appointed as Master of Ceremonies, and, in his comment on that passage, Yen Shih-
ku says that Mien was his given name.   Then he is probably the person referred to here,
and the historian has merely lost his surname.   With regard to Yen Shih-ku's statement
about surnames being given, Chou Shou-ch'ang replies that there was no fixed principle
about citing surnames, and gives examples to prove his point.   With regard to the title of
Chief of the Palace Grandees not being in use at this time, he replies that there are many
such anachronisms.   When Ying Pu was still King of Chiu-chiang, he was called King of
Huai-nan.   The title of Grand Chief of Agriculture was changed in 104 B.C. to Grand
Minister of Agriculture, but in ch. 24 the latter title is sometimes used in dealing of
events before 104 B.C. and the former title is used after 104 B.C.   Hence Hsü Kuang
is right in saying that his title was Chief of the Palace Grandees.

was made a General, and stationed at Chü-chu;[1] General Chang Wu was stationed in the Pei-ti [Commandery]; the Administrator[2] of Ho-nei, Chou Ya-fu, was made a General and encamped temporarily[3] at Hsi-liu. The Superintendant of the Imperial House, Liu Li, was made a General and encamped temporarily at Pa-shang; the Marquis of Chu-tzu, Hsü Li, was made a General and encamped temporarily at Chi-men, in order to be ready for the Hu.

18b

158 B.C.
May/June In the summer, the fourth month, there was a great drouth and locusts.[4] [The Emperor] ordered that the nobles should not pay tribute. He opened [to the common people] the mountains and marshes,[5] reduced the [imperial] robes and the imperial officers, diminished the [regular] number of Gentlemen and officials, and opened the granaries[6] in order to succor the people. The people were allowed to sell [aristocratic] ranks.[7]

157 B.C.

19a In the seventh year, in the summer, the sixth month,
VII on [the day] chi-hai, the Emperor died in the Wei-yang
July 6 Palace. His testamentary decree said, "We have

月大旱蝗令諸侯無入貢弛山澤減諸服御損郎吏員發

為將軍次霸上祝茲侯徐厲為將軍次棘門以備胡夏四

張武屯北地河內太守周亞夫為將軍次細柳宗正劉禮

免為車騎將軍屯飛狐故楚相蘇意為將軍屯句注將軍

六年冬匈奴三萬騎入上郡三萬騎入雲中以中大夫令

---

[1] HS 94A: 15b says that the kingdom of Tai garrisoned Chü-chu and the kingdom of Chao garrisoned the Fei-hu defile.

[2] The present text reads 太守; but commandery administrators were not called by this title until 148 B.C. Ch'ien Ta-hsin (1728–1804) thinks that the first word is an interpolation and should be omitted. The SC at this point does not have the first character. We have omitted it in the translation.

[3] Fu Tsan (fl. ca. 285) says, "To stay one night [at a place] is called 宿; to stay a second night is called hsin 信; more than hsin is tz'u 次." Ho Ch'uo (1661–1722) says, "T'un 屯 [to be stationed] is different from tz'u. For a t'un there is an apportioned region; [an army] that tz'u is ready to be transferred."

[4] HS 27Ba: 24a says, "In the spring there was a great drouth [all over] the world." Yen Shih-ku says, "Locusts are 螽; they eat the sprouts, and cause a visitation 災. Today they are popularly called po-chung[1] 簸蝩."

[5] For hunting and fishing. Cf. Mh II, 485, n. 3.

[6] Ying Shao says, "Granaries [to which grain is] transported by water are called 庾." Cf. also Mh II, 485, n. 4.

[7] Ts'ui Hao (381–450) comments, "Rich people wanted [aristocratic] ranks; poor people wanted money, hence [the Emperor] permitted buying and selling [ranks]."

暑之數哀人父子傷長老之志損其飲食絶鬼神之祭祀以重吾不德謂天下

重服以傷生吾甚不取且朕既不德無以佐百姓今崩又使重服久臨以罹寒

死死者天地之理物之自然奚可甚哀當今之世咸嘉生而惡死厚葬以破業

七年夏六月己亥帝崩于未央宮遺詔曰朕聞之蓋天下萬物之萌生靡不有

倉廙以振民民得賣爵

heard it [said that], of all [plants and animals] that sprout from or are born to any of the beings in the world, all of them, it seems, have to die. Death is a law of Heaven and Earth, and the nature of things. [Then] how could it be [so] greatly lamentable? [But] in the present age all esteem life and hate death; they elaborate burials, thereby ruining their estates; they perform a rigorous mourning, thereby injuring their health. I disapprove of this very much.

"Moreover since We have not been virtuous and have not been able to assist Our subjects, if now that [We] are dead, [We] also cause [people] to perform rigorous mourning and lament for a prolonged period, causing them to suffer [extreme] cold and heat for several [years, We would] make old and young to be afflicted [by our death], and would hurt the feelings of the elders [of the people].[1] To diminish their drink and food, to interrupt the sacrifices to the manes and divinities, thereby aggravating my lack of virtue—what [could We] say to the world [about that]?

"We have had the opportunity to protect the [imperial] ancestral temples, and, [in spite of Our] insignificant person, [We] have been entrusted for already more than twenty years [with a position] above the world's princes and kings. By the aid of the blessing of Heaven [and Earth[2]] and the benediction of the gods of the soils and grains, within the [four] quarters [of the world] there has been peace and contentment and no war.[3] Since We are not intelligent,

---

[1] SC 10:17a has 幼 for the HS 老 and Chavannes (Mh II, 488) translates, "que les esprits des vieux comme des jeunes soient aigris."

[2] Wang Hsien-shen says that the word 地 should be inserted in the text after 天; the parallelism requires it and the SC has it.

[3] Cf. Mh II, 488, n. 1.

267

We have been constantly afraid of committing some
19b faulty action, thereby dishonoring the virtue handed
down by the deceased emperors, [Our father and
elder brother].   In truth, as the years have lengthened out, [We] have been afraid of coming to a bad
end, but now [We] have [ended[1]] happily the years
[assigned to Us by] Heaven, and are permitted to
return to and receive offerings in the [ancestral]
temple of Kao-[tsu].[2]   When Our lack of wisdom
is [thus][3] recompensed, how can there be any
thoughts of mourning?

"Let it be ordered that, when [this] order reaches
them, the officials and people of the empire should
lament for three days [and then] all take off their
mourning garments.   Let there be no prohibition of
taking a wife or of marrying off a daughter, of making
sacrifices or of drinking wine or eating meat.   As to
those who must themselves take part in mourning

何朕獲保宗廟以眇眇之身託于天下君王

之上二十有餘年矣賴天之靈社稷之福方

內安寧靡有兵革朕既不敏常畏過行以羞

先帝之遺德惟年之久長懼于不終令乃幸

以天年得復供養于高廟朕之不明與嘉之

---

[1] Wang Nien-sun says that after the word 年 there has dropped out the word 終;
the comments of Ju Shun (fl. dur. 189–265) and Yen Shih-ku show that it should be
added here and in the corresponding passage of the *SC*.   Chavannes has supplied this
word in his translation; cf. *Mh* II, 489.   This word is of course implied; but adding
it is unnecessary and it spoils the rhythm.   The notion behind this saying is that he
has died a natural death, for something must be wrong with anyone who comes to a
violent end.

[2] The descendant comes from the ancestral temple and after death returns there.

[3] Yen Shih-ku says that *yü* 與 should here be read as 歟, which marks a question.
Liu Pin (1022–1088) and Liu Chang (1017–1068) agree.   But Wang Nien-sun points
out that Yen Shih-ku, in editing the comments on this passage, has excised four words
of Ju Shun (fl. dur. 189–265), which are preserved in the *Shih-chi Chi-chieh* (written by
P'ei Yin, fl. 465–472), "*Yü* is an expletive 與發聲也."   Wang Nien-sun says that *yü*
in this passage is not to be interpreted as 歟, but as an auxiliary word, without
meaning.   As examples of this use of *yü* he quotes sentences from *HS* 1B: 2b; from
the *Tso-chuan* (prob. iv cent. B.C.), Duke Hsi, 23rd year; ibid., Dk. Hsiang, 29th yr.;
ibid., Dk. Chao, 17th yr.; from the *Kuo-yü* (prob. iii cent. B.C.), ch. I, p. 6b; ibid. on
Chin (twice); ibid. on Chou; and ibid. on Yüeh; in all of which *yü* is merely an auxiliary
meaningless word.   It is a conjunctive conveying emphasis.   *HS* 6: 8b has the phrase
嘉與, but that has a different meaning, "am happy to be with; here *yü* is equivalent to 而.

其奚哀念之有其令天下
吏民令到出臨三日皆釋
服無禁取婦嫁女祠祀飲
酒食肉自當給喪事服臨
者皆無踐姪帶無過三寸

ceremonies, wear mourning garments, and lament, let none of them wear unhemmed [mourning] garments;[1] their headbands of hemp or white linen 20a strands[2] and girdles should not be more than three inches [wide]. Do not make a display of chariots or soldiers' weapons,[3] and do not send people to wail and lament in the palaces or halls. Those in the [Palace] Hall who must lament shall all raise their voices fifteen times each morning and evening.[4] When the rites are ended, [this prac-

[1] Meng K'ang (ca. 180–260) and Chin Shao (fl. ca. 275) explain 踐 as 跣 "to walk barefoot"; Yen Shih-ku approves; Chavannes and Wieger, *Textes Historiques*, follow. The *Han-chi* and the *Tzu-chih T'ung-chien* write the second character directly. But Fu Yen (prob. ii cent.) says that the first character above means "to cut off. [The sentence means not to use unhemmed mourning garments 剗也謂無斬衰也." Shen Ch'in-han points out, "In the *Book of History*, [where,] in the Introduction, [it says that] King Ch'eng 踐奄, Cheng [Hsüan, 127–200] reads [the first word] as 翦. The *Shih-ming* [Han period] says, 'The mourning garments for the three years [of mourning] are called "cut off"; do not hem it, merely cut it off 翦斬.' This was the ancient meaning of people in Han times. Fu [Yen's] interpretation is right." Wang Hsien-shen (1859–1922) adds that this interpretation corresponds with the sense of the next sentence. The *HHS*, Treatise 26: 3b, says "The Accessory Officials [and officers] below [that grade], with linen clothes, with cap and mourning hat and mourning cloth girdle not wider than three inches, shall lament in the hall; military officials, with a linen mourning hat and great [ceremonial] cap." Wang Hsien-shen says that with these ceremonial garments, it goes without saying that they would not be barefoot. Hence Fu Yen's interpretation is the correct one.

[2] Ch'ien Ta-chao says that 姪 should be 絰; the Southern Academy ed. (1528), the Fukien ed. (1549), the Official ed., the *SC*, and the *Han-chi* all write the second character.

[3] Ying Shao says, "Do not use linen cloth to cover the chariots together with the soldier's weapons." But Fu Ch'ien (ca. 125–195) says, "Do not send out light chariots, [used on formal occasions; they had no cloth canopies], and armed soldiers." Yen Shih-ku approves Ying Shao's interpretation, but Li Tz'u-ming (1829–1894) agrees with Fu Ch'ien, "The ancient chariots with canopies all used linen. For the mourning ceremonies, plain chariots with white linen cloth would not have been prohibited. This [passage] of course speaks of displaying chariots and arms. If we take Ying [Shao's] explanation, then it is difficult to explain 'soldiers' weapons'; how could the soldiers' weapons be covered with linen?"

[4] Chavannes, (*Mh* II, 489) translates this sentence to mean that fifteen persons shall wail morning and night, but *HHS*, Tr. 6: 5b, in describing the mourning for an

tise] must be stopped: Except for the morning and
evening time for lamenting, let [people] be forbidden
to wail[1] without special permission. [When the
coffin is] already[2] buried, let there be worn deep
mourning for fifteen days, light mourning for fourteen days, and thin [garments] for seven days; [then]
20b take off the mourning garments.[3] Whatever is not
[mentioned] in this order, let it all be done in accordance with [the spirit of] this order, and let it be published and told to the world in order that Our will
may be clearly known.

"Let the mountain and stream at the Pa Tomb[4]

服大紅十五日小紅十四日

夕臨時禁無得擅哭臨以下

夕各十五舉音禮畢罷非旦

宮殿中殿中當臨者皆以旦

無布車及兵器無發民哭臨

emperor, says that after the presentation of his posthumous name, "the Grand Master
of Ceremonies kneels and says, 'Wail.' The Grand Herald transmits [the order], 'Wail.'
Fifteen [times he says], 'Raise your voices,' [then], 'Stop wailing.' "

[1] Li Tz'u-ming says that the SC has no second 臨 after 哭, and since this word
should not be repeated, the second one in the HS is an interpolation. Hsün Yüeh's
(148–209) Han-chi likewise has not this word. Wang Hsien-shen (1859–1922) notes that
the Later Han dynasty followed the practises here specified.

[2] Wang Hsien-ch'ien says that 已 was interchanged with 巳.

[3] Chin Shao (fl. ca. 275) says, "The HS regularly uses 紅 for 功." Yen Shih-ku
says these two words are interchanged. "These mourning practises were made up
by the Emperor Wen following his own ideas, and were not taken from the Chou-li."
Sometimes more than a hundred days elapsed between the death and burial of the Han
emperors, so that mourning was worn considerably more than the thirty-six days herein
ordered. Ti Fang-chin followed this practise; cf. 84: 4b. The Confucian theory had
been to mourn to the third year, which period was ended at the beginning of the third
year (27 months in all). Yen Jo-ch'ü (1636–1704) says, "This rule of the [Emperor] Wen
of the Han [dynasty] was followed for three hundred and seventy years. Emperor
Wu [died 220] of the Wei [dynasty] first ordered that with the burial [the ceremonies]
had been completed, and abolished [the Han rule, ordering that] there should be no
thirty-six days of [wearing] mourning. We do not know later what period used thirty-
six days as the date for taking off mourning without considering [whether the deceased
had been] buried or not. In the mourning for Yüan-[tsung, 713–755] and Su-tsung
[756–762] of the T'ang [dynasty], [the period for mourning] was again reduced [from]
thirty-six days to twenty-seven days. Then the saying [that Emperor Wen, in deter-
mining the length of mourning] changed the days for the months [of the Chou period
of mourning, which had been twenty-seven months] arose first from this [event]."

[4] The Pa Tomb was the sepulcher of the Emperor Wen, which he had, following
custom, prepared for himself. The point of this order was that there should be no
mound raised or any interference with the stream.

纖七日釋服它不在令中者皆以此

令比類從事布告天下使明知朕意

霸陵山川因其故無有所改歸夫人

以下至少使令中尉亞夫爲車騎將

軍屬國悍爲將屯將軍郎中令張武

remain as it has been; let it not be altered. Let [the concubines of the Emperor], the Ladies[1] and those [ranking] lower, down to the Junior Maids, be sent back [to their homes]. Let it be ordered that the Palace Military Commander [Chou] Ya-fu be made General of Chariots and Cavalry,[2] that the [Director of] Dependent States [Hsü] Tao be made General In Charge of Encampments,[3] and that the Chief of **21a** the Gentlemen-at-the-Palace Chang Wu be made the General [In Charge of] Replacing the Earth.[4] Let there be mobilized [for the funeral] sixteen thousand soldiers from the neighboring prefectures and fifteen thousand soldiers of the Prefect of the Capital.[5] The burial of the outer coffin, the opening and replacing of the earth shall be in charge of General [Chang] Wu. Let there be granted to the vassal kings and to those [ranking] below [them] down to the Filially Pious, the Fraternally Respectful, and

---

[1] Ying Shao says, "Below the Ladies 夫人 [who were outranked only by the Empress] there were the Beauties 美人, the Sweet Ladies 良人, the Eighth [Rank] Ladies 八子, the Seventh [Rank] Ladies 七子, the Senior Maids 長使, and the Junior Maids 少使. All were sent back to their homes. He considered important the cutting short of their family lines," i.e. he did not wish them to remain without children. Cf. 97A: 2a. The *Han-chi* says, "His favorite, the Lady [*née*] Shen, and those below, down to the Junior Maids, received an order to be married." Wang Hsien-ch'ien suggests that the Emperor was probably thinking about political matters—the way that the Empress Dowager did away with her husband's concubines and that supposed children of the Emperor Hui were brought forward after his death. For an account of the Emperor's harem, cf. *Han-kuan Ta-wen*, ch. 4, p. 5 ff; *Mh* II, 533; 490, n. 2.

[2] According to the *SC* 22: 11a, the Supervisor of the Household of the Empress and Heir-apparent, Jung Nu, was also made General of Chariots and Cavalry to attend upon the Empress Dowager.

[3] Yen Shih-ku says that the General In Charge of Encampments was to be "in charge of the encamped armies, in order to be prepared for any unexpected [rebellion or danger]."

[4] Ju Shun says, "He was in charge of opening the grave and filling up and burying." Cf. Mh II, 203, n. 1.

[5] Emperor Wen wished to disturb the military dispositions of the empire as little as possible.

the [Deligent] Cultivators of the Soil, gold, cash, and silk, to each a definite amount.''

July 12　On [the day] *yi-szu* [the Emperor] was buried in the Pa Tomb.

In eulogy we say:[1] Emperor Hsiao-wen occupied the throne for twenty-three years. In his palaces and apartments, in his pastures and enclosures, in his carriages and saddle-horses, in his garments and daily needs, he made no addition or increase [over the requirements of his predecessors]. If there was [any activity] that was not convenient [for the people], he at once abandoned it in order to benefit his people. At one time he wanted to make a roofless terrace. He summoned the artisans to count up its [cost], and it would cost [the equivalent of] a hundred [catties of] gold. The Emperor said, "A hundred [catties of] gold is the estate of ten families

21b of medium [means]. I have received the palaces and apartments of the deceased emperors and have constantly been afraid that I should disgrace them; what is the use of building this terrace?"[2]

He personally dressed in thick black[3] silk. The

所增益有不便輒弛以利民嘗欲作露臺召匠計之直
贊曰孝文皇帝即位二十三年宮室苑囿車騎服御無
錢帛各有數乙巳葬霸陵
藏郭穿復土屬將軍武賜諸侯王目下至孝悌力田金
為復土將軍發近縣卒萬六千人發內史卒萬五千人

---

[1] This eulogy (except for the last two sentences) is found in *SC* 10: 16a–17a verbatim (except for a few verbal differences) and translated in *Mh* II, 485–487. Its presence there, interrupting the account, seems to show that it was interpolated into the *SC* from the *HS*, but the differences between the two versions seem to indicate that the *SC* version is the earlier and the *HS* version the more polished one. Perhaps someone interpolated into the *SC* an earlier version of Pan Ku's eulogy.

[2] Szu-ma Cheng (fl. 713–742) quotes Ku Yeh-wang (519–581) as saying, "On top of the Li Mountain south of Hsin-feng there are still the ancient foundations of a terrace." Yen Shih-ku says, "Today on the top of the Li Mountain south of Hsin-feng Hsien there is a Lu-t'ai Village [Roofless Terrace Village], which is very high and conspicuous. There is still the place where the Emperor Wen wished to build a terrace." The Li Mountain 驪山 is located, according to the *Shina Redikai Chimei Yoran*, 2 *li* southeast of the present Lin-t'ung 臨潼, in the Ch'ing dynasty's Hsi-an Fu, Shensi.

[3] Chia Yi (200–168 B.C.) in his memorial to Emperor Wen, entitled *Lun-shih-chen-su*, in *Han, Wei, Liu-ch'ao Pei San-min Chia-chi* writes 身衣皁綈. Shen Ch'in-han suspects that instead of 皁 we should read 帛, making the sentence read, "He personally

因其山不起墳南越尉佗自立為帝召貴佗

下先治霸陵皆瓦器不得以金銀銅錫為飾

夫人衣不曳地帷帳無文繡以示敦朴為天

宮室常恐羞之何以臺為身衣弋綈所幸慎

百金上曰百金中人十家之產也吾奉先帝

clothes of his favorite, the Lady [*née*] Shen, did not trail on the ground. His curtains and canopies had no ornaments or embroidery, thereby showing that in naturalness and simplicity he was the leader of the world. When he constructed the Pa Tomb, he altogether [used] objects of pottery and did not allow the use of gold, silver, copper, or tin as ornaments.[1] He took advantage of [the rise of] the hill [where] his [grave was built], and did not raise a mound [upon his tomb].

When the Commandant of Nan-yüeh, [Chao] T'o, set himself up as Emperor, [Emperor Wen] summoned and honored [Chao] T'o's older and younger cousins and enveloped them with his goodness; thereupon [Chao] T'o declared himself his subject.[2] After he had made peace and friendship with the Huns, and they had gone contrary to their covenant and entered [his territory] to rob, he ordered that the borders

wore thick silk," and adds, "Why should he have fixed upon black for his clothes? The *Ku-chin-chu* [prob. written dur. 265–420] writes, 'Emperor Wen attended court wearing straw sandals.'"

[1] Such pottery mortuary objects are found in museums today. Shen Ch'in-han writes, "The *Chin Dynastic History* [written by Fang Hsüan-ling, 578–648], in the Memoir of So Ch'en, says, 'The people of the three [parts of the territory of ancient] Ch'in robbed and opened the two Han tombs of Pa and Tu [those of Emperors Wen Hsüan; the latter was 50 *li* south of Ch'ang-an] and got many jewels and precious things. Emperor Min [313–317] asked [So] Ch'en, "How is it then that there are so many things in the Han tombs?" [So] Ch'en replied, "When the Han [dynasty] Sons of Heaven had been on the throne for one year, they made their tombs. The tribute and taxes of the empire were divided into three parts: one provided for the ancestral temple; one provided for [the entertainment of] guests; one provided for the tomb. The years that the Emperor Wu of the Han [dynasty] enjoyed were many and long; when he died, the Mou Tomb could not contain any more articles and its trees were already two spans [in circumference]. The 'Red Eyebrows' [a group of bandits, ca. 23 A.D.] took the articles from the tomb, but could not diminish them by half. Today the decayed silk is still left there, and the pearls and jade have not yet been exhausted. These two tombs were parsimonious ones." ' According to what the present Annal says, then, after this Emperor died, his subjects and sons disregarded his acknowledged will."

[2] The Emperor Wen's letter to Chao T'o is considered one of the great pieces of Chinese literature. It is in 95: 9a–10a.

should prepare for defence,[1] but did not send troops deep into [the Hun territory], for fear of burdening his subjects.

When the King of Wu, [Liu P'i], feigned illness and did not come to court, [the Emperor] granted him a stool and a cane.[2] When the officials, Yüan Ang and others, remonstrated [with him], although their words were cutting, he often pardoned them, accepted [their advice], and put it into practise.[3]

22a When Chang Wu and others accepted bribes of gold or cash, and [the fact] was discovered, [the Emperor] gave to them still more presents and grants, in order to shame them.

His sole care was to improve the people by means of his virtue; for this reason [all the country] within the [four] seas was prosperous and opulent and advanced towards proper conduct and right relationships.[4] [During his reign] there were pronounced verdicts [of capital punishment] in [only] several

兄弟以德懷之佗遂稱臣與匈奴結和親後而背

約入盜令邊備守不發兵深入恐煩百姓吳王詐

病不朝賜以几杖羣臣袁盎等諫說雖切常假借

納用焉張武等受賂金錢覺更加賞賜以媿其心

專務以德化民是以海內殷富興於禮義斷獄數

---

[1] Chavannes translates this phrase, "aux commandants préposés à la garde des frontières," but I do not find any officials by this title. Cf. *Mh* II, 486.

[2] Presents made to an honored official over the age of sixty-six. Cf. *Li-chi*, ch. L, pt. i, art. i, sect. 29; *Mh* II, 487, n. 1. Liu P'i rebelled after the Emperor's death. Cf. 5:4a.

[3] Shen Ch'in-han points out that the *Feng-su T'ung-yi* (written by Ying Shao, ca. 140–206), ch. *Cheng-shih*, says, "The Emperor Hsiao-ch'eng [32–6 B.C.] asked Liu Hsiang [76–8 B.C.], saying, 'Later generations all say that Emperor Wen ruled the world until it almost attained perfect peace, and that his virtue equalled that of King Wen of the Chou [dynasty]. From what did this saying arise?' [Liu Hsiang] replied, 'It arose from his practise regarding advice. Emperor Wen respected those who offered advice, in order not to hurt their feelings. When the officials, whether great or small, came [to him], then they could speak to him with ease, and the Emperor would stop his carriage and listen to them. If their advice could be [followed], he called it "Good"; if it could not be [followed], he merely smiled pleasantly. Most of these advisors praised him. Later people saw their transmitted writings, and so considered him to have been as [the writings said].' "

[4] Down to this point, this eulogy is found, practically verbatim, in the *SC*. Cf. p. 272, n. 1.

百 刑 呼	漢	hundred [cases]; [so that he] almost succeeded in
幾 措 仁	書	setting aside punishments [without using them].[1]
致 嗚 哉	四	Alas! How benevolent he was![2]

[1] *HS* 72: 14a says, "[Kung] Yü [a high official, lived 124–43 B.C.] also said, 'In the time of Emperor Hsiao-wen, he honored probity and purity and despized avariciousness and impurity. The adopted sons-in-law of merchants and officials who were sentenced for bribery were always imprisoned and could not become officials. He rewarded goodness and punished wickedness, and did not make his relatives and kin his chief officials. When [anyone's] crime was plain, [the Emperor ordered that person] to suffer his punishment; when it was doubtful, he gave [the criminal] to the people [for public opinion upon his crime; cf. *Chou-Li*, 35: 26, Biot p. 322 f]. He had no law for commuting crimes [by the payment of a fine], hence his orders were carried out and his prohibitions were effective, and the [land] within the [four] seas was greatly influenced [by his example]. In the empire there were pronounced verdicts upon [only] four hundred [cases], which was no different from setting aside punishments [without using them].' "

[2] This concluding sentence is the positive form of the last sentence in the *SC*'s chapter. Cf. *Mh* II, 495. This eulogy of Emperor Wen is largely a criticism of Emperor Wu, who did very much the opposite of what Emperor Wen is here represented as having done. Cf. 6: 39b, the last sentence.

CHAPTER IV

Appendix I

STANDARD WEIGHTS AND MEASURES OF HAN TIMES

The standard weights and measures are given in *HS* 21A: 15b–20a as follows:

"The measures of length are the *fen* 分, the inch 寸, the foot 尺, the *chang* 丈, and the *yin* 引. They are used to measure length. They arose originally from the length of the *huang-chung* [a sonorous tube; cf. *Mh* III, 302, 314–316]. Using medium sized kernels of black millet 秬黍 [which the *Erh-ya* III, p. 8a, defines as black millet], with the width of one [kernel of] millet measure ninety *fen*—[that is] the length of the *huang-chung*.[1] One [kernel of millet] is one *fen*; ten *fen* are an inch; ten inches are a foot; ten feet are a *chang*; ten *chang* are a *yin*—thus the five measures of length are clearly defined. . . .

"The measures of capacity are the *yo* 龠, the *ko* 合, the *sheng* 升, the *tou* 斗, and the *hu* 斛. They are used to measure amounts. They arose originally from the *yo* of the *huang-chung*. They are used to measure quantities and therein to define its volume. Using medium sized kernels of black millet, 1200 [kernels] fill its *yo*, using [clear] well water to level off the grains which stick out above the top of the measure. Double a *yo* makes a *ko* [a pun; the word for *ko* is used to mean 'double']; ten *ko* make a *sheng*; ten *sheng* make a *tou*; ten *tou* make a *hu*. Then the five measures of capacity are excellent [standard instruments].

"The method of [construction of the standard measure is as follows]: Using bronze, [take] a square [which is] a foot [on each side] and circumscribe [a circle] outside of it, [on each] side making a [slight] additional space. Its top is the *hu*, its bottom is the *tou*, its left ear is the *sheng*, and its right ear is the *ko* and the *yo*. Its shape is like a bird-cup (*chio*). . . . Its weight is two *chün*, . . . double 11,520 [*shu*]. . . . The persons who hold the offices of the Great Granarian and of the Grand Minister of Agriculture have charge of them. . . .

"The weights used with a balance are the *shu* 銖, the tael 兩, the catty 斤, the *chün* 鈞, and the picul 石. They are used to weigh things; with a level [balance] as a standard, to know their weight. They

---

[1] *SC* 25: 8a (*Mh* III, 314) says that the *huang-chung* is 8.1 Chinese inches long; but Liu Hsin (i cent. B.C.), Cheng Hsüan (127–200), the *Sui Dynastic History*, and other authorities all give the length of the *huang-chung* as 9 inches.

arose originally from the weight in the *huang-chung*. One *yo* [the volumetric contents of the *huang-chung*] contains 1200 [kernels of] millet and weighs 12 *shu*. Double it is a tael [a pun, the word for 'tael' also means 'double']. Twenty-four *shu* make a tael; sixteen taels make a catty; thirty catties make a *chün*; four *chün* make a picul."

Fortunately we are not ignorant of the units contained in this table. There has been preserved in the imperial palace at Pcking an imperial standard measure that is dated by its inscription in 9 A.D., during the reign of Wang Mang. It came to light in 1924. A hundred of these standard measures are said to have been made and distributed about the empire, of which only this one remains. This measure is plainly alluded to in the passage of the *HS* translated above. The inscription on the *hu* of this standard measure is translated here:

"The lawful admirable [standard] measure. The *hu*.

[The area of its base is obtained by taking] a square [which is] a foot [on each side] and circumscribing [a circle] outside of it.

The additional space on [each] side is 0.095 inch.

The area [of the base] is 162 [square] inches.

Its depth is a foot.

Its volume is 1620 [cubic] inches.

Its capacity is ten *sheng*."

The other measures have similar inscriptions, except for the numerals.

This standard measure is a bronze right cylinder in shape, with a membrane across it one inch from one end, thus making of the two ends a *hu* and a *tou* measure respectively. On one side is attached a similar cylinder containing a *sheng*; on the other side is another cylinder, arranged like the large one, making a *ko* and a *yo* measure. A drawing of this measure is to be found in the *Hsi-ch'ing Ku-chien* 西淸古監, ch. 34; an account of it is in Wang Kuo-wei, *Kuan-t'ang Chi-lin* 觀堂集林, no. 19. An account of the mathematics involved is to be found in the *Yenching Journal of Chinese Studies*, Dec. 1930, no. 8, p. 1493 ff. An excellent description, with photographs, is to be found in Ma Heng, *The Fifteen Different Classes of Measures as Given in the Lü Li Chih of the Sui Dynasty History*, translated by John C. Ferguson, Peiping, 1932.

Mr. H. Ma 馬衡 of the National Palace Museum, Peiping, has very kindly supplied me with measurements of this important standard measure. The *hu*, which is said to be 1 ancient foot deep, measures 0.2310 meters in depth. The other measures are in proportion. The volume of the *hu* is 19968.753 cc. with the others in proportion.

Mr. Ma Heng also very kindly sent me a copy of a paper by the late Dr. Fu Liu 劉復, in which Dr. Liu tells that he examined four weights dating from the time of Wang Mang, which were in the possession of the Peiping 古物保管委員會. These four weights are evidently of 3, 6, 9, and 60 catties respectively, and weighed 730.050 g., 1446.150 g., 2222.870 g., and 14775.000 g., respectively. The first two have no inscription; the third is marked "律九斤 Nine Legal Catties," and the fourth is marked "律二 □ Two Legal [*Chün*]." The legal weight of a catty in Wang Mang times, as determined by these four weights, was 243.350 g., 241.025 g., 246.986 g., and 246.250 g., respectively, the average being 244.028 g. Dr. Liu thinks this weight is quite reliable; we may then take 244 g. as the weight of the ancient catty.

Dr. Liu had previously weighed the standard measure of Wang Mang, which the *HS* says (in the passage quoted above) weighs two *chün*. From that weight he calculated the catty as 226.667 g. I have also checked that weight by millet grains. Wang Hsien-ch'ien says that the millet in terms of which these measures and weights are given is *p'ei* 秠, which is said by the *Erh-ya* to have two kernels in one husk. But the *Erh-ya* seems to distinguish between *p'ei* and *chü* 秬 (the word used in the *HS*); seed experts moreover doubt the existence of any such millet as the supposed *p'ei*, for all known millets have only one seed in a spikelet. It may be a rare sport. *Panicum miliaceum* is of the right size to be the millet referred to; the black veronesh variety is a dark brown and could easily be denoted by the definition of *chü* in the *Erh-ya*, "black millet." Ten of its seeds set side by side measure 21.8 mm., which is only a little smaller than the Han inch. Stein (*Serindia*, I, 374) measured the inch of later Han times as 22.9 mm. Data found on a piece of silk of Han times (cf. Chavannes, *Documents decouverts par Aurel Stein*, p. 118) indicate that the Han inch was 22.7 mm.

Twenty average size seeds were weighed by an expert and the weight of a seed (average of three weighings) was found to be 0.00590 grams, so that the ancient tael weighed about 218 gr. or 14 g. According to the size, this weight should be a little under the standard Wang Mang weight. To check this weight, 111 ancient cash, all with the inscription, "Half tael," and dating from Ch'in and Han times, loaned by Dr. A. W. Hummel, were weighed. Four large cash averaged 96.1 gr. each. The two best medium sized cash averaged 95.7 gr. each. Thirteen medium sized cash averaged 74.8 gr. each. Nine small cash seemingly in good condition averaged 42.2 gr. each. Eighty-five ordinary small cash averaged 38.3 gr. each. Since the Han dynasty regularly issued light-weight cash and permitted private coinage, it is natural that there should have been large variations in the weight of cash. If we take the weight of the largest of these cash as being an actual half-tael, as its inscription says, the ancient tael weighed 192 gr., not far from the weight found from the *miliaceum* seeds. Something should be added to this weight because of the wear and tear on coins. Chavannes (*Mh* II, 103, n. 2) reports a statement in the *Chin-shih-so* (sect. *Chin-sou*, B) that the ancient catty weighed 6 taels of the present weight or 225 grams, which checks well with the weight we found.

To check the volumetric data, the volume of 9600 miliaceum seeds was measured and found to be 81 ml., so that the volume of a *yo* would be 10.1 cc., an amount slightly larger than that in the Wang Mang measure. Laufer (*Chinese Pottery of the Han Dynasty*, p. 293) however notes a pottery ewer inscribed "Contains one *sheng*; weighs 14 taels; 52 B.C. No. 5." He reports its capacity as 790 cc., which is much too large; its weight, about 18 ounces, is also too large; this measure must be rejected as representing a marked variant.

Stein (*ibid.* II, 660, 669) found several foot-rules of Han times in the desert, which measured about 9 inches (Eng. meas.) in length. Wang Kuo-wei (*Jour. N. C. Br. R. A. S.*, 59: 111 ff) reports a foot-measure of the Wang Mang period a little over 9 inches (Eng. meas.) in length; he checked its length by the 'trousers cash,' four of which made a foot.

Using the above data from the Wang Mang standard measure and from the weights, the following table of Han standard measures is obtained:

LENGTH

1 *fen* =		2.31 mm.	= 0.091 in. Eng. meas.
10 *fen*	= 1 inch =	23.10 mm.	= 0.909 in. Eng. meas.
10 inches	= 1 foot =	231.0 mm.	= 9.094 in. Eng. meas.
10 feet	= 1 *chang* =	2.31 meters	= 7 ft. 6.94 in. Eng. meas.
10 *chang*	= 1 *yin* =	23.10 meters	= 75 ft. 9.4 in. Eng. meas.

CAPACITY

1 *yo* =		9.98437 cc. =	0.60927 cu. in.	
2 *yo*	= 1 *ko* =	19.9687 cc. =	1.2185 cu. in.	
10 *ko*	= 1 *sheng* =	199.687 cc. =	12.1856 cu. in.	= 0.36 U. S. dry pint.
10 *sheng*	= 1 *tou* =	1996.875 cc. =	121.8561 cu. in.	= 1.81 U. S. dry quart.
10 *tou*	= 1 *hu* =	19968.753 cc. =	1218.5608 cu. in.	= 0.565 U. S. bushels = 19.9682 liters.

CHAPTER IV

WEIGHT

1 *shu*	=	9.8 gr.	= 0.64 g.
24 *shu*	= 1 tael	= 235.4 gr.	= 15.25 g.
16 taels	= 1 catty	= 8.6 oz. avoir.	= 244 g.
30 catties	= 1 *chün*	= 16 lb. 2.2 oz. avoir.	= 7.32 kilograms.
4 *chün*	= 1 picul	= 64 lb. 8.8 oz. avoir.	= 29.3 kilograms.

These measures are all smaller than present day measures. Wang Kuo-wei (cf. *Jour. N. C. Br. R. A. S.*) has described the causes and manner in which the foot measure was lengthened. Probably similar causes operated with other measures. Whereas in Han times 10 *tou* made a *hu*, later five *tou* made a *hu*. The very existence of a standard measure illustrates forcibly the degree of imperial organization at that time.

CHAPTER IV

Appendix II

THE SACRED FIELD

This was the field in which the emperor opened the agricultural season by himself turning several furrows. Chavannes discussed the derivation and meaning of this word; cf. *Mh* II, 463, n. 2. The Commentator Tsan whom he mentions is Fu Tsan (fl. ca. 285). Cf. also Maspero, *La Chine antique*, p. 231–232.

Ying Shao, in a comment to *HS* 4: 9b, says, "Anciently the Son of Heaven plowed 10 *mou* of the sacred field for the world." Wei Chao adds, "耤 is to borrow. He borrows the strength of the people to cultivate it in order to uphold the ancestral temple and moreover to encourage and lead the empire, causing them to emphasize agriculture." Wang Hsien-ch'ien says that, anciently 耤 and 籍 were interchanged; according to the comment of Ying Shao on *HS* 4: 9b, his text had the latter character; Wei Chao's comment (197–273/4) shows that his text had the former. The Official ed. has the latter character at that point. The word should be written correctly as 耤. In the *Shuo-wen* under this last character "it says, 'The emperor's Sacred Field [contains] 1000 *mou*. In ancient times [the government] employed the people like borrowing them. Hence it was called 耤, from 耒 [to plow] and 昔 giving the pronunciation.' Under 藉 [the *Shuo-wen*] says, 'The sacrificial pad [made of Myriophyllum 藻 or Imperata 茅, on which an offering was placed].' It also says, 'Grass which is not plaited is a wolf's litter (i.e. in great disorder) 草不編狠藉.' Under 籍 it says, 'An account book.'" Then Wei Chao's interpretation, which Chavannes rejects, is correct.

HS 65: 10b says, "The Ku-ch'eng Temple is distant, with no place for sojourning; moreover [the place is entirely] occupied by catalpas, bamboos, and the Sacred Field." Fu Ch'ien [ca. 125–195] comments on a sentence on 4: 12b [cf. p. 249], "The Ku-ch'eng Temple was south of the city of Ch'ang-an." Wang Ch'i-yüan (xix cent.) says, commenting on 4: 9b, "This was the fixed place of the Han [dynasty's] sacred field. Emperor Hsiao-wu plowed [the sacred field] in the Shang-lin [Park; Emperor] Hsiao-chao plowed [the sacred field] in the amusement park [within the Wei-yang Palace] of the Intendant of the Imperial Palace Parks. Hence the annals especially record it [because it was not the usual practise.

HS] 24 [A: 12a] says, 'The Emperor was impressed by the words of Chia Yi to open the sacred field the first time.' " But from the dates in Chia Yi's memorial (24A: 10b), this latter statement seems incorrect.

Tu Yu (735–812) in his *T'ung-tien*, ch. 46, has a long historical account dealing with the practise of plowing the sacred field, beginning with the Chou and ending with the T'ang dynasty. We append a translation of his account dealing with the first two dynasties: "[According to] the regulations of the Chou [dynasty], 'the Son of Heaven in the first month of spring selected [the day] of the first conjunction [of the sun and moon] and, himself carrying the plow and plowshare, placed them in the right [side] of his chariot. Leading the great ministers of the first and second ranks, the nobles, and the grandees, he personally plowed in the sacred field of a thousand *mou* in the southern suburbs [of the capital]. With his [ceremonial] cap with vermillion cap-strings, he himself held the plow, and the Son of Heaven [turned] three furrows' [the foregoing sentences are taken from the *Book of Rites*, Bk. IV, sect. I, pt. I, par. 13] in order to use it to serve Heaven, Earth, the mountains, the streams, the gods of the land and of the grains, and the deceased rulers, using [its products] to make sweet wine, rice or millet wine, millet, and sacrificial grain. Thereupon these products were taken to the *Nei-chai* [the superintendant of the inner apartments in the palace] and 'an imperial edict [summoned] the Empress to lead the persons in the six palaces [within the imperial palace] to make the late and early [varieties of] seed to grow in order to present them to the ancestors' [these sentences are taken from the *Chou-li*, cf. Biot's trans. I, p. 148]. She ordered the ladies of the harem to store the seed to grow it again. The *Tien-szu* [the officer in charge of the laborers] 'put himself at the head of his subordinates and tilled and hoed the King's field, and in season brought [to him its products]' [this sentence is also taken from the *Chou-li*; cf. Biot's trans. I, p. 84].

"Under the Han [dynasty], the decree of Emperor Wen reads, 'Agriculture is the foundation of the world. Let the sacred field be opened. We Ourself lead in plowing in order to provide millet and grain offerings for the [imperial] ancestral temples.' The [*Han-*]*chiu-yi* [composed by Wei Hung, fl. 25–57, pt. II, p. 6b, 7a] says, 'In the beginning of spring, [the Emperor] himself plows in the sacred field east [of the capital]. The officials sacrifice to the God of Agriculture. (The God of Agriculture is Shen-nung, Emperor Yen.) They offer one ox, one ram, and one pig. The many officials all follow him. The Emperor [plows] three furrows, the three highest ministers [plow] five [furrows], the assistants to the three highest ministers and the [other] ministers [plow] ten]furrows], the gentlemen and the common people [finish plowing] the entire *mou*. [The Emperor] grants to [the people of] the three [capital] commanderies within 200 *li*, to the Filially Pious, Fraternally Respectful, and Cultivators of the Fields and to the San-lao, cloth, silk and ten thousand *hu* of seeds of all kinds of grains, in order to establish for them the granary of the sacred field. He establishes a Chief and Assistants for the granary. The grains are all used for the grain offerings at the worship in the sacrifices to Heaven, Earth, in the ancestral temple, and to the many spirits of mountains and rivers.' The Emperor Ching's imperial edict said, 'We Ourselves plow to lead the world [in plowing].' The Emperor Chao, when young, ascended the throne and plowed in the amusement park of the Intendant of the Imperial Palace Parks [within the Wei-yang Palace]."

The ancient word for the Sacred Field implies that this field was one which 'borrows' the forces of the people for its cultivation. The Emperor himself only plowed a few furrows, the actual cultivation was done by others. In Han times, the Imperial Sacred Field was located at the Ku-ch'eng Temple, south of Ch'ang-an, although, on occasion, other places were plowed. The products of the Imperial Field were used for sacrifices in the imperial ancestral temples.

CHAPTER IV

Appendix III

ECLIPSES DURING THE REIGN OF EMPEROR WEN

During this period, six eclipses were recorded in the *SC* and *HS*. We discuss them in chronological order.

i. In the second year, the eleventh month, on the day *kuei-mao*, the last day of the month, an eclipse was recorded (4: 8b). P. Hoang gives this date as Jan. 2, 178 B.C., on which Oppolzer calculated his solar eclipse no. 2447. This was a partial eclipse; calculation shows that at Ch'ang-an it reached a magnitude of 0.20 at 2:48 p.m., local time. The longitude of the sun was 279.0° = 278.2° R.A. *HS* 27 Cb: 13b says that it was one degree in the constellation Wu-nü, of whose stars ϵ and μ Aquarii were then in 281.7° and 283.0° R.A. respectively.

ii. In the *SC*, after the record of the above eclipse, there is the following statement (cf. *Mh* II, 461), "In the twelfth month, on the day of full moon [the fifteenth of the month], there was an eclipse of the sun." This date was, according to Hoang, Jan. 17, 178 B.C.; but eclipses of the sun cannot happen on the day of full moon. They happen only at new moon, whereas eclipses of the moon happen at full moon. Hsü Kuang (352–425) says that the *HS* does not record this eclipse [it is now neither in chap. 4 nor chap. 27], and tells that one copy [of the *SC*] says it was an eclipse of the moon, but that the histories do not record eclipses of the moon. The conjectural emenation of that copy is correct —Oppolzer calculated his lunar eclipse no. 1580 on the evening of Jan. 16, 178 B.C. at Ch'ang-an. If the historian misread in the astronomical records a poorly written 月 as being 日, this mistake could easily occur. This passage seems to show that the court astronomers kept a record of lunar as well as of solar eclipses. The discrepancy in dates indicates that Hoang's calendar is a day in error here.

iii. In the third year, the tenth month, on the day *ting-yu*, the last day of the month, a third eclipse was recorded (4: 11a). This date was Dec. 22, 178 B.C., for which Oppolzer calculated his solar eclipse no. 2449. He charts the umbra of the moon as passing through the Malay peninsula; calculation shows that the eclipse at Ch'ang-an reached a magnitude of 0.35 at 1:58 p.m., local time. The sun was in long. 267.4° = 267.1° R.A. *HS* 27 Cb: 13b adds, "It was 23 degrees in [the constellation] Tou," of whose stars μ, λ, ϕ, σ, τ and ζ Aquarii were then in R.A. 241.1°, 243.5°, 247.2°, 249.8°, 253.3° and 250.6°, respectively.

284

iv. In the third year, the eleventh month, on the day *ting-mao*, the last day of the month, a fourth eclipse is listed (4: 11a). P. Hoang gives this date as Jan. 20, 177 B.C., the first day of the twelfth month. *HS* 27 Cb: 13b adds, "It was 8 degrees in [the constellation] Hsü," whose stars, α Equulei and β Aquarii, were then in R.A. 291.4° and 293.4°. The *Han-chi* 7: 7b dates this eclipse on "[the day] *yi-mao*, the last day of the month," 12 days before the *HS*'s date and on the 18th day of that month.

There was no eclipse on that date, for Oppolzer gives none. In the 22 years from the preceding eclipse to the next correctly dated eclipse in 154 B.C., in which period the *HS* lists 3 eclipses, there occurred 56 eclipses, of which only 10 were visible in China.[1]

In this period, 9 umbral eclipses were visible in China: (1) no. 2452, on June 6, 176 B.C., 23 days after a ting-mao day, sun in long. 70.7° = 69.3° R.A.; (2) no. 2459, on Oct. 10, 174 B.C., 39 days after such a day, sun in long. 193.2°; (3) no. 2460, on May 4, 173 B.C., 36 days after such a day, sun in long. 10.6°; (4) no. 2470, on July 17, 169 B.C., 41 days after such a day, sun in long. 110.2°; (5) no. 2475, on May 28, 167 B.C., 1 day after such a day, sun in long. 61.9°; (6) no. 2477, on May 17, 166 B.C., 55 days after such a day, sun in long. 51.4°; (7) no. 2486, on Mar. 5, 162 B.C., 3 days after such a day, sun in long. 340.9°; but the umbral path of this eclipse ran so far south that I calculated it, and found it invisible in the present Ch'ang-an, Pei-p'ing, Shantung, and Ch'ang-sha. In Wu (present Soochow), the eclipse reached a magnitude of only 0.02 at 4: 34 p.m. local time, so that it was practically invisible; (8) no. 2489, on Aug. 16, 161 B.C., 53 days after such a day, sun in long. 140.1° = 142.5° R.A.; the umbral path of this eclipse ran so far north that I calculated it and found that in Ch'ang-an it reached a magnitude of 0.17 at 5: 16 a.m. local time; (9) no. 2505, on Oct. 10, 155 B.C., 19 days after such a day, sun in long. 193.4°; the umbral path of this eclipse ran so far south that I calculated it and found that in Ch'ang-an the eclipse reached a magnitude of 0.17 at 9: 32 a.m., local time. Westwards and southwards its magnitude was greater.

In this period, 11 partial eclipses occurred in the northern hemisphere, of which only one was visible in ancient China: no. 2481, on Mar. 26, 164 B.C., 13 days after a *ting-mao* day, sun in long. 165.7°. At Ch'ang-an the eclipse reached a magnitude of only 0.02 at 7: 12 a.m., with visibility

[1] Besides those located in Oppolzer, the following 9 partial eclipses were invisible in China because they belonged to initial (i.) or terminal (t.) runs in exeligmos series whose nearest umbral eclipses was located near the south pole: no. 2454 (t.); no. 2457 (i.), no. 2464 (i.), no. 2473 (t.), no. 2498 (t.), no. 2474 (t.), no. 2482 (i.), no. 2483 (t.), and no. 2501 (i.).

better at places north and west. On the longitude of Ch'ang-an, at latitude 40°, in the Ordos region, the magnitude of the eclipse reached 0.14.[2]

It is probable that the eclipse intended by the text was the first umbral eclipse listed above, on June 6, 176 B.C. Then the *ting* 丁- *mao* of the text is an error for *hsin* 辛- *mao* (a natural mistake) and Hoang's calendar is two days in error; this date was the first day of the fifth month, in the fourth year. The heavenly location given for this eclipse is then greatly in error.

v. In the latter part of the reign, the fourth year, the fourth month, on the day *ping-yin*, the last day of the month, a fifth eclipse is listed (4: 17b). The *Han-chi* 8: 15a has the same reading. But there was no *ping-yin* day in that month. *HS* 27 Cb: 13b dates it on the day *ping-ch'en*, and adds, "It was 13 degrees in [the constellation] Tung-ching." This latter date was June 9, 160 B.C., according to P. Hoang. The first star in Tung-ching, μ Gemini, was then in 63.4° R.A. But Oppolzer lists no eclipse on this date.

For the eclipses occurring about this time, cf. the discussion under the preceding eclipse. As to their cyclical days, *ping-yin* is the day before *ting-mao*, and *ping-ch'en* is 11 days before *ting-mao*.

Very possibly the eighth umbral eclipse mentioned previously, on Aug. 16, 161 B.C., is the eclipse referred to in the text. It occurred on a *keng-shen* day, in the third year, the sixth month, the day before the last day of the month, according to Hoang's calendar. This identification would require no alteration in the order of events of *HS* ch. 4, merely a redating of one event; the cyclical day is already in doubt because of the difference between the two recordings. The location of the eclipse in the heavens is about 60° in error.

vi. *HS* 27 Cb: 13b adds, "In the seventh year, the first month, on [the day] *hsin-wei*, the first day of the month, there was an eclipse of the sun." The *Han-chi* has the same recording. P. Hoang gives this date as Feb. 9, 157 B.C. But no eclipse occurred on that date.

For eclipses occurring about this time, cf. sub eclipse iv. *Hsin-wei* is 4 days after *ting-mao*. There was no eclipse visible in China in Emperor Wen's reign after the date we adopted for the preceding eclipse. It seems that Pan Ku considered this eclipse doubtful, for he did not put it into his "Annals," although it got into his chapter on the "Five Ele-

---

[2] The other ten eclipses were all calculated approximately and found to be invisible in China. They were: no. 2455, on May 26, 175 B.C.; no. 2456, on Oct. 20, 175 B.C.; no. 2465, on Mar. 14, 171 B.C.; no. 2466, on Aug. 8, 171 B.C.; no. 2471, on Jan. 10, 168 B.C.; no. 2472, on June 7, 168 B.C.; no. 2490, on Jan. 12, 160 B.C; no. 2492, on Aug. 6, 160 B.C.; 2499, on June 5, 157 B.C.; and no. 2500, on Oct. 31, 157 B.C.

ments," and was copied by the *Han-chi* in its chronological account. It looks as though someone considered that an eclipse was due at this time in order to predict the death of Emperor Wen, so placed an eclipse five months (about an eclipse season) before his death. Pan Ku's rejection of this eclipse in his Annals is a good testimony to his historical judgment.

But the solar eclipse of Oct. 10, 155 B.C., which Hoang dates in Emperor Ching's second year, the ninth month, the day *yi-yu*, the last day of the month, was the only eclipse visible in China after the one identified for the preceding eclipse and before the next and correctly dated eclipse. Since Hoang's calendar may be a day in error, this date may have been the tenth month, the first day, the day *ping-hsü*. It seems stretching things to identify this eclipse with the one listed in ch. 27, yet it is peculiar that, in a period during which only one eclipse was listed, there should have been only one eclipse visible.

CHAPTER IV

APPENDIX IV

SOLAR ECLIPSES DURING THE FIRST FIFTY YEARS OF THE FORMER HAN DYNASTY

Since exactly fifty years elapsed from the accession of Kao-tsu in 206 B.C. down to and including the year of Emperor Wen's death, 157 B.C., it may be useful to summarize the results we have obtained in the discussion of the eclipses during that period. Out of the total number of 119 eclipses occurring, only 23 were visible in China. Four of these were so barely visible that we can hardly expect them to have been noticed. Excluding these, only 19 eclipses were visible in Ch'ang-an in this half-century. Six of them were recorded correctly. For three more listings we were able to suggest plausible dates. If these suggestions are accepted, only 9 out of a possible 19 eclipses were recorded— about half of the total eclipses visible, weather permitting.

In these four reigns, we found 13 records of solar eclipses. Nine referred to actual solar eclipses (accepting the suggested corrections for their dates). One plainly referred to an actual lunar eclipse. In the case of the three remaining we found great difficulties in suggesting any date. For one, we found reason to suspect that it was a later interpolation. For a second, we found that the general opposition on the part of the officials to the Empress Dowager's acts made it possible that an eclipse was fabricated to warn her. The third we found textually doubtful, since Pan Ku had not included it in his "Annals."

The ten plainly visible eclipses that were not recorded were the following: in the reign of Kao-tsu, four: July 6, 206 B.C., Jan. 1, 205, July 26, 197, June 6, 195; in the reign of Emperor Hui, one: Sept. 29, 192; in the reign of the Empress of Kao-tsu, none; in the reign of Emperor Wen, five: Oct. 10, 174, Apr. 4, 173, July 17, 169, May 28, 167, and May 17, 166 B.C. The four others which were barely visible or visible only outside of Ch'ang-an were those of Oct. 8, 201 B.C., May 6, 184, Mar. 26, 164, and Mar. 5, 162 B.C.

Bad weather is a possible cause for the failure to record some of these eclipses. But in Sian (Ch'ang-an), Shensi, during the period 1924–1934, the number of overcast days, as reported by Fr. E. Gherzi, S.J., the Director of the Zikawei Observatory, averaged almost the same for each month in the year, ranging from 7 in July and November to 11 in April and October. The monthly variation of the weather thus cannot account for the omission of these eclipses. Reports could moreover have been secured from places outside the capital.

It is however noticeable that during the years 188 to 175 B.C. all the visible eclipses were recorded,[1] whereas between 175 and 162 B.C. five eclipses were visible and none were recorded. None of these were total in Ch'ang-an; they might easily have been missed if no one was looking for them. Why were they missed? Was it because of a change in the responsible astronomer, who was negligent in his duties? Or was it because it was considered that the good reign of Emperor Wen left Heaven without any necessity of sending eclipses? Emperor Wen in an edict said that an eclipse was an admonition from Heaven (4: 9a). Neugebauer (*op. cit.* II, 73) says that an eclipse is not conspicuous unless it reaches a magnitude of at least 0.75, or, at sunrise or sunset, 0.33, so that, unless people were looking for eclipses, they might easily be missed. Yet Halley's comet appeared in 163 B.C. (cf. p. 261, note), and it too was not recorded. Such a spectacle could hardly have been missed. Perhaps comets were not then being regularly recorded; cf. 5: n. 1.3. In later periods of good rule, such as that of Emperor Hsüan, eclipses are similarily lacking in the records.

Several conclusions emerge from a consideration of these eclipses: First, the Chinese accounts are predominatingly reliable, even for the beginning of the Han period. In the later parts of this period, we shall find them much more reliable.

Secondly, there are errors of recording or transmission of the text. One eclipse (the second one in Kao-tsu's reign) is probably a later interpolation; three others were incorrectly dated, possibly before Pan Ku used them. In the case of the lunar eclipse we found positive evidence that an error had been made in transcribing from the original astronomical records.

Thirdly, we found that the court astronomers, in some cases at least, kept records of lunar as well as of solar eclipses, although the historians did not consider them worth recording.

Fourthly, we found that in one case at least (cf. ch. 2: App., ii) astronomical reports were gathered from places outside the capital. The divergences between the list in the "Annals" and that in ch. 27 regarding this eclipse suggest that the list in ch. 27 came from the court astronomers at the capital.

---

[1] If we adopt the eclipse of 192 for the first eclipse in the Empress Dowager's reign, that period is lengthened from 194 to 175 B.C.

CHAPTER IV

Fifthly, we found that Pan Ku must have had records of eclipses not found in the *SC*, which he inserted into that material.

Sixthly, eclipses were considered as warnings to the ruler from Heaven, so that during an unpopular reign all visible eclipses were recorded, while during a decade in a "good" reign no eclipses were recorded, not even a conspicuous comet.

Seventhly, our tables of correspondences between European and Chinese dates are quite accurate for Han times, but they may be two days in error.

Eighthly, the records of the position of the sun at the time of an eclipse are not reliable. In the case of the six correctly recorded eclipses, that location is fairly good, but in the only one which was total in Ch'ang-an, that of 181 B.C., in which alone the position of the sun among the stars could have been observed at the time of the eclipse, that position is in error by 14°. In the case of the three eclipses for which we suggested emendations in their date, the location of the sun is grossly in error. In the case of the one which seems a later interpolation, the location of the sun was plainly calculated from the calendar. We suspect that all of these records were so calculated. These locations are moreover not given in the "Annals," but only in the "Treatise on the Five Elements," and in two cases not at all. They are thus of little help in identifying an eclipse.

Chapter V

INTRODUCTION

This chapter, like the other Annals, is rather a chronological summary of the reign, amplified by the more important imperial enactments of the period, than what we should today call a history. The history, in the modern sense, is to be found in the "Treatises" and "Memoirs" dealing with the period.

The chief source for this chapter, as for the preceding chapters, was probably the corresponding section of the *SC*, which, in this case, comprises the last part of ch. 10 ("The Annals of Emperor Wen") and the whole of ch. 11 ("The Annals of Emperor Ching"). The foregoing conclusion has however been challenged; Chang Yen, in the third century, declared that *SC* ch. 11 was one of the ten chapters which Pan Ku says were missing from that book; Szu-ma Cheng in the eighth century says that *SC* ch. 11 was taken from *HS* ch. 5. That skeptical view has received wide credence; Liang Ch'i-ch'ao (1873–1929) accepts it without comment in his *Yao-chi Chieh-t'i Chi-ch'i Tu-fa*, p. 51.

Since Chang Yen's exact statement can better be discussed in connection with the next chapter, I shall here merely refer the reader to the introduction of that chapter and the conclusions there drawn. The only sure fact is that Pan Ku found ten chapters missing from the *SC*; Chang Yen seems to have made little more than a poor guess concerning which ones they were. Chavannes, after discussing this matter, says flatly that *SC* ch. 11 is not taken from *HS* ch. 5: "Nous ne voyons aucune raison de mettre en doubte leur authenticité." (*Mh* I, cciv; cf. also *id.* II, p. 496, n. 1). He also says that *SC* ch. 11 is quite incomplete, that it is inferior to Szu-ma Ch'ien's other work, and that hence the latter doubtless did not complete it as he had planned.

With Chavannes's conclusion I am in full accord. *HS* ch. 5 is similar to the preceding chapters in its condensation and amplification of the material in the corresponding chapters of the *SC*. *SC* ch. 11 is rather sketchy; Pan Ku filled it out, chiefly from the collection of imperial edicts which he found in the imperial files, so that this chapter contains much that is not in the *SC*. Sometimes, however, Pan Ku condensed *SC* ch. 11. That chapter contains a long list of the alterations in official

291

titles made by Emperor Ching. Pan Ku transferred them to his treatise dealing with the bureaucracy. Mentions of ministerial appointments are similarily transferred. The estimate of Emperor Ching in the concluding paragraph of SC ch. 11 is moreover quite different from that in this chapter, so much so that Pan Ku seems to be combating the unfavorable impression given by Szu-ma Ch'ien in that paragraph. These are precisely the phenomena we should expect if Pan Ku were basing his account upon that of Szu-ma Ch'ien.

Perhaps the most nearly conclusive evidence for the originality of SC ch. 11 is the curious mistake made in HS 5: 5a. Evidence from other parts of the HS and SC shows that the text of the HS at this point is in error (cf. n. 5.6); that error is moreover merely a condensed repetition of the corresponding passage in SC ch. 11. The SC moreover contains at this point additional statements omitted from the HS, so that the HS is plainly condensing the account in the SC and has fallen into error by copying that account. If Pan Ku had been compiling his account independently, he would hardly have made the same mistake that SC ch. 11 does, and would in more likelihood have given the correct information obtainable from other parts of his own and of Szu-ma Ch'ien's book.

There is then every reason to conclude that Pan Ku followed mainly the corresponding chapter of the SC in preparing this chapter. The sort of material he added is the same as that in ch. 4, and has been discussed in the introduction to that chapter.

* * *

The outstanding event during the reign of Emperor Ching was the rebellion of the Seven Kingdoms in 154 B.C. Because it lasted only a few months, only one paragraph is devoted to it in the Annals. Yet it was the most serious revolt during the Former Han period. The leaders of this rebellion were Liu P'i, King of Wu, and the descendants of Liu Fei, King of Ch'i. A full account is given in the relevant Memoirs, from which this abstract in condensed.

There had previously been serious trouble between Liu P'i and the imperial family. When Emperor Ching was still Heir-apparent, while playing an ancient game, resembling dice, he had a drunken quarrel over precedence with his second cousin, Liu Hsien, who was the son and heir of Liu P'i. The future Emperor took up the dice board, struck, and killed Liu Hsien. The Heir-apparent seems to have been in the right, for he was not punished, and the body was sent to Wu for burial. But Liu P'i was angry and sent the body back to Ch'ang-an. Emperor Wen smoothed the matter over and buried the murdered prince. Liu P'i thereafter alleged that he was ill and refused to come annually to

Ch'ang-an to pay court as was required. Such conduct was almost equivalent to rebellion, but Emperor Wen, after investigation, again smoothed matters over, granting to the offended King a stool and cane, symbols of age, and excusing him from attendance because of his infirmities. Liu P'i then maintained peace as long as Emperor Wen was alive.

There had also been bad feeling between the royal family of Ch'i and the imperial family. That royal family had descended from Kao-tsu's eldest son, Liu Fei, who did not succeed Kao-tsu because he was the child of a concubine. When the Empress of Kao-tsu died, Liu Fei's eldest son, Liu Hsiang, naturally thought that he would be given the imperial throne, but Kao-tsu's followers selected Emperor Wen, a son of Kao-tsu by another concubine. Liu Hsiang had put into the field his army and that of the oldest active member of the imperial clan, while the future Emperor Wen had done nothing. Hence Liu Hsiang and his clan thought the selection unjust and were bitterly disappointed.

Chia Yi, perhaps the greatest statesman of Former Han times, warned Emperor Wen about the possibility of rebellion by the various vassal kingdoms, and urged weakening their power. Emperor Wen saw the cogency of his reasoning, but also had the wisdom to see that if he tried to take any territory from the feudal princes, such action would induce, rather than avoid, rebellion. He rejected Chia Yi's advice and sent him away to Ch'ang-sha, far from the court, thus placating the vassal kings. When Liu Tse, King of Ch'i and son of Liu Hsiang, died without heirs in 164 B.C., Emperor Wen put into practise Chia Yi's advice, dividing the large kingdom of Ch'i into seven kingdoms, which were given to Liu Hsiang's six brothers who had not yet been given kingdoms. Another kingdom, Ch'eng-yang, had also previously been made out of a section from Ch'i.

Emperor Ching favored Ch'ao Ts'o greatly, and, soon after he ascended the throne, made the latter his Grandee Secretary. Like Chia Yi, Ch'ao Ts'o realized the danger to the throne from the vassal kingdoms. The strongest kingdom was Wu, rich in copper ore. Its king, Liu P'i, minted cash and made salt from sea-water in the southern part of his kingdom. These two enterprises produced so much revenue that he dispensed with taxation. Ch'ao Ts'o was not willing to wait to enfeeble Wu until the death of this king, who was already over sixty, for he had heard that Liu P'i was making preparations for rebellion and would rebel as soon as those preparations were complete. So Ch'ao Ts'o urged upon Emperor Ching the importance of curtailing immediately the power of the various vassal kings.

293

In doing so, he took advantage of the Han laws, which seem to have been so numerous and flexible that hardly anyone could avoid violating some of them. The King of Ch'u was first charged with having broken the rule requiring continence during mourning. Ch'ao Ts'o reported his crime and suggested that he be sentenced to execution so that Emperor Ching might take away a large slice of his territory in commutation of his sentence. Ch'ao Ts'o next made other accusations against the King of Chao, part of whose territory was likewise confiscated. The same treatment was given to the kingdom of Chiao-hsi. Thus the vassal kings were thrown into consternation, wondering who would suffer next.

The King of Wu knew that, as the richest and strongest of the vassal kings, he would undoubtedly be attacked, and seems to have had private information that the officials in the capital were planning to take away most of his territory. He took the lead in arousing the vassal kings against the imperial government, especially the descendants of the King of Ch'i. His messengers arranged a coalition against the Emperor. He especially sought the King of Chiao-hsi, who was known for his military prowess. When a order arrived in Wu, commanding that his fairest provinces, including the copper region, should be taken from him, the King of Wu mobilized his army and six other kingdoms followed suit.

The news of the revolt threw Emperor Ching into a panic. Urged by his ministers, he however promptly made arrangements to meet the rebellion. The Han dynasty kept a very large body of troops, numbering many tens of thousands, at the capital (cf. p. 206, n. 4). Emperor Ching selected his father's ablest generals to lead the three armies sent against the three groups of rebels, and made his maternal cousin, Tou Ying, the Commander-in-chief, putting him in charge of the reserve army to be stationed at Jung-yang.

The King of Wu had sent a letter to all the vassal kings, blaming Ch'ao Ts'o for the conditions which led to the revolt, and urging them to join in executing Ch'ao Ts'o. A private enemy of this powerful minister secured an imperial audience and told Emperor Ching that if Ch'ao Ts'o were executed and the territory of the rebels were restored to them, they would submit. The Emperor was ready to catch at a straw. His ablest advisors, who could have corrected him, were away with the armies; when Emperor Ching secretly proposed the matter to three of his high ministers, they servilely agreed and prepared a secret memorial accusing Ch'ao Ts'o of capital crimes and begging for his execution, together with that of his relatives. Emperor Ching secretly approved this memorial and sent his Military Commander at the Capital to arrest Ch'ao Ts'o. The latter had no suspicion of the plot; when summoned, he dressed in his court garb and mounted his chariot to attend court. At the market-place he was stopped, was made to get down, and was cut in two at the waist.

This cowardly sacrifice of a loyal minister helped Emperor Ching not at all. Some days later an aged colonel told him that Liu P'i had visions of setting up an independent empire with himself as Eastern Emperor; Ch'ao Ts'o's death had merely aided the rebels by removing a faithful and far-seeing servant of the Emperor and by discouraging bold and loyal imperial subjects.

The rebelling kingdoms included four of the seven kingdoms that had been made out of Ch'i, viz. Chiao-hsi, Chi-nan, Tzu-ch'uan, and Chiao-tung, together with the three other kingdoms that had been curtailed, Wu, Chao, and Ch'u. The three other kingdoms formed from Ch'i remained loyal. The King of Ch'i went back on his agreement to rebel and guarded his cities. The King of Chi-pei said that his city-wall was broken and needed to be repaired. Nothing is said about the King of Ch'eng-yang. The King of Huai-nan, the famous Liu An, had also planned to rebel, but his plan was thwarted by his Lieutenant Chancellor. The high officials of the vassal kings were all appointed by the Emperor and were expected to watch their kings; in Ch'u and Chao four loyal officials lost their lives in attempting to prevent the revolt (cf. n. 6.5). In Huai-nan the Lieutenant Chancellor induced his King to make him General-in-Chief. In time of war, by custom, even a king had to obey his General-in-chief. This official then closed the gates of the cities and declared for the Han dynasty! An imperial general was sent to aid him; thus revolt was averted and the king kept his throne.

Thus of the ten or more kingdoms that planned to rebel, only seven actually put their forces into the field. The rebels were located in three regions: Wu and Ch'u in the lower Yangtze valley, the four kingdoms made out of Ch'i in the present Shantung, and Chao in the present western Hopei. Chao was isolated; it sent its troops to its western border, intending to join with the forces of Wu and Ch'u when they came north, secure aid from the Huns, and advance upon the imperial capital. Chao was unable to take any active part in the campaign.

The kingdoms formed from Ch'i were held back by the defections in their ranks. They gathered to besiege the capital of Ch'i. Its king sent a palace official to the Emperor for aid. Just when, against the wishes of his officials, the King of Ch'i was arranging to surrender, this palace official returned. He was captured by the besiegers and was allowed to speak to his King from the foot of the city-wall, on condition that he would falsely report the defeat of the relieving army. The man agreed, but, when he had his opportunity to speak, he sacrificed his life in order to give his message that the relieving force had been victorious and would soon arrive. Thus surrender was prevented. The troops of these four kingdoms were thus held near their bases and did little to aid the revolt.

The brunt of the fighting fell upon the troops of Wu and Ch'u. The King of Wu assembled his troops at Kuang-ling, crossed the Huai River, went west, made a junction with the troops of Ch'u, and attacked the kingdom of Liang, which was ruled by Emperor Ching's full brother, Liu Wu. The forces of Liang were routed at Chi-pi, where it is said that several tens of thousands were killed. The King of Liang sent another army against the rebels, but it was also defeated, so his troops fled into his capital, Sui-yang, which was defended.

Chou Ya-fu, who was made the imperial general against the armies of Wu and Ch'u, proposed, as his plan of campaign, to cut their communications and allow them to wear themselves out before he attacked them. They came from the Yangtze valley, where horses were scarce, hence were weak in light soldiers and cavalry, while the imperial force was strong in cavalry. Chou Ya-fu sent his cavalry to cut the communications by which food was brought to these armies.

The King of Liang sent a messenger to Chou Ya-fu for aid. But Emperor Ching was jealous of his brother, for Liu Wu was the favorite child of his mother, the Empress Dowager *née* Tou. The Emperor could not openly oppose his mother, but he would not have been sorry if his brother had suffered harm, for, probably by prearrangement with the Emperor, Chou Ya-fu refused to send aid to Liang. When Liu Wu got Emperor Ching to order that Chou Ya-fu should send aid to Liang, Chou Ya-fu did not pay any attention to the order, yet he was never called to account for his disobedience of an imperial edict.

Time was with the imperial forces, and Chou Ya-fu's plan of campaign proved wise. It was winter and the rebels had little food, for they could not capture the cities, in which food was stored, and their communications were interrupted. The rebels were finally defeated by Liang and came to Hsia-yi, where Chou Ya-fu had concentrated his troops, but Chou Ya-fu would not come out of his entrenchments to fight. Not until more than a month after the rebellion had begun, when the troops of Wu were scattered, had lost many through desertion, and were famished, did Chou Ya-fu fight a pitched battle. He routed the troops of Wu and Ch'u. The King of Wu fled from the army by night and the King of Ch'u committed suicide.

Liu P'i fled across his kingdom to the south, where he took refuge with the barbarians of Eastern Yüeh and attempted to gather troops for another attempt. But the emissaries of Emperor Ching induced the people of Tan-t'u to stab Liu P'i as he was out encouraging his troops. His head was sent to Ch'ang-an.

When the imperial forces had routed the besiegers of the capital of Ch'i and relieved its siege, it was discovered that the King of Ch'i had originally agreed to revolt. He committed suicide. Emperor Ching however pardoned his heir and appointed him to succeed his father. The kings of the four revolting kingdoms made from Ch'i either committed suicide or were executed; their kingdoms were abolished and made into commanderies.

When the Huns heard that Wu and Ch'u had been defeated, they did not come to the aid of Chao. Its king retreated to his capital, Han-tan, where he was besieged. The river was finally used to breach the city-wall, and the King of Chao committed suicide.

Thus the imperial line was firmly established on the throne and a break-up of the empire was prevented. Thereafter it became the set policy of the dynasty to enfeeble the vassal kingdoms by dividing the territory of a kingdom among all the heirs of a king, and by taking away some territory whenever a king committed a misstep. The vassal kings were carefully watched and supervised by their own officials (who were appointed by the imperial court). These kings became so unimportant that the Emperor could utterly disregard their wishes and Wang Mang could reduce them to private life without difficulty.

* * *

The reign of Emperor Ching shows the deterioration in character that was inevitable when an emperor had been raised in a harem and protected from close contact with the world of action. The decay and fall of the dynasty was eventually produced by this deterioration. Emperor Ching indulged his petty personal feelings, allowing his likes and dislikes to guide him in his choice and treatment of his ministers. He showed in practise an acute distaste for frank admonitions, and allowed palace intrigues to influence the government.

Chou Ya-fu was the most distinguished general and official in the reign. He was a faithful and capable servant, who put down the rebellion of the Seven Kingdoms and in reward was made Lieutenant

Chancellor, the highest position in the government. But he did not always trouble to bring himself into accord with Emperor Ching's likes and dislikes. After the Emperor had divorced his first Empress and had appointed his second Empress, the Emperor's mother suggested that the new Empress's brother, Wang Hsin, should be made a marquis. The procedure of ennobling the close relatives of an empress or even those of a favorite concubine, which later became common, had not yet become a custom, and Chou Ya-fu protested. He is reported to have said, "Emperor Kao-tsu made a covenant with his generals that, except for members of the Liu clan, no one should be made a king, and, except for those who have done distinguished [military] service, no one should be made a marquis. Now, although Wang Hsin is the older brother of the Empress, he has done no distinguished service; to make him a marquis would be contrary to the covenant." Emperor Ching had accordingly to drop the matter. Later Chou Ya-fu also protested against enfeoffing as marquises five Hun kings and nobles who surrendered to the Chinese: "These people have turned traitor to their king and have surrendered to your Majesty; if your Majesty makes marquises of them, then how will you be able to reprove your subjects who do not keep faith with you?" Emperor Ching did not think his arguments were apposite. He enfeoffed the lot, and Chou Ya-fu resigned his position on account of illness.

The Emperor could not forget criticism and resolved to even the score. He summoned Chou Ya-fu to a feast in the forbidden apartments of the palace and had set before him large slices of meat without having them cut up and without any chopsticks wherewith to eat. Chou Ya-fu fell into the trap, and, with the easy familiarity of one who was used to command, turned to the Master of the Mats, saying, "Bring some chopsticks." Such a request however implied criticism of the imperial arrangements, and Emperor Ching looked at him, laughing sarcastically, "This too cannot be unsatisfactory to you, sir?" Chou Ya-fu begged pardon, but the Emperor merely said, "Rise," whereupon Chou Ya-fu hastened out. Emperor Ching looked after him and said, "This man is tormented by desire; he cannot be a satisfactory official for the young lord my successor."

After such an imperial condemnation, the officials merely awaited a pretext to end his career. Before long his son purchased five hundred suits of armor from the imperial Department of Works for use in his father's funeral. A mistreated workman informed against the son, and Chou Ya-fu was arrested. He proudly refused to answer the questions put him by the officials. When Emperor Ching heard of it, he cursed him, saying, "I have no more use for him," and sent him to the Commandant of Justice's jail. There he was again questioned and charged with planning rebellion. Chou Ya-fu answered that these arms were merely burial articles, whereupon an official replied, "If you, sir, do not intend to rebel on earth, then you merely intend to rebel below the earth." The officials pressed him harshly; he refused to eat and died in five days. Thus was rewarded a faithful servant of the dynasty who had opposed the imperial will for the good of the empire.

Although Emperor Ching continued the practise of his father in his edicts, asking the officials to recommend for the bureaucracy persons who "can speak frankly and admonish unflinchingly," yet by his actions he tacitly encouraged sycophancy and discouraged any opposition to his will. A century later advice contrary to the imperial will could be denominated a crime and punished. Chou Ya-fu was the outstanding example of the Emperor's indulgence in petty dislikes; the able and proud Tou Ying was kept from high office all through the reign because he had opposed the Emperor's change of his Heir. Emperor Ching tolerated no opposition.

* * *

Intrigue showed itself most prominently in the change of the imperial heir. Emperor Ching had fourteen sons (and numerous daughters) by six different women of his harem, the largest number of children by any emperor of the Former Han dynasty. He first chose as his Heir-apparent his oldest son, Liu Jung, a son of the Concubine *née* Li. His other sons, including Liu Ch'ê, the future Emperor Wu, were made kings.

The first Empress, *née* Po, had been appointed through the influence of Emperior Ching's grandmother, the Grand Dowager Empress *née* Po, to whose clan the Empress belonged. But the Empress had no children and lost her husband's favor; four years after the death of the Grand Empress Dowager, the Empress *née* Po was dismissed. The favorite women of the Emperor thereupon intrigued for the vacant position.

Emperor Ching's eldest sister, Liu Piao, who was entitled an Elder Princess, recommended to him the women of his harem whom he favored with his attentions. She wanted to marry her daughter to the Heir-apparent, as was often done, for the two children were of different surnames. But the Heir-apparent's mother, the concubine *née* Li, was jealous of the Elder Princess's influence with the Emperor and refused to consent to the marriage.

The Elder Princess thereupon suggested marrying her daughter to Liu Ch'ê, the Emperor's son by a Lady *née* Wang. The Lady *née* Wang agreed, although her son was then less than four years old. From that time on, the Elder Princess slandered the Concubine *née* Li to Emperor Ching and praised the Lady *née* Wang. When the latter knew that the Concubine *née* Li was definitely out of favor with Emperor Ching, she moved to crystallize his feelings by sending someone to urge upon the officials the propriety of asking for the appointment of a new Empress. An official promptly suggested the mother of the Heir-apparent, the Concubine *née* Li, as the Empress. Emperor Ching became thoroughly wrathful at this idea and had the official who had made the suggestion tried and executed. Then he dismissed from his position as Heir-apparent the son of the Concubine *née* Li, Liu Jung, for it was the custom that the mother of the Heir-apparent should become the Empress. Emperor Ching next appointed as Empress his favorite, the Lady *née* Wang, and then made her son, Liu Ch'ê, the Imperial Heir-apparent. Three years later, the first Heir-apparent, Liu Jung, was imprisoned for usurping temple land and committed suicide. Thus Emperor Wu came to the throne because of palace intrigues.

There were other such palace intrigues: the memoirs of the important personages of the reign are full of them. Liu Wu, Emperor Ching's younger brother, was the favorite son of Emperor Ching's mother, and she tried to have Liu Wu made the Heir-apparent of Emperor Ching. Her nephew, the bold Tou Ying, advised Emperor Ching against such a move, thus incurring the enmity of the Empress Dowager, who banished him from the court. Later she renewed her entreaties for Liu Wu, but Yüan Ang opposed the move. In revenge Liu Wu had Yüan Ang assassinated. Emperor Ching was enraged and had the assassins traced to Liu Wu's palace. The Empress Dowager wept incessantly and refused to eat for fear that her younger son would be executed. Emperor Ching was told by the official sent to investigate, "If now Liu Wu is not executed, the law of the Han dynasty will not be carried out; if he is executed, the Empress Dowager's food will be tasteless and her sleep troubled. This trouble will come upon your Majesty." Filial piety thus kept Emperor Ching from carrying out the law, and Liu Wu was finally pardoned in spite of the Emperor's dislike for him.

Such incidents throw deep shadows upon Emperor Ching's reign. They seem quite inevitable when the ruler has grown up in the luxury and indulgence of an imperial harem. These intrigues are not told in the "Imperial Annals," because they belong to the private life of the individuals concerned, rather than to the official actions of the government, which latter were alone thought to belong in the "Annals." They are mentioned here to show the extraordinary wealth of information contained in this encyclopedic history and to urge the reader to go behind the "Annals" to the real history of the reign, which is often to be found in the "Memoirs." An abstract of the pertinent "Memoirs" will be found in the Glossary.

* * *

Szu-ma Ch'ien, in his summary of this reign (*Mh* II, 509), does not award the slightest praise to Emperor Ching; Wieger, in his *Textes historiques*, I, 452 f, condemns the Emperor roundly. Pan Ku, in his eulogy (5: 10b), on the other hand equates Emperors Wen and Ching with Kings Ch'eng and K'ang of the Chou dynasty, which seems to be high praise. Many of the additions made by Pan Ku to Szu-ma Ch'ien's "Annals," especially those in the latter years of the reign, seem designed to counteract the low impression of Emperor Ching given in the *SC*—these additions show an attempt on the part of the Emperor to be a beneficent ruler over his people, limiting severities, punishing wrongdoing, and improving the administration. Emperor Ching does not deserve Wieger's condemnation. In spite of the fact that many of his deeds cannot bear scrutiny, and that his self-indulgence of petty whims sometimes brought calamity to the highest personages, yet in general the administration of the government was good, and the Emperor attempted to continue the beneficence and economy of Emperor Wen.

Szu-ma Kuang, in his *Tzu-chih T'ung-chien* 15: 19b ff, quotes Pan Ku's eulogy and points out that the period of Emperors Wen and Ching was in general a time of peace and plenty, when wealth accumulated and properity was restored, but when growing wealth also brought about the beginning of the extravagance and luxury that was, together with continual military expeditions, to result in the economic collapse under Emperor Wu. The *SC* says little of King K'ang except that his reign was a period of peace, so that, during his reign and that of his father, "the mutilating punishments were set aside and not used for a period of forty years." Inasmuch as Emperor Ching's reign was largely a period of peace (the revolt of the Seven Kingdoms lasted only a few months), and inasmuch as he attempted to continue the excellent tradition left by his father, Pan Ku's comparison of Emperor Ching with King K'ang seems quite apt.

Chapter V

THE FIFTH [IMPERIAL ANNALS]

THE ANNALS OF [EMPEROR HSIAO]-CHING

孝　母　月　皇
漢　景　曰　文　帝
書　皇　竇　帝　位
五　帝　皇　崩　尊
　　文　后　丁　皇
景　帝　後　未　太
紀　太　七　太　后
第　子　年　子　薄
五　也　六　卽　氏

Emperor Hsiao-ching was the Heir-apparent of Emperor Wen. His mother was called the Empress [*née*] Tou. In the seventh year of the latter [part of Emperor Wen's reign],[1.1] in the sixth month, Emperor Wen died; on [the day] *ting-wei* the Heir-apparent took the imperial throne.[1.2] He honored the Empress Dowager *née* Po, entitling her the Grand Dowager Empress. The Empress [*née* Tou] was entitled the Empress Dowager. In the ninth month a comet appeared in the western quarter [of the sky].[1.3]

157 B. C.

July 6
July 14

Oct.

[1.1] The reign of an emperor continues, for chronological purposes, to the end of the calendar year in which he dies. The *Tzu-chih T'ung-chien* (1084) includes the events in an emperor's reign previous to the beginning of his first year, including his accession, in the previous emperor's reign.

[1.2] This date was two days after the burial of Emperor Wen. *SC* 10: 18b (*Mh* II, 491) says that he took the throne "in the Temple of Kao-[tsu] and on [the day] *ting-wei* he inherited the title and was called 'Emperor.'" The *Kung-yang Commentary* (iii cent. B.C.) 25: 7b (Dk. Ting, I), says, "Arrange the coffin between the two [central] pillars, and then only take the throne." Shen Ch'in-han (1775–1831) remarks, "The regulation, [used by] later generations, of taking the throne before the encoffined corpse, came thus from the explanation in the *Kung-yang [Commentary]*. This [practise] is honoring [the customs] of later antiquity."

[1.3] *HS* 27 Cb: 22b adds, "Its trunk was straight [in the constellations] Wei₃ and Chi, and its end pointed to [the constellations] Hsü and Wei₁. It was more than ten feet long and reached the Heavenly Han [River (the Milky Way)]. On the sixteenth day it disappeared." This comet is no. 17 in J. Williams, *Chinese Observations of Comets*.

The Chinese phraseology in recording a comet is very expressive, e.g., 有星孛于西方, lit. "There was a star which bushed out [or 'cometed'] in the western quarter [of the sky]." When we remember that a comet often appears at first as a mere star wandering among the other stars and later puts forth a tail, the Chinese expression appears apt.

Before the time of Emperor Ching only two comets are mentioned in Han times: one in Aug./Sept. 204 B.C. (27 Cb: 22a) and the other in the summer of 172 B.C. (4: 13b).

I   In the first year, in the winter, the tenth month,
Nov. an imperial edict said, "We have indeed heard that
the ancients regarded as founder him who achieves
great deeds and as exemplar him who possesses
1b virtue.[1.4]   In establishing rites and music, each [ele-
ment of the ceremonies] should have its corresponding motive.   Songs are the means of expressing virtue.   Dances are the means of manifesting great
deeds.[1.5]   When, in the Temple of Kao-[tsu], the

日　皇　于　元　聞
太　太　西　年　古
皇　后　方　冬　者
太　九　　　十　祖
后　月　　　月　有
皇　有　　　詔　功
后　星　　　曰　而
曰　孛　　　蓋　宗

Even Halley's comet, which passed perihelion on May 20, 163 B.C., was not recorded.
Did Emperor Ching install an astrologer who was really interested in watching the
heavens? Szu-ma T'an did not begin his official career until after 140 B.C., when he
became Grand Astrologer (SC 130: 3a).

In 157 B.C. there was ended the last of the vassal kingdoms not ruled by a scion of
the Liu family. Wu Jui had been moved from the kingdom of Heng-shan to that of
Ch'ang-sha in 202 B.C. (1 B: 4a); in 157 B.C. the last king of his line died without
heirs, and the kingdom was abolished, later to be given to a son of Emperor Wu. All
the other vassal kingdoms not in the hands of a member of the imperial clan had been
ended by 196 B.C.

[1.4] Ying Shao (ca. 140–206) says, "The one who first takes the empire is the Founder
(tsu 祖). That Emperor Kao was entitled Kao-tsu [lit. "the Eminent Founder"]
is an instance [of this use]. The one who first governs the empire well becomes the
Exemplar (tsung 宗). That Emperor Wen was entitled the Grand Exemplar (t'ai
太-tsung) is an instance [of this use]." Yen Shih-ku, with his usual cocksureness,
writes, "Ying [Shao's] explanation is wrong. Tsu [means] first; he first received the
mandate [of Heaven]. Tsung [means] honorable; being virtuous he deserves to be
honored." Liu Pin (1022–1088) replies, "Yen [Shih-ku's] saying is mistaken. The one
who first received the Mandate [of Heaven] is entitled the Great Founder (t'ai-tsu).
Those who perform great deeds are also entitled tsu. [Emperor] Tsu-chia [said to have
reigned 1258–1226 B.C.] of the Shang [dynasty] was an instance [of this use]." Cf.
Mh II, 491, n. 1.

Wang Ch'i-yüan (xix cent.) writes, "That 'the Founder has merit and the Exemplar
has virtue' is said in the K'ung-tzu Chia-yü [forged by Wang Su, fl. 386–534, based on
an ancient book and later interpolated], ch. "Miao-chih," to be a saying of Confucius.
Although this is not adequate proof, in the HHS, An. 1: [1a], the commentator [Li
Hsien, 651–684] quotes these words and attributes them to the Rites, which is probably
a lost treatise on the rites."

[1.5] Wang Ch'i-yüan calls attention to a passage in the Po-hu-t'ung Te-lun (said in
HHS, Mem. 40 B: 9a to have been composed by Pan Ku; said by W. Hung to have been
composed between 213–245), A: 22a, which reads, "The singers are placed above [in
the hall]; the dancers are placed below [the hall]. Why? Because the singers symbolize virtue and the dancers symbolize great deeds. The superior man places virtue
above and great deeds below."

304

有 禮 有 者 發 eighth month wine[1.6] [is offered], there are per-
德 樂 由 所 德 formed the Dances of Military Virtue, of the Peace-
制 各 歌 以 也 ful Beginning, and of the Five Elements.[1.7]　When,

[1.6] Chang Yen (prob. iii cent.) explains, "On the first day of the first month they make wine; in the eighth month it is completed. It is named *chou* 酎 [the word in the text]. It is called *chou* because it is pure. At the time of Emperor Wu, because in the eighth month, when [the Emperor first] tastes this *chou*, there was an assembly of the nobles in the [imperial ancestral] temple, at which they paid money to assist in [defraying the expenses of] the sacrifice, it was hence called the eighth month wine money 酎金." Yen Shih-ku adds, "*Chou* is a thrice-repeated agitated and purified wine. Its taste is rich, hence it is used as an offering in the ancestral temples." Cf. 6: App. III for a description of the ceremonies connected with this wine.

[1.7] *HS* 22: 13b says, "The Dance of Military Virtue was made in the fourth year of Kao-tsu (203 B.C.) in order to symbolize that the empire is happy because military power has already been used to do away with confusion. The Dance of the Peaceful Beginning was originally Shun's *Shao* Dance. In his sixth year (201 B.C.), Kao-tsu changed its name to the Peaceful Beginning to show that he [did] not copy [what Shun had done]. The Dance of the Five Elements was originally a dance of the Chou [dynasty]. In his twenty-sixth year (221 B.C.), the First Emperor of the Ch'in [dynasty] changed its name to the Five Elements."

Meng K'ang (ca. 180–260) adds, "In the Military Virtue, the dancers hold shields and battle-axes. In the Peaceful Beginning, the dancers hold feathers and flutes. In the Five Elements, the dancers' ceremonial hats and clothes imitate the colors of the five elements. Cf. the 'Treatise on Music' [*HS*, ch. 22]."

Ying Shao, in a note to *SCHC* 10: 44, remarks, "According to my opinion of what the present passage says about the dancing in the Dances of Military Virtue, of the Peaceful Beginning, and of the Five Elements, their music in general was like the music of King Wu [of the Chou dynasty, 1122–1117 B.C.]. The meaning was that Kao-tsu used military means to conquer the world, hence he showed that he was not copying [what King Wu had done, and could make a new beginning, just as King Wu did]. When they begin to perform music, they first perform the Peaceful Beginning. Using feathers, flutes, and ornamented and embroidered clothes, they make the first [performance]; then they immediately perform the Five Elements. The Five Elements is a military dance; they hold shields and battleaxes and in their clothes they have the colors of the five elements."

In a comment to the *Chou-li* 23: 7b, sub the *Ta-hsü*, Cheng Chung (ca. 5 B.C.–A.D. 83) says, "The *Han Code Concerning the Music Master* [now lost] says, 'The children of humble people are not permitted to dance at the offering of the eighth month wine in the [imperial] ancestral temples. Officials who have been appointed to [positions ranked at] two thousand piculs down to six hundred piculs, together with those [holding noble ranks from] Kuan-nei Marquis down to Fifth Rank Grandee first pick their heirs who are seven feet [63 in. Eng. meas.] tall or more, in their twelfth year to their thirtieth year, whose features and appearance are harmonious, and whose body and members are healthy, and use them for the dancers.' "

in the Temple of [Emperor] Hsiao-hui, the eighth month wine is offered, there are performed the Dances of the Peaceful Beginning, and of the Five Elements.

"When Emperor Hsiao-wen administered the empire, he opened [free] the [customs] barriers and bridges,[1.8] making no difference between [near and] distant regions; he suppressed [the punishments for] speaking ill and criticizing,[1.9] and did away with mutilating punishments;[1.10] he bestowed and granted [pensions] to elders and the aged;[1.11] he took care of and pitied the orphans and the childless,[1.12] in order to satisfy [the desires of all] living [persons]. He restrained his likes and desires and did not receive any presents, not enriching himself with [such] ad-

2a vantages.[1.13]　[In the punishment] of criminals [he did not involve] their wives and children;[2.1] he did not punish those who had committed no crimes; he suppressed the punishment of castration,[2.2] and sent

舞者所以明功也

舞孝惠廟酎奏文始五行之舞孝文皇帝臨天下通關梁不異遠方除誹謗去肉刑賞賜長老收恤孤獨以遂羣生減者欲不受獻罪人不帑不誅亡罪不私其利也除宮刑出美人重絕人

舞武德文始五行之

高廟酎奏

1.8 Cf. 4: 14a.

1.9 Cf. 4: 10b.

1.10 Cf. 4: 14b.

1.11 Cf. 4: 7a, b.

1.12 Cf. p. 238, n. 1; 4: 14b.

1.13 The clause translated, "not enriching himself with such advantages," now stands after the clause, "did not punish those who had committed no crimes." It has been moved in accordance with its meaning, following the Fukien ed. (1549) and the *SC*, at the suggestion of Ch'ien Ta-chao and Wang Hsien-ch'ien.

2.1 Cf. p. 233 & n. 3.　The text reads 帑; Yen Shih-ku says that this character "should be read as 孥." Ch'ien Ta-chao remarks, "The Mao [text of] the *Book of Odes*, the *Li-ki*, and the *HS* all write" the first character; "the *Book of History* and the *Mencius* write" the second character.　"It is a corrupt form, and arose from Lü Shen's [fl. 265–330] *Tzu-lin*. Cf. Chang Ts'an, *Wu-ching Wen-tzu* [776]."

2.2 The *SC* reads 肉 instead of 宮, repeating what is said above (5: 1b); cf. *Mh* II, 492, n. 5.　This reading in the *SC* may be a corruption arising from conflation with this passage of the *HS*, as Wang Hsien-ch'ien thinks, or it may be an error in transcribing an original 腐.　Wang Hsien-ch'ien remarks that the last part of this sentence shows that castration, not mutilation, is the original meaning.　Ch. 23 does not say that Emperor Wen specifically abolished castration independently of the other mutilating punishments.　But 5: 7a says that the Emperor allowed those who had been sentenced to

曰陛下永思孝道立昭德之舞以明孝文皇帝之盛德皆臣嘉等愚所不

無窮朕甚嘉之其與丞相列侯中二千石禮官具禮儀奏丞相臣嘉等奏

爲孝文皇帝廟爲昭德之舞以明休德然後祖宗之功德施于萬世永永

厚侔天地利澤施四海靡不獲福明象乎日月而廟樂不稱朕甚懼焉其

之世也朕既不敏弗能勝識此皆上世之所不及而孝文皇帝親行之德

the Beauties [of Emperor Hui] out [of the palace to their homes,[2.3] because] he considered important the cutting off of these persons' posterity.

"Since We are not intelligent, [We] are not able to know everything. [It however appears to Us] that these things were all beyond the attainment of previous generations, yet they have been achieved by Emperor Hsiao-wen himself. The depth of his virtue was equal to that of Heaven and Earth; the benefits of his favor were extended to [the borders of] the four seas, [so that] no one failed to receive happiness. His brilliance was like that of the sun and moon, yet the music in the [imperial ancestral] temple is inadequate [to express it]. We are very much awed. Let there be made for the Temple of Emperor Hsiao-wen the Dance of Glorious Virtue,[2.4] in order to make manifest his praiseworthy virtue. Then only the glory and virtue of the founder and exemplar[2.5] will be exhibited for ten thousand generations, for ever and ever without end. We approve most highly of this. Let [the proper officials], with the Lieutenant Chancellor [Shen-t'u Chia], the marquises, [officials ranking at] fully two thousand piculs,[2.6] and the officials [set over] the rites, prepare a memorial concerning these rites and observances."

[In reply], "the Lieutenant Chancellor, your subject [Shen-t'u] Chia" and others memorialized [the Emperor], saying, "Your Majesty is always thinking of the Way of filial piety and has established the

capital punishment to be castrated instead, so that probably in the time of Emperor Wen castration had really been abolished.

[2.3] Cf. 4: 14a.

[2.4] *HS* 22: 14a says, "[Emperor] Hsiao-ching selected from the Dance of Military Virtue to make [the Dance of] Glorious Virtue, in honoring the Temple of the Great Exemplar."

[2.5] The *SC* at this point adds, "will be written upon bamboo and silk" (the writing materials of the time). Cf. *Mh* II, 493.

[2.6] Cf. Glossary, sub Salaries.

Dance of Glorious Virtue in order to make manifest the abundant virtue of Emperor Hsiao-wen. The stupidity of us, your subjects, [Shen-t'u] Chia and the others, prevents us from attaining to all [these matters]. Your servants have carefully discussed [this matter], and say:[2.7]

2b "In achievements, no one has been greater than Emperor Kao-[tsu]; in virtue, no one has been more abundant than Emperor Hsiao-wen—the Temple of Emperor Kao-[tsu] should be made the Temple of the Great Founder of Emperors and the Temple of Emperor Hsiao-wen should be made the Temple of the Great Exemplar of Emperors.[2.8] The Son of Heaven should from generation to generation make offerings in the Temples of the [Great] Founder and of the [Great] Exemplar. The commanderies, the kingdoms, and the nobles should each establish a Temple of the Great Exemplar for Emperor Hsiao-wen; delegates from the vassal kings and the marquises should attend at the sacrifices which the Son of Heaven offers [yearly] in the Temples of the [Great] Founder and of the [Great] Exemplar.[2.9]

及臣謹議世功莫大於高皇帝德莫盛於孝文皇
帝高皇帝廟宜為帝者太祖之廟孝文皇帝廟宜
為帝者太宗之廟天子宜世世獻祖宗之廟郡國
諸侯宜各為孝文皇帝立太宗之廟諸侯王列侯
使者侍祠天子所獻祖宗之廟請宣布天下制曰

[2.7] Wang Hsien-ch'ien suggests that, since the 世 in the text is inappropriate and the *SC* and the *Tzu-chih T'ung-chien* do not have it, it is a mistake for 曰, which is in the *SC*. We have adopted this emendation in the translation.

[2.8] The titles "Great Founder" and "Great Exemplar" became the "temple names" of Emperors Kao-tsu and Hsiao-wen respectively, and are used with their posthumous names in the headings of the chapters devoted to them in the *Tzu-chih T'ung-chien* and other histories.

[2.9] Wang Hsien-ch'ien points out that the *SC* has 歲 for the *HS*'s 所, and that Chang Yen (prob. iii cent.) explicitly uses the former word in his comment; Yen Shih-ku uses the latter character. We have adopted this emendation.

Chang Yen says, "The kings together with the marquises, yearly, at the correct seasons, sent delegates to visit the capital and attend the sacrifices to assist at the sacrifices." Ju Shun (fl. dur. 189–265) says, "It is exactly [the case] as the Temple of [Emperor] Kuang-wu [25–58] is at the Chang Tomb and the Grand Administrator of the Nan-yang [Commandery], being entitled a delegate, went to sacrifice [there]. The marquises and kings are not sent to make the sacrifices, [because] the nobles of the imperial house are not permitted to take as their ancestor the Son of Heaven; [they worshipped

可春正月詔曰間者歲比不登

民，多乏食夭絕天年朕甚痛之或

郡國或磽陿無所農桑毅畜或

地饒廣薦草莽水泉利而不得

徙其議民欲徙寬大地者聽之

We beg that this be proclaimed and published to the world." [The Emperor's] decree said, "It may be done."

In the spring, the first month, an imperial edict said, "Recently, for successive years there have not been good harvests, so that many people are lacking food; early death is cutting short their natural [span of] years. We are very much pained at this [circumstance]. In some of the commanderies and kingdoms there are stony and narrow [regions] and there is no place for agriculture or sericulture or the feeding and rearing [of domestic animals],[2.10] [whereas] in other [commanderies and kingdoms] there are fertile and broad regions, abundant in tall grass,[2.11] and the streams and wells are advantageous,

156 B. C.
Jan./Feb.

their imperial ancestors as subjects, not as descendants]. All [nobles] who attend the sacrifices at the ancestral temples act as attendants [not as sacrificers] at the sacrifices." Yen Shih-ku adds, "Chang [Yen's] explanation is correct. Since it says, 'The temple where the son of Heaven makes offerings to the [Great] Founder and the [Great] Exemplar,' it does not speak of the temples in the commanderies and kingdoms."

[2.10] Wang Nien-sun (1744–1832) says that the *T'ung-tien* (compiled by Tu Yu, 735–812) in its first chapter on "Foods and Goods," quotes this passage, and that before the words 磽陿 there is the word 地, which is lacking in the present text, and should be supplied. It is parallel with the same word in the next sentence.

Yen Shih-ku says, "毅 is an ancient form of 繫; it means to fatten and rear them; 畜 means to put out to grass."

[2.11] Ju Shun explains, "Chuang Chou [iv cent. B.C.] says, 'What deer eat is called grass (*chien* 薦).' It is also said that when the grass is thick it is called *chien*; when it is long it is called *mang* 莽 [translated, 'tall grass']." But Wang Nien-sun replies, "If you interpret *chien* as grass, then the phrase, '*chien*, grass, and *mang*' is repetitious. I say that *chien* means *chü* 聚 [together, dense]. It means that the region is fertile and broad and that in it the grass and tall grass is dense. *Chien* is used for *ch'ien* 荐. The *Tso-chuan* [iv. cent. B.C., Dk.] Hsiang, IV [Legge 422¹⁴], says, 'The Jung and Ti live in groups (*ch'ien*),' while the [*Kuo*]-*yü* [iv or iii cent. B.C., in the chapters on] Chin, says, 'The Jung and Ti dwell in groups (*ch'ien*).' Wei [Chao (197–273/4)] and Tu [-284)] both comment, saying, '*Ch'ien* is *chü*.' HS ch. 84: [20a, says], 'He planted it heavily (*chien*) with thorns,' and Yen Shih-ku comments, '*Chien* should be read as *ch'ien*. *Ch'ien* is heavily, together (*chü*).'" Chou Shou-ch'ang (1814–1884) adds, "HS ch. 69: [11b, says], 'Now the caitiffs [Huns] have lost their beautiful land and *chien* grass.' The T'ang History, 'Memoir on the Ch'i-pi-ho-li,' [says], 'They

yet the people have not been allowed to migrate [to
3a these places]. Let it be discussed that the people
who wish to migrate to [such] broad and large regions
may be permitted to do so."

Apr./May   In the summer, the fourth month, an amnesty was
granted to the empire and the common people were
given one step in noble rank.[3.1]

[The Emperor] sent the Grandee Secretary [T'ao]
Ch'ing-ti[3.2] to Tai[3.3] to make peace and friendship
with the Huns.

令田半租秋七月
與匈奴和親五月
大夫青翟至代下
民爵一級遣御史
夏四月赦天下賜

followed the dense (*chien*) grass and fine water for their livelihood." This [passage]
speaks of the density of the grass and the advantageousness of streams and springs.
The ancients changed the word-order in using [passages with] parallel [phrases]."

[3.1] The *Tzu-chih T'ung-chien* 15: 16 dates this amnesty on the day *yi-mao*, May 18.

[3.2] The *SC* says that the Huns had invaded the region of Tai, hence this treaty.
This man's personal name has been the subject of discussion. *HS* 19 B: 10 says,
"The Grandee Secretary T'ao Ch'ing [sic] was made Lieutenant Chancellor." *Ibid.* 9b
says, "T'ao Ch'ing became Grandee Secretary." Shen Ch'in-han writes that the *Wen-
yüan Ying-hua* (publ. ca. 978), ch. 873 tells that Hsiao Lun's (ca. 508–551) stele to T'ao
the Hermit (T'ao Hung-ching, 452–536) says, "The son of T'ao She, [T'ao] Ching-ti
[occupied] positions up to that of Lieutenant Chancellor." A Lieutenant Chancellor
of Emperor Wu was named Yen (or Chuang) Ch'ing-ti; Yen Shih-ku, Shen Ch'in-han,
Ch'ien Ta-hsin, and Ch'i Shao-nan think that the last word of his name may have been
added by confusion to that of T'ao Ch'ing.
But Yang Shu-ta (1885–   ), in his *Han-shu Pu-chu Pu-cheng* 2: 30, remarks, "Duke
Wen of Chin [636–628 B.C.] was named Ch'ung-erh; the *Tso-chuan*, [Dk.] Ting, IV, in
recording the oath at Chien-t'u, however says, 'Chung of Chin.' Shou Chen-to of Ts'ao
is called 'Shou Chen' in the [*Kuo*]-*yü*, [ch. on] Chin; the *SC* calls him 'Shou To.' Duke
Yin of Lu [722–712 B.C.] was named Hsi-ku; *SC* ch. 33 calls him only 'Hsi.' Anciently
there was the practise of calling [given] names [composed] of two words by one word
for short. *HS* ch. 19 [in mentioning T'ao Ch'ing-ti] has not the word *ti*, for it copies
the text of *SC* 22: [11b], this text [i.e. *HS* 5: 3a] therefore completes [the name]. The
Superintendent of the Imperial House, Liu Hsi, in *SC* ch. 120, is called Liu Hsi-chi in
the *HS*—this is a clear proof that the *SC* [uses] a shorter name and Pan [Ku] added to
it and that the explanations of Ch'i [Shao-nan], Shen [Ch'in-han], and Ch'ien [Ta-hsin]
are all incorrect. Cf. my *Ku-shu Yi-yi Chü-lieh Pu.*"

[3.3] The word *hsia* 下 is sometimes added to a place-name which is composed of only
one word in order to make a binomial. For example, in *SCHC* 47: 91 and *HS* 81: 14b,
K'ung Fu is said to have died at Ch'en₂-hsia; in the *K'ung-ts'ung* B: 34a, sect. 19, near
the end, he is said to have died at Ch'en₂. *SCHC* 11: 3 (*Mh* II, 497) says under this
date, "The Huns entered Tai and [the Emperor] made a treaty of peace and friendship
with them," hence it was natural that T'ao Ch'ing-ti should have been sent to Tai.

詔曰吏受所監臨以飲食免重受財物賤買貴賣
論輕廷尉與丞相更議著令廷尉信謹與丞相議
曰吏及諸有秩受其官屬所監所治所行所將其
與飲食計償費勿論它物若買故賤賣故貴皆坐
臧爲盜沒入臧縣官吏遷徙免罷受其故官屬所

In the fifth month [the Emperor] ordered that the cultivated fields should pay half of their [former] tax.[3.4]　**May/June**

In the autumn, the seventh month, an imperial edict said, "When officials receive food or drink from those who are superintended or governed by them, dismissal [from their positions and noble ranks is too] heavy [a punishment]; when they receive valuables and articles [from such persons], or when they purchase [things] cheaply and sell dearly, their sentences have been [too] light. [Let] the Commandant of Justice discuss [this matter] anew with the Lieutenant Chancellor [in order to establish] a statutory ordinance."　**July/Aug.**

The Commandant of Justice Hsin carefully discussed [the matter] with the Lieutenant Chancellor [Shen-t'u Chia], and said, "If an official or anyone who has [official] rank has received anything from his official subordinates, whether from those superintended by him, or those under his rule, or those of whom he is [temporarily] in charge, or those whom he commands [as a military leader], let those who have received food or drink and who calculate [its value] and repay this expense not be tried [for crime; those who receive] other things, [not food or drink, and officials who] have purposely bought things cheap and purposely sold them dear must all be sentenced for having received bribes, and treated as robbers; **3b** their bribes shall be confiscated and paid to the government.[3.5] If officials have been removed, exiled,

[3.4] Emperor Wen had exempted agriculturists from taxes; cf. 4: 14b. Now that tax was re-established at half its former rate. The *Tzu-chih T'ung-chien* 15: 16b adds that this tax was at the rate of 1/30.

[3.5] Szu-ma Cheng (fl. 713–742) in a note to *SCHC* 57: 23 says, "The *hsien-kuan* 縣官 is the Son of Heaven. The reason that the state is called the *hsien-kuan* is that in [the *Chou-li*, sub] the Ministers of Summer, [it says,] 'The inner prefecture (*hsien*) of the imperial central domain is the capital of the state.' The king controls (*kuan*) the world. Hence he is called the *hsien-kuan* [i.e. controller of the capital prefecture]." The *Chou-li* does not seem to contain this statement; the two words referring to that book may be an interpolation.

311

dismissed, or their offices discontinued, and receive from their former official subordinates who have been under their [military] command or under their superintendency or control, the gift of any valuables or things sent them, their noble ranks shall be taken away from them and they shall be made common soldiers, [but] shall be relieved of [any further punishment].[3.6]   If they have no noble rank, they shall be fined [the equivalent of] two catties of gold and it shall be ordered that [the amount] they have received shall be confiscated and paid [into the treasury].   Anyone who is able to arrest or inform [of bribery] shall be given [the amount of] the bribe which is received [by the accused]."

II
155 B. C.
Jan./Feb.
In the second year, in the winter, the twelfth month, a comet appeared in the southwest.[3.7]   [The Emperor] ordered that young men of the empire should be first enregistered [for military service and taxes] in their twentieth year.[3.8]

Apr./May
In the spring, the third month,[3.9] [the Emperor] established his Imperial Sons: [Liu] Tê as King of

臧
金二斤令沒入所受有能捕告畀其所受
將監治送財物奪爵爲士伍免之無爵罰

子年二十始傅春三月立皇子德爲河間
二年冬十二月有星孛于西南令天下男

[3.6] Li Ch'i explains, "Those who had noble ranks were to have [their ranks] taken from them and to be made common soldiers; those who had official positions were to be dismissed from their positions." But Shen Ch'in-han replies that the case of those who have already left their positions is different from those who are in official positions, since in the former case they could not compel their subordinates to pay bribes; hence in such cases they were to be punished by merely having their noble titles taken away from them and were excused from further trial. He adds that the Han practise was, at the first crime, to dismiss a person from official position, and, when he was tried a second time, to take away his noble rank.

[3.7] This is comet no. 18 in John Williams, *Chinese Observations of Comets*, London, 1871. His date is incorrect; this month was Jan. 18–Feb. 15, 155 B.C. The *Han-chi* 9: 1b erroneously dates this comet in the eleventh month; the *Tzu-chih T'ung-chien* reads as the present text does.

[3.8] Yen Shih-ku explains "[According to] the old law, in their twenty-third [year] they were enregistered (cf. p. 80, n. 2)]; now this [edict sets the age at] twenty, a change to a different [dynasty's] code." But Shen Ch'in-han replies, "Originally those who were in their fifteenth year and over had to pay the poll-tax (*suan*) in cash [cf. p. 93, n. 1]; now [the Emperor] liberalized it, making it the twentieth year."

[3.9] HS 14: 14a, 15a dates these appointments on the day *chia-yin*, May 12.

Ho-chien, [Liu] O as King of Lin-chiang, [Liu] Yü₂ as King of Huai-yang, [Liu] Fei₁ as King of Ju-nan, [Liu] P'eng-tsu as King of Kuang-ch'uan, and [Liu] Fa as King of Ch'ang-sha.

In the summer, the fourth month, on [the day] June 9 *jen-wu*, the Grand Empress Dowager [*née* Po] died.

In the sixth month the Lieutenant Chancellor, July/Aug. [Shen-t'u] Chia, died.

[The Emperor] enfeoffed [Hsiao] Hsi, a grandson of the former Chancellor of State, Hsiao Ho, as a marquis.

In the autumn, [the Emperor] made peace and 4a friendship with the Huns.   Autumn

In the third year, in the winter, the twelfth month, III an imperial edict said, "[Chi] K'uei-yüeh, a son of 154 B.C. the Marquis of Hsiang-p'ing, [Chi T'ung]-chia,[4.1] has Jan./Feb. been unfilial and has conspired to revolt, intending thereby to kill [his father, Chi T'ung]-chia, which is treason and inhumanity. Let [Chi T'ung]-chia be pardoned and be [again] made Marquis of Hsiang-p'ing, and, together with his wife and children, who should be condemned with him, let him be restored to his former noble rank; let [Chi] K'uei-yüeh, together with his wife and children, be sentenced according to the law."[4.2]

In the spring, the first month, there was a visita- Feb./Mar. tion [of fire] in the Main Hall at the Palace of the King of Huai-yang [Liu Yü₂], and the King of Wu, [Liu] P'i, the King of Chiao-hsi, [Liu] Ang, the King of Ch'u, [Liu] Mou, the King of Chao, [Liu] Sui, the King of Chi-nan, [Liu] Pi-kuang, the King

---

[4.1] According to 16: 43b, the Marquis of Hsiang-p'ing was Chi T'ung. Here he is called [Chi] Chia. We have understood this as merely another case of a double given name for one person; cf. n. 3.2.

[4.2] Ju Shun says, "According to the Code, when there is a case of 'treason and inhumanity,' the father, mother, wife, children, and brothers and sisters should all be publicly executed." Evidently Emperor Wen's abrogation of extending punishment to the relatives of a criminal (4: 5b) did not extend to treason and inhumanity.

of Tzu-ch'uan, [Liu] Hsien, and the King of Chiao-tung, [Liu] Hsiung-ch'ü, all mobilized their troops and rebelled. [The Emperor] granted a general amnesty to the empire and sent the Grand Commandant, [Chou] Ya-fu, and the General-in-chief, Tou Ying, with troops, to attack them.   [The Emperor] had the Grandee Secretary, Ch'ao Ts'o, beheaded in order to excuse himself to the Seven Kingdoms.   In

Apr. 4 the second month, on [the day] *jen-tzu*, the last day of the month, there was an eclipse of the sun.[4.3] The generals routed the Seven Kingdoms, cut off more than a hundred thousand heads, pursued and beheaded the King of Wu, [Liu] P'i, at Tan-t'u.

4b The King of Chiao-hsi, [Liu] Ang, the King of Ch'u, [Liu] Mou, the King of Chao, [Liu] Sui, the King of Chi-nan, [Liu] Pi-kuang, the King of Tzu-ch'uan, [Liu] Hsien, and the King of Chiao-tung, [Liu] Hsiung-ch'ü, all committed suicide.[4.4]

July In the summer, the sixth month, an imperial edict said, "Recently the King of Wu, [Liu] P'i, and others, rebelled and raised their troops to coerce [Us], leading astray their officials and people.   Their officials and people could not do otherwise [than follow them].   Now that [Liu] P'i and the others have already been exterminated, let the officials and people who should be sentenced [for being accomplices of Liu] P'i and the others, together with those who have absconded and fled or deserted the army, all be pardoned.   [With regard to Liu] Yi₄, the son of King Yüan of Ch'u, [Liu Chiao], and others, who rebelled with [Liu] P'i and the others, We cannot bear to apply the law [to them].   Let [their names] be expunged from the register [of the imperial house] and do not let them defile the imperial house.   We establish the Marquis of P'ing-lu, Liu Li, as King of

兵反大赦天下遣太尉亞夫大將軍竇嬰將兵擊之斬御史大夫晁錯以謝七國

二月壬子晦日有蝕之諸將破七國斬首十餘萬級追斬吳王濞於丹徒膠西王

卬楚王戊趙王遂濟南王辟光菑川王賢膠東王雄渠皆自殺夏六月詔曰廼者

吳王濞等為逆起兵相脅詿誤吏民吏民不得已今濞等已滅吏民當坐濞等及

逋逃亡軍者皆赦之楚元王子藝等與濞等為逆朕不忍加法除其籍毋令汙宗

[4.3] This dating is incorrect.   For a discussion of the eclipses in this chapter, cf. App. II.
[4.4] For an account of this rebellion, cf. Introduction.

室立平陸侯劉禮爲楚王續元王後立皇子端爲膠西王勝爲中山王賜民

爵一級

四年春復置諸關用傳出入夏四月己巳立皇子榮爲皇太子徹爲膠東王

六月赦天下賜民爵一級秋七月臨江王閼薨十月戊戌晦日有蝕之

五年春正月作陽陵邑夏募民徙陽陵賜錢二十萬遣公主嫁匈奴單于

Ch'u, to continue the posterity of King Yüan." [The Emperor also] established his Imperial Sons, [Liu] Tuan as King of Chiao-hsi and [Liu] Sheng as King of Chung-shan, and granted to the common people one step in noble rank.

In the fourth year, in the spring, [the Emperor] reestablished the various [customs] barriers [and ordered] the use of passports for going out and in.[4.5]　**IV 153 B.C. Spring**

In the summer, the fourth month, on [the day] *chi-szu*, [the Emperor] established his Imperial Sons, [Liu] Jung as Imperial heir-apparent, and [Liu] Ch'ê as King of Chiao-tung, and in the sixth month an amnesty was granted to the world and the common people were granted a step in noble rank.　**May 16　June/July**

In the autumn, the seventh month, the King of Lin-chiang, [Liu] O, died, and in tenth month, on [the day] *mou-hsü*, the last day of the month, there was an eclipse of the sun.　**July/Aug.**

In the fifth year, in the spring, the first month, [the Emperor] built the Yang Tomb and the town [of Yang-ling]. In the summer, [the Emperor] solicited common people to move to Yang-ling, granting them two hundred thousand cash.　**152 B.C. 5a V Feb./Mar. Summer**

He sent a Princess to be married to the *Shan-yü* of the Huns.　**151 B.C.**

In the sixth year, in the winter, the twelfth month, there was thunder and prolonged rain.　**VI Jan.**

In the autumn, the ninth month, the Empress *née* Po was dismissed.[5.1]　**Sept./Oct.**

In the seventh year, in the winter, the eleventh month, on [the day] *keng-yin*, the last day of the　**VII 150 B.C.**

4.5 In 169 B.C. these barriers had been abolished. Cf. 4: 14a. The *SC* dates the present order in the intercalary ninth month (Oct./Nov., 153) and says, "He re-established the fords and [customs] barriers." Cf. *Mh* II, 500. Ying Shao says that this re-establishment was "because the Seven Kingdoms had just rebelled and to be prepared for any untoward circumstance."

5.1 She had no children, had lost the favor of Emperor Ching, and her protectress, the Grand Empress Dowager *née* Po, had died.

Jan. 22 | month, there was an eclipse of the sun, and in the
Feb./Mar. | spring, the first month, [the Emperor] dismissed the Imperial Heir-apparent [Liu] Jung and made him King of Lin-chiang.[5.2]

Mar./Apr. | In the second month, [the Emperor] abolished the office of the Grand Commandant.[5.3]

June 6 | In the summer, the fourth month, on [the day] yi-szŭ, [the Emperor] established the Empress née

June 18 | Wang [as Empress]. On [the day] ting-szŭ, [the Emperor] established the King of Chiao-tung, [Liu] Ch'ê, as Imperial Heir-apparent, and granted to those common people who would be the successors of their fathers one step in noble rank.[5.4]

I | In the middle [part of the reign],[5.5] the first year,

月罷太尉官夏四月乙巳立皇后
春正月廢皇太子榮爲臨江王二
七年冬十一月庚寅晦日有蝕之
后薄氏廢
六年冬十二月雷霖雨秋九月皇

[5.2] SC ch. 11 (Mh II, 501) dates this dismissal in the winter of 151/150 B.C. HS 14: 17a dates his appointment as king "in the eleventh month, on [the day] chi-yu," which day was only possible in the tenth and twelfth months of that year. SC 17: 21b dates the dismissal and appointment both "in the eleventh month, on [the day] yi-ch'ou," which was Dec. 28, 151. The Tzu-chih T'ung-chien 16: 12b follows HS 14: 17a. The Han-chi 9: 12b follows HS 5: 5a.

[5.3] The Grand Commandant, Chou Ya-fu, was made Lieutenant Chancellor on Apr. 7, according to Mh II, 501, and, according to HS 19 B: 11a, after Aug. 5.

[5.4] For the intrigues leading to this change of heirs, cf. Glossary sub Wang, Empress née; Mh II, 501, n. 5.

[5.5] The name for this year is usually written today as if there had been a year-period by the name of Chung-yüan 中元. There is also tacitly assumed to have been a year-period Hou-yüan 後元. Both the SC and the HS however only write the first of these two pairs of characters. In the SC, the Chinese for the various years is 中二年, etc. In the HS, only the first year of the part of the reign is preceded by 中; in that year the word yüan 元 is plainly intended to indicate the "first" year of that part of the reign. In the "Tables," the Chinese dates for the latter two parts of this reign are always written 中二年, 後五年, etc. Cf. 14: 17b, 19a; 15 A: 8a; 16: 7b, 8a, 9a, 14a, b; 17: 1b, 4a, 6a; 18: 7b. There is an exception: 16: 13b has 景後元元年, but Chu Yi-hsin (1846–1894) says that the Wang ed. (1546) is correct in reading only one yüan, for the second yüan is dittography. Wang Hsien-ch'ien, in a note to 5: 8b, also uses the single character to indicate this part of the reign, but Shen Ch'in-han, in a note to 5: 8a, uses two characters, making it the name of a year-period. Emperor Ching was merely imitating the practise of his father, Emperor Wen, in beginning anew the numbering of the years in his reign. Reign-periods were not introduced until 114 or 113 B.C., in the reign of Emperor Wu. Cf. p. 260, n. 1; ch. 6, App. I.

王氏丁巳立膠東王徹爲皇太子賜民

爲父後者爵一級

中元年夏四月赦天下賜民爵一級封

故御史大夫周苛周昌孫子爲列侯

二年春二月令諸侯王薨列侯初封及

in the summer, the fourth month, an amnesty was granted to the world and the common people were granted one step in noble rank. [The Emperor] enfeoffed the grandson and son of the former Grandee Secretaries Chou Ho and Chou Ch'ang as marquises.[5.6]

In the second year, in the spring, the second month, [the Emperor] ordered that when vassal kings die, and when marquises are first enfeoffed and go to their states, the Grand Herald should memorialize [the Emperor] concerning [respectively] their posthumous names and eulogies and their charters [of appointment]. When marquises die and when the nobles' Grand Tutors are first appointed and go to their offices, the Grand Messenger shall memorialize [the throne concerning respectively] their post-

149 B. C.

May/June

5b

11

148 B.C.

Mar.

[5.6] The words for "grandson and son" seem to be a mistake on the part of Pan Ku in which he follows the text of SC ch. 11. HS 16: 45a tells that the Marquis of Kao-ching, Chou Ch'eng, was enfeoffed because of his father, Chou Ho, and that in 159 B.C. his marquisate was abolished, but that in 149 B.C. (the present year) Chou Ch'eng's grandson, Chou Ying, was enfeoffed as Marquis of Sheng. SC 18: 45a (Mh III, 130, no. 25) says the same. Then Chou Ying was Chou Ho's great-grandson.

HS 16: 15b, 16a tells that Marquis Tao of Fen-yin, Chou Ch'ang, transmitted his marquisate to his son and grandson. The latter was punished and the marquisate abolished, but in "the second year of the middle [part of the reign] of [Emperor] Hsiao-ching, [Ch'ien Ta-chao remarks that it should be the "first year"], [Chou] Tso-ch'ê succeeded to enfeoffment because he was a grandson of [Chou] Ch'ang" and became Marquis of An-yang. SC 18: 12a says the same. HS 42: 4a also says that Chou Tso-ch'ê was Chou Ch'ang's grandson.

Then these two new marquises were the great-grandson and grandson of these Grandee Secretaries. SC ch. 11 (Mh II, 502) says, "[The Emperor] appointed [Chou] P'ing [who was the son of Chou Ying, according to SC 18: 45a and HS 16: 45a], the grandson of the former Grandee Secretary Chou Ho, as Marquis of Sheng and [Chou] Tso-chün [chün 軍 instead of the ch'ê 車 in HS 16: 15b], the son of the former Grandee Secretary Chou Ch'ang, as Marquis of An-yang." The HS seems here to have clearly been abstracting from the corresponding passage in the SC.

humous names and eulogies and their charters [of
6a appointment].[5.7] When kings die, an Imperial
Household Grandee shall be sent to condole, provide
grave-clothes, sacrifical food, funeral horses and
carriages, oversee the mourning ceremonies and on

官大行奏諡
太傅及初除之
侯薨及諸侯
奏諡誄策列
之國大鴻臚

[5.7] Ying Shao writes, "When the Emperor entertains the vassal kings or treats kings
and nobles as his guests, they are all under the charge of the Grand Herald. Hence,
when they die, he memorializes their deeds and grants them posthumous names, together
with funeral eulogies."   Ch'ien Ta-hsin adds, "The posthumous name and eulogy are
used for the dead; charters are used by those who are newly enfeoffed and go to their
states."

Fu Tsan (fl. ca. 285) says, "Emperor Ching in this year had already established a
Grand Herald, yet HS 19 [A: 13b] says, 'In 104 B.C. Emperor Wu changed [the title
of the Chief Grand Messenger] to be the Grand Herald,' which is, according to this
passage, incorrect."   The use of the title, Grand Herald, here may however be an
anachronism.   Yen Shih-ku says, "The Grand Herald was originally named the Director
of Guests; later [his title] was changed to be Grand Herald.   The Chief Grand Messenger
was originally named the Messenger, which was a subordinate office to the Director of
Guests.   [His title] was later changed to be Chief Grand Messenger.   Hence, in honorable and important matters, [the Emperor] sent the Grand Herald, and in less honorable
or important ones, [the Emperor] sent the Grand Messenger.   According to the text of
this 'Annals,' Emperor Ching had already changed [the title of] the Director of Guests
to be Grand Herald, and changed the Messenger to be the Grand Messenger.   Yet HS
19 [A: 13b] says, 'In 144 B.C. Emperor Ching changed the title [of the Director of
Guests] to be Chief Grand Messenger.   In 104 B.C. Emperor Wu changed the title
[of the Chief Grand Messenger] to be Grand Herald . . . and changed the title of the
Messenger to be the Chief Grand Messenger.'   According to the text [of ch. 5], ch. 19
is mistaken."

According to HS 53: 2b, when King Hsien of Ho-chien, Liu Tê, died in 130 B.C., the
Chief Grand Messenger memorialized his posthumous name.   The passage regarding
posthumous names, etc., is not in SC ch. 11; Pan Ku probably found the law regarding
the memorializing of posthumous names, eulogies, and charters in the form it assumed
after the titles of the participating officials had been changed, and inserted it in the
"Annals" at the time when it was originally enacted, so that the titles of the officials
are merely anachronisms.   The title in this passage, Imperial Household Grandee, is
also an anachronism, for according to HS 19 A: 9a that title was not established until
104 B.C.

Ying Shao misunderstood the meaning of ts'ê 策 in this passage.   Here it is the term
for the charter given an official upon his appointment.   Ch'ien Ta-hsin (1720–1804)
corrects him, saying, "When marquises are first enfeoffed and go to their states, the
Grand Herald has charge of memorializing their charter.   Ying [Shao] considered
that the ts'ê was a 'funeral eulogy,' which is a mistake."   Such charters are to be
found in HS 99 A: 6b, 21a, etc.   Another is translated in Appendix I.

誄策王薨遣光祿大夫弔襚祠賵視
喪事因立嗣子列侯薨遣大中大夫
弔祠視喪事因立嗣其薨葬國得發
民輓喪穿復土治墳無過三百人畢
事匈奴入燕改磔曰棄市勿復磔三

the same occasion enthrone the son who succeeds to [the kingdom]. When marquises die, a Grand Palace Grandee[6.1] shall be sent to condole, offer sacrifical food, oversee the mourning ceremonies, and on the same occasion enfeoff the heir. When they[6.2] are buried, their states shall be allowed to mobilize not more than three hundred common people for the whole matter of pulling the hearse and mourning, digging and replacing the earth, and building the tomb.

The Huns entered into [the kingdom of] Yen.[6.3]

[The punishment of execution and] quartering [the body] was changed to that of public execution, so that no one was any more to be quartered.[6.4]

In the third month, the King of Lin-chiang, [Liu] Apr.

[6.1] Wang Hsien-ch'ien's text writes 大; the Official ed. (1739) writes 太, so does *HS* 19 A: 8b, 9a.

[6.2] The text at this point has the word 薨, which is superfluous and interrupts the meaning. It seems to have crept in through dittography from the preceding three instances of that word. It is not in *Han-chi* 9: 3a. Following Wang Nien-sun, we have omitted it.

[6.3] *SC* ch. 11 (*Mh* II, 503) adds at this point, "Thereafter there ceased to be peace and friendship [between the Chinese and the Huns]."

[6.4] This is one of the classic texts dealing with these two punishments. Ying Shao says, "Before this time those who were punished with death were all *chê* in the market-place 磔於市. Now it was changed and called public execution 棄市. From [this time], except for monstrous [crimes] and rebellion, they did not again *chê* anyone." Chavannes *Mh* I, cxi, n. 2), Couvreur, (*Dict. Classique*) and the *Tz'u-yüan* say that *chê* means "to quarter" (the latter writes 分裂肢體). In support of this interpretation is the use of the word *chê* in the Book of Rites for the cutting up of victims offered in some sacrifices (cf. Couvreur, *Li-Ki*, I, 352, 406). The existence of a punishment which consisted in quartering 分裂 is established by the use of those words in *HS* 100 A: 9a.

But Yen Shih-ku writes, "*Chê* means exposing his corpse 磔謂張其尸也; public execution is to kill him in the market-place 棄市殺之於市也. It means that when someone is to be publicly executed, there is employed [the principle stated in the *Li-ki* III, ii, 11 (Legge I, 215; Couvreur I, 274)], 'A person should be executed in the market-place, [thus] being done away with (*hsi*) with the participation of the crowd.'" The *K'ang-hsi Dictionary* gives both meanings for *chê*: "張也開也裂也." Perhaps Yen Shih-ku was attempting to make an ancient practise appear more humane than it really was.

Jung, was found guilty of encroaching upon the land of the Temple of the Great Exemplar. He was summoned [to the capital], went to [the quarters of] the Palace Military Commander, and committed sui-

Apr./May cide. In the summer, the fourth month, a comet appeared in the northwest.

[The Emperor] established his Imperial Sons, [Liu] Yüeh as King of Kuang-ch'uan and [Liu] Chi as King of Chiao-tung.

July/Aug. In the autumn, the seventh month, [the Emperor] changed [the titles of] Commandery Administrators to be Grand Administrators, and Commandery Commandants to be Chief Commandants.

Sept./Oct. In the ninth month, [the Emperor] enfeoffed the sons of four persons who had been the former [Grand] Tutor, Chancellors, and Prefect of the Capital at [the kingdoms of] Ch'u and Chao, who had previously

6b died [because of] what they had done, and made [these sons] marquises.[6.5]

On [the day] chia-hsü, the last day of the month, there was an eclipse of the sun.

III In the third year, in the winter, the eleventh

Dec./Jan. month, the offices of Grandee Secretaries were abol-

147 B.C. ished in [the courts of] the nobles.

Feb./Mar. In the spring, the first month, the dismissed Empress [née Po] died.[6.6]

月臨江王榮坐侵太宗廟地徵詣中尉自殺夏四月有星孛于西

北立皇子越爲廣川王寄爲膠東王秋七月更郡守爲太守郡尉

爲都尉九月封故楚趙傅相內史前死事者四人子皆爲列侯甲

戌晦日有蝕之

三年冬十一月罷諸侯御史大夫官春正月皇太后崩夏旱禁酤

[6.5] Wen Ying (fl. ca. 196–220) says, "The Chancellor of Ch'u, Chang Shang, the Grand Tutor [of Ch'u], Chao Yi-wu, the Chancellor of Chao, Chien-tê, and the Prefect of the Capital [at Chao], Wang Han—these were the four persons. Each had admonished his king not to bring about a revolt, [but their kings] would not heed and killed all of them. Hence their sons were appointed." HS 17: 3a, b, 4a and SC 19: 21b, 22a, b (from which the above information was taken) note these four persons as all appointed in the fourth month, on the day yi-szu, May 26, 148 B.C. SC ch. 11 (Mh II, 503) dates these appointments "in the summer," putting the words for "in the ninth month" after this notice.

[6.6] There is some mistake in the text. At present it reads, "The Empress Dowager died." But the Empress Dowager née Tou did not die until 135 B.C. This notice of a death is not in the SC or the Han-chi. Fu Tsan (fl. ca. 285) quotes Wang Mou (fl. before 265) as saying, "The Empress [née] Po of Emperor Ching died in this year;

320

酒秋九月蝗有星孛于西北戊戌晦日有蝕之

立皇子乘爲清河王

四年春三月起德陽宮御史大夫綰奏禁馬高

五尺九寸以上齒未平不得出關夏蝗秋赦徒

作陽陵者死罪欲腐者許之十月戊午日有蝕

In the summer there was a drought,[6.7] and the sale of wine was prohibited. In the autumn, the ninth month, there were locusts,[6.8] and there was a comet in the northwest.[6.9] On [the day] *mou-hsü*, the last day of the month, there was an eclipse of the sun.

[The Emperor] established his Imperial Son [Liu Fang]-sheng as King of Ch'ing-ho.[6.10]

In the fourth year, in the spring, the third month, the Tê-yang Residence was built.[6.11]

The Grandee Secretary [Wei] Wan memorialized [the throne] that horses five feet and nine inches and more in height whose teeth were not yet smooth should not be allowed to go out through the [customs] barriers.[6.12]

In the summer, there were locusts.

In the autumn, an amnesty was granted to the convicts who had built the Yang Tomb. Those who had committed capital crimes and wished to be cas-

Summer
Oct./Nov.

Nov. 10

IV
146 B. C.
Apr./May

7a
Autumn

I suspect that it was she. It should say the 'dismissed Empress,' " i.e., read 廢 instead of 太. Wang Mou may be taking as his authority *HS* 97 A: 8b, which says that this Empress died the fourth year after she was dismissed. The latter date was 151 B.C. (5: 5a); then she died in 147 B.C. We have followed Wang Mou's emendation in the translation.

There are however very serious objections. Yen Shih-ku points out that the death of a dismissed empress is not recorded and that the particular word here used for "died" would never be used of a dismissed Empress. Cf. p. 260, n. 3. Ch'ien Ta-chao concludes that the whole sentence is an interpolation.

[6.7] *HS* 27 Ba: 24a calls it a "great drought" and dates it in the autumn.

[6.8] These locusts are also mentioned in *HS* 27 Bb: 20a.

[6.9] This is no. 24 in Williams, *Observations of Comets*.

[6.10] *HS* 14: 18b dates this appointment in the third month, on the day *ting-yu*, May 13, 147 B.C.

[6.11] This was to be Emperor Ching's funerary temple. Ch'ien Ta-chao notes that the Fukien ed. (1549) mistakenly has interchanged the words in this temple's name.

[6.12] This height is about 52 in. Eng. meas. Fu Ch'ien explains, "When horses are in their tenth year, the surfaces of their teeth become smooth." The *SC* (*Mh* III, 544) says that in the time of Emperor Ching, additional horse pastures were established in order to increase the public resources.

trated [instead of being executed] were permitted [to be thus punished].[7.1]

145 B. C.
Mar. 26

In the tenth month, on [the day] *mou-wu*, there was an eclipse of the sun.

V
Summer
June/July

In the fifth year, in the summer, [the Emperor] established his Imperial Son [Liu] Shun as King of Ch'ang-shan.[7.2]   In the sixth month an amnesty was granted to the world and the common people were granted one step in noble rank.

Sept. 11

In the autumn, the eighth month, on [the day] *chi-yu*, there was a visitation [of fire] at the Eastern Portal of the Wei-yang Palace.[7.3]

The titles of the nobles' Lieutenant Chancellors were changed to that of Chancellors.[7.4]

Oct./Nov.

In the ninth month, an imperial edict said, "The laws and ordinances, the measures and weights are for the purpose of preventing violence and of stopping wrongdoing.   Criminal tribunals are the great [determiners] of peoples' fate, [for] the dead cannot come to life again.   Some of the officials do not uphold the laws and ordinances: they make a business of presents and bribes; they form parties and cliques and practise favoritism; they consider merciless inquisition as penetration and exacting

吏或不奉法令以貨賂爲市朋黨比周以苟爲察以刻爲
法令度量所以禁暴止邪也獄人之大命死者不可復生
八月己酉未央宮東闕災更名諸侯丞相爲相九月詔曰
五年夏立皇子舜爲常山王六月赦天下賜民爵一級秋
之

[7.1] Ju Shun explains that castration was called 腐, i.e., rottenness, because it was being like a rotten tree, which could not bring forth any fruit.   *HS* 97 A: 21b tells that when Hsü Kuang-han had committed a capital crime, an edict of Emperor Wu invited him to enter the silkworm room of the palace, (i.e., to be castrated instead of executed).   In the *San-kuo Chih* (by Ch'en Shou, 233–297) Chung Yu (a Grand Tutor and a famous calligraphist) says to Emperor Ming (58–75), "It is proper that, like the ordinance of [Emperor] Hsiao-ching, whoever should be publicly executed and wishes [instead] to cut off his right toes should be permitted to do so."   Chou Shou-ch'ang remarks that castration accordingly does not seem to have been the only way of commuting the death penalty.

[7.2] *HS* 14: 19a dates this appointment in the third month, on the day *ting-szu*, an impossible month and day, according to Hoang, *Concordance*.

[7.3] *HS* 27 A: 11a blames this fire on the dismissal and suicide of the first heir-apparent, Liu Jung, and the dismissal of Chou Ya-fu.   Cf. Glossary, *sub vocibus*.

[7.4] The purpose of this change, as of that abolishing Grandee Secretaries in kingly courts, was to exalt the imperial court and to distinguish imperial from kingly titles.

明令亡罪者失職朕甚憐之有罪者不
伏罪姦法爲暴甚亡謂也諸獄疑若雖
文致於法而於人心不厭者輒讞之
六年冬十月行幸雍郊五畤十二月改
諸官名定鑄錢僞黃金棄市律春三月

cruelty as perspicacity, so that they cause the inno- **7b**
cent to lose their positions (We pity them greatly),
and the guilty do not suffer for their crimes. They
violate the laws and act tyrranously. It is utterly
unspeakable. Whenever a judicial case is doubtful,
although [the decision] may have been made out as
if it fits the law, if yet it does not satisfy peoples'
minds, [the case] shall be specially referred to a
superior."[7.5]

In the sixth year, in the winter, the tenth month, VI
[the Emperor] travelled and favored Yung [with a Nov./Dec.
visit, where he] performed the suburban sacrifice at
the altars to the Five [Lords on High].[7.6]

In the twelfth month, he changed the names of the 144 B. C.
officials[7.7] and established the statute [fixing] public Jan./Feb.
execution for coining cash or [making alchemistic]
counterfeit gold.[7.8]

s

[7.5] Chou Shou-ch'ang says, "The *T'ung-tien*, ch. 4 on Punishments, "Miscellaneou
Discussions," pt. A, says, 'The Chief Justice sent to the Emperor a prisoner, Fang Nien.
His step-mother, [Fang] Ch'en, had murdered Fang Nien's father. Fang Nien therefore killed [Fang] Ch'en. According to the Code, a matricide should be sentenced as
having committed treason. The Emperor doubted [the justice of such a sentence].

" 'The [future] Emperor Wu was at this time in his twelfth year and was Heir-
apparent. He was by [the Emperor's] side. The Emperor thereupon asked him [about
the case]. The Heir-apparent replied, saying, "Now a step-mother is like a mother,
[but] it is plain that she is not equal to a mother. Because of his father, she is similar
to a mother. Now this step-mother acted wrongly. With her own hand she murdered
his father; then from the day that she put forth her hand [against his father], his
indebtedness to her as a mother was already ended. He should be sentenced as a person
who has killed another, and should not be sentenced as one who has committed treason."
[The Emperor] followed his [judgment].' From this [account we see that] this affair
happened in precisely the year [of the edict in the text]."

[7.6] *SC* 11: 5a (*Mh* II, 505) says that this visit was in the second month, on the day
chi-mao, Apr. 9, 144 B.C.

[7.7] For details, cf. *Mh* II, 506; *HS* ch. 19 passim.

[7.8] Ying Shao writes, "Emperor Wen, in his fifth year (175 B.C., cf. 4: 12b), allowed
people to coin [cash], a law that had not yet been abrogated. At earlier times there
had been made much [alchemistic] counterfeit gold. [But] counterfeit gold cannot
really be made, and vainly [causes] loss and expense, so that it turns to mutual boasting
about one's brilliancy. When [these alchemists become] poor, then they rise up and
become brigands and robbers, hence [the Emperor] established this law." Meng K'ang
(ca. 180–260) quites a popular "saying, 'If gold could be made, the world could be

Apr./May   In the spring, the third month, snow fell,[7.9] and
May/June   in the summer, the fourth month, the King of Liang,
[Liu Wu₃], died.[7.10]   [The Emperor] divided Liang
into five kingdoms and established all the five sons
of King Hsiao [Liu Wu₃] as kings.

June/July   In the fifth month an imperial edict said, "Now
the officials are the teachers of the people.   It is
proper for their carriages and quadrigae, their clothes
and robes to be proportionate [to their station].
Officials [ranking at] six hundred piculs and above
8a   are all important officials.[8.1]   Persons negligent of
the rules sometimes do not [wear] their official robes,
so that when they go in and out of the villages they
[appear] no different from the common people.   [We]
order that on the carriages of important officials
[who are ranked at] two thousand piculs, both side-
screens should be made vermillion;[8.2] and on those

令長吏二千石車朱兩轓千石至六百石
也亡度者或不更服出入閭里與民亡異
也車駕衣服宜稱吏六百石以上皆長吏
子五人皆爲王五月詔曰夫吏者民之師
雨雪夏四月梁王薨分梁爲五國立孝王

measured.' "   This edict of 144 B.C., together with these comments of the second and
third century of our era establish the existence of alchemy in China at this early date.

Cash had been largely coined in the kingdom of Wu, under its King, Liu P'i.   Now
that he had rebelled and had been executed, private coinage was forbidden.

[7.9] *HS* 27 Bb: 13a says that this snow prognosticated a Hun raid and the death of
Chou Ya-fu.

[7.10] Ch'ien Ta-chao says that the omission of the King's personal name must probably
have been due to a copyist's error.

[8.1] Chang Yen (prob. iii cent.) comments, "The position of six hundred piculs was
that of Grandees."   This may be the only place where 長吏 is used in the sense of
"important officials."   Elsewhere it is the title of certain subordinate officials.

[8.2] Ying Shao explains, "They are the ears of a carriage which open out.   They are
the means whereby one protects (*fan*) and covers himself against dust and mud.   [Offi-
cials ranking at] two thousand piculs make the pair of them vermillion; those of lower
rank do it for the left side only.   They are made of bamboo matting, or leather is used."
Ju Shun says, "*Fan* 轓番 is pronounced as 反; they are the two screens of a small
carriage."   Yen Shih-ku adds, "According to the explanation of Hsü Shen [fl. 100] and
Li Teng [fl. dur. 220–265], *fan* is the covering of a carriage. . . . They were screens to
cover the carriage.   To say that they 'are the ears of a carriage which open out' is
mistaken."

Wang Hsien-ch'ien notes that the Supplement to the Official ed. (1739) says, "吏 is
erroneously written 史.   Following Sung [Ch'i's] ed. [ca. xii cent.], it is emended."

HHS, Tr. 29: 10b (by Szu-ma Piao, ca. 240–304) says, "In 145 B.C. there first was
an edict granting permission to [officials ranked at] six hundred piculs and above to use
bronze for the five ends of their carriage screens and on their yokes to have *chi-yang*
pipes."

朱左轓車騎從者不稱其官衣服下吏出入閭巷亡吏

體者二千石上其官屬三輔舉不如法令者皆上丞相

御史請之先是吏多軍功車服尙輕故爲設禁又惟酷

吏奉憲失中廼詔有司減笞法定箠令語在刑法志六

月匈奴入鴈門至武泉入上郡取苑馬吏卒戰死者二

[of officials whose positions are ranked from] one thousand to six hundred piculs the left screen should be made vermillion. If their carriages or the horsemen in their retinue are not proportionate to the office [of their master], or if the robes of petty officials, when they go out and in the hamlets, are not according to their official dignity, [officials ranking at] two thousand piculs should report what are the offices to which [such officials] belong; [in the capital districts] the Three Adjuncts[8.3] should report any who do not act in accordance with the laws and ordinances [on this point]. All shall be reported to the Lieutenant Chancellor or [Grandee] Secretary, who shall beg [the throne to order them punished]."

Previous to this time most of the officials [had owed their appointments to] their military achievement, so they had paid scant attention to their carriages and robes, hence [the Emperor] made this prohibition. He moreover reflected that cruel officials, using the sanction of the law, might depart from equity, hence he issued an imperial edict [ordering] that the high officials should [propose] a law lightening [the punishment] of beating, and an ordinance fixing [the size of] the stick. A discussion is in the "Treatise on Punishments and Laws."

In the sixth month, the Huns entered into the Yen-men [Commandery] to Wu-ch'üan, and entered into the Shang Commandery, where they took the horses of the imperial pastures.[8.4] Two thousand

8b

23 :14b–15a
July/Aug.

[8.3] "Three Adjuncts" (q.v. in Glossary) is probably anachronistic here; this title was not used until 104 B.C. According to *HS* 19 A: 20b, until 155 B.C. there was only a Prefect of the Capital; in that year Western and Eastern Prefects of the Capital were appointed. Ch'üan Tsu-wang (1705–1755) thinks that perhaps the Western and Eastern Prefects of the Capital, together with the Military Commander at the Capital, governed the capital city, and had covertly divided it into the "Three Adjuncts" (which title denotes also the three districts governed by those three officials). Wang Hsien-ch'ien suggests, "The use of the title, 'Three Adjuncts,' is perhaps an anachronistic change by a historian. In this book this sort of thing is quite frequent."

[8.4] Ju Shun comments, "The comment in the *Han-[chiu]-yi* [written by Wei Hung,

officers and soldiers died in battle, and in the autumn,
Sept. 8 the seventh month, on [the day] *hsin-hai*, the last
day of the month, there was an eclipse of the sun.

I   In the last [part of the Emperor's reign], the first
143 B. C. year, in the spring, the first month, an imperial edict
Feb./Mar. said, "A trial at law is an important matter.   [Some]
people are wise and [some are] stupid; [some] offices are superior and [some] inferior.   When, in a
trial it is doubtful [what to decide, the case] should
be referred to the high officials; what the high officials cannot settle should be transferred to the Commandant of Justice.   If it is ordered that a matter
should be referred [to a superior judge], and later
[it is found that] it should not have been referred,
[that reference] does not constitute a fault.   [We]
desire to bring it about that those who judge law-
suits should above all take care to be lenient."

Apr.   In the third month, an amnesty was granted to
the empire, the common people were granted one
step in noble rank, and [officials ranking at] fully two
thousand piculs and Chancellors of the nobles [were
granted] the noble rank of Senior Chiefs of the
Summer Multitude.   In the summer, universal drinking [was
allowed] for five days and the people were permitted
to buy and sell wine.[8.5]

June   In the fifth month there was an earthquake.   In
Aug. 28 the autumn, the seventh month, on [the day] *yi-
szŭ*, the last day of the month, there was an eclipse
of the sun, and the Marquis of T'iao, Chou Ya-fu,
was sent to prison, where he died.[8.6]

fl. dur. 25–57, says], 'The various pastures [under the care of] the herdsmen of the Chief
of the Stud [number] thirty-six.   They are divided and spread over the northern and
western borders.   Gentlemen are used as Superintendants of the Pastures; thirty
thousand male and female slaves care for three hundred thousand horses.' "   Yen Shih-
ku adds, "Places for rearing birds and beasts are comprehensively named pastures
Hence it says that a place for herding horses is a pasture."

[8.5] Buying and selling wine had been forbidden since 147 B.C.   Cf. 5: 6b.

[8.6] Wang Hsien-shen (1859–1922) argues that this date is mistaken and that Chou

四月詔曰雕文刻鏤傷農事
登禁內郡食馬粟沒入之夏
死發車騎材官屯春以歲不
匈奴入鴈門太守馮敬與戰
二年冬十月省徹侯之國春

In the second year, in the winter, the tenth month, **9a**
[the Emperor] dispensed with the marquises going **II**
to their states.[9.1]　　　　　　　　　　　　　**Oct./Nov.**

In the spring the Huns entered into the Yen-men **142 B. C.**
[Commandery] and its Grand Administrator, Feng **Spring**
Ching, died in battle with them. Chariots, cavalry,
and skilled soldiers were sent to garrison [the Yen-
men Commandery].

In the spring,[9.2] because in the [previous] year
there had not been a [good] harvest, in the commanderies under [the Prefects] of the [Imperial]
Capital,[9.3] feeding horses with grain was prohibited
and they were confiscated to the government.

Ya-fu died in 147 B.C., which is the date given in the *SC* (*Mh* II, 504). According to *HS* 19 B: 12a, he was dismissed from his position as Lieutenant Chancellor in 147 B.C., and 40: 28a tells that soon afterwards he was insulted by the Emperor. When his son had purchased arms for use in his funeral, Chou Ya-fu was arrested and committed suicide by starvation. *HS* 16: 13a notes that he was made a marquis in 162 B.C., (Chu Yi-hsin says that the Wang. ed. (1546) is correct in reading 161 B.C.) and was dismissed from his title of marquis in the eighteenth year after, which would be 145, 144 or 143 B.C. *HS* 40: 28b moreover says that the same year that he died, Emperor Ching enfeoffed his son as Marquis of P'ing-ch'ü; *HS* 16: 13b dates that appointment in 143 B.C., so that the date of his death in 5: 8b is corroborated.

[9.1] In 179 B.C. (cf. 4: 8b), Emperor Wen ordered the marquises to go to their states, which order is now dispensed with. Chavannes (*Mh* II, 508) translates quite differently, "on examine si les seigneurs avaient été envoyés dans leurs états." The nobles had however evaded Emperor Wen's order that they should go to their estates (cf. p. 246). Emperors regularily enfeoffed the relatives of their mothers and favorite concubines; we do not hear of any such nobles thereupon disappearing from the capital; on the contrary they continued to figure in intrigues even when they did not hold office. According to 8: 9a, in 67 B.C. the Emperor "granted to each of the eighty-seven marquises who were at their estates twenty catties of actual gold." But, according to the "Tables," there were at that time more than two hundred marquises, so that the vast majority of the marquises were in the capital. Marquises were moreover sometimes sent to their estates as a punishment, cf. *HS* 45: 18a, also Glossary, *sub* Marquis.

The original term for marquis 徹侯, which is here used in the text, was tabooed because the word *ch'ê* was the personal name of Emperor Wu. Chou Shou-ch'ang says that this reading is a copyist's chance error.

[9.2] Wang Hsien-ch'ien points out that "the spring" has been previously mentioned and that this word is here an interpolation. The *SC* dates the invasion of the Huns in the third month and the prohibition of feeding grain in the first month.

[9.3] *SC* 11: 6a reads 內史君郡, in which phrase the *HS* omits the middle word. Yen Shih-ku says that what were confiscated were the horses.

Apr./May   In the summer, the fourth month, an imperial edict said, "Carved ornaments and chiseled engravings are matters that injure agriculture. Brocade, embroidery, vermillion silk ribbons, and braided ribbons harm women's work.[9.4]   Injury to agriculture is the source of hunger; harm to women's work is the cause of [suffering from] cold. Verily when hunger and cold both come at the same time, there are few who will be able to keep from doing wrong.[9.5]   We Ourself plow and the Empress herself cultivates silkworms in order to lead the empire by furnishing the millet, the sacrifical grain, and the sacrificial robes for the [imperial] ancestral temples. [We] have not accepted the [yearly] offerings;[9.6] [We] have reduced [the supplies of] the Grand Provisioner; [We] have diminished the amount of public service and the poll-taxes, wishing that the empire

9b should stress agriculture and sericulture and should constantly have stores and provisions in order to be prepared for visitations and calamities, the strong should not rob from the weak, the many should not do violence to the few, the aged and those over sixty should die a natural death, and the young and orphans should be allowed to grow to maturity.

者也錦繡纂組害女紅者也農事傷則飢之本也女
紅害則寒之原也夫飢寒並至而能亡爲非者寡矣
朕親耕后親桑以奉宗廟粢盛祭服爲天下先不受
獻減太官省繇賦欲天下務農蠶素有畜積以備災
害彊毋攘弱衆毋暴寡老者以壽終幼孤得遂長令

[9.4] Ying Shao writes, "*Tsuan* 纂 are the present laces of many colors. Silk stuff of variegated colors (*tsui* 綷) is this [material]. *Tsu* 組 is the present seal-ribbon. Intermixed silk cords 紛條 is this [material]." But Fu Tsan (fl. ca. 285) writes, "Hsü Shen [who wrote the *Shuo-wen*, ca. 100] says, "*Tsuan* is vermillion *tsu*," " and Yen Shih-ku writes "[Fu] Tsan's explanation is correct. *Tsui* is *hui* 會 [many-colored embroidery] and *hui* is many [colored] *ts'ai* 綵 [many-colored flowered silk]. At present it is called *ts'o-ts'ai* 錯綵 {woven multicolored stuff]. It is not *tsuan*."

Women's work was especially raising silk-worms, weaving, and sewing. Raising food is men's work; making cloth and clothes is women's work.

· [9.5] The foregoing sentence is found in a conversation about punishments between Marquis Wen of Wei[h] and Li K'o or Li K'uei (cf. Duyvendak, *Book of Lord Shang*, p. 43, n. 2), in the *Shuo-yüan* (written by Liu Hsiang, 77–6 B.C.), ch. "*Fan-chih*."

[9.6] The taxes paid to the emperor by commanderies and nobles.

歲或不登民食頗寡其咎安在或詐僞爲吏吏以貨賂爲市漁奪百

姓侵牟萬民縣丞長吏也奸法與盜盜甚無謂也其令二千石各脩

其職不事官職耗亂者丞相以聞請其罪布告天下使明知朕意五

月詔曰人不患其不知患其不勇患其爲暴也不患

其不富患其亡厭也其唯廉士寡欲易足今訾算十以上迺得宦廉

"Now for some years there have not been good harvests and the food of the common people has been quite scanty; where does the fault lie? Perhaps dishonest and hypocritical officials make a business of presents and bribes, taking by fraud or by force the peoples' [property], encroaching upon and consuming the many common people.[9.7] An Assistant Prefect is a Chief Official; [for him] to pervert the laws and rob with the robbers is utterly unspeakable.[9.8]

"Let it be ordered that [officials whose positions rank as] two thousand piculs should each look after their own charge. As to those who do not occupy themselves with their official duties or who govern unintelligently, the Lieutenant Chancellor should report it and beg [the throne to order punishment] for their crimes. Let this be published and told to the empire and cause Our will to be clearly known."

In the fifth month, an imperial edict said, "A May/June person should not be disquieted if he is ignorant, [but] he should be disquieted if he acts deceitfully. He should not be disquieted if he is not brave, [but] he should be disquieted if he acts tyrannously. He should not be disquieted if he is not rich, [but] he should be disquieted if he is not satisfied [i.e., is covetous]. Only incorrupt gentlemen make their desires few and are easily satisfied. [But] now [a person must have] capital [sufficient to be required to pay at least] ten or more [times] the poll-tax (suan) before he is permitted to become a palace official.[9.9] The [number of] poll-taxes [which can 10a

[9.7] Yü Yüeh (1821-1906), in his *Hu-lou Pi-t'an* 4:4, suggests that one *wei* and one *li* are due to dittography. A parallel passage is found in *HS* 6: 17a.
Li Ch'i (fl. 220-265) writes, "*Mou* 牟 is an insect that eats the roots of cereals. 侵牟 is to eat up the people like this *mou*."
Yen Shih-ku explains *yü* 漁 by *lieh* 獵 (hunting), but Chou Shou-ch'ang replies, "To invade and take by force without choosing [any particular things] is called *yü*. *Yü* and *lieh* are two [different] things."
[9.8] Ch'ien Ta-chao notes that the Fukien ed. (1549) mistakenly reads 異 for 謂.
[9.9] Fu Ch'ien (ca. 125-195) comments, "Those whose *tzu* 訾 (capital or property)

329

is ten thousand cash [pay]·as a poll-tax (*suan* 算 [cf. p. 184, n.1]) 127 [cash]." Ying
Shao explains, "Anciently [people] hated that officials should be covetous. 'If their
clothes and food are enough, they know [how to distinguish between] honor and disgrace.' [A quotation from *Kuan-tzu*]. So [official position] was restricted [to those
whose] capital (*tzu*) [was sufficient so that they paid at least] ten [times] the poll-tax
(*suan*) and then only were people permitted to become officials. [Those who paid]
ten [times] the poll-tax [possessed] a hundred thousand [cash]. Merchants who had
wealth were not permitted to become officials; incorrupt gentlemen who had no capital
were also not allowed to become palace officials (*huan*). Hence [the Emperor] reduced
[the required] capital to [enough to require the payment of only] four [times] the poll-tax
[as the amount required before they] were permitted to become palace officials (*huan*)."

Ho Ch'uo (1661–1722) adds "What Tung Chung-shu said [in the *HS*] 'To select
Gentlemen and officials according to their wealth and capital (*tzu*)' points to this *tzu*
and *suan*. [*HS* 57 A: 1a says that] Szu-ma Hsiang-ju, 'by his capital (*tzu*) and poll-
taxes (*suan*) became a Gentleman.' " The Han dynasty had a tax upon property or
capital; each ten-thousand cash of property paid one poll-tax (which tax was different
in amount at different times; cf. Glossary *sub* Poll-tax). Poor people were kept out of
office in order to avoid securing high officials who sought profit in holding office.

Yao Nai (1732–1815) however says, "When this [passage] says palace officials (*huan*
官), it means Gentlemen. [But cf. below]. At the beginning of the Han [period],
Gentlemen had to furnish ornamented robes and horses before they were permitted to
wait upon the emperor, hence [they were appointed] according to their capital (*tzu*)
and poll-taxes (*suan*). The saying of Chang Shih-chih [*HS* 50: 1a], 'Being a palace
official (*huan*) for a long time reduced my [older brother] Chung's possessions' and that
General Wei Ch'ing ordered that the members of his suite should all furnish their
saddles, horses, deep red garments, jade, utensils, and swords is about this [matter].

"In Han [times], when a person [wanted to] enter official life, in general there were
three ways: [1] as a Gentleman or [Palace] Attendant, [2] by holding office in a province
or commandery or in the yamen of a minister, or [3] by an imperial summons. Gentlemen were attendants upon the emperor. Without capital, they were not allowed to
become attendants upon the emperor, but naturally they could hold office in the commanderies or prefectures or in the yamens of the ministers. At the time of Emperor Wu,
schools were established and the filial and incorrupt were recommended; after that,
Gentlemen did not need capital [on which to pay] poll-taxes in order to be promoted;
yet they contributed sheep and contributed grain in order to be given a vacancy among
the Gentlemen, which was a very much greater [payment] than the former [require-
ment] of capital [on which to pay] poll-taxes. All this did not exist before the time
of Emperor Ching. When Ying [Shao] says, '[Official position] was restricted to those
whose capital [was sufficient so that they paid at least] ten [times] the poll-tax, and then
only were they permitted to become officials,' he did not comprehend that this regulation
did not apply to all officials."

Wang Hsien-ch'ien says that the Official ed. (1739) and the Academy ed. (1124)
read *kuan* 官 (offices) instead of *huan* (palace officials) both in the text and in Ying Shao's
comment, at the places indicated by [9.9] or by (*huan*). If this emendation is accepted

士算不必眾有市籍不得宦無訾又不得宦朕

甚愍之訾算四得宦亡令廉士久失職貪夫長

利秋大旱

三年春正月詔曰農天下之本也黃金珠玉饑

不可食寒不可衣以爲幣用不識其終始開歲

be paid by] incorrupt gentlemen are not inevitably many. [Just as] those who are enregistered in the market-places [as merchants] are not allowed to become palace officials,[9.9] [so] those who have not [sufficient] capital are also not allowed to become palace officials.[9.9] We very much deplore this. If the capital [of incorrupt gentlemen is sufficient so that they pay] four [times] the poll-tax, they shall be allowed to become palace officials,[9.9] so as not to let incorrupt persons be kept for a long time from office and covetous fellows to profit continuously."

In the autumn there was a great drought.   Autumn

In the third year, in the spring, the first month, III an imperial edict said, "Agriculture is the foundation 141 B. C. of the world. As to real gold, pearls, or jade, when Feb./Mar. one is hungry, they cannot be eaten; when one is cold, they cannot be worn. They are considered and used as objects of value, [but] one does not understand how their final or original [value came to be].

(and the first part of Ying Shao's comment uses the word *li* 吏 for "officials," so that he may not have had *huan* in his text), Yao Nai's restriction that only palace officials were required to have property falls to the ground.

This emendation is however making a difficult reading easy and hence is operating on a wrong principle. Dr. J. J. L. Duyvendak remarks that it is not likely that an original *kuan* should have been changed to *huan* and that such a change does not make a proper sentence, inasmuch as in the *HS kuan* is used to mean "office" rather than "official." For "official," the word *li* would have been used.

Emperor Ching seems to have been thinking that entrance into the government bureaucracy is normally through first becoming a Gentleman in the imperial palace, where the Emperor could get to know him, and from which position persons were promoted to governmental offices. He deplored that only very wealthy persons could thus enter the government service, hence he lowered the amount of property required for service in the palace. At a later time Commandery Administrators and other high officials recommended persons as filial and incorrupt, etc., whereupon such persons were sent to the quarters of the Major in Charge of Public Carriages or to the Yellow Gate in the imperial palace, where they became Expectant Appointees and were given a small allowance. Later such persons were given positions in the bureaucracy, seemingly without being made Gentlemen. Hence Yao Nai is correct in pointing out that not all officials first became Gentlemen, at least in the time of Ying Shao. Whether that was the case before the time of Emperor Ching is difficult to determine.

"Recently for some years there have not been good harvests. In [Our] opinion this is because those who do non-essential things [merchanizing and craftsmanship] are many, [whereas] the common people who make agriculture [their profession] are few. Let it be ordered that the commanderies and kingdoms shall stress the encouragement of agriculture and sericulture, and increase the sowing and planting, [in order that] there may [thus] be obtained articles for clothing and food. If officials, in mobilizing the common people or in taking from them substitute-[money, employ them] to collect real gold, pearls, or jade, [such officials] shall be condemned [as having taken] booty and treated as robbers. [Offi-

10b cials ranking at] two thousand piculs who permit [such actions, shall be punished] with the same punishment [as other officials]."

The Imperial Heir-apparent [Liu Ch'ê] was capped,[10.1] and those people who would be the successors of their fathers were granted one step in noble rank.

Mar. 10   On [the day] *chia-tzu*, the Emperor died in the Wei-yang Palace.[10.2] In his testamentary edict, he granted to the vassal kings and to the marquises two teams of four horses each, to officials [ranking at] two thousand piculs, two catties of actual gold, and to the [lower] officials and the common people, a hundred cash to each household. He freed the women of the [imperial] harem and sent them back to their families, exempting their persons [from taxation] for life.[10.3] In the second month, on [the day]

Mar. 18 *kuei-yu*, he was buried in the Yang Tomb.

[10.1] Cf. p. 182, n. 2.

[10.2] Fu Tsan (fl. ca. 285) writes, "The Emperor was in his thirty-second year when he came to the throne; he reigned to his sixteenth year; he lived to his forty-eighth year." Then he was born in 188 B.C.

[10.3] Wang Ming-sheng (1722–1798) remarks, "When Emperor Wen died, he sent home

吏民戶百錢出宮人歸其家復終身二月癸酉葬陽陵

于未央宮遺詔賜諸侯王列侯馬二駟吏二千石黃金二斤

石聽者與同罪皇太子冠賜民爲父後者爵一級甲子帝崩

可得衣食物吏發民若取庸采黃金珠玉者坐臧爲盜二千

或不登意爲末者眾農民寡也其令郡國務勸農桑益種樹

民醇厚周云成康漢言文景美矣　漢書五
孝景遵業五六十載之間至於移風易俗黎
掃除煩苛與民休息至于孝文加之以恭儉
信哉周秦之敝罔密文峻而姦軌不勝漢興
贊曰孔子稱斯民三代之所以直道而行也

In eulogy we say: Confucius eulogized, "These people! They are whereby the three dynasties pursued their straight course."[10.4] It was true indeed; the error of the Chou and the Ch'in [dynasties] was that although the net [of their laws] was fine and their enactments were severe, yet they could not overcome the ways of the wicked.[10.5]

When the Han [dynasty] arose, it swept away [such] vexations and harshness and gave the common people repose and rest. [Emperor] Hsiao-wen added [the virtues of] respectfulness and frugality; [Emperor] Hsiao-ching followed his practises. In the course of fifty or sixty years,[10.6] [these Emperors even] altered the people's customs and changed their usages, [so that] the many common people[10.7] became pure and sincere. The Chou [dynasty] talked about [Kings] Ch'eng and K'ang; the Han [dynasty similarly] speaks of [Emperors] Wen and Ching. How splendid!

[his concubines], from his Ladies down to his Junior Maids, [hence] when Emperor Ching died, he also freed the women of his harem. In [the time of Emperors] Wu and Chao there came to be the practise [that members of an emperor's harem] should uphold [his worship] at his tomb. When Emperor P'ing died, Wang Mang again freed [the Emperor's] concubines and sent them all home."

[10.4] *Analects*, XV, xxiv, 2. Yen Shih-ku explains, "He means that the people of this time were the same as those governed by the Hsia, Yin, and Chou [dynasties], when, because of the government's cultural influence, purity, and unity, [the people] could follow a straight path in their actions. He regrets that at this time [the situation] was different."

[10.5] The Ch'in dynasty enacted many and severe laws, which applied to everyone, high and low. These were the "fine net" and "severe enactments." The Lord of Shang, who established the severe laws of Ch'in, is said to have even had the nose of the Grand Tutor of the Heir-apparent, Prince Ch'ien, sliced off in punishment. Cf. J. J. L. Duyvendak, *The Book of Lord Shang*, p. 19.

[10.6] Wang Hsien-shen (1859–1922) says that the words 至於 are an interpolation; the *T'ai-p'ing Yü-lan* (978–983) ch. 88, quotes this passage without these two words.

[10.7] On the meaning of this phrase, cf. 10: n. 6.7.

AN OFFICIAL'S CHARTER

When important officials or nobles were appointed, they were given a charter; cf. n. 5.7. The *Han-chiu-yi* (by Wei Hung, fl. 25–57) A: 12a, contains such a charter, which shows that these charters consisted of admonitions by the ruler to the appointee:

"A [certain] charter for a Grandee who was newly installed says,

" 'Verily, in [the year-period] Wu-feng, the third year, the first month, on [the day] *yi-szu* [Feb. 19, 55 B.C.], the Grandee Secretary took office and the Emperor invited him to mount [the steps to the throne] and in person gave him an imperial edict, which said,

" ' "Let the Grandee Secretary approach, empty himself [of his notions], and receive Our words. We are ignorant of the Great Way, [yet We] have had the opportunity to protect the [imperial] ancestral temples, [so that We are] very fearful and humble. Day and night [We] think of [Our] own faults without taking leisure, joy, or repose. During the day We think that the people have not yet been able to be tranquil. Alas! Let the Grandee Secretary apply himself with all his mind and do his best in supplying Our deficiencies. Alas! Let the nine high ministers, the grandees, and all the officials be careful. If you are not earnest in your duty, there is the regular law. Go and apply yourself with all your mind in harmonizing, enriching, and opening [the way for] capable persons, enabling the capable to have the means of returning to their proper places [in the bureaucracy, and so of] directing the people. Do not keep silence before Our Self. The multitude [of people] in the world receive commands from Us and consider the law as [determining] their fates. [Then] can you fail to be careful? Alas! O Grandee Secretary, be warned." ' "

The list of officials in *HS* ch. 19 B does not give any appointment on the date in this document, and from the dates in that chapter it does not seem at all likely that this date is correct. *Ibid.* p. 23a however lists the appointment of Wang Yen-kuang in the third year of T'ai-ch'u, the first month. According to this suggestion, the year and month are correct, and *yi-szu* is a mistake for *chi-szu* (a common error). Then the date is Feb. 18, 102 B.C. The phrasing may well be that of Emperor Wu.

SOLAR ECLIPSES DURING THE REIGN OF EMPEROR CHING

During this period of sixteen years, ten eclipses are recorded in the *SC* or *HS*. We consider them in their chronological order.

i. In *Ch'ien* III (the third year of the first part of the reign), the second month, on the day *jen-tzu*, the last day of the month, a solar eclipse is listed (*HS* 5: 4a). But, according to P. Hoang, *Concordance des chronologies néoméniques chinoise et européenne*, there was no *jen-tzu* day in the second month. *HS* 27 Cb: 13b dates this eclipse "on [the day] *jen-wu*, the last day of the month. It was two degrees in [the constellation] Wei₄." This date was Apr. 5, 154 B.C. The *Han-chi* (ii cent.) 9: 5b however dates this eclipse "in the second month, on [the day] *hsin-szu*, the first day of the month," which was Apr. 4, 154 B.C., according to Hoang.

Oppolzer calculates his solar eclipse no. 2506 on Apr. 4, 154 B.C., which date Hoang calculates as the day before the last day of the month.

Oppolzer calculates the sun as in long. $10.9° = 10.0°$ R.A.; the stars of Wei₄ were then in $11.2°$ to $12.8°$ R.A.

ii. *HS* 5: 4b says, In *Ch'ien* IV, "the tenth month, on [the day] *mou-hsü*, the last day of the month, there was an eclipse of the sun." *HS* ch. 27 and the *Han-chi* both fail to list this eclipse. The listing in ch. 5 is moreover peculiar, since here the tenth month, which really began the year, is noted at the *end* of the year.

Another eclipse in the tenth month at the end of a year is noted in *Chung* IV, on the day *mou-wu*. Because of the similarity of these two dates, there is a possibility of conflation between these two recordings. *HS* ch. 27 lists neither of them.

P. Hoang, in his *Catalogue des éclipses de soleil et de lune dans les documents chinois* ("Variétés sinologiques", n. 56) suggests Oppolzer's solar eclipse no. 2507, but that was visible only in the southern hemisphere. Chu Wen-hsin, in his *Li-tai Jih-shih K'ao* (1934) suggests Oppolzer's no. 2510, but that eclipse was also invisible in China. Liu Pin and Chou Shou-ch'ang think that this eclipse is an interpolation, because of the peculiar month, because *HS* ch. 27 does not list it, and because of the similarity to the one listed for *Chung* IV. Ho Ch'uo suggests that since the *SC* lists an "intercalary ninth month" in this year, this intercalary month is intended. Hoang does not however put any *mou-hsü* day in that intercalary month, making such a day the twenty-fifth of the regular ninth month, Oct. 12, 153 B.C.

In the four years between the preceeding correctly recorded eclipse in 154 B.C. and the next such a one in 150 B.C., there occurred eight solar eclipses, of which only two were visible in China.[1] The eclipse of Aug. 7, 152 B.C. was invisible in Ch'ang-an, but calculation shows that at the present Peiping it reached a magnitude of 0.08 (totality = 1.00) at sunrise. This day was in *Ch'ien* V, the sixth month, on the day *ting-yu*, the day before the last day of the month. Calculation shows also that the eclipse of Feb. 2, 151 B.C. reached a magnitude of 0.03 at Ch'ang-an at 10:08 a.m., local time; at the present Ch'ang-sha it reached a magnitude of 0.15 at 10:27 a.m., local time. This date was in *Ch'ien* VI, the first month, the day *ping-shen*, the first day of the month.

Ping-shen is two days before *mou-hsü* and *ting-yu* is the day before *mou-hsü*. Since Hoang's calendar (from which these datings are taken) might be as much as three days in error, either of these two eclipses might be the one referred to in this recording, as far as the cyclical days go. These eclipses were however both quite small and would easily be missed. Since our other sources do not list this eclipse, it is more probably an interpolation into the text, possibly a conflation or dittography for the other peculiar eclipse in *Chung* IV.

iii. In *Ch'ien* VII, the eleventh month, on the day *keng-yin*, the last day of the month, a third eclipse of the sun is recorded (5:5a). *HS* 27 Cb: 13b also records it and adds, "It was 9 degrees in [the constellation] *Hsü*." The *SC* (*Mh* II, 501) mistakenly dates this eclipse on the last day of the twelfth month.

Hoang gives this date as Jan. 22, 150 B.C.; Oppolzer calculates his solar eclipse no. 2515 for that date. He calculates the sun's longitude as 299.1° = 301.2° R.A. The two stars of Hsü were then in 291.8° and 293.9° R.A.

iv. In *Chung* I, the twelfth month, on the day *chia-yin*, the last day of the month, a fourth solar eclipse is listed in *HS* 27 Cb: 13b; ch. 5 and the *Han-chi* do not mention this eclipse. Hoang gives this date as Feb. 10, 149 B.C. There was no eclipse on that date.

In the three years between the preceding eclipse and the next correctly

[1] Besides those located by Oppolzer, three were partial. Of those, no. 2508 was near the south polar regions; the other two, upon cursory calculation, were also found located outside China.

recorded one in 147 B.C., there were 7 solar eclipses, of which only one was visible in China.[2] This one occurred on June 7, 149 B.C., in *Chung* I, the fifth month, on the day *jen-tzu*, the last day of the month. Oppolzer charts the moon's umbra as passing into northern Siberia, so that this eclipse was visible as a small partial eclipse in northern China.

Chia yin is the second day after *jen-tzu*; it is likely that Hoang's calendar is here two days in error and that "fifth" was misread as "twelfth," so that the eclipse of 149 B.C. is the one intended in this recording. Then the *Han-chi* did not list all the eclipses given in the *HS*, and missed this one because it is listed only in *HS* ch. 27.

v. In *Chung* II, the ninth month, on the day *chia-hsü*, the last day of the month, a fifth solar eclipse is recorded (5: 6b; 27 Cb: 13b; *Han-chi* 9: 14b). Hoang gives this date as Oct. 22, 148 B.C. No eclipse happened on that day.

If we are correct in identifying the preceeding eclipse with that of 149 B.C., there was no solar eclipse visible in China between the two eclipses of 150 and 147 B.C.

This listing is probably dittography for the next eclipse. Both were listed in the ninth month, one on the day *chia-hsü* and the other on the day *mou-hsü*; one in the second year and the other in the third year. In the list of eclipses in ch. 27 this dittography is quite plain. There two groups, each of eleven characters, follow each other, differing only in two characters. If, possibly in copying the original astronomical records, the word for "three" had been carelessly written "two," and someone had added the correct notation of the next eclipse and had also noted that *mou-hsü* is incorrect for that month of the second year and had changed *mou* to *chia*, the list would stand as it is now. Its insertion into the Annals would naturally have followed.

vi. In *Chung* III, the ninth month, on the day *mou-hsü*, the last day of the month, a sixth solar eclipse is recorded (5: 6b; 27 Cb: 13b; *Han-chi* 9: 14b). Ch. 27 adds, "It was almost total. It was nine degrees in Wei₃."

Hoang gives this date as Nov. 10, 147 B.C., for which Oppolzer calculates his solar eclipse no. 2523. He charts the moon's umbra as passing approximately through the present Urga, Mongolia, and Shan-hai-kuan, Hopei. Calculation shows that the eclipse reached a magnitude of 0.77 in Ch'ang-an at 10:58 a.m., local time.

---

[2] The one partial eclipse, no. 2517, was located near the south pole. Five other eclipses are charted as invisible in China.

The sun's longitude was 224.9° = 222.4° R.A. The nine stars of Wei₃ ranged in R.A. from 218.2° to 230.7°.

vii. In *Chung* IV, at the end of the record for the year, there is listed an eclipse of the sun in the tenth month, on the day *mou-wu* (5: 7a; Han-chi 9: 14b). *HS* ch. 27 does not list this eclipse. There could of course be no tenth month at the end of the year, for the tenth month was the first month in a year.

In the three years between the preceeding eclipse and the next correctly recorded one in 144 B.C., there were six solar eclipses, of which only one was visible in China.[3] This one occurred on the morning of Mar. 26, 145 B.C. It was invisible at Ch'ang-an and even in the ancient Lu, the modern Ch'ü-fou, Shantung. But at Jung-ch'eng, on the eastern tip of the Shantung peninsula, the eclipse reached a magnitude of 0.16 at sunrise, according to calculation. This day was in *Chung* V, the second month, the day *keng-shen*, the last day of the month, according to Hoang.

Mou-wu is the second day before *keng-shen*. There thus occurred an eclipse within a few months of the time when this eclipse is said to have occurred, on a cyclical day which was possibly the same cyclical day as that for which it was listed (since Hoang's calendar might be two days in error). At sunrise an eclipse must reach a magnitude of 0.33 to be conspicuous, and an eclipse of 0.16 is visible to the naked eye. It is possible that some official in eastern Shantung reported this eclipse to the imperial court and that somehow the record got into the "Imperial Annals" in a garbled form. Since the list in ch. 27 seems to represent the records of the court astronomers, it is natural that this eclipse did not get into that list.

viii. In *Chung* VI, the seventh month, on the day *hsin-hai*, the last day of the month, an eighth eclipse is recorded (5: 8b; 27 Cb: 14a; *Han-chi* 9: 15b). Ch. 27 adds, "It was 7 degrees in [the constellation] Chen₃."

Hoang gives this day as Sept. 8, 144 B.C., for which Oppolzer calculates his solar eclipse no. 2530. He charts the path of totality as passing near the present Canton.

He calculates the sun in long. 161.6° = 163.2° R.A. The stars of Chen₃ then ranged from 155.7° to 161.4° R.A.

---

[3] Three were partial eclipses; two, nos. 2525 & 2526 were near the south pole. The other, on Apr. 6, 146 B.C. was calculated and found invisible, in Chinese longitudes south of 60° N lat. The two other eclipses are charted as plainly invisible in China.

ix. In *Hou* I, the seventh month, on the day *yi-szu*, a ninth solar eclipse is recorded. *HS* 5: 8b says it was on the last day of the month; 27 Cb: 14a however says it was "one day before the last day of the month," and adds, "It was 17 degrees in [the constellation] Yi."

Hoang gives this date as Aug. 28, 143 B.C., the day before the last day of the month, for which day Oppolzer calculates his solar eclipse no. 2532. He charts the path of totality as passing through Siberia and the island of Yezo.

He calculates the sun's longitude as 150.8° = 152.9° R.A. The stars of Yi then ranged from 136.0° to 144.7° R.A.

x. Under *Hou* III, the tenth month, which was Nov. 16–Dec. 14, 142 B.C., the *SC* (*Mh* II, 508) says, "The sun and the moon were both eclipsed and red for five days." The *HS* does not mention this matter either in the Annals or in ch. 27. The only solar eclipse visible in China between that of 143 B.C. and the next correctly recorded one in 138 B.C. was that of Aug. 8, 141 B.C., which may have been separately recorded in ch. 6.[4] This record seems to refer to a dust-storm.

---

[4] In this period of 5 years there were 12 solar eclipses, of which 6 were partial. Nos 2534 & 2543 were near the south pole. The remaining four were calculated and found invisible in China. There was no eclipse of the moon in Nov./Dec. 142 B.C.

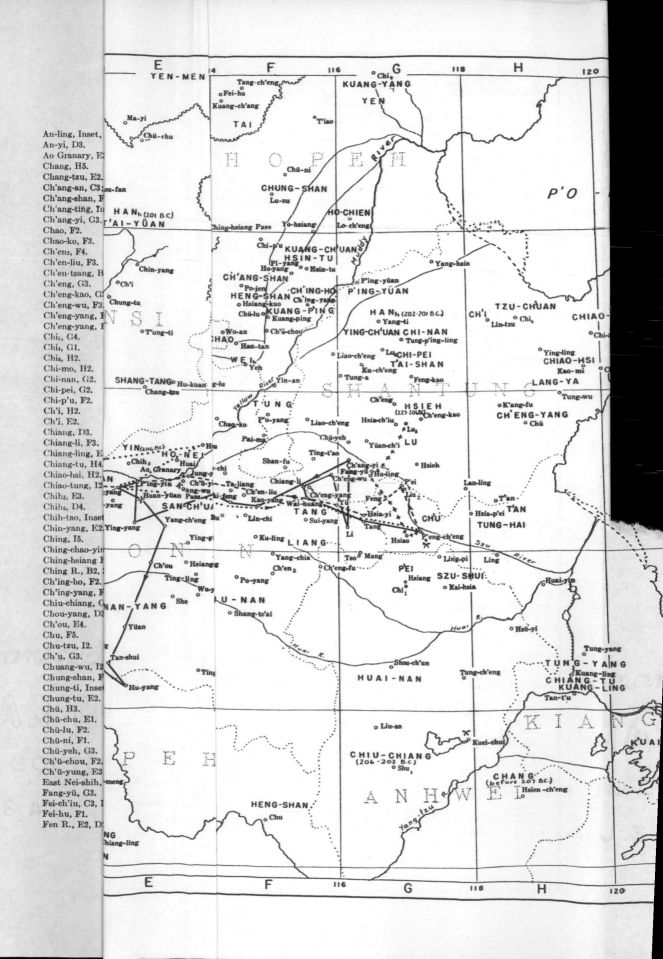

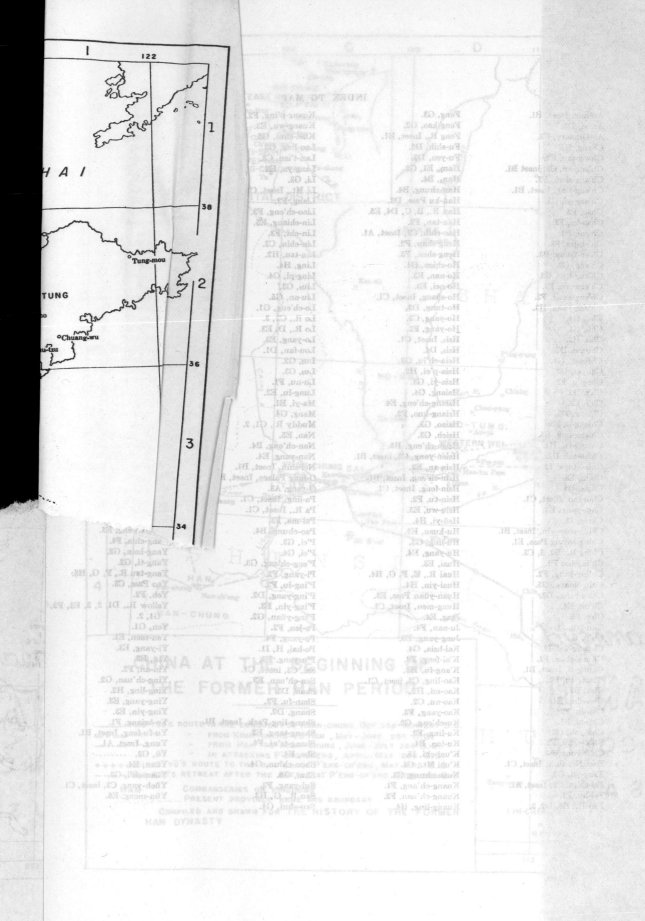